DATA GATHERING
Experimental Methods
Plus

MILTON L. BLUM
Florida International University

PAUL W. FOOS
Florida International University

1817

HARPER & ROW, PUBLISHERS, New York
Cambridge, Philadelphia, San Francisco,
London, Mexico City, São Paulo, Singapore, Sydney

To
Naomi
Rebecca
Clarence
Arlen

Sponsoring Editor: Susan Mackey
Project Editor: David Nickol
Cover Design: Paul Chevannes
Text Art: Reproduction Drawings, Ltd.
Production: Willie Lane
Compositor: ComCom Division of Haddon Craftsmen, Inc.
Printer and Binder: The Maple Press Company

DATA GATHERING: EXPERIMENTAL METHODS *PLUS*

Library of Congress Cataloging in Publication Data

Blum, Milton L., 1912–
    Data gathering.

    Bibliography: p.
    Includes index.
    1. Social science--Research--Methodology. 2. Social
surveys. I. Foos, Paul W. II. Title.
H62.B5868   1985   300′.72   85–24875
ISBN 0–06–040777–8

85 86 87 88 9 8 7 6 5 4 3 2 1

85-24875
30272
B625D
67234

Contents

Preface vii

PART I COMMONALITIES OF METHODS OF DATA GATHERING

Chapter 1   Introduction 1

Rationalism 3
Experience ≠ Data Gathering 4
Science and Pseudoscience 4
Misrepresentation and Science 5
Cause-and-Effect Confusion 10
The Science of Data Gathering 11
Problem Solving 12
And in Conclusion 14

Chapter 2   Scientific Data 15

Measurement 17
Reliability 24
Validity 27

Chapter 3   Scientific Thinking: Theory and Related Concepts 34

Scientific Explanation 36
Scientific Theory 39
Scientific Understanding 48

iii

Chapter 4   Methods of Data Collection 49

Selection Factors 50
Choosing and Using Participants 54
Data Analysis 58
Overview of Methods 58

Chapter 5   Measuring Instruments 62

Instrument Value and Limitation 63
Uses 64
Choosing an Instrument 66
Types of Instrumentation 67

Chapter 6   The Computer and Impact on Research 77

Some Concerns 81
For the Future 84

PART II EIGHT METHODS FOR DATA GATHERING

Chapter 7   Observation 86

What Is Observable 88
Subjective Observations 91
Objective Observations 92
Instrumentation 93
Recording Observations 94
Variables 94
A Checklist 95
The Observation Gestalt 96
Observations of a Second Order 99
Personal Applications 101

Chapter 8   The Experimental Method: Basics 102

Cause and Effect 102
Operational Definitions and Variables 106
Internal Validity 112
Between-Subject Design 121
Special Problems 125

Chapter 9   The Experimental Method: Matched Subjects, Within-Subjects,
and Single-Subject Designs 129

Matched-Subject Designs 130
Within-Subject Designs 136
Single-Subject Designs 146

Chapter 10   The Experimental Method: Complex Designs 154

Factorial Designs 155
Design Selection 162

Chapter 11   The Field 168

The Lewin Point of View 169
The Quasi-Experimental Point of View 170
A Field Study 173

Chapter 12   Archives 179

Uses of Archives 181
But Is Archival Research Scientific? 182
Archival Sources 183
Special-Interest Groups 192
Archives of a Different Order 202

Chapter 13   Case Histories 207

Case History Situations 208
Advantages 216
Limitations 218

Chapter 14   Group Discussions 223

Concept Description 225
What Is Measured 226
Role and Training of Discussion Leader 228
Role of Assistant to Group Leader 234
Group Characteristics and Recruiting 235
The Discussion Guide 237
An Illustration 239
The Findings 250

Chapter 15   Surveys 255

The Ajzen-Fishbein Theory 260
Components of a Survey 263
An Illustration 268

Chapter 16   Simulation 282

Type A and B Simulations 283
Blends 283
Type A Illustrated 283
Type B Illustrated 285

References 291

Appendix A Primer in Statistics 303

Index 315

Preface

We have a number of reasons for writing this book on data gathering. First, it is intended to be a text for courses on research methods in the social sciences. We describe the major data-gathering methods or systems that can be useful in advancing the state of knowledge in a number of different but related disciplines.

After considering the characteristics and standards necessary for data-gathering methods to be scientifically acceptable, we then describe such methods as observations, the experimental method, field research, archives, case histories, group discussions, surveys, and simulation.

We believe there is a compelling need to emphasize that facts, as well as generalizations, can be no better or meaningful than the method used to obtain them. Herein lies the most succinct difference between scientific and nonscientific data. The importance of data-gathering methods is quite independent of the social scientific branch of knowledge being considered.

A commonality of methods for data gathering, as well as a vast potential for such commonality, exists in such diverse yet overlapping fields as psychology, sociology, economics, the business sciences, home economics, political science, and ethnology, as well as the various health sciences from medicine to nutrition. In addition, these overlapping fields deal with an overlapping variety of societal problems such as aging, poverty, and war or peace.

This book acknowledges the need for more and better data as a result of the use of more and better data-gathering methods. As a corollary, we suggest that information acquired as a result of such data gathering might lead to less pontification by self-ordained experts by exposing their methods or positions as being without data or based on inadequate or biased data.

A second, but somewhat more narrow, reason for this book is that we believe courses in experimental psychology should be broadened in scope to include the additional data-gathering methods we present, if only for comparison purposes. Psychologists should be familiar with and be able to evaluate and use data-gathering methods in addition to the experimental methods.

One of the goals of this book is achieved if students of research, regardless of their formal training, will broaden their data-gathering horizons beyond their favorite method or the favored method of their discipline. A number of methods are equally acceptable for scientific data gathering and should be considered. It is our belief that problems are best studied when a variety of methods are used.

This book is organized in two parts. Part I consists of Chapters 1 through 6 and includes what we regard as the commonalities of the various methods, forms, or systems of data gathering enumerated in the book. This section distinguishes between scientific data and what we choose to call rationalisms. It also describes the commonalities and characteristics of scientific data, instrumentation, and the derivation and evaluation of theories.

Part II begins by presenting the fundamental role of *observation* as a data-gathering technique. It then proceeds to recognize and emphasize the importance of the *experiment* and its role in the scientific schema. In addition, it presents a series of somewhat less used data-gathering techniques in a novel and unique manner (in our opinion). Included are *field research, archives, case history, survey,* and *simulation.* Also included is a chapter on *group discussion,* which primarily summarizes the work of Blum over a number of years and reports the research and conceptual development of this data-gathering technique.

A capsule view of the highlights of the chapters follows:

Chapter 1   distinguishes rationalisms and scientific findings, and considers the limitations of experience as a source of data. The characteristics of the science of data gathering, the need for concept prior to instrumentation, and the difficulties of solving problems in the social sciences are presented.

Chapter 2   emphasizes measurement, reliability, and validity; particular attention is given to tests.

Chapter 3   covers theories and models.

Chapter 4   compares-contrasts methods of data gathering and gives an overview of different techniques.

Chapter 5   presents varieties of measuring instruments.

Chapter 6   considers computer use in the social sciences.

Chapter 7   deals with the importance of objective observations as a data-gathering technique and considers the need for the observer to be unobtrusive.

Chapter 8   covers basic between-subjects designs, basic issues of control, and cause-effect conclusions.

Chapter 9   presents matched-subjects designs, all repeated-measures designs, and single-subject experiments.

Chapter 10   covers factorial designs and interactions and an overview of the experimental method.

Chapter 11   considers the quasi-experiment and Lewin's field theory, and illustrates field research by an in-depth study of reasonably equated groups living in different home settings.

Chapter 12   reviews the wide variety of archival resources, the role of investigative reporting, and the importance of archives as a source of data for researchers.

Chapter 13   considers the value of the case history/study and offers some in-depth illustrations.

Chapter 14   covers the research efforts of the first author in developing the data-gathering technique of group discussion. Excerpts from various research projects using the technique are included.

Chapter 15   reviews the trials and tribulations of the survey method and draws in depth on a survey comparing a national sample with various "leader" groups.

Chapter 16   covers simulation by constructing a dichotomy of simulators using instruments and apparatus in comparison with those that essentially have people following or creating scenarios as if both were the "real thing."

An Appendix presents the major statistical concepts used in the social sciences.

A word about potential users. We believe that this book is appropriate for courses in research methods and experimental psychology (for example, experimental design and analysis; experimental methods; research methods; advanced general psychology; data gathering). The book has also been written for research methods courses in *all* social sciences (for example, psychology, sociology, economics, health science, and cultural anthropology).

It may also be considered as a supplementary or second text for any introductory course in such disciplines as the health sciences; sociology; economics; home economics; cultural anthropology; political science; and public administration.

Practitioners (for example, advertising agencies, market research centers, research and development centers, corporations with a consumer affairs interest) wishing to explore and compare various methods will also find this book quite helpful. Prior to problem solving, the fundamental research decision is to select from among many methods the one(s) most appropriate. To accomplish this, one must be familiar with a wide variety of methods. This book describes and defines the fundamentals of the major data-gathering methods.

The book is intended to encourage learning about how to gather data and the use of such data as the basis for decision making.

In brief, this book has been written to emphasize and broaden the horizons of data gathering. It includes, but goes beyond, the experimental method. Its ultimate goal is to provide the source for adding facts and generalizations to existing knowledge.

A word about the writing of this book. The authors agreed that each would do the first draft of eight chapters and then review and edit the other's work. We chose the chapters according to our background and predilection. Both of us recognized, in advance, that the substance or subject matter of each chapter would dictate the writing style. It was our purpose to have each chapter's style be a function of its substance.

We acknowledge with gratitude the suggestions of Drs. James Rotton and Ron Fisher and two anonymous reviewers. We recognize the conscientious efforts of Ruth Kuestner and Grace Holden in helping us to prepare the manuscript for publication.

We invited Drs. Toby Berk and Sam Shapiro to present relevant information on computers (Chapter 6) and statistics (Appendix) and we thank them for their efforts. We thank our many students for helpful suggestions. Finally, we appreciate and respect George Middendorf for maintaining the Harper & Row tradition. He is the very essence of a gentleman and a scholar.

Milton L. Blum
Paul W. Foos

DATA GATHERING
Experimental Methods *Plus*

chapter *1*

Introduction

The theme of this book is data gathering. It postulates that data gathering is primary. The method or methods of most parsimoniously and effectively gathering data useful in solving a problem are a matter of choice. A major goal of this book is to facilitate the making of such a choice by describing the "how to do" and the "why do" of a number of different data-gathering methods. This knowledge can transform the data gatherer from an automaton to a creative planner who can explain why the data gathered contribute to the solution of the problem.

Relevant data gathering is the key to appropriate problem solving and correct decision making. However, many individuals resolve their problems, as well as those of others, without the benefit of data—or the benefit of the analysis and synthesis of objectively obtained data. Such "solutions" are sometimes called "common sense" or "nonscientific," depending on one's bias or naiveté.

When verifiable data are gathered and analyzed, then one approaches the realm and province of science. It should be recognized that as one strives toward the pinnacle of science, data gathering is exactly a function of the method used. Different methods can be used for accumulating different types of data. Further, these different methods can lead to similar, as well as supplemental, results and decisions—provided the method used is not flawed or the data have not been finagled.

The methods this book will emphasize include: experiment, observation, group discussion, interviewing, case histories, simulation, archives, and field research. Each, when used appropriately and correctly, is capable of producing data that meet the criteria and standards considered scientific.

Whether one is, or aspires to be, a psychologist, sociologist, home economist, nutritionist, economist, political scientist, or cultural anthropologist, it is necessary to know and use various methods of data gathering. The experimental method has considerable value, but also valuable are the other methods included in this book.

Common to all science is data gathering by defined and verifiable methods. Within science there are classifiable subject matters. Such a major classification is physical and social. The province of this book is the social.

Basic to the needs and goals of social scientists is problem solving as a result of data gathering. However, such needs and goals should not be limited to social scientists. All individuals should be encouraged to take advantage of the methods that social scientists develop so that they can attempt to make decisions related to solving their personal problems or helping others to do so—be they family, friends, or society.

It should be noted that scientific methods are equally appropriate in the laboratory or in the real world not only as a means of solving problems, but also as a part of the decision-making process. Unfortunately, decision making may or may not be a result of objectively analyzing obtained data. Too often, decisions are made without the information that data can provide. Examples can be offered from a wide variety of circumstances, such as buying certain brands of food, clothes, a car, or even a home. Other examples might include the decision to meet a friend, the choice of a college, or the choice of an occupation.

All people can benefit as a result of using appropriate, but varied, data-gathering methods. Their use can lead to objective and more accurate decisions. Such decisions lead to more satisfactions and fewer failures.

Conclusions are dependent upon the findings obtained as a result of data gathering. Although there are many commonalities among data-gathering techniques, such as participant selection, measurement, and data analysis, the researcher must know how various techniques differ. Researchers need this information to decide which technique is likely to be most appropriate in solving the problem under investigation. Given the problem of why and which marriages end in divorce, it should be clear that any of several different data gathering techniques might be used. One might attempt to *observe* (Chapter 7) the conditions under which marriages break up, or search existing *records* (Chapter 12) of marriages and divorces, or *interview* (Chapters 5 and 15) couples who have been divorced or are contemplating a divorce. One might also conduct *group discussions* (Chapter 14) or conduct an *experiment* (Chapters 8, 9, and 10). To aid the researcher in selecting an appropriate data-gathering technique, a familiarity with its advantages and limitations is important. All techniques have both. Such knowledge will enable the researcher to choose with more confidence the one (or ones) most appropriate to the specific problem being studied.

The methods of the scientist are neither mystical nor difficult. They are learned readily. They are as capable of being applied to personal problems as they are capable of producing academic tomes. The reader will be encouraged to become a practitioner who more often uses any of various methods to gather data objectively and less often uses what we choose to call rationalisms.

RATIONALISM

A rationalism occurs when a person invents a reason to explain the occurrence of an event, situation, or phenomenon. Rationalisms are also offered to explain the behavior of a person or a group. The primary characteristic of a rationalism is that the reason offered as the explanation is a product of one's thinking, wish, experience, or perception. It is *not* based on data that have been gathered in a fashion that meet scientific standards.

It should be noted that both rationalisms and data-based conclusions are capable of being either correct or incorrect. Both may be generally accepted or rejected. Rationalism can best be described as dataless reasoning. Data-based conclusions require that the reasoning include or be based upon data that have been gathered in a clearly defined manner. Further, the conclusion reached must be confined to the data, their analysis, and their synthesis.

The term rationalism as just defined has its antecedents in the branch or school of philosophy known as rationalism. Briefly, this doctrine states that reason is the source of knowledge and the knowledge that is derived can be obtained independently of experience. Rationalism also encompasses the view that every effect has a cause and that one can attribute a cause to an effect by the process or power of reason. As we shall see in Chapter 8, the scientific approach in attributing causation is not as simple.

A major problem is that rationalism can occur by "just sitting there and reasoning." Since this is so much easier than systematic data gathering, it is widespread and rather commonly used by people in the course of everyday life. It is also used by scientists and experts.

A segment of a newspaper item can serve as an example. In an article by Hillery (1982) in the *Wall Street Journal* it was reported that the Dow-Jones industrial average went down and on the preceding day it went up almost three times as much. Amusingly, the article refers to the reasoning or rationalism of four experts. They have quite different explanations for the same event. We also find that one of these experts mentions that "psychology was warming up again" and another states, "it just took a spark to set off a wave of emotional buying." It should be emphasized that psychologists do not understand such language, except as rationalisms.

What rationalisms have in their favor is that individuals can make up reasons for whatever takes place and for almost anything. People do not hesitate to offer reasons that disregard and even run counter to facts and data.

It is "dull" not to be able to explain to yourself, and especially to others, what has or will happen. It is "sharp" to offer reasons. Sometimes research establishes a fact, but the reason for the fact is supplied by the researcher. It is more appropriate for the researcher to obtain both fact and reason from the data.

EXPERIENCE ≠ DATA GATHERING

Experience has certain advantages as well as disadvantages in our daily living. It can be an impediment or obstacle in the data-gathering process. Experience prepared us very well for yesterday, but it only helps us in the present or future to the degree that the elements, variables, and responses will be identical or similar to those that existed in the past. Does the experience of being the parent of 10 children result in becoming a better parent? Hardly! Does being married four or more times provide the experience of being a better spouse than someone who has only been married once? Hardly. Or maybe!

An example of the limitations of experience may be offered by recognizing that the continued experience of living prepares one better for yesterday than for tomorrow. Are people in their twenties prepared for the thirties or forties, or do they have to live through them? Being 60 or 70 years old does not really provide one with the experience to adjust to being older. Becoming older, however, does allow one to talk about or relive the past. Memory of the past, however, may be accurate or inaccurate.

For most research projects one needs to review the experiences and data gathered by others. In addition, one should consider and select the method(s) for gathering current data. To illustrate, if one is researching unemployment, inflation, auto driving safety, or any other topic, one should review what others have done and then add one's own data. The solutions to past problems may not be lasting solutions.

In the social realm, solutions to problems often create additional questions. For example, does public housing create slums or does it provide housing for the underprivileged? Or, does bilingual education increase English literacy or decrease it? There is a need to solve existing problems by gathering data that consider the variables which confound the present setting and which did not exist in the past. An advantage of being familiar with data-gathering methods is that it should encourage us to be less dependent on our former experiences and more alert for the newer variables that need to be recognized, considered, and manipulated as we attempt to solve today's problems. Housing, crime, peace, health, and safety are just a few problems for which solutions are needed.

SCIENCE AND PSEUDOSCIENCE

A cogent discussion of the differences between science and pseudoscience can be found in the work of Radner and Radner (1982). Pseudoscience includes a number of constantly recurring themes such as astrology, unidentified flying objects, flat earth, ancient astronauts, and psychic phenomena. It is distinguished from science by a characteristic unwillingness to accept disconfirming data.

Pseudoscientists typically take a position that makes them immune to criticism. The only data recognized are those that support the claims of the pseudoscientist. As an illustration, the official policy of the *Journal of Parapsychology* is not to publish negative reports. The major defense for pseudosciences has been to say that "anything is possible." Radner and Radner point out that "it is a mistake to suppose, however, that what has not been proven to be impossible has been proven to be possible" (p. 82).

Science, however, recognizes all data that have been gathered by using appropriate methods. Those methods are the ones discussed in the second part of this book. Although science does not yet have all the correct answers, science does have the methods for deciding whether answers are or are not correct. Pseudoscience lacks such a collection of careful and effective data-gathering methods. It is not data per se that distinguish science from pseudoscience but the methods used to gather data and the uses to which data are put (e.g., science does not ignore negative results).

MISREPRESENTATION AND SCIENCE

Because scientists are people, it can be predicted that their motives, goals, and personalities will resemble those of the population found in their specific cultures and societies. This means that in addition to possessing desirable moral and ethical values, they also may possess undesirable qualities. For instance, they may offer disingenuous explanations, present theories that are biased, or seek notoriety by being sensational.

The necessary admonition is: do not believe everything you read or hear, even from the mouths of scientists, whether they work for corporations, universities, or the government, have sponsored research grants, or are unemployed.

Blum (1977) refers to the two major sins of research as stupidity and dishonesty. However, such labeling does not convey the complexities of the problems related to the spreading stain of scientific fraud. Broad (1981) lists some examples:

●John Long, a researcher with $750,000 in federal funds at Massachusetts General Hospital, forged data and for seven years watched over a cell line for the study of Hodgkin's disease that proved to be absolutely useless.

●Vijay Soman, a researcher at Yale medical school, plagiarized a rival's paper, fabricated data, and received for 1980 alone some $100,000 in NIH support. Eleven papers were retracted. He ultimately returned to his home in India, but left his coauthor and boss, Philip Felig, in an administrative and ethical tangle.

●Elias A. K. Alsabti, a young researcher from Jordan, pirated almost word-for-word at least seven papers and published them in obscure journals.

●Marc Straus, a Boston University researcher who in three years was awarded nearly $1,000,000 in cancer research grants, submitted reports containing repeated falsifications. He resigned under fire, insisting that he was the victim of a conspiracy by select members of his 20-person staff. More than two years later, after the Boston *Globe* ran a five-part series on the affair, the National Cancer Institute (NCI) initiated an investigation.*

*Reprinted with permission from *Science,* vol. 212, pp. 137–141, April 10, 1981. Copyright 1981 by the AAAS.

Whereas some scientists espouse the view of a self-correcting mechanism whereby scientific inquiry is subject to rigorous policing, others believe that academic research centers foster intense pressure to publish, to obtain research and renewals of grants, or to qualify for promotion. Still others believe that finagling is endemic and that public exposure is to be continually encouraged.

Another confusing and corrupting influence occurs when a sponsor or a view is immune from scrutiny. Burt's studies of identical twins is an outstanding example of this. It required about 40 years to have some researchers conclude that Burt may have either doctored or invented his data. A rather good and succinct summary exists in the last paragraphs of Broad's article:

> No matter why they come forth, the recent cases illuminate much. They disclose a gap between the ideal and the real, between reliance on automatic self-policing and the fact that mechanisms such as immunity from scrutiny often prevail. They hint at support of philosophical views that say finagling of one sort or another may be endemic to the research enterprise. Perhaps further study of the dark side will disclose more about the structure of science. At the very least, the recent cases illustrate that "organized skepticism" and the self-policing nature of science need themselves be taken with a little more skepticism.

Another reference might be made to a column by Suzanne Garment (1980) writing on the Food and Nutrition Board, a voluntary committee of the National Academy of Sciences. An excerpt from the column is as follows:

> But modern day public science—with its aggrieved public agencies, vested-interest private organizations, attendant congressional committees and concerned editorialists—quickly got itself together and began to rake the board over the coals. It raised the Imbalance Charge, asserting that the board had no epidemiologists and therefore had ignored the epidemiological evidence. It raised the Confusion Problem, accusing the board of acting only to befuddle the public. And most of all it raised the specter of Conflict of Interest, pointing out triumphantly that one of the board members had actually done consulting for the American Egg Board. It was with these whiffs of scandal tantalizingly displayed that the House subcommittee finally opened its proceedings.
>
> But somehow the hearings flopped. Not one real impropriety was turned up, not a true incompetence exposed, not even a witness left cowering.

Another example of "Is it or is it not accurate" concerns a study conducted in 1970–71 by Mark Sobell and Linda Sobell. According to Kathleen Fisher (1982):

> The Sobell study, conducted in 1970–71 indicated a better outcome for alcoholics who were taught through behavior modification techniques to modify their drinking than for a control group who were treated with the traditional abstinence approach.

Fisher also states:

> In a July *Science* magazine report on a follow-up of the Sobells' subjects, two California psychologists, Mary Pendery, Irving Maltzman and Joylan West dispute the Sobells' findings. And in newspaper interviews, Maltzman has gone beyond suggestions of sloppy research or even bias and accused the Sobells of fraud.
>
> The Pendery study, published in *Science* July 9, says that "most subjects trained to do controlled drinking failed from the outset to drink safely" and "the majority were rehospitalized for alcoholism treatment within a year after their discharge from the research project." After 10 years only one of the 20 had successfully moderated his alcohol consumption they claim.*

It might be noted that in the same issue of the *American Psychological Association Monitor,* Fisher (1982) reported that a special committee appointed by the Alcoholism and Drug Addiction Research Foundation in Toronto, where the Sobells are employed, upheld the integrity of researchers Mark and Linda Sobell. It was also reported that the Pendery group did not cooperate in the committee's investigation on the advice of an attorney.

Even further, a segment of the March 6, 1983, television network program "60 Minutes" was devoted to "The Sobell Experiment." The following are excerpts from the transcript of the program:†

> HARRY REASONER: There is no way an alcoholic can become a social drinker. The only hope for an alcoholic is to give up drinking altogether. That has always been what doctors and psychologists have told men and women with a drinking problem. It's the first thing a drinker learns when he joins Alcoholics Anonymous. Now comes a new theory. An alcoholic can learn to drink in moderation, can be a social drinker.
>
> The new theory followed an experiment conducted by a couple of behavioral psychologists some 10 years ago in California. How successful was the experiment? If you look at the books it spawned, it was a howling success. If you talk to the alcoholics who took part, it was a miserable failure.
>
> What has come to be known as the Sobell Study is now firmly embedded in the literature, in books on the treatment of alcoholism and in standard textbooks on psychology and behavior modification. You're looking at some of them in front of me now. The question is: just how valid was that study?
>
> The idea of the experiment was to train the alcoholics by means of behavioral conditioning. They could drink whatever they liked, but if they ordered their liquor straight or drank too fast or too much, they were given a mild electric shock. Another component of the program was counseling, trying to teach the men problem-solving skills so they could handle their lives and their drinking better.
>
> On the strength of the study, the Sobells gained an international reputation and substantial government grants.

DR. PENDERY: The federal government has spent close to a million dollars just on their work, and many more millions on people whose work was perhaps stimulated by their work.

REASONER: All told, 14 of the 20 men who had been taught to control their drinking were back in the hospital again, for alcoholism, within a year after their discharge.

As a result of her investigation, Dr. Pendery felt that the discrepancies between the Sobells' statistics and the men's lives were so great that she decided to publish her findings. They appeared in *Science* magazine this past summer and created quite a stir, especially in Toronto, Canada, where the Sobells have been working for the past couple of years. They hold senior positions at a world-famous institution, the Addiction Research Foundation.

In response to the questions raised by Dr. Pendery, the foundation appointed a committee to look into the matter. And last fall, after reviewing the Sobells' records, the committee concluded that there was no reason to doubt the scientific or personal integrity of the Sobells. The Sobells feel that they have been vindicated and have declined an interview. They have also not responded to our request to review their records.

DR. PENDERY: People don't understand that that committee was just addressing whether or not they had committed fraud, which wasn't the question I was interested in at all. I was interested in, you know, what's the validity of their work; did this treatment work or did it fail? It failed.

REASONER: The people on the Canadian committee did not talk to any of the men who had been in the study.

DR. PENDERY: No. To my knowledge they contacted none of them, nor did they review any of the hospital records.

REASONER: But with their report, which the Sobells say exonerated them—

DR. PENDERY: Yeah.

REASONER: —are the Sobells still in good standing in the scientific community?

DR. PENDERY: Oh, yes. I would say probably better than ever, within the discipline of psychology—and even in the field of alcoholism.

REASONER: If the Canadian committee had been in touch with the men, they might have seen a different picture from that portrayed by the Sobells' data. This is a blow-up of the Sobells' bar graph for the last six months of their two-year follow-up. Here are the 20 men, listed by their initials, and the vertical bars show how well they were doing on a scale of a hundred. It looks impressive. According to the Sobells, there was every reason to believe that this successful pattern would carry into the future, and they claimed that 19 out of the 20 men were "functioning well" by the end of two years.

DR. PENDERY: I found the other way around, that 19 out of 20 found that it had completely failed and paid a very high price for trying it.

The article shown in Box 1.1 appeared in a September 1983 issue of the *American Psychological Association Monitor.*

Box 1.1 'CONTROLLED DRINKERS' SUE SOBELLS

Patients who were the "controlled drinkers" in Mark and Linda Sobell's 1971–72 study have filed a claim for $80 million against the two psychologists, the hospital where the study was conducted and the state of California.

The patients are alleging fraud and medical malpractice in the study, in which the Sobells reported that the 20 subjects who were taught to drink in a controlled manner functioned better during the two years of the study than another group who were instructed to abstain from consuming alcohol.

Eleven of those patients joined in a claim against the defendants in mid-July, asking for $40 million in general damages from the state, Patton State Hospital and the Sobells, and $40 million in punitive damages from the Sobells. California law allows defendants 45 days to pay a claim before a suit can be filed.

Harry Scolinos, of Dunne, Scolinos, Falvey, McCollough and Marsh in Pasadena, Calif., said he expected the other five surviving controls to join the suit by the time it is filed with U.S. Superior Court in Los Angeles on Sept. 1.

Scolinos said they are charging that the care given the plaintiffs was below minimal standards. "I think our most damaging testimony will come from our clients," he said. He charged that the Sobells did not obtain proper consent, were not well-qualified or properly supervised.

A spokesperson at the Addiction Research Foundation in Toronto, where the Sobells now work, said they were unwilling to comment on the legal action.

Several procedural questions will have to be addressed before the case can go to trial, Scolinos said. For example, injured parties normally have only 100 days after they become aware of their injury to file a claim, and the court will have to agree to waive that limitation.

Similiar cases handled by the firm, which specializes in medical malpractice and personal injury, often don't go to trial for four to five years, he said. But several of the plaintiffs are older than 70, he said, in which case the state allows cases to go to trial within a year.*

*Reprinted with permission from the *American Psychological Association Monitor,* vol. 11, no. 9, September 1983. Copyright 1983 by the American Psychological Association.

Finally, Fisher (1984) reported the results of a federal investigative team, whose report concluded that the Sobells were "ambiguous but not fraudulent." The investigative team indicated that their report was inconclusive because parties on both sides failed to cooperate fully. Their report found that the Sobells were "careless in preparing their manuscripts for publication."

Scientists have different biases toward one or another theory or one or another point of view. Also, their employers may be universities, corporations, foundations, or government, and such organizations may need money to continue to exist.

One must weigh evidence carefully and not believe everything. The public and private sectors may be equally noble, but different. To weigh evidence, one must know something about the data-gathering method(s) used to obtain it.

CAUSE-AND-EFFECT CONFUSION

In the social sciences, including psychology, researchers sometimes establish relationships or associations between the characteristics/behavior of people and events. These relationships can also be expressed in numbers and are then known as correlations. It is most important to recognize that such relationships or correlations do not necessarily mean that a cause-and-effect relationship has been established. We will discuss cause and effect more fully in Chapter 8, but for the present it is important to recognize that science does not accept the view that cause and effect operates, no matter how formidable a relationship appears. When two events are related, one may or may not be the cause of the other.

A delightful illustration is the "Super Bowl Stock Market Predictor." Accompanying the Super Bowl hype each year is the "remarkable fact" that since 1967, the New York Stock Exchange index rises every year a National Football Conference team wins. Conversely, every year an American Football Conference team wins the market falls. This fact is as good an example as any to indicate that relationships do not establish cause and effect—unless someone wants (unscientifically) to attribute cause and effect to this phenomenon.

Among other "indicators" of a rise in stock market indices mentioned by R. F. Winans (1984) are such items as snow on the ground on Christmas Day in Boston and the rising of women's hemlines.

Those of us with a touch of mysticism or quaintness must surely ask how it is possible for the NFC team to win 11 times and the Standard & Poor's Index to rise each time without there being a meaningful or causal relationship. When an AFC team wins, the index goes down. There has been only one exception, and even this exception was a cliff-hanger: the index rose only 0.1%. Those of us with a bent toward science recognize that a football team affiliation cannot in any way cause a rise or fall in the Standard & Poor's index, even if it did happen 16 out of 17 times.

Another, but quite different, relationship considers changes in animal or human behavior and the lunar phase cycle. In a column in the *Wall Street Journal* by M. Loeb (1983), reference is made to two professionals who believe, or at least report, data establishing a relationship.

In his book "The Lunar Effect: Biological Tides and Human Emotions," Arnold L. Lieber traced 1,887 homicides in Dade County, Fla., between 1956 and 1970. A graph he devised plotting the murder rate showed "a striking correlation with the lunar phase cycle," Dr. Lieber said. "The homicides peaked at full moon."

In Chicago, Ralph Morris, a professor at the University of Illinois College of Pharmacy, says his research "indicates a correlation between the week of the full moon and a greater incidence of bleeding ulcer attacks, as well as coronary attacks in angina patients." He concludes that "stress-related diseases are most likely to have their crises, whether behavioral or physical."

Again, the reader can choose between either no relationship, no cause and effect, or the popular lunar belief.

One must remember that even when a relationship has been established, many possible causal explanations are always possible. Data gathering aids one in sorting out these explanations and in rejecting those that are merely rationalisms.

THE SCIENCE OF DATA GATHERING

Gathering data in a defined, prescribed, and systematic fashion is the cornerstone of science. A role of the researcher is to select the method or methods that will gather the data most appropriately and effectively. Data gathering leads to data analysis and synthesis, which, in turn, lead to problem solving and decision making.

Although not all data-gathering methods meet the requirements of science, those that do must satisfy two sets of conditions. The *first set* is related to considering three types of variables: *independent, dependent,* and *confounding.* The independent variable is the one the researcher chooses, selects, or decides to manipulate. This manipulation produces varying responses. These responses become variables of the second type, known as the dependent variables. In addition, other variables enter the situation because the researcher has been unable to anticipate their existence or influence, or because such variables were not eliminated or controlled. These are known as the confounding variables.

It is essential to recognize that regardless of the data-gathering method used, these three types of variables are part of the data that have been gathered. To be sure, they are somewhat different from one data-gathering system to another, but they are clearly identifiable and recognizable. Table 1.1 is intended to serve as a partial illustration of each of these variables for the eight different data gathering systems included in this book.

The *second set* of basic conditions requires an awareness of the measurement, reliability, and validity of the data. Although concern with variables takes place either concurrently, as an antecedent, or subsequently, the data that are gathered must meet certain standards. These standards include measurement, reliability, and validity.

At the outset it should be recognized that data can be presented in either a quantitative or a qualitative fashion. Such presentation requires decisions regarding the development and use of measuring instruments, be they rating scales, tests, or observation charts.

The need for estimates of reliability and validity is fundamental to all measurements if they are to have scientific credibility. For different methods of data gathering there may be somewhat different definitions to demonstrate reli-

Table 1.1 ILLUSTRATION OF VARIABLE TYPE

Gathering system	Independent	Dependent	Confounding
Observation	The selection or determination of the place or scene	What people do	An environmental change that was not anticipated (rain)
Experiment	What researcher manipulates	Response of subjects	Uncontrolled events that interfere with results
Field research	The locale in which data are obtained	The demographics and behavior of people in that field	Inadequate sampling because of unpredicted circumstances
Survey	The inquiry developed to obtain data	The responses	The dropouts
Case history	Selection of subject	The actions and thinking of the subject	Errors of memory distortion and bias
Group discussion	The guide used to lead the discussion	The reactions and interactions	The excessive influence of an aberrant
Archives	Selecting the source(s)	Extracting from existing data	Incomplete data in original or secondary source
Simulation	The adequacy of the facsimile	The responses of subjects	Whether transfer to the "real thing" will work

ability and validity, but no data can be accepted as having some scientific basis without knowing how the measurement was obtained, that the measurement will be similar upon repetition (i.e., reliability), and that the measurement is an accurate portrayal of the existing reality—whether it is one's intelligence quotient, or the prediction of an election, or any of many different concepts (i.e., validity).

PROBLEM SOLVING

Sarason (1978) published some cogent comments worthy of serious consideration. He stated:

A problem has been "solved" (a) when it does not have to be solved again because the operations that led to the solution can be demonstrated to be independent of who performs them, (b) when the solution is an answer to a question or set of related questions, and (c) when there is no longer any doubt that the answer is the correct one. If there are competing answers, the problem has not yet been solved. Problem solving is a venerable and sprawling field in psychology. I wish to note two of its characteristics. The first is that almost without exception the human subject is presented with a problem that is solvable, although the correct answer may be arrived at in different ways.

A second characteristic of the problem-solving literature is that the types of problems used in research almost defy categorization. It is an exaggeration to say that each researcher develops his or her own stimulus problem, but it is not a gross exaggeration. It would be understandable if someone concluded that when researchers used the words *problem solving,* they were far more interested in *solving* than they were in *problems.*

In science, problems may be extraordinarily difficult, but they can never be viewed as intractable, and if some fool says a problem is intractable it is because he or she is not posing the problem correctly or does not have the brain power to work through to the solution. In science, fools are people who say problems are intractable. In the realm of social action, fools are people who say all problems are tractable.*

In other words, the social sciences cover many problem areas. Some problems are readily tractable and find their way into the professional journals. It must be recognized that social sciences study social problems that could lead to varieties of social actions. Some of these problems are poverty, war, drugs, aging, inflation, nutrition, and housing. Research in such areas often finds solutions that create additional problems requiring solutions.

Sarason asked:

> Just as technology depends on basic science, don't both depend on or reflect the wishes of the larger society? What will happen if and when the social world changes and the relation between society and psychology is altered so that psychology is asked and willingly attempts to solve social problems it never encountered, and never could encounter, either in the laboratory or through employment of any of its research strategies? Will psychology be found inherently wanting?

Well-meaning laypersons often ask, "If we can put a man on the moon or return a space ship to earth, why can't we solve societal, economic and psychological problems?" Probably the question indicates a lack of understanding about what social scientists can and cannot do. The man on the moon and the space ship are problems that can be solved by mechanical, technical, electronic, and mathematical processes. The problems are essentially physical and the variables are known and controllable or correctable. Problems in social science are confounded by not appropriately identifying the problem, not recognizing that more than one solution is possible, and, most frustratingly, not being able to eliminate, control, or hold constant the imponderable variables that are continually changing the environment for the problem solver.

*Reprinted with permission from *American Psychologist,* vol. 33, pp. 370–380, 1978. Copyright 1978 by the American Psychological Association.

As Sarason has indicated, we do better at problem changing than we do at problem solving. We also seem to do much better at offering solutions than at defining and solving the problem. An illustration is provided by individuals who repeatedly go on different diets or attempt to stop smoking or drinking. Another illustration is provided by politicians who propose either lowering or increasing taxes as a solution to the problem of unemployment.

AND IN CONCLUSION

Probably as good a way as any to end an introductory chapter of a book on data gathering is to refer to the writing of Kaplan (1964):

> In addition to the social pressures from the scientific community there is also at work a very human trait of individual scientists. I call it *the law of the instrument,* and it may be formulated as follows: Give a small boy a hammer, and he will find that everything he encounters needs pounding. It comes as no particular surprise to discover that a scientist formulates problems in a way which requires for their solution just those techniques in which he himself is especially skilled. To select candidates for training as pilots, one psychologist will conduct depth interviews, another will employ projective tests, a third will apply statistical techniques to questionnaire data, while a fourth will regard the problem as a "practical" one beyond the capacity of a science which cannot yet fully predict the performance of a rat in a maze. And standing apart from them all may be yet another psychologist laboring in remote majesty—as the rest see him—on a mathematical model of human learning.
>
> The law of the instrument, however, is by no means wholly pernicious in its working. . . . What is objectionable is not that some techniques are pushed to the utmost, but that others, in consequence, are denied the name of science. The price of training is always a certain "trained incapacity": the more we know how to do something, the harder it is to learn to do it differently. . . . I believe it is important that training in behavioral science encourage appreciation of the greatest possible range of techniques.

chapter 2

Scientific Data

Data gathering serves as both an aid and a necessity in reaching conclusions, but one should be aware that data can be obtained by using any of many appropriate, but different, techniques.

One must first, however, establish what data are. The Oxford English Dictionary (1971) defines a *datum* as "something known or assumed as fact and made the basis of reasoning or calculation." This definition certainly reinforces our theme of using data, rather than rationalisms, for making reasoned decisions. Data are facts that serve as the basis of reasoning. But what exactly are facts? The same dictionary defines a *fact* as "something that has *really* occurred or is actually the case; a datum of experience" (emphasis ours). Well, that helps to clarify the situation: data are facts and facts are data. They are things that really exist, have really happened, and are not merely the products of our imagination. Although it may not always be easy to separate reality from imagination, most of the time we all have the feeling that we know which things are factual and which are not. For example, consider the following statements and decide which are facts and which are not:

(a) The moon is made of green cheese.
(b) Santa Claus lives at the North Pole.
(c) 2 + 2 = 4.
(d) Humans need oxygen to live.
(e) People enjoy laughing.
(f) We are being observed by extraterrestrials.
(g) Misery loves company.
(h) All humans have an immortal soul.

Most people will say that statements (a) (the moon is made of green cheese) and (b) (Santa Claus lives at the North Pole) are not facts and that statements (c) $(2 + 2 = 4)$ and (d) (humans need oxygen to live) are. Statement (a) is not a fact because we have been able to observe the moon through telescopes, walk on it, and bring pieces of it back to the earth for scientific study. We have found no evidence at all for the notion that the moon is made of green cheese. That is, such a view is not supported by more exacting observations.

Statement (b) is not a fact; it is a myth. We all know that it is a story told to young children. In this case there seems to be no need for observation; we all know it just is not so. If Santa Claus lives anywhere, but in parking lots and department stores, it is in the hearts of young children (and parents too).

Statement (c) is certainly true but it is not what we usually mean by a fact. It is true by definition rather than by observation. The statement is, in a sense, redundant. It is the same sort of "fact" as the statement "a horse is a horse" or "the day after Sunday is Monday." We need gather no data to determine the veracity of such claims.

Statement (d), about oxygen, on the other hand, is both true and factual. The claim is supported by a wealth of reinforcing observations. Without some observation one would not know whether the statement was a fact or an *hypothesis. An hypothesis is a tentative solution, an educated guess, as to what the true state of affairs is.*

Statements (e) through (g) are all hypotheses with varying degrees of observational support. For example, the statement that people enjoy laughing seems to have quite a bit of support and, thus, might be considered a fact. The support, however, comes mostly from rather unsystematic, if not biased, observation. We see people laugh and they seem to be enjoying themselves, but people also laugh when they are shy or nervous or tense. Some people never seem to laugh. Maybe all of the people you know enjoy laughing, but you do not know all people. It is probably safest to withhold judgment on the factual basis of this statement until more observations are made.

As mentioned, statements (f) (we are being observed by extraterrestrials) and (g) (misery loves company) are also hypotheses. There is very little support for the statement that extraterrestrials are observing us, while there seems to be a fair amount of support for the statement that misery loves company (at least under some circumstances). We do not, however, have enough observations to allow us to conclude with certainty that statement (g) is a fact and that statement (f) is not. This may seem a bit unfair at first. After all, how much observation is needed? Well (as we shall see later in this chapter), one must consider the quality as well as the quantity of the observations. None of us should be willing to call something a fact unless we have several consistent and reinforcing observations. By way of example, if you eat a bag of potato chips you expect (perhaps not consciously) several observations to support that "fact." You can see, feel, taste, smell, and hear (crunch) the chips. Suppose you could taste the chips (i.e., one observation to support the hypothesis that you are eating chips) but saw none, felt none, smelled none, and heard none. Most people would probably believe that, in such a case, the taste observation was an illusion. We demand several pieces of consistent and supporting evidence before concluding that something is (or is not) a fact. We often do this automatically and unconsciously; scientists must do it systematically and consciously.

Finally, statement (h) (all humans have an immortal soul) is an hypothesis but not one subject to scientific investigation. No observations can be obtained to determine whether the statement is or is not a fact. It is a question of belief. This statement cannot be supported by data or observation. This and similar beliefs are unsubstantiated.

Consistent with the scientific point of view, we will from now on use the term hypothesis only to refer to statements that can be tested through observation.

Let us summarize what we have so far. Data are facts provided they are supported by reinforced observations. *They are observed.* Hypotheses are not facts. Hypotheses must be checked against observations to see if there is any support for them; their validity is tested through observation. Box 2.1 illustrates this difference between data and hypotheses.

The exercise of determining whether statements (a) through (h) were facts should have made it clear that observation(s) is very important for such determinations. Scientists must be very careful in gathering data through observation and are generally very concerned with criteria that can be used to separate "good" data (i.e., real facts) from bad. These criteria fall under the general headings of measurement, reliability, and validity.

MEASUREMENT

Scientific data are facts that have been measured. Although there are many different forms of measurement, all are designed to obtain data as objectively as possible. Personal bias or convictions should never influence data gathering and it is absolutely necessary to eliminate such data-gathering bias by using objective measures. *Objective measures assign labels to data by using a scale.* The use of a scale is intended to eliminate subjectivity from our data gathering. Scientists generally classify their measures by using two kinds of labels and four kinds of scales.

Labels

One usually thinks of measurement as involving numbers that specify different *amounts* of something. For example, different amounts of length might be specified in number of centimeters, different amounts of income in number of dollars, and different amounts of intelligence in number of IQ points. Numbers, which do specify amounts, are called *quantitative* labels. Most measures in science are quantitative.

The other kind of label is called *qualitative*. Qualitative labels do not specify amounts, they specify *kinds* of things. For example, the labels male and female specify different kinds of individuals, as do the labels native and foreign; black and white; and butcher, baker, and candlestick maker.

One should not conclude that the difference between quantitative and qualitative labels is the same as the difference between number and word labels. It is not. There are instances in which numbers are used qualitatively and in which

Box 2.1   FACTS AND HYPOTHESES

Hypotheses are tentative; they represent our best guess about the way things are. Hypotheses are checked by gathering data. When enough data are gathered (no one can say *exactly* how much is enough) to support the hypothesis then the hypothesis is accepted as a fact. Unfortunately, what we see on television or read, as well as what is (with some frequency) presented by scientists, are hypotheses with little or no supporting data. The problem is that they are presented as if they were facts. This is dangerous and our readers should be alerted to avoid such confusions.

For example, Bent and Rossum (1976) state that "The common belief among many policemen that they operate in an unsympathetic, critical, and uncomprehending community leads them to isolate themselves from the community and to seek peer group alliances with fellow officers" (p. 191). This appears to be a statement of fact. This "common belief" produces isolation and alliances with fellow police officers. Are there data to support this? Cohn and Viano (1976) say "the police community perceives itself as a minority group, disadvantaged and discriminated against" and that the "dynamics of this self-perception . . . involve reinforced defensive group solidarity, intensified feelings of alienation and polarization" (p. 402). Again, no data are offered in support of the claim.

Are there any data? Radelet (1980) reports "relevant" data from a 1969 survey in which police officers of all ranks were asked a series of questions about their jobs. The International Association of Chiefs of Police conducted the survey and found that only 40% felt that the police image was favorable in the community where they worked and 16% said that there was little respect for the profession from outsiders. Radelet reports that "Only 14% thought the most pressing problem was lack of understanding and support by citizens" (p. 102). The data support, to some extent, the notion that police do perceive themselves to be unaccepted by the community.

The view that this leads to isolation and/or alienation is, however, just an hypothesis. It is difficult to separate hypothesis from fact when information is presented in this manner. It appears to be factual, but is it? Clark (1979) argues strongly for better and more frequent data collection on police-community relations and we wholeheartedly support the hypothesis that more data are (always) needed. Or is that a fact?

words are used quantitatively. For example, zip code numbers are qualitative labels that inform one where an address is. Verbal labels like better-worse, taller-shorter, and faster-slower, on the other hand, tell one about *amounts* of goodness, height, and speed, respectively.

Generally, scientists prefer to use numbers over words and quantitative over qualitative labels in an effort to increase precision and objectivity. When quantitative measures are considered, verbal labels are always somewhat less precise. For example, if measures of intelligence were "very little, not very much, a little bit, almost an average amount, an average amount, more than average, a goodly amount, quite a lot, a whole lot," it would be difficult to place individuals appropriately into such categories. It is not at all clear where the boundaries are between such categories, or for that matter, exactly what the categories really mean. Numerical measures such as points on an IQ test are far more precise, although, as we will soon see, they too are far from perfect. Many writers (e.g., Asimov, 1960; Hull, 1920) claim that science tends to progress from qualitative to quantitative measures. Initially, sciences are busy discovering, naming, and differentiating, that is, doing qualitative work. Later, sciences are busy quantifying these discovered qualities. Science strives toward quantification of the relevant domain. Although this seems to be generally true, such a claim must not be interpreted as denigrating qualitative measures. One should always use the best measure available, and in many instances that measure is a qualitative one.

Scales

Measurement scales are generally divided into four different types (Stevens, 1951). The scales represent different kinds of measurements, progressing from qualitative measures on the first scale to quantitative on the remaining three. The scales are called nominal, ordinal, interval, and ratio.

Nominal Scale.   Nominal scale measures are qualitative measures; as implied by the title "nominal," they name things. They serve to differentiate one collection of data from another and carry no implication of relative or absolute quantity. Examples include numerical labels such as those found on the jerseys of football players (they imply assigned position, not excellence of play) and verbal labels such as male-female, democrat-republican, and psychologist-psychiatrist. Although people often have the initial impression that number labels always imply quantities, nominal scale numbers do not. The player wearing jersey number 40 is not necessarily a better player than the one wearing jersey number 20. These nominal scale numbers only tell us that they are different players and the position played, but not who is better or best.

Ordinal Scale.   Ordinal scale measures name things and, as the name implies, also order things along some dimension. For example, the labels might order things from biggest to smallest, fastest to slowest, or best to worst. Thus, these labels do tell us something about quantity or degree. It is easiest to understand what they tell us by looking at an example. Suppose we conduct a survey of all the patients in a certain hospital ward. We ask them to rank the eight members of the nursing staff from best to worst on quality of care administered. We then combine all these rankings into an overall ordering of the staff as follows:

No. 1: Nurse Mary
No. 2: Nurse Ron

No. 3: Nurse Janet

No. 4: Nurse Art

No. 5: Nurse Lorrain

No. 6: Nurse Gary

No. 7: Nurse Joan

No. 8: Nurse Harold

The numbers 1 through 8 are ordinal scale numbers. They tell us two things. First, they tell us that each number represents a different case; it "names" a different nurse. Second, they tell us that, in terms of quality of care, nurse no. 1 is better than no. 2, no. 2 is better than no. 3, no. 3 is better than no. 4, and so on, according to the patients in the ward who are receiving the care. That, however, is all that the numbers tell us. We do not know *how much* better no. 1 is than no. 2, or no. 2 is than no. 3, and so on. It may be the case that the nurse ranked no. 1 is head and shoulders above all the rest and that the other seven are very similar. Or perhaps the first three are very similar with only a slight difference among them, whereas all the rest are considerably lower in quality of care. The rank order from first to eighth does not answer questions about differences or intervals between numbers.

Verbal labels that are used quantitatively are best thought of as being on an ordinal scale. They certainly indicate different amounts of something, but rarely, if ever, are the intervals between labels made specific. For example, "excellent" is better than "good" and "good" is better than "fair," but the difference between excellent and good may or may not be the same as the difference between good and fair. Even more complex is the fact that one person's excellent might be another's good. We do, however, know that good is not as good as excellent.

Interval Scale.   Interval scale measures name, order, and also place equal intervals between things. The difference between adjacent labels is meaningful; it is always the same. Calendar year numbers are interval scale labels. The interval between 1492 and 1493 is the same as the interval between 1984 and 1985. Degrees Fahrenheit (centigrade also) are interval scale labels. The difference in amount of measured heat, between 20° and 30°, is the same as the difference between 75° and 85°. Although the difference in measured heat is the same in these two conditions (i.e., 20°–30° vs. 75°–85°), the difference in perceived heat is not. One typically feels a bigger change from 20° to 30° than from 75° to 85°. Interval changes in physical inputs (e.g., measured heat) do not typically produce interval changes in perception (e.g., felt heat).

Let us return to our example of evaluating the nursing staff in a hospital ward. Table 2.1 shows the rank ordering we previously discussed and an interval scale measure as well. The interval scale involves, in this case, asking how many patients named a particular nurse as best in the ward. This assumes that each patient's ranking of a number one nurse is the same. That is, receiving a number one ranking from the cardiac patient in bed 3 is no better or worse than receiving a number one ranking from the patient with severe allergies in bed 12. Now we can see what the differences between ranks reflect. The difference between nurse 1 and nurse 2 is the same as that between 2 and 3 (i.e., two "number one" ranks). Interval scale numbers give us information about how much more of the thing measured a certain datum has.

Ratio Scale.   Ratio scale measures name and order, have equal intervals, and also have an absolute (or natural) zero. That is, zero on the scale really means zero amount of what is being measured. For example, zero centimeters (not 0.0000000001 centimeters) means no length. Zero degrees Kelvin means no measurable heat. Ratio scale numbers tell us about *absolute levels* of the dimension (e.g., length, heat) being measured. Forty degrees Kelvin is twice as hot as twenty degrees.

   Most scientists rely on statistics to help them make sense of the data they have collected. Statistics help describe the collected data and are an aid in drawing inferences about the significance of collected data. For example, it is usually the case that a scientist will want to describe a typical datum and will resort to the calculation of a mean or average. It is also important to describe how different or dispersed the data are, and scientists will thus calculate some index of variability such as the standard deviation. Although all kinds of statistics and mathematical operations are appropriate for ratio scale measures, the same is not true for the other scales. For example, it makes little sense to add up all of the telephone numbers (nominal scale labels) in a directory and calculate the mean telephone number. It is not that one could not do this; it would just be nonsense to make such a calculation. The same can be said for calculating the average football jersey number, zip code, or any other nominal scale number. Statistics are generally very robust and may be calculated on several different scales of measurement, but one should always use good judgment when selecting a statistic for a certain scale.

   Once statistics have been calculated, one uses them in interpreting data and drawing conclusions. Conclusions and interpretations are dependent upon the scale of measurement being used. This is particularly true in the social sciences, since few of our measures can be called ratio scale measures. For the most part we are dealing with ordinal or interval scales and there is frequently considerable

Table 2.1   ORDINAL AND INTERVAL MEASURES OF NURSING STAFF

Ordinal measure Rank	Nurse	Interval measure[a] Number of patients giving a no. 1 rank
1	Nurse Mary	18
2	Nurse Ron	16
3	Nurse Janet	14
4	Nurse Art	7
5	Nurse Lorrain	6
6	Nurse Gary	5
7	Nurse Joan	2
8	Nurse Harold	0

[a]This measure can also be considered a ratio scale.

debate about which of these two scales is being used. To illustrate these difficulties of interpretation, let us assume that we wish to measure intelligence. Figure 2.1 shows the underlying property that is being measured—intelligence—and the four scales used to measure that property.

When we use a nominal scale, the numbers (or words) in the scale tell us only that we are at different points on the underlying dimension. For example, the numbers 100, 0, and 120 on this scale tell us that we have different amounts of intelligence but not what those amounts are in any relative, let alone absolute, sense. In this case, a score of 100 does *not* represent more intelligence than a score of 0. This is difficult to imagine since 100 is clearly a bigger number, but when used nominally the numbers (or any labels) only name things. It is as if we distributed IQ scores by reaching into a hat, pulling out a score, and assigning it to the next individual in line. If two individuals have two different scores on this scale, all we can conclude is that they have somewhat different amounts of intelligence; we do not even know (from the scores) who has more or less.

When we use an ordinal scale we are in a position to say something about the relative amounts of intelligence. That is, someone with a score of 120 has more than someone with a score of 110, and the person with a score of 110 has more than someone with a score of 90. We cannot, however, say how much more. While we might calculate a number of statistics (e.g., means or measures of variability) using ordinal scale numbers, we must exercise caution in reaching conclusions. Suppose, for example, that we measure the intelligence of three different groups: comedians, politicians, and scientists. The mean scores for these three groups are 120, 110, and 121, respectively. We might refer to some statistical test (e.g.,

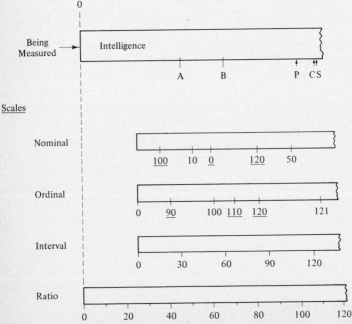

Figure 2.1 Four ways to measure intelligence (or anything else).

analysis of variance) and find that there is no significant difference between the mean scores of comedians (i.e., 120) and scientists (i.e., 121) but that both of these means are significantly higher than the mean score of politicians (i.e., 110). What can we conclude? First, looking at the underlying dimension of intelligence, it is clear that the interval between the data points 120 and 121 is actually greater (in terms of amounts of intelligence) than the interval between points 110 and 120. Thus, the results of our statistical test are nonsense. [Hays (1963, p. 74) points out that "If nonsense is put into the mathematical system, nonsense is sure to come out"—or, more simply, "garbage in—garbage out".] With ordinal scale measures, we must use statistical tests that are designed for that scale. Second, since the intervals between points on the scale are not equal, all that can be said with any certainty is that scientists, who scored 121, have more intelligence than comedians, who scored 120, and that both of these groups have more than politicians, who scored 110. This conclusion says nothing about the magnitude of the differences between the three groups. Finally, we should point out that such problems are very evident when we can see the underlying dimension as in Fig. 2.1. In actuality, of course, one can rarely see the underlying dimension, and it is thus easy to be misled by the numbers. Extreme care must be taken in interpreting and drawing conclusions from ordinal scale numbers.

With an interval scale we are in a much better position to draw conclusions about the magnitude of differences. The intervals between adjacent data points are equal. Thus, if we conduct the same statistical analysis on scores for politicians, comedians, and scientists and again find no difference between the mean scores of comedians and scientists (i.e., 120 and 121) but a significant difference from the mean score for politicians (i.e., 110), we feel confident in concluding that comedians and scientists have about the same amount of intelligence, whereas politicians have significantly less. (Remember, this is a hypothetical example.) One can plainly see this by comparing the mean scores on the interval scale to the quantities on the underlying dimension, which are marked P (politicians), C (comedians), and S (scientists). Even with an interval scale, however, there are some conclusions that cannot be drawn. Notice, for example, that zero on the scale does not correspond to zero amount of intelligence. Because of this, one cannot make statements that describe absolute amounts of the property being measured. For example, one cannot say that someone with a score of 60 has twice as much intelligence as someone with a score of 30. These two points (i.e., a score of 30 and a score of 60) are marked A and B on the underlying dimension of intelligence. Here one can clearly see that point B is *not* twice as much intelligence as point A. To repeat, the danger with an interval scale is, of course, that one cannot really see the underlying dimension and must exercise caution in drawing conclusions.

With a ratio scale, all of these problems are removed. One can make statements about absolute quantities of the property in question. Zero on the scale does correspond to zero amount of the property being measured. There are not many ratio scales in social sciences. Some, which are occasionally treated as ratio scales, are measures of age, income, number of siblings, and reaction time.

It should be clear from our discussion thus far that scientists measure things and strive for precise and objective measures when data are collected. Measures, however, must meet the criteria of reliability and validity.

RELIABILITY

Reliability refers to the *consistency* of measures. If we measure the same thing twice and get the same result each time, we have a reliable measure. If we get different results each time, we have an unreliable measure.

Another indication of reliability involves the concept of *measurement error*. We can think of the scores (i.e., numerical labels) on our measuring instrument as having two components: a true score and some amount of random error. The error may make the obtained scores larger than they should be by adding to the true score, or smaller than they should be by subtracting from the true score. Reliable measures are those with a relatively small amount of measurement error; unreliable measures have a relatively large amount. To help clarify this, let us consider another example. Suppose we want to measure the length of a table top and we have two "rubber" yardsticks that we can use. The tabletop is actually 150 cm long; that is, 150 cm is the true score. The first yardstick gives us a score of 135 cm one time and a score of 165 cm another time. The second yardstick gives us a score of 145 cm one time and 155 cm another time. Considering these measurements, there are three points to be made. First, both yardsticks have a certain amount of measurement error. Neither of them is perfectly reliable. Second, the first yardstick we used has far more measurement error than the second one. The second yardstick is more consistent in the measures it provides. Third, neither of the yardsticks is accurate. However, reliable instruments are not necessarily accurate instruments, and we will have more to say about this problem when we discuss validity.

It can be said that in many instances social scientists use rubber yardsticks. That is, few, if any, of our measures are perfectly reliable; there always seems to be some amount of measurement error. This is due, in part, to the abstract nature of many of the things we try to measure. It is easier to measure length and speed than it is to measure scholastic aptitude, personality, recession, health, or learning. Nevertheless, all scientists strive for as much reliability as possible in their measures. To choose the more reliable measure we must, of course, have some way to assess reliability. One way social scientists do this is to compute a correlation coefficient.

Correlation

From our discussion thus far, it should be clear that reliability can be assessed only when one has at least two measures of the same thing. *A correlation is a statistic that quantifies the relationship between two measures.* For present purposes it is not so important to understand how a correlation is computed as it is to understand the end result, the coefficient of the correlation. To obtain a correlation, one must have two measures from the same individuals. The more individuals measured the better. For example, if we wanted to assess the reliability of a new measure of scholastic aptitude we would want to measure the aptitude of as many individuals as we could. Furthermore, we would need to have two measures on these same individuals. Remember, reliability can be assessed only if we measure the same thing each time. To measure the same scholastic aptitude each time we must obviously measure the same people.

The computed correlation can range in value from −1.00 through 0.00 to +1.00. The strength of the relationship is in the absolute measure or value, while the direction is in the sign. A positive correlation means that high scores on one measure tend to go with high scores on the other measure, low scores with low scores. A negative correlation means that high scores on one measure tend to go with low scores on the other measure (and low scores with high scores). For example, one might expect to find a positive correlation between the amount of time spent studying and performance on a test. That is, people who spend a great deal of time studying (a high score on our measure of study time) should also obtain a high score on the test; people who spend less time studying should score lower on the test.

We might expect to find a negative correlation between amount of time spent studying and amount of time spent watching television, presuming, of course, that people who are studying are not watching TV.

In the social sciences it is very rare to find a correlation of −1.00 or +1.00. Correlations of .20 to .60 are more common. For the purpose of establishing reliability, a correlation of +.90 is desirable.[1]

Finally, we should emphasize (again) that the *strength* of the relationship is in the number itself and not in the sign. A correlation of −.80 indicates a much stronger relationship than one of +.20. While this is so, it is also the case that when we use correlation to assess reliability, only positive correlations are desired. A negative correlation would imply that on one measure of the property in question we obtained a high score and on the other measure of the same property we obtained a low score (e.g., a length of 20 cm, an IQ of 40; a length of 200 cm, an IQ of 140).

Reliability refers to consistent measurements of the same property (e.g., length, IQ) taken at different times.

Types of Reliability

While reliability refers to the consistency of measurement and is generally assessed by obtaining a correlation coefficient, there are several ways of obtaining the two measures necessary. Those ways are referred to as types of reliability (Anastasi, 1982).

Test-Retest Reliability. A most obvious way to obtain two measures of the same thing is to measure it once (e.g., test) and then measure it again (retest) at

[1]Of course, sample size is the crucial issue.

a later time. One can then correlate the two sets of measures to obtain an estimate of reliability.

There are some problems associated with test-retest reliability that limit its usefulness. In the first place, it is unlikely that all the individuals tested in situation one will be available in situation two, particularly when the interval between the two measures is fairly long. Some individuals are almost always lost. A more serious problem is the assumption that the "same individual" is being retested. That is, the individual may be different when tested again. She or he has, for example, now had some practice on this particular test and may perform better. Certain pleasant or unpleasant experiences, illness, stress, and so on, that occurred during the interval may have changed the individual property (e.g., intelligence, maturity, aptitude, interest) being measured. Finally, if the interval is short, one might remember particular responses made on the test the first time and simply repeat those responses from memory. This would artificially inflate the estimate of reliability. Test-retest reliability depends too heavily on the measure being relatively unaffected by repeated application (e.g., tests of sensory-motor abilities).

Alternate-Form Reliability. One way of avoiding some of the problems intrinsic with test-retest reliability is to use two alternate forms of the test and administer one on one occasion and the other on another occasion. This prevents the individual from simply remembering and making the same responses when tested again. It does not solve the difficulties of using the same individuals with the same attributes for the second testing. But, constructing an alternate form of a test is not an easy job.

Split-Half Reliability. One can obtain an estimate of reliability while administering the test only once. One simply correlates scores on one half of the test with scores on the other half. This avoids all of the problems of retesting the same individuals, effects of practice, and memorizing responses, and is thus a technique used quite often.

The test is usually split into odd and even items and the scores on these two halves are then correlated to estimate reliability. An exception to this procedure occurs when there is a subset of items dealing with a single problem (e.g., comprehension questions for a single passage). In such cases, the entire group of items dealing with a particular problem is placed in one or the other half of the test.

Observer Reliability. When behaviors are being observed it is a good idea to use at least two observers. A rough comparison of the two sets of observations (e.g., percent agreement) can be used to estimate their reliability. For example, one might have two examiners score the same set of tests to determine whether or not the examiners are reliable.

Although there are still other kinds of reliability (e.g., Kuder and Richardson, 1937), the important point is that our measures must be as reliable as possible.

VALIDITY

Methods, and observations, as well as tests and measurements, if valid, must measure what they are intended to measure: intelligence, reaction time, an hypothesis, behavior of people, and so forth. When such a specific dimension measures what it purports to measure, then it has *validity*. Although this is true in a very general sense, there are many different kinds of validity, depending on the context in which the term is used. These contexts can be divided into two general categories: methods and test-measurements.

Validity of Methods

We shall spend some time discussing the validity of data-gathering techniques and methods when we discuss those techniques in the second part of this book. For now, we shall simply define two kinds of validity associated with general methodology: internal and external.

Internal validity refers to the ability of a method to isolate an effect and point clearly to the factor(s) responsible for it. For example, we may wish to know if a hungry animal will respond more quickly than a satiated animal. Suppose we take two different animals, starve one and feed the other, and then test their responsiveness. Suppose further that we find a difference in favor of the hungry animal. Is hunger responsible for this effect? Perhaps one animal (the hare) is naturally faster than the other (the tortoise). Perhaps one is younger, older, healthier, bigger, or more experienced on the measurement we devised. To attribute the difference in responsiveness to hunger, we must be able to rule out such variables or alternatives. For example, one might use two of the same species of animal of similar age, health, size, and so on. Using methods that rule out such alternatives contributes to internal validity; failing to do so lowers internal validity.

External validity refers to the generality of a finding. Do the results extend beyond the particular data collected? For example, are hungry animals always faster, or is that only true for the two particular animals and/or amounts of hunger we tested? If it is generally true that hungry animals are faster, then we have external validity.

More about internal and external validity will be discussed in Chapters 8 through 10. Now let us examine the validity of tests and measures.

Validity of Tests and Measures

Most tests and measures have names that specify what they are intended to measure. For example, the Wechsler Intelligence Scale for Children (WISC) is intended to measure intelligence in children; the Minnesota Multiphasic Personality Inventory (MMPI) is intended to measure dimensions of personality adjustment. The problem concerning validity is whether or not tests *really* measure what they are intended to measure. Does the WISC really measure intelligence? Does the MMPI really measure personality adjustment? Or do these tests measure something else such as test-taking ability, general knowledge, conformity, or "fakeability"? There are quite a number of ways to answer such questions and, thus, there are several different kinds of validity associated with tests and measures. These kinds of validity can be classified according to whether they are or are not assessed by using a correlation coefficient. Criterion-related and construct validity are assessed by using correlations; content and face validity are not. We shall discuss content and face validity first.

Content validity refers to the *representativeness* of the test. Do the items on the test adequately sample and represent the property being measured? If we adequately cover the content of the property (dimension, trait, etc.) then we have content validity. If we have a poor sampling of the content then we have poor content validity.

Content validity should be considered when the questions that make up the test are being assembled. One must carefully consider what is to be measured and build a test that covers the domain. Most professors concerned with content validity do just that. He/she examines the material covered in text and lecture and writes (and/or selects from a test manual) appropriate test items. For example, after five weeks of a class in Introductory Psychology, one may have spent one class defining basic terms, two on research methodology, two on physiology, three on learning, and two on motivation. For a 20-item test, one might then ask 2 questions on basic terms, 4 on methods, 4 on physiology, 6 on learning, and 4 on motivation. What is more, each of the questions included on the test would sample each of the topics covered. For example, if four kinds of motivation were discussed, then one might ask one question about each kind. As you might suspect, building a test with high content validity takes considerable effort.

For tests that are built around very specific domains, such as the contents of a course, it is not too difficult to determine whether or not the domain has been adequately covered in the test. When the domain is not so specific, such as the "contents" of intelligence or personality adjustment, one can never be certain whether a test adequately represents the domain or not. The difficulty in such cases is that the contents of the domain are in the mind of the test constructor. Consider for a moment the sorts of things that should be measured to assess personality adjustment. A large number of traits could be included, such as sociability, dominance, sensitivity, stability, assertiveness, creativity, cautiousness, optimism, openness, imagination, and nervousness. Even if we were certain that the list was complete, we might never agree on the correct weights or proportions to assign to each of the traits. In addition, adequately sampling and representing the contents of each individual trait (e.g., sociability) is a problem in its own right. Because of problems such as these, content validity raises serious questions that are not easily answered. In other words, content validity, as an indicator of test validity, has very real limitations.

Face validity refers to whether or not a test seems appropriate to those who take it or to those who administer it. Accordingly, it only offers indirect information on whether the test does or does not measure what it is, or what the author, intended to measure. Face validity can be said to be cosmetic since it primarily refers to appearances. At the same time, it is desirable that tests appear valid so that persons who give and take them will accept them as measures and not reject them out of hand. As Blum and Naylor (1968) suggest, it may be the case that some of the bad publicity associated with tests is due to the fact that the test constructors overlooked the need for face validity. Individuals who construct tests should always strive for a certain amount of face validity. It is important to avoid the view that the test or its items are spurious. For example, a test to measure mechanical skills should involve the use of tools.

Criterion-related validity is assessed by measuring the property in question (e.g., intelligence) using the test to be validated and another, but independent, measure of the same property. The other independent measure is known as the criterion. An example might be grades in school as a criterion for an IQ test. The two sets of scores can then be correlated to provide a quantitative estimate of validity. Criterion-related validity can be of two different kinds: concurrent and predictive.

When one wishes to assess an existing situation to measure things as they now are, one uses *concurrent validation.* The test is administered and related to a criterion administered at the same, or a previous, time. For example, one might devise a test to measure how well students are doing in college. The test is intended to reveal the students' current status. One might correlate test scores by using the student's current grade point average (GPA) as the independent criterion measure of current status. If the resulting correlation is acceptably high (what is acceptable depends on a number of factors such as sample size), the test can be said to have concurrent validity. It would be a valid measure of the current status of college students.

In a number of situations it is important to have a valid measure to assess current status. Such a measure can provide quick and much needed information. This is particularly true in matters of health and safety. A doctor may want to know, through the results of tests, if a patient has or does not have a contagious infection, an illness such as AIDS (acquired immune deficiency syndrome), measles, or, for that matter, any other illness or problem in need of immediate attention.

When a test is designed to predict future performance, one assesses its *predictive validity.* Tests are quite frequently used to predict future performance. Will Arlo do well in college? Will John succeed in this job? Will Cherie respond to this type of therapy? These are some of the kinds of questions that we try to answer by administering tests with predictive validity. In assessing the validity of these tests, the criterion measure is administered *after* the test and the two sets of scores are then correlated. For selection purposes (e.g., admission to college, hiring decisions, selecting appropriate treatments or therapy), predictive validity is most important since it duplicates the situation in which individuals will be selected. When the tests are used as selectors or eliminators, the predictive validity is, however, often not fairly assessed, for the individuals who score low are not admitted to college, given the job, or treated with that therapy. Thus, we do not know whether the test predicted correctly, since we do not know how the eliminated individuals would have performed if they had not been eliminated by their score. Because of this difficulty, it is frequently the case that a criterion measure is administered at the same time as the test. Unfortunately, concurrent validity does not always assure predictive validity and may not really be assessing performance in the future.

There are no easy solutions when assessing predictive validity. One must often admit everyone who takes the test (and the more the better) to college, the job, or therapy where performance is to be predicted. This can be costly, since many individuals will be selected who should not have been selected. For example, many individuals who will not do well in a job will be hired and overall productivity may thus decline. Of course, this cost may be worth it in the long run if it turns out that the predictive validity of the test is high and it can be used in future decisions regarding employment.

Once the predictive validity of a test has been established, one must make certain decisions regarding how the test is to be used. Will it be the only predictor, or one of several, used in determining who is admitted to college, hired, or treated? Will there be some minimum test score such that those who score below it are not admitted, hired, or treated? Decisions such as these can be made to maximize correct choices (e.g., admitting people to college who will do well) and/or minimize incorrect choices (e.g., admitting people to college who will not do well). Several fine texts (e.g., Blum and Naylor, 1968; Cronbach, 1984; Guion, 1965; Nunnally, 1978) illustrate the procedures involved in such decision making.

In assessing criterion-related validity (i.e., concurrent and predictive) one must be careful to maintain independent measures of the property in question. For example, IQ test scores are good predictors of performance in school. The correlation between IQ score and GPA is about +.60 (Anastasi, 1982). But GPAs are not only earned by students but also given by teachers. When a teacher knows that a given student has scored high on an IQ test or in previous courses, that student might be given the benefit of the doubt and receive a higher grade in situations where another student, known to have a low IQ, might be given a lower grade. On another dimension, teachers might have different expectations

Table 2.2   VALIDITY OF TESTS AND MEASURES

Type of validity	Brief description	How assessed
Content	Test adequately *represents* domain being measured.	By comparison of test and domain.
Face	Test *appears* to measure appropriate domain.	By appearance.
Criterion-related: Concurrent	Test measures *current* status.	Correlation with current criterion.
Predictive	Test predicts *future* performance.	Correlation with future criterion.
Construct	Test measures a construct.	Factor analysis and/or convergent/discriminant validation.

for students who have different IQs. While there is considerable debate over the power of such expectations, they do seem to have some influence on performance (Crano and Mellon, 1978). In such instances, the correlation between IQ and GPA can be artificially inflated. The test would appear to be a better predictor than it really is. When validating a test, the criterion measure must be independent.

Construct validity. A construct is an abstract property assumed to account for performance. Terms such as intelligence, altruism, mechanical aptitude, friendliness, motivation, and so on are constructs that social scientists use when describing or explaining human behaviors. For example, Janet did better than Art because she has more _____ (fill in a construct). *Construct validity refers to how well a test measures a certain construct.* It is frequently assessed by correlating test scores with several criteria rather than a single criterion. Although there are several procedures used to assess construct validity, two are particularly important.

The first is the statistical procedure known as *factor analysis.* Factor analysis is a technique for analyzing the interrelationships of a number of measures attributed to a construct. One might, for example, administer a dozen different tests and correlate each one with every test given. Some sets of tests would correlate very highly with one another and thus might be measuring the same factor. Other sets may be measuring different factors. At least they are not correlated with the first set. Factor analysis is a statistical technique for determining how many factors there are, and which test(s) measures which factors. We may determine that a given test measures one factor and that factor is also measured by other tests called intelligence tests. In that case, we will have demonstrated some degree of construct validity for the test; it does seem to measure the construct, intelligence.

The second procedure relies on two additional types of validity: *convergent* and *discriminant* (Campbell, 1960; Campbell and Fiske, 1959). Certain constructs should be related to one another and unrelated to other constructs (i.e., theoretically). For example, intelligence should be related to scholastic aptitude and verbal comprehension but unrelated to sociability and physical stamina. A test with construct validity should correlate highly with tests that measure related constructs and not with tests that measure unrelated constructs. For example, an intelligence test should correlate highly with tests of scholastic aptitude and verbal comprehension but not with tests of sociability and stamina. The former is referred to as convergent validation and the latter as discriminant validation. Together they yield information concerning the construct validity of a test.

Table 2.2 provides a summary of the validity of tests and measures. Ideally, tests should possess all types of validity. For example, we would be very happy (perhaps smug) if our new test of intelligence *adequately covered* the domain of intelligence and, furthermore, *appeared valid* to those who give and those who take the test. This would mean that the test had content as well as face validity. If the test also correlated well with current and future GPAs, we would have concurrent and predictive validity, respectively. Finally, if factor analysis showed that the test measured a factor (or factors) measured by other intelligence tests, and if it correlated well with tests of related domains (i.e., convergent validation) but not with tests of unrelated domains (i.e., discriminant validation), we would have evidence for its construct validity. There are few, if any, tests that can be so well constructed or exist.

Relationship of Validity to Reliability

Tests and measures may be either reliable, or valid, or both, or neither. The relationship of validity to reliability depends on the type of validity being discussed. For example, the attainment of content and face validity does not, in principle, depend on the test's reliability. A test with very low reliability may still cover the domain under investigation (i.e., content validity) and appear to be a good measure (i.e., face validity). Conversely, a highly reliable test may have little or no content or face validity. Content and face validities are independent of the test's reliability. The same cannot be said for criterion-related and construct validities.

A test with low reliability cannot attain a high criterion-related or construct validity. A test with low reliability will not obtain the same scores for the same individuals who take the test. For example, it may obtain an IQ score of 80 in one instance and a score of 120 in another instance when testing the same individual. Such unreliable scores will not correlate highly with the criterion being used (e.g., GPA) to assess concurrent or predictive validity. Construct validity is also assessed by correlation and will also be low when the measures used have low reliabilities. The obtained validity declines as the reliability of the correlated tests declines (see Blum and Naylor, 1968, for an algebraic expression of this relationship).

On the other hand, a test with high reliability will not necessarily obtain a high validity. A reliable test is certainly measuring something but may not be measuring what it is intended to measure. For example, the following two-item test is very reliable.

Question 1: What is the sum of 2 plus 1?
Question 2: What is the sum of 1 plus 3?

People who answer the first question correctly almost always answer the second question correctly (split-half reliability). The test itself, however, is intended to measure personality adjustment. Its criterion-related (not to mention construct) validity, perhaps assessed by correlating performance with scores on the MMPI, is extremely low. In fact, its content and face validities are also, obviously, low. A test, to be valid, must have a high reliability, but a test with high reliability may or may not be valid.

Finally, we should point out that, regardless of the type of validity being discussed, tests can have high reliability with high validity or neither high reliability nor validity. The former is the situation we always strive for; the latter is the situation we hope to avoid. A test with neither reliability nor validity is a useless instrument.

In this chapter we have examined scientific data, which are measured facts. We found that there are a number of different kinds of objective measurement, and that scientists must always be concerned with the reliability and validity of their methods and measures. These concerns, and the care taken to assure high levels of reliability and validity, lead to the belief, and confidence in the belief, that our conclusions based on scientific data are conclusions that are far more consistent and accurate than those based on rationalisms. Data are the basis of scientific reasoning. Reliable and valid reasoning is based upon obtaining reliable and valid data.

chapter *3*

Scientific Thinking: Theory and Related Concepts

Scientific thinking can be differentiated from "ordinary" thinking insofar as it is more disciplined, confined, and restricted. Thinking is considered scientific when it is based on data that meet the criteria of measurability, reliability, and validity. Scientific thinking may be either the antecedent of data gathering or the interpretation of the data after gathering is complete. Usually it is both, but when it is the antecedent of data gathering it does not confuse facts and hypotheses and it does not reach premature conclusions because it recognizes the need for data. As previously stated, scientific thinking and rationalisms differ although both may be imaginative and creative. One is disciplined and the other may resemble a "wild cannon".

Scientific thinking generates hypotheses, laws, models, and theories within a paradigm (Kuhn, 1962). Such constructs integrate and summarize one's thinking as a result of the data gathered. Once reported, others can either replicate or null the position taken. More important, the goals of predicting and controlling behavior are or are not achieved as hypotheses and theories are established as valid or invalid.

The achievement of such scientific goals requires discovery, description, and explanation of the phenomenon being studied. Figure 3.1 illustrates the dynamic relations among these various concepts and sets the parameters of scientific thinking.

When investigating a phenomenon, one starts by gathering data to determine if the phenomenon is real or not, or valid or invalid. This is the stage of *discovery.* If the phenomenon is not real, there is no need for further investigation. If the phenomenon is real, or at least appears to be, one proceeds to a *de-*

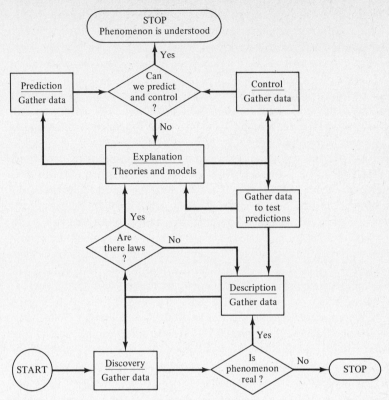

Figure 3.1 The scientific investigation of a phenomenon.

scription of the phenomenon. This also involves gathering data and testing hypotheses about the relations between the phenomenon under investigation and other phenomena. This gathering of data, which describe the phenomenon, enhances further discovery. At this stage, description may lead to the discovery that the phenomenon is not real.

When the phenomenon is real, data gathering eventually results in laws concerning the phenomenon. *Laws are statements about the regularity of phenomena; they state the continuing association between two or more events.* They allow us to predict and repeat phenomena in specified situations. All sciences have laws. Some are specifically labeled as such (e.g., law of supply and demand); others are not. For example, there is a frequent and general association between frustration and aggression. Different forms or kinds of frustration produce different kinds or measures of aggression. This regular association between frustration and aggression is a law, although it is not ordinarily labeled as a law (e.g., law of frustration and aggression).

The emergence of laws calls for *explanation.* Scientific explanations are referred to as models and theories and are meant to show how a phenomenon "works" and how it enters into lawful relations with other phenomena. From explanations, one derives hypotheses that are tested by further data collection.

These explanations are then supported, altered, or rejected by the gathered data. Whether an explanation is supported or not, collected data lead to further attempts at explanation and more description.

From Fig. 3.1, one can see that explanations also lead to attempts to *predict* and *control* the phenomenon. To know if attempted predictions and control have been successful, one must, of course, gather data. As discovery, description, and explanation become complete, prediction and control are enhanced. When one is able to completely predict and control the phenomenon under investigation, one has attained *scientific understanding*.

As Fig. 3.1 suggests, explanation is at the core of scientific understanding. Prediction and control of a phenomenon are quite dependent upon having an adequate explanation. It should also be clear from the figure that data gathering occurs at every step on the way to understanding. Data are the lifeblood of the system. Data are gathered in many different ways and we shall examine many techniques of data gathering in the second part of this book. It is also important to realize that work in all five areas—discovery, description, explanation, prediction, and control—proceeds at the same time but at different rates of progress. Discovery is completed earlier while the goals of prediction and control are completed later. Finally, we should make clear that Fig. 3.1 is our version of scientific investigation and the attainment of scientific understanding. Many other versions have been offered (e.g., Hempel, 1966; Kuhn, 1962; Lauden, 1977). This figure is meant only as one way to conceptualize some of the important interrelations among the various concepts. Now let us examine scientific explanation in general and scientific theory in particular.

SCIENTIFIC EXPLANATION

Scientific explanations are meant to tell *how* a phenomenon "works" and *how* it influences and/or is influenced by other phenomena. In doing this, most explanations focus on the laws that have emerged from data collection. Although it is important to explain irregularities and exceptions, the major focus is on regular, lawful relations.

In everyday conversations, regularities are sometimes ostensibly "explained" by attaching a label to them or naming them. This is not, however, a true explanation and should be guarded against. Labels and names identify phenomena, but do not explain them. For example, if asked why teenagers have problems of identity and often experience role confusion, we might respond by saying that this is due to the "crisis of adolescence." The "crisis of adolescence," however, is only a name for the problems of identity and role confusion that occur; it does not explain them. Considering another example, if asked why so many people are out of work, one might answer by saying that it is due to unemployment. This again is a label, not an explanation. Such labels cannot even be considered rationalisms. Rationalisms for the problems of adolescence or the many people out of work might maintain that the former is produced by cosmic karma during puberty and the latter by the full moon. Rationalisms *are* explanations, but they are based on reason (or lack thereof) alone. They are not scientific because they are not dependent on data. The point to be made here is that naming something or labeling some phenomenon, does not in any way explain it. It is not even a rationalism. Box 3.1 offers further examples of these nonexplanations.

Scientific explanation does not occur in a vacuum. That is, the explanations that are offered for the regularities and phenomena of a science depend not only upon data but also upon the current *paradigm*. A paradigm is an all-encompassing view held by the members of a scientific community. It includes the terms, methods, concepts, data, and explanations of that science (Kuhn, 1962). Different sciences have different paradigms and the same science will progress by moving from one paradigm to another on the way to further scientific understanding. A classic example of a paradigm shift within a science is the change from a physics based on the ideas of Newton to one based on the ideas of Einstein. In social science the change from a strict behaviorist orientation to an information-processing, cognitive approach is sometimes considered a paradigm shift.

The *same* regularities or laws are explained in different ways by scientists who operate under different paradigms. For example, many explanations can be offered for the tendency to ingest food around noon every day. A physiologist might focus on the depletion of the body's resources after a morning of work and the tissue need for nutrients. A psychologist might focus on the hunger drive or the learned habit of eating at lunch time. A sociologist-anthropologist might focus on the cultural norm of eating lunch at noon and social-peer pressures.

When paradigms change, it should be clear that explanations also change. Explanations, however, do not just change when a paradigm changes; they also change within a single paradigm. They are altered by data that reveal gaps and/or inadequacies in an existing explanation. At any one point in time there are always competing explanations, most of which can be predicted to change over the course of time. As Underwood (1957) points out, the explanations offered by science provide "no more than a momentary picture, a picture which would be considerably changed by the flux which is science, were a second analysis made a few years hence" (pp. 174, 175). The picture of science that results is one of a dynamic, continually changing enterprise.

In this enterprise, scientific explanations are known as theories. Before examining scientific theory, two points should be made about scientific explanation in general and reductionism. *Reductionism* is a term that refers to explanations of complex phenomena in terms of simpler phenomena. Two kinds of reductionism need to be considered.

The first is called reduction to the familiar and occurs when an unfamiliar phenomenon (e.g., the structure of atoms or the phenomenon of feedback) is explained in terms of a familiar phenomenon (e.g., the solar system or a thermostat, respectively). Such explanations are usually quite welcome for they are easier to understand. On the other hand, scientific explanations are not always reductions to the familiar. As Hempel (1966) points out, it is frequently the case that scientific explanations are in the other direction. That is, a familiar phenomenon is explained in unfamiliar terms. An outstanding example is Einstein's theory of relativity, where seemingly familiar phenomena (e.g., time, space) are explained in novel ways (e.g., warps, light speed).

Box 3.1 WHAT'S IN AN EXPLANATION?

Psychologists are in the business of investigating mental events, and so we study mental phenomena until we comprehend them thoroughly. The explanation, you might think, should flow smoothly once we fully comprehend the phenomenon. Unfortunately, the explanation often turns out to be less than illuminating. As the following anecdote illustrates, explanations are sometimes just disguised forms of phenomena rather than sources of insight about the phenomena.

While working at one of the computer terminals in my laboratory at UCLA, I noticed that one of the keys on the keyboard did not work properly. The shift (upper/lower case) key on the left side of the keyboard was stuck. That is not absolutely debilitating, because one can use the right-hand shift key all the time, but it is annoying when one has to type uppercase H, J, K, L, N, M, O, and the like. Since everyone in the lab uses the same terminal, I thought I would tell Charlie, our resident computer and mechanical expert, about the problem. He might be able to fix it, and he, in his infinite mechanical wisdom, could explain to me why it was not working. "Charlie," I said, "the left shift key on the keyboard isn't working properly; it's stuck. Do you know why it doesn't work?" Instantly, Charlie's computer-like mind retrieved the answer and formulated an elegant, rigorous explanation, "Yeah, 'cause it's broken."

Rarely have I been so overcome by the power of explanation. My understanding of mechanics took a quantam leap forward. The shift key did not work *because it was broken*.

Now, this anecdote would not be so pathetic if it were unique to Charlie, our resident computer whiz. Unfortunately, it is omnipresent, as the following all-too-common excerpts suggest. "Why does gasoline cost more now than last year, sir?" "Because the prices went up." "Your shirt doesn't go with your pants, dear. What's wrong with them?" "They don't look good together."

Were trained psychologists to refrain from this restatement-as-explanation policy, we could show a bit of disdain toward our fellow explainers. A quick examination of some of our most rigorous journals, however, shows that we are as guilty as others. Thus, we find statements like, "The better recall of words at the beginning of the list was due to primacy effect." Where will it end?

Perhaps we should think more seriously about what constitutes an explanation before offering them so cavalierly.

SOURCE: Prepared by Ron Fisher.

The other type of reductionism is across, rather than within, sciences. In simple terms, the position is that social phenomena and sciences can be explained by biology, and biology, in turn, by chemistry, and, finally, chemistry by physics. This view fosters the relief that all the sciences and the phenomena they study will eventually be reduced to physical explanations. At present, no one can be certain whether or not such a reductionism will occur. There have, of course, been attempts to explain social phenomena in biological terms (Wilson, 1975). We side with those (e.g., Morowitz, 1982) who believe that such a reductionism is unlikely, and that explanations will always be needed on different levels (e.g., physical, biological, psychological, sociological). Which position will prove to be correct is far from clear at this time.

In sum, scientific explanations are not, necessarily, reductionistic. They are attempts to show how a phenomenon works. They are concerned with the laws and regularities among phenomena that emerge as data collection continues. They are called theories.

SCIENTIFIC THEORY

In this section we shall examine the defining properties of scientific theory, the types of theories, and the ways in which theories are evaluated.

Defining Properties

McBurney (1983) points out that the term "theory" is used differently in science than it is in everyday language. In everyday language, it is common to ask whether a statement is a fact or "just a theory." For example, is it a fact that video games are harmful, or is that just a theory? This is different from scientific use of the term theory and for a number of reasons. First, the statement that video games are harmful is an hypothesis, not a theory. It states a relation but offers no explanation. Data must be collected to determine the veracity of this hypothesis and if enough supporting evidence is accumulated, we will regard it as factual. A theory would offer an explanation for any obtained lawful relationship between video games and resulting harm (or benefit). Second, a theory is not, and never can become, a fact. Theories are offered to explain facts and may be valid or invalid, but are never facts.

Another example of common usage revolves around the distinction between theory and "practice." For example, in theory, cramming is a poor way to prepare for a test, but in practice it does not work that way since this is what students do quite frequently. This usage suggests that theories exist on paper (e.g., in books and articles) and that the real world is very different. Scientific theories, however, are meant to explain the real world. In science, if it is not true in practice then it is not true in theory either. Incidentally, cramming works only when it functions as a review (i.e., you have already studied the material).

Generally, scientific usage of the term theory is more narrow and specific than everyday usage. *A scientific theory is a collection of related statements that organize data, explain lawful relationships, and make predictions concerning a variety of phenomena.* The greater the variety of phenomena and the fewer the explaining statements, the better the theory. That is, the best theories explain a great deal of data without having to say very much. A good example is Einstein's theory of relativity.

The collection and *organization of data* is very important for science. Without some organizational framework we would be swamped with stacks of data describing phenomena and their relations to other phenomena. Theories organize these mountains of data by stating what is and/or should be related to what else. Theories *predict* laws and relations that are not yet documented by data. They can lead to new research and give direction to our data collection efforts.

Theories *explain lawful relationships* in a number of ways. They may, for example, explain one relationship by showing it to be an instance of a more general law. For example, rhymes (e.g., "thirty days hath September . . .") produce better memory than rote learning. This finding is explained by, and offers support for, theories that emphasize the importance of organization for memory storage and retrieval. That is, rhymes are an instance of an organizational scheme and, thus, improve memory when compared with an unorganized strategy like rote learning.

Theories may also discover and designate newer concepts to explain a set of data. For example, social behaviors such as helping someone in need, obeying authorities, and liking certain people may be explainable in terms of *attribution.* Attribution is not a name for the social behaviors; it designates an internal process that underlies different social behaviors. That is, you may behave in certain ways toward others, depending on the factors that you think are responsible for *their* behavior (Kelly, 1973). If you attribute someone's need for help to their own carelessness, you may be less inclined to help than if you attribute it to unforeseen circumstances. Such attribution is, of course, never directly observed and, thus is an abstract concept used to explain observable behavior. Theories abound in such abstract concepts, which are often referred to as internal principles (e.g., Hempel, 1966). Because of their abstract nature they must be related to observables by other statements, called bridge principles. That is, theories, which use abstract concepts, must relate those concepts to the observed and observable data that are to be explained. The different ways in which this is done help to distinguish the various types of theories.

Theory Types

There is no universally accepted classification for theory types. Our classification overlaps that of Marx (1963) and describes *deductive, inductive,* and *functional* theories, and *models.*

Deductive Theories. The term deduction refers to reasoning from the general to the particular. For example, it is generally true that when individuals are asleep and a REM (i.e., rapid eye movement) state is measured, they are having a dream (Aserinsky and Kleitman, 1953). On the basis of this generality we can *deduce* that a particular person is dreaming because we can observe that she/he is asleep and is in a REM state. We can test our deduction by waking the person at that time to ask if she or he was dreaming.

Deductive theories are usually quite formal and general. They offer explanations for phenomena and predict new lawful relationships. *After* such explanations are formulated, they are *then* tested in particular cases by collecting data. To be recognized is that explanation comes first.

A classic example of such a theory is the one proposed by Hull (1943) and later by Spence (1956). This theory attempted to unite and explain the lawful relationships that had been found in classical and operant conditioning. This was done by introducing new concepts like habit strength (H), drive (D), and incentive motivation (K) and writing general laws. For example, where R is the speed of running in a maze, $R = H \times D$. These general laws and concepts were tied, by means of bridge principles, to observables and the theory was tested again and again. For example, H is tied to the observable "number of trials" and D is tied to the observable "hours of deprivation." Collected data fed back into the theory and produced modification as time went on. For many researchers this is the way science should progress. Hull said, "Scientific theory in the best sense consists of the strict logical deduction from definite postulates of what should be observed under specified conditions" (1953, p. 17). From this point of view, a guiding theoretical framework is *always* necessary for data collection. One collects data only when some theoretical deduction is being tested. Such theories are said to be not really ever rejected by data; data are only used to modify the theory.

Such formal deductive theories are quite popular with philosophers of science but are infrequent in social science practice. Perhaps we will see more deductive theories as social sciences grow older. Deductive theories abound in physics (e.g., theory of general relativity).

Inductive Theories. The term induction refers to reasoning from particular instances to the general. For example, we might find that when we wake someone who is in a REM state, he or she reports having a dream. And when we do the same to a few more people, we find the same thing. On the basis of these particular data we might *induce* that it is generally true that people dream while in a REM state.

Inductive theories are built in that fashion. They are derived from particular data. As data accumulate, regularities emerge, and explanations for those regularities are induced. This approach is sometimes referred to as *atheoretical* since data collection proceeds without reference to theory and theory is formulated, if at all, only after data have been collected. Such an approach is favored by strict behaviorists (e.g., Sidman, 1960; Skinner, 1950) who see no need to go beyond the observed data to posit new, abstract concepts. General laws will emerge from the lawful relations apparent in the collected data. A deductive theory, on the other hand, may blind one to important, but theoretically ignored data. As Sherlock Holmes said, "It is a capital mistake to theorize before one has data. Insensibly one begins to twist facts to suit theories; instead of theories to suit facts" (Doyle, 1930, p. 163).

There are also few, if any generally acceptable inductive theories in the social sciences at present. Perhaps more data must be collected, or the approach is too risky or too time-consuming.

Functional Theories.   Inductive and deductive theories can be considered as opposite ends of a continuum of theory types. Such theoreticians take exactly opposite approaches toward achieving scientific explanation (see Mitroff and Kilmann, 1975, for portraits of these extreme theoreticians). Functional theories exist between these extremes. They are both inductive and deductive. That is, they propose general explanations that lead to deductions testable by data, and also induce general explanations from collected data. Typically, they deal with relatively small areas of investigation, and for that reason they are often referred to as minitheories (Marx, 1963). The use of abstract concepts is held to a minimum and the theory is closely bound to the data.

Functional theories abound in the social sciences. An explanation for some data will be proposed, tested, altered or rejected, and tested again. Theory and data are continually interacting. Data modify the theory and the theory leads to further data collection.

Take, for example, data on the processing of comparative and locative sentences. Comparative sentences compare two nouns on some scale. For example, Tom is taller/shorter or better/worse or faster/slower than Steve. Locative sentences specify the location of one object with reference to another. For example, the bank is north/south/east/west of the park. When one knows the location of some objects and must add a new object to this known array, one sentence is always easier than the other. In Fig. 3.2, for example, three objects—the supermarket, school, and park—are already known and the bank is to be added in the position shown (x marks the spot).

Data show that the sentence "The bank is south of the park" is processed more quickly and easily than the sentence "The park is north of the bank" (e.g., Huttenlocher, 1968). The question to be answered is, why?

Huttenlocher (1968) offered the first explanation by noting that the item to be added to knowledge—that is, the new item—was the subject of the easy sentence (i.e., The bank is south of the park) but the object of the difficult sentence (i.e., The park is north of the bank). She proposed that individuals generally regard sentence subjects as active items, and thus when the new item is placed in the active subject position it is easier to process. Potts and Scholtz (1975) argued that the real explanation centered on the sentence adjective (e.g., north vs. south) rather than the grammatical status (i.e., subject or object of the sentence) of the new item. They claimed that when the sentence adjective was congruent with the new item's placement, processing was easier. For example, since the bank is to be added on the south side, *any* sentence using the adjective south will be easier to process than one using the adjective north.

These two explanations were tested by Foos (1980), using sentences like "The park has the bank on its south side" and "The bank has the park on its north side." According to Huttenlocher, the second of these sentences should be the easy one since the new item (i.e., the bank) is the subject. According to Potts and Scholz, the first sentence should be the easy one since it contains the congruent

N

W   E

S

Figure 3.2 My little town.

adjective (i.e., south). The data supported the Potts and Scholz explanation and Huttenlocher's explanation was rejected.

Foos (1982) then proposed another explanation. Comparative and locative sentences contain reference points. They say "The *item* is north/south/east/west of the *reference point.*" It was proposed that individuals listening to such sentences search their memory for the reference point first. If it is found, they can then add the new item to their knowledge; if it is not found, they must search memory for the other item presented in the sentence. When the reference point is in memory (i.e., is an old item), that sentence will be processed quickly and easily. Data supported this new explanation, and the current (probably not the final) explanation of easy comparative and locative sentences is in terms of memory search for reference points. And so, explanation leads to data, which lead to further explanation, and so on with functional theories.

Models.   Models are analogies. They are often considered as a first step toward the formulation of a formal theory; they are very popular in psychology. The analogies used are frequently based on physical, electrical, or computer technology. For example, a model for the way in which people focus attention is provided by a common flashlight. The flashlight beam can be brought close to an object and focused on it; the beam is very intense. One can also back away and shine the light toward the object. Now many things are in the wide, dimmer beam besides the object of interest. Attention can also be narrowly focused and intense, or widely dispersed and dim. A wide focus is analogous to more shallow processing. Concentrated processing produces better memory for the object to which attention is directed (e.g., Craik and Lockhart, 1972).

Models have a more narrow focus than theories and serve four basic functions (Lachman, 1960). First, models provide a *representation* of a phenomenon. In this way they aid in organizing data. A flashlight beam is a way of representing attention. Second, models function as *rules of inference.* They bridge the gap between abstract concepts and observable events. We see what happens when a flashlight beam is close to an object and when it is farther away. From this we can infer that a focused attention is also more intense than a dispersed attention. Like the beam of light, processing is more intense with a narrow focus and should lead to better memory. Third, models aid in the *interpretation* of data. Data may show that the performance of individuals in a memory experiment can be interpreted by a model. Some remembered a little information, quite analogous to a focused flashlight beam, while others remembered a great deal but not in much detail, like a dispersed flashlight beam. Finally, models provide a *pictorial visualization.* They permit us to "see," in terms of images, how a phenomenon works. One can easily image the focus of a flashlight beam.

Models are sometimes considered an impediment to the goal of explanation. There are many, many models and they cannot be easily integrated. They may produce a "patchwork theoretical structure" (Kantowitz and Roediger, 1978, p. 12) and no overall explanation. The subareas of a discipline may grow farther and farther apart.

This contrasts with the opinion that models are aids rather than impediments to explanation and that they serve very useful functions, as previously outlined (e.g., Hesse, 1966). We do not believe that a simple model or analogy will be found to serve as an overall explanation of social phenomena, but we firmly believe that models serve as ministeps toward such an overall explanation.

Evaluating Theories

Theories are evaluated by gathering data. This is what distinguishes theoretical explanations from rationalisms. Data are important for determining whether a theory is or is not tenable. There are, however, many additional factors involved in evaluating theories.

We will examine nine factors that should be considered in evaluating theories. It is rare for a theory to receive high marks on all nine factors. To be scientific, a theory *must* be testable and falsifiable (factor 1), *must* have some empirical support (factor 2), and *must* make predictions (factor 3). Beyond these first three requirements, theories are better as they are more clear and precise (factor 4), are more parsimonious (factor 5), are logical (factor 6), have deductive capacity (factor 7), are general (factor 8), and account for individual differences (factor 9).

1. *Testability-Falsifiability.* Theories must be testable. That is, the case must be made that one can gather data that support the correctness of the theory.

Explanations that cannot be tested are not scientific theories. Furthermore, the tests must be capable of proving the theory wrong; theories must be falsifiable (Popper, 1981).

For example, consider the personality theory of Freud. One of the stages in this theory of personality development is known as the phallic stage. Presumably, children between the ages of three and five go through a period of competition with the same-sexed parent for the affections of the opposite-sexed parent (Oedipus and Electra complexes). This claim may be testable if we can find good measures of competition and affection. Suppose, however, that in spite of our good measures we find no evidence for the theory's claim. The theorist's answer in this case is not "Whoops, guess I was wrong about that." It is more likely to be claimed that the competition was unconscious and the behavioral manifestations, if there were any, were disguised. The behavior that occurred *was* competition for affection because the theory said it occurs in this stage. This theory is not a scientific theory because it cannot be falsified; it always has an answer for seemingly disconfirming data.

Falsifiability is extremely important because, logically, theories cannot be proved true, but only false. This is a result of the implicative relationship between theory and data. If this theory is correct, then these data should occur. If the data do occur, is the theory proved correct? No. There may be many other theories that are also supported by such data. One can, in principle, always come up with another theory; thus, any single theory can never be proved true. If, however, the data predicted by the theory do not occur, then the theory can be proved false. While this is true in principle, usually the theory is simply modified rather than rejected as false.

When one tests a scientific theory by gathering data, one should obtain data that can, in principle, fairly evaluate the possibility that the theory is false. This provides a fair test of the theory. Confidence in a theory increases as it survives tests that could falsify it. Individuals seem, however, to have difficulty in choosing data that could falsify a theory (Wason, 1968; Mynatt et al., 1978). For example, consider the following task taken from Wason (1968). Four cards are placed in front of you and they have the following symbols.

E   K   4   7

You know that each has a number on one side and a letter on the other side. You are to select the card(s) that would determine whether a hypothesis is true or false. The hypothesis is: If a card has a *vowel* on one side, then it has an *even number* on the other side. What card(s) would you select?

Most people say either "E and 4" or "only E." In fact E is a useful datum to examine but 4 is not. Card 4 can only support the hypothesis by having a vowel on the other side; if there is a consonant on the other side, no information regarding the hypothesis is obtained. The card with a 7 is the valuable datum because it can potentially falsify the hypothesis by having a vowel on the other side. Individuals rarely select the potentially falsifying datum. Scientists must learn to do so.

2. *Empirical Support.* Empirical support refers to the quantity and quality of collected data that support or confirm the theory. Generally, a theory with

more empirical support is likely to be more valid. It is important to stress that the empirical support for a theory cannot be measured by counting the number of studies (i.e., quantity) that have collected supporting data. Remember, the best support for a theory is when it survives a test that could have falsified it (i.e., quality). A theory must have some empirical support. As we said earlier, if it is not true in practice then it is not true in theory either.

3. *Predictive Capacity.* Theories must do more than explain existing data and laws; they must predict new laws and tell us what to expect in new situations. A theory that only organizes existing data fails to be a useful theory in terms of progress toward the goals of science. Theories must reach forward into the future as well as explain the past. Remember, making predictions is one of the important defining properties of scientific theory.

4. *Clarity/Precision.* It almost goes without saying that a theory must be clear. It must avoid ambiguities. It must be as precise as possible. The individuals who test the theory by gathering data must have no doubts about what the theory claims. Precision and clarity are achieved by minimizing the number of abstract concepts, using bridge principles to relate the theory's abstractions to observable phenomena, and striving for quantitative laws. A mathematical theory is generally more precise and, thus, to be preferred, all other things being equal.

5. *Parsimony.* Simple, parsimonious explanations are preferred to complex explanations. Scientists attempt to avoid the proliferation of entities beyond necessity. As we said previously, the theory that can explain a great deal without having to say very much is a better theory.

This preference for simple explanations is a logical part of our progress toward scientific understanding. It makes little sense to propose complex theories, discover that they are wrong, and then not know which way to go. That is, should we then propose a more complex or a simpler theory? Starting with simple theories allows one to steadily progress in one direction, toward complexity, on the way to scientific understanding.

6. *Logical Consistency.* Theories must be logical. They must not contradict themselves or lead to contrary positions in considering the same phenomenon. There is something illogical about a theory that claims "absence makes the heart grow fonder" while also claiming "out of sight, out of mind."

7. *Deductive Capacity.* A theory should offer sufficient generalized statements so that deductions to particular instances can be made. This is true for inductive, deductive, and functional theories as well as models. That is, even though the theory's claim has been induced from particular instances, it should still be possible to deduce further particulars from it. Bridge principles play an important role in deduction since they help specify the observable phenomena (e.g., hours of food deprivation or recall of information) that define an abstract theoretical concept (e.g., drive or retrieval from memory). Later, (Chapter 8) we will see that such specifications of abstract concepts in terms of observables are referred to as operational definitions and that they are a crucial part of data collection.

8. *Generality.* Theories should not be too restrictive; they should strive for some degree of generality. Theories that explain many phenomena are, all other

things being equal, more valuable than theories that explain few phenomena. For example, the statement that "overcrowded dormitory rooms produce decrements in performance on complex mazes," is not as valuable, theoretically, as the statement that "high social density produces decrements on complex tasks." Even more general, and thus more valuable, would be a statement such as "high density produces arousal and, in conformity with the Yerkes-Dodson law (Yerkes and Dodson, 1908), arousal interferes with performance in complex, but not simple, tasks." The latter statement is very general and shows how particular regularities may be instances of a more general law. Many of the current theories in social science are lacking in generality.

9. *Individual Differences.* A good theory should account for individual differences in performance (Underwood, 1975). A theory directed, for example, toward explaining the behavior of children exposed to violence on television should be able to account for individual differences in the behavior of these children. Why are some children more influenced than others? Underwood has developed a procedure to assess a theory's ability to account for such individual differences.

For example, suppose our theory says that there is an additive relationship between the child's initial level of aggressiveness (IA) and the violence witnessed on TV (V). Together those two factors produce aggression in the child. That is, IA + V = aggression. To assess the adequacy of the theory for accounting for individual differences in the resulting aggression, one must take two independent measures of IA and determine whether individual differences on one of these measures is related to individual differences on the other measure (e.g., correlate the scores on the two measures). If they are related, the theory has passed the test. The concept that is used to account for individual differences (in this case individual differences in IA) does vary in an orderly way among people. A theory that cannot account for individual differences needs further elaboration, since individual differences are always present.

Before leaving the topic of theories, two additional points should be made. First, theories are better thought of as being useful or not rather than as being true or false. A theory that has been falsified is a useless theory since it does not explain the state of affairs as revealed by collected data. Theories can never become facts, but they can serve as useful ways of conceptualizing, explaining, and understanding facts. Theories are useful ways of thinking about the world, but they cannot be substituted for the world (or real thing).

The other point to be made is that conflicting theories, including those quite opposed to each other, are likely to be offered by scientists. More often than not, theories presenting extremists' views receive considerable attention and notoriety but, over time, do not prevail. Movement tends to occur from the extremist views toward a more central position. For example, nature and nurture are extreme positions offered to explain a child's acquisition of language, an individual's intelligence, and any number of other human behaviors. One position (i.e., nature) claims that genetic inheritance explains everything, while the other position (i.e., nurture) claims that environment is the explanation. The most useful explanation lies somewhere between these extremes; both nature and nurture are involved. The initial tendency to take extreme positions is ubiquitous and probably worthwhile. When an extreme position is rejected, there is only one direction to move in and that is toward the center.

SCIENTIFIC UNDERSTANDING

Earlier in this chapter we said that scientific understanding is attained when one can completely predict and control a phenomenon. Furthermore, prediction and control often depend upon the availability of a useful scientific explanation of the phenomenon under investigation. Explanation, prediction, and control all rely on data.

It is possible, at least in principle, to achieve prediction and control, and thus scientific understanding, without having an explanation of the phenomenon. For example, one can predict that an object thrown into the air will fall to earth without having any explanation for how this occurs. Predictions can be made from the lawful relationships that emerge from data collection. One can learn how to control migraine headaches by learning (perhaps by using biofeedback) to warm the hands and/or relax the frontalis muscle. Again, one can do this without an explanation for how the warming and relaxation accomplish the reduction in headache pain. Control can be achieved on the basis of known lawful relationships that have emerged from data collection. Data are necessary for successful prediction and control; explanations are not.

While explanations are not, in principle, necessary for the attainment of scientific understanding, they do greatly facilitate such attainment. In fact, phenomena for which no useful explanations exist never seem to progress beyond the stages of discovery and description. Extrasensory perception (ESP) is an example of such a phenomenon. Although one cannot at present say whether ESP is (or is not) a real phenomenon, it is clear that one of the major hurdles faced by workers in the area is the lack of explanations for such phenomena. The phenomena themselves cannot be easily fit into existing explanations and overall, scientific paradigms. Because this remains true, it is extremely unlikely that scientific understanding will be achieved.

In sum, gathering data is necessary at *every* step toward scientific understanding. Explanations are, while not necessary, extremely useful for attaining scientific understanding.

chapter *4*

Methods of Data Collection

Data collection is a most fundamental prerequisite if one is to perform the tasks of scientific discovery: description, explanation, control, and prediction. Such data must meet certain specific standards if they are to be accepted as reliable and valid. We emphasize that data can be collected by using any of many acceptable methods.

In this book, we present eight different, but somewhat overlapping, methods of collecting data. They are (in our order of presentation): observation, experiment, field research, archives, case history, group discussion, survey, and simulation.

Although researchers within different disciplines may prefer specific methods for gathering data, it is important to recognize that most of these methods, while different, may be equally good. All researchers should be thoroughly familiar with the various systems of data gathering, and then, and only then, should it be decided which one of which combination is likely to be most appropriate for the gathering of data that it is hoped will solve some problem.

Rather than introduce each of these methods in this chapter in a purely descriptive fashion, we have decided to illustrate the use of each of these kinds of data gathering by selecting a single topic. For each of the many disciplines in the social sciences and for each of the data-gathering methods included, the frame of reference will be poverty.

Poverty presents enormous problems in need of solutions. These problems are of interest to social sciences such as psychology, sociology, geography, economics, anthropology, criminal justice, social work, urban and regional planning, public affairs, government and public administration, history, political science, and related fields. More important, it is a problem that can be investigated by using *all* of the major methods of data collection. A researcher interested in investigating poverty, or any other problem, must consider a number of factors when deciding which method of data collection to use.

SELECTION FACTORS

A number of factors lead to the selection of a method of data collection. Some factors are specific to certain methods. Examples might include which kind of experiment among the various kinds, or which survey technique from among many, is most appropriate and will produce the most valid results within a given time frame and research budget.

In addition, there are many factors of a general variety such as familiarity, research objectives, practical considerations, level of measurement, type of measurement, previous work conducted, and pilot studies. These factors also should be considered when a particular method of data collection is selected.

Familiarity

It may be unfortunate, but many researchers select a method of data collection simply because they are most familiar with it. They tend to use it again and again through all of their professional lives. Individuals who are familiar with a particular method will probably use that method effectively. It is our belief, however, that even if particular scientists tend to restrict their data collection efforts to the method or methods they know best, particular problems are best solved when many different methods of data collection are employed. Frankly, familiarity with a method is not the best reason for choosing to use it but it is a reason nonetheless. It is, therefore, imperative to become acquainted and familiar with a number of different methods.

Research Objectives

The objectives of the research project are also important for the selection of an appropriate method. In research, we refer to the things that are manipulated and/or observed and/or measured as variables. A *variable* is anything that varies, that has different levels or values. Poverty is a variable. Research projects dealing with the variable poverty may have a number of different objectives. For example, an objective might be to describe the conditions of poverty. This may lead one to select an observational technique. Another objective might be to determine if, and to what extent, poverty is related to other variables such as social mobility, self-esteem, divorce rates, family size, political preference, and so on. To achieve such objectives one might conduct surveys and interviews, examine archives, or do field research. An objective might be to describe in detail the lives of individuals or groups living in poverty. The case history study technique would then be appropriate.

Perhaps the objective is to learn something about how different groups perceive poverty, or to have different groups share their perceptions of poverty with one another. In this instance, group discussion would be appropriate. Perhaps a further objective is to examine the causes of poverty or to examine poverty as a cause of other social phenomena. Causes are best examined by conducting experiments. Finally, to understand the complexity of poverty one might try to simulate such conditions and derive new insights from the attempted simulations.

For the moment and without fully understanding the how and why of these different methods, it should be clear that different methods are able to satisfy different objectives. The research objectives should always be considered when an appropriate method is being selected.

Practical Considerations

Time, money, and effort are (unfortunately) involved in the selection of a method of data collection. All research takes time, but some methods take more time than others. The same is true for money and effort. One may want to obtain thorough case histories for all the members of an impoverished community but may not have enough time, money, or staff. Perhaps a phone survey of a handful of members is all that can be accomplished, but are people on the poverty level likely to have phones? One should always select methods that can be completed with the resources available and without sacrificing sampling requirements.

Level of Measurement

By level of measurement, we refer to the size and specificity of the measures. This can be viewed as a continuum from macro- to micromeasures. *Macromeasures* are large measures of a system or variable as a whole. *Micromeasures* are small measures of parts or components of a system or variable. With respect to a problem such as poverty, both macro- and micromeasures are desirable. However, some methods of data collection are more appropriate for one or the other level of measurement. For example, when one wishes to take an overall view; a macromeasure may be most appropriate. If one wishes a focused view of a small component, a micromeasure may be most appropriate. Most data-gathering techniques can serve macro- and micromeasurement purposes.

Type of Measurement

By type of measurement we refer to the previously discussed difference between qualitative and quantitative measures. Generally, qualitative measures are used for differences in kind and quantitative measures are used for differences in degree. Although all methods have the potential to use either type of measurement, generally observation, case histories, and group discussions provide qualitative measures while experiments, field research, archives, and surveys provide quantitative measures. But there is considerable overlap.

These differences between different levels (macro- and micro-) and types (qualitative and quantitative) of measurement can be illustrated by four studies conducted to investigate different aspects of poverty.

Macro-, Qualitative Measurement.   Fried (1969) examined the relationship between poverty and migration. Poverty was assessed by examining the occurrence of economic and/or social crises in the country of origin (e.g., the great famine in Ireland); migration was assessed by examining immigration for different years (1870 to 1914) from different countries (e.g., Germany, England, Ireland, Sweden, Italy, Austria-Hungary, Russia, and Greece). These are large-scale macromeasures and are qualitative. That is, the immigrants from Germany are not better/worse than those from England, they simply have different points of origin. Fried found that "cycles of prosperity or depression, at home or abroad, can only account for relatively small proportions of the total volume of migration from any given country" (p. 116).

Macro-, Quantitative Measurement.   Srole (1962) examined the relationship between poverty and mental illness. Poverty was measured by socioeconomic status and mental illness was measured by psychiatric diagnoses ranging from well to mild, moderate, and impaired mental health categories. These are large-scale macromeasures that are quantitative. That is, the classification "impaired" means less mental health than the classification "moderate," "moderate" less than "mild," and "mild" less than "well." Srole found significantly more cases of "impairment" among the lowest socioeconomic class and significantly more cases of "well" among the highest socioeconomic class. There was a clear linear relationship between the measures of poverty and mental health. Such a study does not establish causality; it does reveal association or relationship.

Micro-, Qualitative Measurement.   Work by Bennett et al. (1969) illustrates micro, qualitative measurement. In their studies rats were exposed, from birth, to enriched or impoverished environments to determine what effect such environmental differences produce in the adult rat brain. Enriched environments contained many rats (10 to 12), large cages, platforms, wheels, and other "rat toys." Impoverished environments were qualitatively different as rats were housed singly without "toys." After 80 days the rats were sacrificed and chemical and anatomical comparisons of their brains were made. Enriched-environment rats had different brains; they had a thicker and heavier cortex, better blood supply, different chemicals, and fewer synapses (i.e., "links" between neurons).

Micro-, Quantitative Measurement.   Michelotti (1978) examined the relationship between years of education and poverty. Education measures were numbers of years of schooling; poverty was assessed in terms of unemployment. As expected, unemployment and poverty were higher for those with less education.

At this point, one might be struck by the absence of a clear dividing line between micro- and macromeasurement as well as quantitative and qualitative. Quantitative measures refer to different *amounts* of something (e.g., years of schooling, degree of mental health, annual income) while qualitative measures refer to different *kinds* of things (e.g., coming from Ireland as opposed to Sweden, different kind of brain anatomy).

Micro- and macromeasurements can be considered as end points on a continuum, and it is more difficult to classify measures that fall in the middle than those at an extreme. It is reasonable to assume that most measures fall into this middle range and are neither very microscopic nor macroscopic.

Previous Work

In selecting a method for data collection, previous work and methods used by others should be a very important consideration. As stated above, it is our belief that problems are best solved when data are collected by using a variety of methods. If everyone else has used methods *a, b,* and *c,* that, in itself, may be reason enough to try method *d.* For the study of poverty, Rossi (1969) suggests a progression from surveys, case histories, and archives as appropriate methods for the early stages of an investigation to experiments and field research methods for the later stages. Such a progression, change, or evolution of methods may well be an important consideration as research is planned.

Pilot Work

Pilot work or pilot studies refer to situations where a researcher has selected a method of data collections and tests it on a small scale before beginning the major study(ies). A pilot study may be considered similar to a dress rehearsal. It can provide valuable information about the probability of completing the major work, the likelihood that the major work will pay off (i.e., provide useful information), and especially the presence of unforeseen difficulties. A pilot study might encourage the researcher to continue with the method selected, alter some of the details, or abandon the method altogether and try a different approach. A pilot study can, thus, be cost-effective since it can prevent wasting of time and money in "undoable" projects.

Pilot studies can be very useful, provided such studies are well planned. That is, one should *always* try to put together the best possible procedure and choose the most appropriate method for data collection whether it is planned as a pilot or a major study. In practice, and as data collection proceeds, some studies will fail. That is, before they are completed, it becomes clear that the method is not working. On the other hand, if the method works then the study conducted may be regarded as a continuum between the pilot and the major study. One should never deliberately design a pilot study to be different in quality from a major study.

Other factors that influence the selection of a particular method of data collection will be discussed when we focus on specific methods later in this book. Now let us examine the selection and treatment of research participants and the importance of data analysis.

CHOOSING AND USING PARTICIPANTS

The selection of participants for a research project is usually discussed under the general heading of sampling. We will follow this tradition here and also discuss the ethical use of the chosen participants.

Sampling

A *sample* is a subset of a population; *sampling* refers to how that subset is chosen. A *population* is the whole number of people in a group or area. One can rarely, if ever, obtain the total population for a study and, thus, one must rely instead on a selected sample. Even the census studies do not obtain the total population but they do come close for some of their measures.

For example, one may be interested in examining the relationship between crime and poverty. More specifically, is crime concentrated in the poorer areas of cities? In answering this question, one would like to be able to make a statement about cities in general. It is probably not feasible, however, to gather and assimilate the data on crime for all cities, even if one restricts the question to relatively large cities (e.g., over 250,000 people). Instead, one would gather data on a selected sample of cities (perhaps a single city) and then generalize to the population of cities on the basis of what is found in the sample data. Clinard (1970) found that in Milwaukee 13.7% of the population lived in a poor slum area where 60% of the murders were committed. Generalizing from this sample and projecting the results to other populations depends upon a number of factors (see Angoff, 1971, for a detailed discussion of these factors).

One important factor is the *size* of the sample. Generally, a large sample tends to be more stable than a small sample because extreme aberrations have less influence. A *stable* sample is one that gives results that are similar to those for other such samples. That is, they are consistent with other samples. In addition, stability depends not just on sample size but also on "clustering" (Mehrens and Lehman, 1984). For example, if one used a sample of cities that are all clustered in the same geographic location, such as Milwaukee, Chicago, Des Moines, and Minneapolis, *and* had reason to believe that geographic location influenced the relationship between crime and poverty, then one would not have obtained a stable sample of cities in general. In this case, a stable sample would include cities from different geographic locations (e.g., Milwaukee, Atlanta, Boston, and Los Angeles). Were the sample used by Clinard (i.e., Milwaukee) the only one for which data had been collected, one would be justifiably concerned about the stability of the sample.

A sample should also be *representative* of the population. Size alone does not guarantee that the chosen sample truly represents the population of interest. A representative sample is one that has been selected without bias, regardless of its size. To reduce sample bias, one should *select randomly*. For example, one might put the names of all the cities to which one would like to generalize (i.e., the population) on separate slips of paper and toss them all in a bowl (be sure to mix well). One could then reach in and draw out the city(ies) that would comprise the sample. *A random sample is obtained when each member of the population has an equal chance of being selected.*

Such random sampling is rarely accomplished. In many cases it is simply not possible. For example, if one wished to describe the characteristics (e.g., number of children, number of wage earners, level of education) of poor families one would like to use a stable, representative sample of poor families. Random sampling, however, can be done only when the population is known. If there were a complete list of all poor families, one would select a random sample from that list. No such list, however, exists. Hsieh (1979) used data on poor families obtained from the Bureau of the Census. The census provides a very useful list and important data but it is clearly not complete. Few people believe that every person (poor or otherwise) in the country has been included in the census. Hsieh examined 5450 poor families and it can probably be assumed that his sample was both stable and fairly representative. Table 4.1 shows some of his findings for these families. The sample used by Clinard (i.e., Milwaukee) was probably a sample of convenience rather than a random sample. That is, it was more convenient to use a Milwaukee sample because the data collectors were residents of Milwaukee.

Because of the difficulties involved in obtaining a truly random sample, researchers have devised a number of strategies to aid in the selection of an unbiased sample (e.g., Moser and Kalton, 1972). A typical procedure is to select as unbiased a sample as possible and then try to determine the population to which one can generalize. That is, what population does the selected sample represent? Can the sample be considered a random sample from some larger population? Some of the specific sampling procedures used by researchers will be discussed later (in Chapter 15). In many cases, the sample is composed of individuals who volunteer and/or are paid to participate. In such cases, it is always possible that the findings will hold only for those who possess the characteristics (whatever they my be) of volunteers.

The need to rely on voluntary participants in a research project is a major reason why truly random samples are rarely used. If it were the case (and it rarely is) that one had a list of *all* members of a population (e.g., the poor in the United States) and truly selected a random sample from that list, the sample used in the research would still include only those willing to participate. It might, thus, be

Table 4.1   SOME CHARACTERISTICS OF POOR FAMILIES

Number of children (under age 18)	Percentage	Number of wage earners	Percentage	Level of education (for family head)	Percentage
None	23.4	None	45.5		
1 or 2	41.5	1	37.5	Elementary (8 years)	41.8
3 or 4	24.0	2	11.9	High School (4 years)	48.0
5 or more	11.0	3	5.1	College	10.2

SOURCE: Hsieh, 1979.

considered a random and representative sample of the poor *who would willingly participate;* it would not be a random sample of all the poor. Those who are selected randomly but who are unwilling to participate leave the researcher with a potentially biased sample because it contains only willing participants.

Quite a large number of texts discuss the many different sampling techniques used by researchers (e.g., Jessen, 1978; Kress, 1979; Som, 1973). Some of these techniques (e.g., stratified sampling) will be presented when we discuss the survey method of data collection (Chapter 15). For now, it is important to realize that in selecting a sample the researcher must always answer three important questions. First, is the sample affordable? All research depends upon the time and money available. One may want a sample of 100,000 but be able to afford only a sample of 100. Second, is the sample stable and representative? As we have already pointed out, several factors (e.g., clustering, voluntary participation) must be considered when answering this question. Finally, is the sample adequate? Is it of sufficient size to inspire confidence in the results? It is generally the case that bigger samples produce much more confidence but, remember, size alone is not enough.

In an experiment, we must start with samples that can be assumed to be the same in designated characteristics (e.g., age, years of education) and manipulate some variable(s) to see if such manipulation will result in differences. That is, the sample must come from one population. The previously described work by Bennett et al. started with rats taken from the same population (i.e., littermates weaned in the same environment) and exposed them to enriched or impoverished environments. These different environments resulted in important differences between the groups where originally there had been none.

Quite different from animal samples, human members of a sample must be willing to participate. From a scientific standpoint, individuals who are coerced may not behave as they ordinarily would and, thus, may become unrepresentative simply because of the coercion.

Ethics

One should always treat research participants ethically. Scientific progress depends upon the willingness of individuals to give of their time and effort. The American Psychological Association (1973) has put forth 10 general principles to guide the researcher in the use of human participants. It is hoped that when such principles are followed, individuals will be willing to participate in social science research. The 10 principles are:

1. In planning a study the investigator has the personal responsibility to make a careful evaluation of its ethical acceptability, taking into account these principles for research with human beings. To the extent that this appraisal, weighing scientific and humane values, suggests a deviation from any principle, the investigator incurs an increasingly serious obligation to seek ethical advice and to observe more stringent safeguards to protect the rights of the human research participant.

2. Responsibility for the establishment and maintenance of acceptable ethical practice in research always remains with the individual investigator. The investigator is also responsible for the ethical treatment of research participants by collaborators, assistants, students and employees, all of whom, however, incur parallel obligations.

3. Ethical practice requires the investigator to inform the participant of all features of the research that reasonably might be expected to influence willingness to participate and to explain all other aspects of the research about which the participant inquires. Failure to make full disclosure gives added emphasis to the investigator's responsibility to protect the welfare and dignity of the research participant.

4. Openness and honesty are essential characteristics of the relationship between investigator and research participant. When the methodological requirements of a study necessitate concealment or deception, the investigator is required to ensure the participant's understanding of the reasons for his action and to restore the quality of the relationship with the investigator.

5. Ethical research practice requires the investigator to respect the individual's freedom to decline to participate in research or to discontinue participation at any time. The obligation to protect this freedom requires special vigilance when the investigator is in a position of power over the participant. The decision to limit this freedom increases the investigator's responsibility to protect the participant's dignity and welfare.

6. Ethically acceptable research begins with the establishment of a clear and fair agreement between the investigator and the research participant which clarifies the responsibilities of each. The investigator has the obligation to honor all promises and commitments included in that agreement.

7. The ethical investigator protects participants from physical and mental discomfort, harm, and danger. If the risk of such consequences exists, the investigator is required to inform the participant of that fact, to secure consent before proceeding, and to take all possible measures to minimize distress. A research procedure may not be used if it is likely to cause serious and lasting harm to participants.

8. After the data are collected, ethical practice requires the investigator to provide the participant with a full clarification of the nature of the study and to remove any misconceptions that may have arisen. Where scientific or humane values justify delaying or withholding information, the investigator acquires a special responsibility to assure that there are no damaging consequences for the participant.

9. Where research procedures may result in undesirable consequences for the participant, the investigator has the responsibility to detect and remove or correct these consequences, including (where relevant) long-term after-effects.

10. Information obtained about the research participants during the course of an investigation is confidential. When the possibility exists that others may obtain access to such information, ethical research practice requires that this possibility, together with the plans for protecting confidentiality, be explained to the participants as a part of the procedure for obtaining informed consent.

The principle underlying all of these principles is *informed consent.* The potential participant has the right to be informed of all aspects of the research project that might influence her/his willingness to participate (i.e., principle 3). It is necessary to have participants in research leave a project no worse off, and hopefully better off, than when they entered.

DATA ANALYSIS

After data are collected, it is important to make an accurate interpretation of the results obtained. One cannot be sure that the measures are reliable or valid simply by looking at them. Researchers often have hypotheses that may bias their interpretations. Statistics are the tools we use to make sense out of our collected data. The reader will find a general discussion of statistics in the Appendix. The simple point to be made here is that researchers rely on statistics to aid them in the *objective* interpretation of collected data. It is important for all social scientists to have some knowledge of statistics and such courses and texts are offered in all colleges and universities.

OVERVIEW OF METHODS

We said earlier that a major social problem like poverty can, and should, be approached by using a variety of data-gathering methods. In the second part of this book we shall examine a variety of these methods in some detail. For now we shall take an overview of these methods as they have been used by social scientists to investigate different aspects of poverty. The methods are those which were introduced in Table 1.1 of Chapter 1.

Observation (Chapter 7) underlies all the methods of data gathering and is also a method in its own right. In the area of poverty, an example of unobtrusive observation can be found in the work of Briggs (1978) and Yanis-McLaughlin (1978), who observed poor Italian immigrants. Results showed that immigrant poor were acculturated and absorbed into society fairly rapidly. Nonimmigrant poor (Indians and Blacks, in particular) have often been held back by such conditions as lower wages, poorer education, and poor housing and have not had the same access as immigrant poor to better education, higher wages, and better housing. Nonimmigrant poor tend to remain poor whereas immigrant poor do not.

We have already offered an example of an *experiment* (see Chapters 8, 9, and 10) concerned with the effects of poverty. The work of Bennett et al. (1969) sought to determine whether and how impoverished environments influenced brain anatomy, chemistry, and physiology. Rats taken from the same litters were randomly assigned to enriched or deprived environments. Although these rats were initially the same, exposure to different environments resulted in different brains with different characteristics. This work has been repeated a number of times and clearly shows the unfortunate effects an impoverished environment can produce when compared to an enriched environment. One might, of course, argue that rats are very different from humans and that the environments used in the studies are not the same as human (impoverished or enriched) environments. This may be so, but experiments are often justifiably conducted far from the real world of ultimate interest to the social scientist. At the same time, experiments do have a relatively narrow and concentrated focus which makes them excellent tools for examining causal relationships. If such environments produce differences in the brains of rats, it is not unreasonable to suppose that human brains are also influenced by environmental differences. It would not have been possible to do the experiment in the same way with human participants. Experiments are necessary, but not sufficient, for understanding complex social problems like poverty.

Data gathering that takes place in the real world instead of a laboratory, even though it does not quite have the concentrated focus of an experiment, is known as *field research* (Chapter 11). Such research often strives for as concentrated a focus as possible, which is difficult in the complex field of real-world events. The work of Scheirer (1983) on the households of welfare families is an example of field research. Five different kinds of welfare families were compared on a number of variables (e.g., education). The five family types were: mother with children; mother, children, and father or stepfather; mother, children, and one or more grandparents; mother, children, and other adult (relative or nonrelative); and motherless family. Over all these family types, the likelihood of continued schooling was compared. In families with mothers, the probability of the mother being in school was less as the age of the mother increased. For mothers who were less than 24 years old, families with live-in grandparents were most likely to have mothers attending school. In all comparisons, Scheirer attempted to achieve some of the focus of an experiment by equating the different family groups on age and posteducational level. This does not, of course, make the groups the same, except for family type, as would be the case in an experiment. At the same time, field research is frequently the closest one can come to, and is often preferable to, a laboratory experiment. It is, after all, events in the real world, the field, that we are striving to understand.

The previously discussed studies by Fried (1969) and Michelotti (1978) are examples of *archives* (Chapter 12). In such cases, one "collects" data that have already been collected. That is, one examines existing records or archives in an attempt to investigate relationships among variables, such as poverty and migration (Fried), or poverty and education (Michelotti). Fried's data were taken from historical records on social and economic crises in Europe and from U.S. government immigration records. No strong relationship between the two measures was found. Michelotti's data come from the U.S. census and employment statistics. Unemployment was greatest among the least educated. Because of the abundance of archives, it is possible to find micromeasures (Michelotti) and macromeasures (Fried), or quantitative (Michelotti) and qualitative (Fried) measures. There is a wealth of informative data already collected awaiting the interested researcher.

Another way to investigate poverty would be to do a detailed study of a single individual or family. Such a detailed biography is called a *case history* (Chapter 13). Case histories and case studies provide a wealth of information on a very limited sample and can frequently reveal patterns and suggest hypotheses that might otherwise be missed. Lewis's (1964) case history of Clarence Earl

Gideon reveals much about the impoverished inmate, the workings of the courts, and prison life in general. This story was shown by the CBS television movie *Gideon's Trumpet* (1980) based on Lewis's book. The case resulted in the Supreme Court ruling that free counsel at trial be provided for all felony defendants who are poor.

The *group discussion* (Chapter 14) method of data gathering is a relatively recent development which grew out of the original work of Blum. It has not yet been used to investigate aspects of poverty with the possible exception of the effects of inflation on lower income households.

Basically, a group discussion involves the careful assembly of a group of participants to discuss a topic of concern. The discussion is guided by a trained group leader, who uses a written discussion guide. Such a technique could be very useful for investigating the attitudes of middle-class or upper-class individuals toward federal programs for the poor (e.g., food stamps). One might even compare the results of group discussions conducted with upper-, middle-, and lower-class individuals to see what differences and similarities exist.

There are quite a large number of *surveys* (Chapter 15) which deal with poverty-related issues. Interviews and questionnaires are examples of survey techniques. For example, Hagan and Albonetti (1982) surveyed individuals from different socioeconomic classes to find out how they perceived criminal injustice. Participants were asked to indicate the strength of their agreement or disagreement with statements like:

(a) Law enforcement officials/police do not treat poor suspects the same as well-to-do suspects.
(b) Lawyers do not treat their poor clients the same as their well-to-do clients.
(c) Courts do not treat poor people as well as well-to-do people.

Regardless of race, members of the lower class were far more likely to agree with these statements than were members of other classes. Mirowsky and Ross (1983) surveyed individuals living in El Paso, Texas, and Juarez, Mexico, and found social class differences in perceived locus of control. Locus of control refers to the belief that you are in control of the events in your life (i.e., you are referred to as an "internal") or that outside forces control the events in your life (i.e., an "external"). In their study, belief in external control was strongly associated with low socioeconomic status, Mexican heritage, and being female. Survey techniques are used quite frequently in the social sciences.

Simulation (Chapter 16) techniques involve an imitation or copying of real events. Much can be learned about real events and interrelationships simply by trying to simulate them. Panning (1983) has tested a model of deprivation and political stability by simulating different levels of total relative deprivation and inequality (in terms of wealth) in a simulated society. Results show that the total level of relative deprivation is reduced by a reduction in inequality and that these reductions enhance political stability in a society.

We will have more to say about observation, experiments, field research, archives, case histories, group discussion, surveys, and simulation later in this book. As social scientists, it is important to become familiar with these techniques. Social science problems are best solved when data are gathered by using a variety of methods. A recent article by Kimble (1984) reinforces this view that social science is starting to investigate many new areas by using many and varied methods. Kimble says.

In psychology a trend of this sort appears to be in progress. The most important theme in this development is a liberalized viewpoint that permits an easy acceptance of topics for research that would have been unacceptable 40 years ago. Mental imagery, the distinction between remembered and imagined voluntary behavior, self-awareness and self-control, conceptually driven processing, helplessness and coping, risk taking, metaphoric expression, and inferential memory are a few of these topics, all of which are identified by phrases that catch important ideas in the humanistic tradition.

Similar things are happening in the area of methods. Quasi-experimental designs with unobtrusive measures, field studies of animal behavior, investigations of eyewitness testimony, studies of the oral tradition and autobiographical memory, the use of hypnosis as an experimental method, the move from serial anticipation to methods of free recall, and, unless I miss my guess, a renewed interest in case histories are some of the important new features on the methodological scene, all of which again are identified by phrases that catch important ideas in the humanistic tradition.

5

Measuring Instruments

As previously indicated, measurement is a necessary prerequisite for reporting findings that are considered to be scientific. Although any of many methods can meet acceptable standards within the framework of science, all must have in common the use of some form of instrument that is capable of reliably measuring the existence of the phenomenon being investigated.

The problem is that a myriad of measuring instruments exist. Some are more applicable than others, depending upon the methods used to solve the existing problem. Another difficulty is that instruments vary in their accuracy of measurement. For example, human temperature measurements vary depending upon whether the instrument measures body temperature orally, rectally, axillarily, or on the skin surface. The researcher must decide which instrument is most appropriate to use. Considering the research laboratory that is an integral part of any psychology department, one finds quite an array of measuring instruments. They can be classified and fitted into such categories as "brass," electronic, or pencil-and-paper varieties.

Such instruments have various purposes. Three such purposes include: presenting stimuli, measuring responses, and exercising control by limiting the extraneous factors that might otherwise influence the results.

This chapter focuses on the value as well as use of measuring instruments and the factors to be considered in the selection of an appropriate instrument for data gathering. We will also briefly examine the categories or types of instruments available and furnish a few examples.

INSTRUMENT VALUE AND LIMITATION

Measuring instruments provide the opportunity to standardize measurements; without their use we would have hopeless subjective chaos. For example, in a survey, unless the same questionnaire is used, it is impossible to compare the responses of the people included in the sample. Similarly, if one wished to compare the intelligence quotients (IQs) of rural and urban children or compare the intelligence of professors and their students, it would be necessary to select and use one instrument that is generally accepted as measuring intelligence. One cannot use two or more different instruments in such a situation and assume that they equally measure the same thing, especially if one instrument is used on one group and the other instrument is used on the other group.

The use of a standardized instrument allows for the comparison of measurements across different samples, different settings, different times, and different investigators. It is the common denominator that tends to produce valid findings.

Instruments standardize measurements and are the vehicle for obtaining evidence of reliability and validity. Another advantage that measuring instruments offer is that there is less opportunity for extraneous influences to contribute to measurement error. With reduced measurement error, one obtains greater reliability. Reliability is a prerequisite for validity (Chapter 2).

Researchers continually develop and introduce new instruments to open new areas of research. In fact, testing new hypotheses often awaits the appropriate new technology and its accompanying instruments. For example, computers (see Chapter 6) have made it possible for researchers to examine previously unmanageable mountains of data and to conduct complex analyses in incredibly short periods of time. The technology for recording the activity of single nerve cells has opened new research opportunities in the study of brain activity. Satellite photography enables us to see and make macromeasures of weather and its influence on earthbound populations. Succinctly, instruments advance the frontiers of researchable problems.

Finally, instruments can provide the investigator with an exact replica of the data as they unfold. They provide what can easily be transcribed to a written record, tape, or film, so that the data can be examined again and again, and not just by the original investigator. Such records or protocols help to minimize the chances of error of interpretation as more individuals are able to examine the same data.

Researchers should be familiar with the widest variety of available instruments. Scott and Wertheimer (1962) caution against "falling in love" with a certain instrument. An investigator may become a little too enthusiastic about a brand new instrument, particularly if she or he has played a role in designing the instrument. One should not become so fixated with an instrument that it begins to dictate which studies should be conducted. Instruments are a means to aid research, not guide it.

One must also be watchful for instances in which instruments might introduce error into a research project rather than help to minimize it. Yaremko et al. (1982) describe three such instances. First, instruments may produce changes in the physical environment which can alter a participant's behavior. For example, we may wish to study learning that takes place while a participant is in a relaxed state. To accomplish this we place the participant in a specially constructed and enclosed small isolated space to prevent any interruptions or extraneous noises. The enclosure may, however, have exactly the wrong effect. Rather than becoming relaxed, the participant may become aroused by the confinement in an isolated place. In this instance, instruments meant to control variables (e.g., noise, interruptions) which would prevent relaxation end up themselves preventing relaxation.

Second, instruments may alter behavior by creating an environment that is unlike the natural setting. For example, a pretest might sensitize participants to the measuring instrument and lead them to respond in certain ways that are different from the way they would ordinarily respond. Third, instruments may lose accuracy and precision as they grow older or are not properly maintained. One should always check the proper functioning of instruments before using them in a research project.

To avoid such errors, one should always check the instruments. Additionally, one might add a group of participants who receive no pretest to see if the pretest itself altered behavior. One might take an independent measure of relaxation to ascertain whether or not participants are relaxing. Researchers must be mindful of possible errors due to the instruments used and attempt to eliminate these errors.

USES

A researcher uses instruments to facilitate data gathering while at the same time increasing its objectivity. This is achieved because using an instrument tends to reduce or eliminate the many judgmental factors that might otherwise enter into the researcher's interpretation of the measurement of the data. Many instruments are capable of measurement quite independently of the researcher's judgment. It is not that a researcher may deliberately distort the measurement of the things observed, although that may happen. It is, rather, that our perceptions are altered, in often subtle ways, by our beliefs, attitudes, and expectations. Instruments, without the bias of beliefs, attitudes, and expectations, are far more objective in what they record.

Humans are often not as objective as the measuring instruments they construct. Humans process information from the moment such data impinge on the sense organs. The limitation is that our eyes are not cameras, and our ears are not tape recorders. Data may also be obscured when we recognize that memory does not infallibly recall what has occurred. Cameras and tape recorders do not process information; they record it as it takes place. Such instruments do have infallible "memories." They record what exists.

Another complication is that people are likely to be selective in observing even the most simple event. Instruments are much less likely to be selective and more likely to record the total event. Instruments are capable of both larger macromeasures and finer micromeasures than are humans. With instruments we can take measures that could not otherwise be recorded. In this way, instruments facilitate the collection of a more complete range of data.

Instruments are used by scientists to *present* stimuli, *measure and record* behavior, and *control* variables. These three uses are not mutually exclusive and an instrument may function in any combination of these ways.

Stimulus Presentation

Some instruments of data gathering not only measure events that occur, they create such events. Instruments present stimuli for participants to respond to and then measure those responses. In such instances it is important for stimuli to be presented in a standard and consistent fashion. Instruments are designed to do just that. Examples include a slide projector or a tape recorder. Other examples include a guide to conduct a group discussion, or a questionnaire to obtain responses from a sampling of the population.

Recording Behavior

Recorded behavior is the very essence of data and instruments can record behavior with accuracy. Examples include videotapes, tape recordings, or minicomputers. Somewhat less reliable or accurate are the written responses as observed or heard. In addition, responses of relevance and interest are those which the participants record (e.g., in questionnaire research or in a memory experiment). Ordinarily, one might not think of "paper and pencils" as being instruments of scientific research, but in fact they are probably the most widely used instruments in social science research. They are quite frequently used by researchers in psychological laboratories.

Controlling Variables

Instruments can also be used to control variations in unwanted variables such as noise, temperature, lighting, and so on when such variables might influence the data gathering. Instruments can hold noise level, temperature, and lighting quite constant in a laboratory experiment. This is often necessary so that such ambient conditions do not influence the results.

A printed questionnaire standardizes the manner and order in which questions are asked, so that variations do not influence the results. Tape-recorded instructions can control variations such as tone of voice and rate of speaking, which might otherwise potentially influence the data gathering.

Instruments, then, are very useful for presenting stimuli, recording responses, and controlling variables. Instruments are valuable because they introduce objectivity and at the same time facilitate the collection of data.

CHOOSING AN INSTRUMENT

A major factor in the choice of an instrument, when gathering data, is the *previous work* reported in the area being studied. One should not try to measure intelligence by giving a test that measures a knowledge of physics or chemistry or algebra. Each of these subjects has some degree of positive relationship with scores on an intelligence test, but this relation or correlation is far from a perfect one.

Briefly, one should choose, from among instruments, ones that at least are similar to those others have used. This enables one to compare current data with previously collected data. Any familiarity with the literature suggests that it is rare that a researcher would have no interest in, or need for, making such comparisons. In addition, one should always choose a direct measure rather than an indirect measure when both are available. In this connection, *direct* and *indirect* measures should be perceived as end points on a continuum rather than as discrete categories. Suppose, for example, that we decide to investigate whether there is a need to expand an existing parking lot. Since several new stores have opened in the complex it is possible that present parking facilities are inadequate. Before making a decision to expand the number of available parking places one should gather some data about the present situation. Decisions are best based on data and, thus, one should measure the current use of the present parking lot. Listed below are several possible measures:

1. For one week, we will count the number of empty spaces in the lot at various times such as 10 A.M., 1 P.M., 4 P.M., and 8 P.M., every day.
2. For a weekday and a weekend we will count the number of cars that drive by the complex. By averaging the traffic that passes the complex and recognizing that additional stores increase the complex size by 4%, we might then assume that there might be a 4% increase in cars that park.
3. For one week we will administer a short questionnaire to shoppers asking them to rate the adequacy and convenience of the present parking lot.
4. We will compare the number of spots available in our lot with the number of spots available in lots of similar-sized shopping complexes within a 7-mile radius.

From the viewpoint of data gathering, the first of these four measures is the most direct. It measures use of the lot by actually counting the number of unused spots at various times of day for all days of what is hoped is a typical week. It is the measure to be preferred. The other measures are somewhat less direct.

The second measure is based on an assumption that may be faulty. The third measure seems fairly direct since it is the shoppers whom we wish to please. In this instance the shoppers may be providing less direct information than cars. This is so because several shoppers may have been passengers in the same car and, thus, provide duplicative information (e.g., "I found a good spot"). Some shoppers may feel the parking is inadequate, not because the lot is not big enough but for other reasons (spaces are not big enough, lighting is inadequate, entry is difficult, there are no valets, etc.). The fourth measure is also fairly indirect. After all, we do not really know if these other lots are adequate.

One should choose, whenever possible, instruments that provide the most direct measure(s). Indirect measures provide data but one must be concerned with how well the obtained data address the problem under investigation. Sidowski says, "The farther a hypothesis is removed from publicly verifiable physical events, the less any single experiment contributes to the confirmatory evidence" (1966, p. 4). Hypotheses are tied to publicly verifiable physical events by using the most direct measures available.

TYPES OF INSTRUMENTATION

In this section three categories of instrumentation will be considered. They are "brass," electronic, and paper and pencil.

"Brass"

"Brass" instrument technology previously tended to dominate research in the psychology laboratory. Such instruments are more often mechanical than electrical and are often rather large and bulky; they are almost never made of brass. Although they were very frequently used in anthropology and psychology during the first half of the twentieth century, their use has declined (see Guthrie, 1976). Examples of such instruments include:

1. *Anthropometer.* A graduated rod with a movable horizontal arm. It measures sitting or standing height.
2. *Calipers.* An instrument used for measuring the distance between two points that are separated by some object (e.g., doing cranial measurements).
3. *Metronome.* A timer used to standardize the presentation of stimuli and beat out rhythm.
4. *Vernier chronoscope.* An instrument that measures reaction time.

Electronic

Most of the instruments used today are electronic. The use of transistors and silicon chips has made electronic instruments affordable and portable, and they can be found in many variations in every university in the country. They function in presenting stimuli, recording behavior, and controlling variables; they number in the hundreds (perhaps thousands). Some examples are described below.

Figure 5.1 The large apparatus on the left is the tachistoscope. Participants look through the dark viewer. On the table underneath the scope is a button (hand held) which, when pressed, stops the clocks to the right of the scope. The clocks are seated on top of the scope's controls and measure the response time of participants to various presented stimuli.

Tachistoscope.   Figure 5.1 shows a tachistoscope or t-scope (Gerbrands). This instrument permits highly controlled presentation of visual stimuli. The investigator can control the level of illumination and the duration of stimulus presentation down to a single millisecond (i.e., a thousandth of a second). Such control can be very important, particularly in research on perception.

The t-scope has been used quite frequently in investigations of functions of the left and right hemispheres of the brain (Springer and Deutsch, 1981). The participant looks into the viewer on the t-scope and focuses on a centered, fixation point. Soon a stimulus is presented in the left or right visual field. The t-scope permits rapid presentation (100–200 msec) so that the participant is unable to shift focus toward the presented stimulus. As Fig. 5.2 shows, stimuli presented in the right visual field are routed to the left visual cortex and vice versa. One can measure time to respond in an attempt to determine which hemisphere processes which stimulus types. Several studies (Mishkin and Forgays, 1952; Bryden, 1965) show that normal, right-handed individuals are better able to identify words presented in the right, rather than left, visual field. This suggests that words are processed in the left hemisphere.

Biofeedback.   Figure 5.3 shows a biofeedback laboratory (Cyborg). The participant is seated in a comfortable chair while various biological functions (e.g., brain

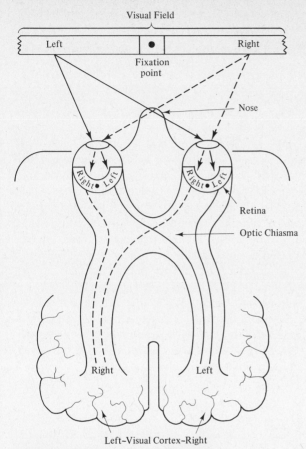

Figure 5.2   From visual field to visual cortex.

waves, heart rate, muscle tension, skin temperature) are monitored. The television screen provides visual feedback (e.g., a moving bar) to the participant concerning one or more biological functions. Auditory feedback is also provided through a small speaker. When individuals are given feedback on various biological functions, they can learn to consciously control those functions (Brown, 1977; Green and Green, 1977).

Biofeedback research has practical as well as theoretical implications (e.g., *how* people learn to gain control over their biology). For example, learning to warm the hands, by increasing blood flow to the hands, has been shown to be an effective treatment for many cases of migraine headaches (Peper, 1973; Sargent et al., 1972). As blood flow to the hands is increased, blood flow to the temples and forehead is decreased, thus minimizing the headache pain. One learns to warm the hands by trying different strategies (e.g., imagining one's hands are in a hot oven) and noting their effects on the biofeedback instrument. When a successful strategy is found, the biofeedback is no longer needed. For hand warming, simple and small circles of liquid crystals that change color (like the old "mood rings") as temperature changes can be an effective biofeedback instrument. These "Biodots" (Medical Services Corp.) are inexpensive and somewhat reliable indicators of skin temperature. Many drugstores and supermarkets sell such instruments as thermometers indicating degrees of fever (see Chapter 14 for an example).

Videotape.   Figure 5.4 shows some videotape instruments (e.g., camera, microphone) and a monitor (Panasonic). Such equipment is very useful for recording complex social and nonverbal behavior, which can later be coded by raters. With videotapes, the behavior can be played and replayed until it is correctly coded (e.g., as an instance of, or degree of, aggressive or nonaggressive behavior).

Videotaping equipment, home video recorders, and television arcade games have become very popular. In fact, researchers have begun to examine the use of different kinds of arcade games as training supplements for various kinds of work (S. Tkacz, personal communication, 1983). Perhaps extensive practice on such arcade games may produce more efficient air traffic controllers. If established, this would confirm that transfer of training exists at least in that instance.

Other.   Our sample of electronic instruments is a sample of convenience (the instruments were available). There are other types almost too numerous to mention. A reasonably complete catalog is provided by Sidowski (1966). Another source is the professional journal *Behavior Research Methods and Instrumentation,* which is available in many college and university libraries.

Figure 5.3 Author Milt Blum learns to control his skin temperature while receiving visual feedback on a television monitor.

Figure 5.4   The left panel shows researcher Cherie Clark adjusting the television monitor while, the right panel shows the camera and the author's child (Arlo Clark-Foos) in a free-play situation in another room.

Paper and Pencil

Paper-and-pencil measures are frequently used to gather data. Box 5.1 documents the use of various kinds of equipment reported in papers published in the 1982 volume of the *Journal of Experimental Psychology* (three journals). Paper-and-pencil measures rank third. Paper-and-pencil measures are inexpensive, very portable, and generally easy to use. They can be classified in three general categories: standardized tests, rating scales, and direct response measures.

Standardized Tests

Standardized tests numbering in the many hundreds are commercially distributed. Such tests provide a fixed set of test items, in a fixed order, administered with standardized instructions, and usually with a prescribed time limit. Scoring procedures are uniform and carefully described in an accompanying manual. Norms for comparison purposes are almost always provided. Such tests usually have known reliability and validity, which are reported in the manual.

Standardized tests measure aptitude, achievement, interest, and personality. Comprehensive information about such tests can be found in Buros (1978). Anastasi (1982) and Mehrens and Lehman (1984) also provide extensive coverage of standardized tests and their uses. We will very briefly examine the types of standardized tests and their use as instruments of research.

Aptitude Tests.   Intelligence tests are the most frequent kind of aptitude tests and are used quite often in research. For example, considerable interest has been

**Box 5.1   ONE YEAR OF INSTRUMENT USE AS BASED ON ARTICLES
PUBLISHED IN THE *JOURNAL OF EXPERIMENTAL PSYCHOLOGY***

Weber and Foos (1983) examined one year of articles published in the *Journal of Experimental Psychology: Animal Behavior Processes, JEP: Human Perception and Performance,* and *JEP: Learning, Memory and Cognition.* They compiled the following list of the 15 most used instruments. It should be noted that some studies used more than one instrument (the total adds to more than 1.0).

Instrument	Proportion of use
Computer	0.35
Cathode-ray tube (CRT)	0.22
Paper and pencil	0.19
Tone synthesizer	0.12
Timer	0.11
Slide projector	0.10
Shock generator	0.09
Rat cages	0.08
Speakers	0.07
Keyboard	0.07
Skinner box	0.07
Oscilloscope	0.05
Telegraph key	0.05

The two most frequently used instruments were computers and CRTs. A CRT is a cathode-ray tube for displaying stimuli which is programmed by a computer. Computer hardware and software have become the most frequently used instruments in many areas of social science (e.g., experimental psychology). Instruments that were used in fewer than 5% of the studies included counters, hand-held response buttons, tape recorders, stopwatches, memory drums, light and sound meters, T-mazes, polygraphs, rod and frame, and even flashlights. In total, 121 different instruments were counted in a total of 413 studies. All 413 studies used at least one instrument.

directed toward improving the IQ scores and the intelligence of disadvantaged children (Detterman and Sternberg, 1982). Such studies relate to the ever present nature-nurture controversy.

Garber and Heber (1982) selected 40 seriously disadvantaged families in Milwaukee who had newborn children. Half of the families were given a rehabilitation program for the mothers and an education program for the children; the other half were not given such programs. Starting at age two, *all* children were periodically given the Stanford-Binet IQ test. Average scores for the treated children (IQ = 120) were consistently higher than for the nontreated children (IQ = 94). Across the first four grades of school, the treated children scored higher on the Metropolitan Achievement Test and the WISC (Wechsler Intelligence Scale for Children). The implication is that intelligence can be improved by environmental influences (but see Sommer and Sommer, 1983).

Achievement Tests. Achievement tests measure an individual's current skill or ability in a specific area. To be recognized is that the same test is sometimes considered to be both an achievement test and an aptitude test, depending upon whether it is measuring present skill or predicting future performance. The SAT (Scholastic Aptitude Test) and the GRE (Graduate Record Exam) are such examples. An example of a more clear-cut achievement test would be a standardized typing test. The subject is given a specific text and asked to type as rapidly and accurately as he or she can. The score is based on the amount typed and the number of errors on the amount typed in a specified time. The score is then compared with the performance of others to determine how well or poorly the subject did.

Interest and Personality Tests. Interest tests are generally used for occupational and educational guidance as well as for aids in clinical diagnosis. Research (Dolliver and Will, 1977) has been done to investigate the stability of interests across different age groups. Interests of adults tend to be more stable than those of adolescents. For example, the Kuder Preference Record measures nine fields of interest: mechanical, computational, scientific, persuasive, artistic, literary, musical, social service, and clerical. The Stroz Interest Blank measures degrees of interest in different vocations such as accountant, lawyer, and psychologist.

Personality tests are generally divided into two categories: objective and projective. An objective test is one in which the "answers" are provided and the participants select one from among a number of possibilities. For example, it might be a multiple choice test or a scale on which one expresses degree of agreement or disagreement with some statement (e.g., "Do you make friends easily?" or "Are you frightened in the middle of the night?").

Projective tests either ask open-ended questions or sentences (e.g., "I love —") or offer an abstract or ambiguous statement or picture to which the response is determined by what the respondent perceives. The intention is for the participants to "project" some of themselves into the test (e.g., Rorschach ink blot test). In research, objective tests are used much more frequently than projective tests because objective tests are easier to score and are generally considered to be less controversial when interpreting results.

Rating Scales

In cases where there is no standardized test available or where such tests are not appropriate, rating scales are often constructed. Although there are a great many standardized tests, they tend to measure a relatively limited number of properties. For example, there are many types of tests for measuring intelligence but few standardized tests for measuring attitude. It is often the responsibility of the researcher to create or adopt a general rating scale as a measuring instrument, such as occurs in cases where one wishes to measure attitudes. Generally, rating scales are very useful for evaluating products, procedures, personal or social development (Gronlund, 1981), and attitudes as well as perceptions and images.

The measurement of attitudes occurs very frequently in sociology and social psychology. Particular interest has focused on comparing and contrasting the attitudes of different groups (e.g., young vs. old, northerners vs. southerners, men vs. women), investigating factors that seem to produce changes in attitude (e.g., credibility of information source, emotionality of appeal, direct experience), and investigating the ways in which attitudes influence perceptions (see Cvetkovich et al., 1984, for a summary of all of this work).

Attitude measurements, however, have a special problem that many other types of measures (e.g., aptitude, achievement, personality) do not have. That is, attitudes can exist for or against anything. One might want to measure attitudes toward abortion, product prices, crime control, television shows, landlords, the weather, working mothers, communism, the space shuttle, and even the kitchen sink! Because of this difficulty it is most inappropriate to devise a standardized attitude test. Instead, researchers have generally used any of four methods for measuring attitudes. These methods are used to measure any of many attitudes. All are rating scales. These four are called Likert, Thurstone, Guttman, and Osgood scales.

Likert scales are scored by summing the ratings given. Table 5.1 is an example of a Likert scale. In this case, the participant notes her/his level of agreement/disagreement with a number of statements by checking the appropriate box. Number values (i.e., 1, 2, 3, 4, and 5) are assigned to each level of agreement/disagreement for each item. Scales typically have five or seven categories so that a neutral response is the midpoint (i.e., no opinion). For the scale in Table 5.1 the maximum total score is 15 (a negative attitude toward television) and the minimum score is 3 (a positive attitude toward television). The assignment of number values to categories for each item depends upon how the item is worded. The ratings given in the table would be scored as a 1 on the first item, a 3 on the second item, and a 2 on the third item for a total score of 6. Likert scales provide *ordinal* measurement. A score of 12 means a less positive (more

Table 5.1 LIKERT SCALE METHOD FOR MEASURING ATTITUDES TOWARD TELEVISION

Statement	Strongly disagree	Disagree	No opinion	Agree	Strongly agree
1. People who watch television are wasting their time.	X				
2. Television is responsible for a national decline in literacy.			X		
3. Television provides inexpensive and worthwhile entertainment				X	

negative) attitude toward television than a score of 6. One cannot assume equal intervals or equivalent differences between the scores.

Thurstone scales have equal-appearing intervals. Table 5.2 shows an example of a Thurstone scaling procedure. Participants are given a large number of statements concerning some object or event. They are told to sort the statements into a specific number of piles (usually 7 or 11) so that adjacent piles are separated by the same, subjectively determined, interval. Typically, the number of statements to be sorted is quite large.

After a number of participants have sorted the statements, one can calculate the median or mean value for that statement and, thus, create an overall scale with equal-appearing intervals. Scores from such a scale are then treated as interval numbers.

Guttman scales use a technique of cumulative ratings. Items are arranged so that participants who respond favorably to a particular item are likely to respond favorably to all the remaining items of lower rank. Table 5.3 shows a Guttman scale. A participant who responds favorably to the first item is likely to respond favorably to all of the remaining items. A participant who responds favorably to the second but not the first item is likely to respond favorably to the third and fourth items, and so on.

The fourth example is Osgood's *Semantic Differential* (Osgood et al., 1957), a very useful scale for measuring attitudes. The Semantic Differential involves rating an item (a product, procedure, object, event, etc.) on a number of seven-

Table 5.2 THURSTONE SCALING METHOD FOR MEASURING ATTITUDES TOWARD CASINO GAMBLING

Sort the following statements into seven piles ranging from most favorable (pile 1), through neutral (pile 4), to least favorable (pile 7) so that the piles are *equally* separated.

1. Casino gambling allows the state to tax the owners and gamblers who participate and, thus, relieve the tax burden on homeowners.
2. Casinos in a community increase property values.
3. Casinos in a community bring organized crime.
4. Drug abuse increases as casino gambling increases.
5. Casinos offer healthy adult entertainment.
6. Prostitution increases as casino gambling increases.
7. Casinos are neither good nor bad.
8. Communities with casino gambling are favorite tourist attractions.
9. Casinos create a bad environment for the youth of a community.

and so on.

Table 5.3 GUTTMAN SCALE METHOD FOR MEASURING ATTITUDES TOWARD HOME COMPUTERS

1. Home computers are the best product to become available to consumers in the twentieth century.
2. Home computers are one of the best products to become available to consumers in the last twenty years.
3. Investing in a home computer is one of the best buys a consumer can now make.
4. In many cases, home computers pay for themselves in the long run.

and so on.

**Table 5.4   OSGOOD SCALE METHOD FOR MEASURING ATTITUDES TOWARD MASS
TRANSPORTATION**

Instructions

Check (✓) the blank line between each pair of adjectives (bad-good, high-low, etc.)
that most closely corresponds to your feeling about the stimulus:

Mass Transportation

bad	——	——	——	——	——	——	——	good
high	——	——	——	——	——	——	——	low
active	——	——	——	——	——	——	——	passive
clean	——	——	——	——	——	——	——	dirty
happy	——	——	——	——	——	——	——	sad
empty	——	——	——	——	——	——	——	full
strong	——	——	——	——	——	——	——	weak
clear	——	——	——	——	——	——	——	hazy
fast	——	——	——	——	——	——	——	slow

point scales. Each scale is anchored by a pair of bipolar adjectives (e.g., good-bad,
fast-slow, weak-strong). Table 5.4 shows a semantic differential for rating attitudes toward mass transportation. Although the scale was originally intended to
measure the connotative meanings of words, it is now used very generally for
measuring attitudes toward products, procedures, and services.

Direct Response Measures

Direct response paper-and-pencil measures are different from standardized tests
or rating scales. They are used when the behavior being investigated is a written
or oral *self-report.* For example, in a laboratory experiment, individuals might be
presented with a number of words to memorize. After some interval of time, they
are instructed to write down all the words that they can recall. This written record
of words recalled is a direct response measure.

In another study, individuals might be given different instructions to determine how they influence problem solving. Some are told that they will receive a
number of "enjoyable" problems to work on, while others are told that the
problems being given "measure intelligence." The written responses-answers to
the problems are a direct response measure. Such direct response measures are
used very frequently in research on cognition.

In sum, instruments are very useful in the gathering of data. They facilitate
and increase the objectivity of data gathering. The problem is to choose the most
appropriate instrument when gathering data. Finally, the reader should be aware
that the instruments presented in this chapter are but a few of the many used by
social scientists.

chapter 6

The Computer and Impact on Research

Computers continue to play an increasing role in our lives, whether we know it or not. Computers, with their ability to simplify and automate complex information manipulation and calculations, have had a revolutionary impact in many areas of contemporary life. The ability to perform millions of calculations in seconds has made possible computational tasks that were outside the realm of possibility 40 years ago. Such ability has provided access to information that was undreamed of prior to the development of the computer.

Accordingly, we shall examine the ways in which computers are used by social science researchers, ranging from statistical calculation to experiment control and word processing. We shall then examine some of the ways in which computers have changed the basic nature of social science research. Finally, we will look at the future and make some predictions about how rapidly changing computer technology will have an impact on researchers of the future.

It is not our purpose to provide a general education in computer literacy or in computer programming. Rather, what we shall attempt to do here is briefly to show some of the reasons why students of the social sciences should become familiar with computers. Rather than attempt an exhaustive listing of the uses of computers, we will illustrate by considering a single research study and inspect the uses of computers in that one project. The study was conducted by Russell Church and Warren Meck, and has been reported in Church (1983).

The experiment was designed to study the effect that administration of the drug physostigmine had upon the memory of rats for time intervals. It was part

NOTE: This chapter was written by Dr. Toby Berk.

of a series of experiments designed to study the influence of various psychoactive drugs on animal timing, memory, and decision processes. The experimental procedure is shown in Box 6.1.

At the planning stage of the study, a computer-based literature search was conducted by the experimenters. By using available computer data bases, they were able to search *Psychological Abstracts* back to 1967. They obtained 576 references to "acetylcholine," 15,307 references to "memory," but only 28 references to both acetylcholine *and* memory. The researchers were able to have complete references to those articles and their abstracts printed at a computer terminal.

After the experimental procedure was designed, it was necessary to construct the equipment to provide the stimuli to the rats, to control food dispensing, and to record the responses of the rats. Further, it was necessary to do this for 10 rats simultaneously. For this task, the researchers made use of a Digital Equipment Corporation PDP-12 computer with a special software system (set of computer programs) to control all 10 of the boxes and rats at once. The computer timed all 10 boxes, turning the signals on and off, arming and disarming the food

---

Box 6.1

Twenty male albino rats were used as subjects. They all received daily injections. On alternate days, the injection was of a neutral saline solution, and on the other days, the injection was of the psychoactive drug (physostigmine salicylate).

Each rat was trained in a box that had a retractable food lever, a food dispenser, a light, and a speaker.

The procedure was as follows: A signal (either light or sound) would be turned on. On half of the trials (randomly selected) the food lever was "armed" 20 seconds after the signal. (When armed, the lever would dispense a food pellet when pressed.) On the other half of the trials, the food lever was not armed at all. When the rat pressed the lever and got food, or after the signal had been on for 50 seconds, whichever came first, the signal was turned off and the trial was over. Trials were repeated at 2-minute intervals. Ten rats were trained at a time in ten separate boxes.

The number of responses (presses of the lever) of each rat was recorded for each 1-second interval after the signal was turned on.

It had been shown elsewhere that, with no drug administered, the responses of the rats should begin slowly after the signal was turned on, reach a peak at 20 seconds, and then drop off. The time of the "peak" response was used as a measure of the time memory of the rats.

The change in the peak response time was used as a measure of the effect of the drug on the subjects' time memory. It was expected that, because it increases the amount of the neurotransmitter substance acetylcholine, the drug would have the effect of reducing the time of the peak, among other effects.

levers, and recording the time whenever a rat pressed its food lever. The computing equipment used was somewhat obsolete, although it performed its function well. Today, a microcomputer would probably be used to control the experiment. Prior to the availability of computerized control, this experiment would have required connecting hundreds of electromechanical relays and switches. Data would have been manually collected from counters after each trial and then combined by hand. Now, the experimenters were able to use a computer for both the control of the equipment and the recording of the results without manual work. The results were recorded on computer tape for later analysis. Today, a small floppy diskette would probably be used.

The data were then combined, using a computer program written for a different computer (a PDP-11). The computer was used to provide a plot of the number of responses per minute as a function of time since the beginning of the trial, for trials following administration of the drug and for trials following administration of the neutral saline solution. The graphs indicated the type of change that the experimenters predicted. This step could have been done by hand, but it would have been rather tedious and error-prone. As the experimenter observed, "One advantage of data analysis by computer is that the user has confidence that the results are accurate" (Church, 1983, p. 123). This is true, however, only for programs that have been carefully tested and validated, and when the programs are properly used. It should be pointed out that, although software for performing a large variety of statistical tests is often available, it is not uncommon for some special-purpose programs to be needed for "manipulating data" prior to analysis. Often such programs can be easily written in a simple language such as BASIC.

The researchers who performed this experiment have a theoretical model for explaining time memory. A complete explanation of that model would require far more discussion than is appropriate for this section. Nevertheless, we can still discuss some of the problems involved in validating the model. The model assumes a component called the *pacemaker* that acts like a master timer, sending out *pulses* at some rate with a given mean and standard deviation. Those pulses are counted in an *accumulator* and compared against a *threshold,* which holds the "remembered" time. When the number of pulses counted is close enough to the threshold, the remembered time is considered to have passed. In order to determine what behavior is predicted by the model, a value for the threshold is determined as a random quantity with certain statistical properties. Although this can be done by hand from published tables of "random" digits, it is far easier to generate these "random" values from a computer program and then to use them to *simulate* the behavior of the model. In fact, the model used by these researchers is more complicated, and the computer simulation is also more complex. It should be noted that this model is obviously influenced by the internal structure of computers, which have master "clocks" that emit "timing pulses."

In order to determine whether the observed responses match those predicted by the theory, statistical analysis was performed. This was, of course, also done by a set of computer programs. Much of the tedious and error-prone hand work was avoided by the fact that both the predicted and the observed data were in computer-readable form.

Even at this point, with the experiment completed and the results analyzed, there remain a few more applications of computers as part of the research. Figures for the final publication of the results were produced by using a computer-driven plotter, and the text of the article presenting and explaining the results was written and edited on a microcomputer-based word processing system. Box 6.2 lists the ways in which computers were used by Church and Meck.

It is important to observe that the great usefulness of computers in a study such as this can obscure the fact that subtle and serious errors can also arise in their use. These errors are, almost without exception, human errors rather than computer errors. Nevertheless, the fact that a computer is being used often leads people to have unwarranted faith in the results. Let us examine some of the ways in which such errors might have occurred in the Church and Meck study if the researchers had not been extremely careful.

The program that controlled the experiment might have had an error (a "bug") which caused it to administer stimuli at incorrect times, or to record response times incorrectly, or to mix responses from two different rats.

There could have been an error in the data combining program, or the wrong data could have been used as input (perhaps from a trial run).

An error in the data plotting program, or in the instructions given to it, or in the data supplied to it could have resulted in a plot that did not actually reflect the results obtained.

The program that generated the "random" values for simulating the model might have had a bias toward certain values, thus distorting the simulation.

In summary, it must always be remembered that although computers are extremely fast, reliable, and accurate, this does not in any way imply that their results are always correct. The possibility of human error still remains when computers are used. In fact, because of the faith that is placed in computers,

---

Box 6.2   USES OF COMPUTERS IN EXPERIMENT BY CHURCH AND MECK

Search of literature
Control of experiment
Recording of results
Storage of data
Manipulation of data
Analysis of results
Development of theoretical model
Simulation of theoretical model
Comparison of data with theory
Preparation of figures
Preparation of manuscript

Box 6.3   SIGNIFICANT VARIABLES USED BY WOLFINGER AND ROSENSTONE FROM CENSUS DATA

Education
Income
Occupation
Employment status (employed, unemployed, not in labor force)
Employer (private, government, self)
Age
Sex
Race
Place of residence (metropolitan area, farm, neither)
Registered to vote
Voted
Reason given for not registering or voting
Hispanic ethnicity (Chicano, Puerto Rican, Cuban, other)
How long at present address
How long unemployed
Live in a trailer

---

the possibility of undetected human error may be greater when computers are used.

SOME CONCERNS

Listing and elaborating the various ways in which computers are employed in social science research is useful and important to anyone studying social science or conducting research in a social science. Mere examination of these applications, however, ignores the significant ways in which the availability of computing power has changed the very nature of social science research. The computer has qualitatively changed the very nature of the research activity and the meaning of research. As we shall see, there is by no means universal agreement that these changes have, in fact, all been positive.

The most obvious changes in research have been, as one would expect, a consequence of the phenomenal reduction in the time required to perform statistical analysis. This reduction in time (and cost) has made feasible studies that were previously impossible. This is especially true of studies involving several variables and, specifically, longitudinal studies (performed over time).

As an example, let us consider the important study of voting behavior by Wolfinger and Rosenstone (1980), which made use of data gathered by the U.S. Bureau of the Census in November of 1972 and 1974. In the 1972 census survey, 93,339 people were interviewed and a large number of data items were obtained (see Box 6.3). By using these data, the authors were able to analyze voter participation in terms of a number of different factors.

Because of the size of the sample and the ability to perform computationally complex statistical tests in a reasonably short time, the authors were able to measure the effect of a large number of variables under the assumption that other factors remained constant. For example, the authors were able to show that for people with four years of college, who were between the ages of 32 and 36, being married and living with a spouse had the effect of increasing the probability of voting by 4%. It would be absolutely impossible to perform such a study without significant computing power. In fact, it is safe to say that without significant computer use the Bureau of the Census would not even have endeavored to collect the data that were used in this study.

Although there can be no doubt of the benefit to researchers that comes from the power of computers when applied to statistical analysis, there is some concern about the danger of improper conclusions being drawn as a result. It has long been an important principle of research that a hypothesis should be first constructed, and then tested. Many researchers condemn the gathering of data and then examining the data for statistically significant relationships after the fact. Nevertheless, this "data snooping" is common practice. It may appear to be a reasonable practice at first, but one must be careful in interpreting results so obtained. If a relationship is considered significant only if its probability of chance occurrence is less than .01, that still means that out of 100 relationships tested, it is expected that one will appear significant by mere chance. When a large number of relationships are so tested, spurious relationships are frequently obtained.

The ease of performing statistical tests has made problems such as these much more common. Data snooping was relatively infeasible when calculations required long periods of hand labor. Now that it is nearly trivial, few researchers can avoid the temptation to look for unanticipated relationships in their data.

In the past, when the cost of testing hypotheses was relatively great, studies tended to be undertaken only when they tested an important hypothesis, and one which had a high expectation of confirmation. Consequently, theoretical analysis was of great importance. With low-cost computerization of data analysis, it has become relatively inexpensive to test hypotheses. Some scholars claim that this has led to a large number of trivial studies of unimportant hypotheses. Hypotheses are frequently constructed after the data analysis has been done. Although no one can doubt that insights, which come from the data, are often of great importance, some feel that the situation has gotten out of hand. Also, the pressure for publication that is imposed upon university researchers has combined with easy data analysis to create a large number of uninteresting, unimportant studies, some of which may also have questionable methodology.

The ease of statistical analysis that has resulted from ready availability of computing power has not only made data analysis easier, it has also changed the basic paradigms of the entire research community. The basic nature of what is meant by a question and by an answer in social science is now very different from what it was some 30 years ago. There has been an increasing tendency toward limiting study to things that can be easily quantified and subjected to statistical analysis. This has caused a decline in the relative status and emphasis of specialties that are not quantitative in nature, such as political theory as a part of the discipline of political science.

Thirty years ago, for example, before the rise of the empiricist school (which emphasized quantitative measurement), typical political science research included case studies of bills, attempts to sort out the effect of various groups, analysis of particular laws and their effects, political biography, and similar work which depended considerably on the observational skills, insights, and theoretical views of the investigator. Recently, there is a very strong focus on the measurement of "behavior," and attitudinal changes, which can be operationally defined in a quantitative manner. In particular, a great amount of work is being done that measures small changes in public opinion. Some claim that this tends to lead to measurement of the status quo and, thus, to a defense of the status quo. (See Box 6.4).

The journals that shape the direction of social science have been accused of publishing too many studies which are methodologically correct but trivial in substance and in contribution to new knowledge. Because of the dominance of statistical analysis, there has been a significant turning away from analyses that depend on the analyst's own insights and observations.

Critics observe that there is now little place for observational studies such as the classic *Middletown* (Lynd and Lynd, 1929), for ethnological studies based on observation, such as those which were fundamental to the formation of anthropology as a discipline, or for works like the significant sociological studies of the 1950s, such as *The Lonely Crowd* (Riesman, 1950) or *The Organization Man* (White, 1956). What kind of audience would a new Freud find for his theories in this quantitative age?

Related to this is a tendency to impute truth to the results of any methodologically correct study, such as the so-called scientific poll. Although researchers are usually careful to state the assumptions underlying their conclusions and to point out the uncertainty of their results, these warnings are often ignored, especially when results are subsequently used by others. For example, consider the tremendous impact of opinion polls on public policy.

If computers, as tools, tend to define problems and solutions, the availability of computer-accessible data also shapes the direction of research. The very availability of data, and therefore the feasibility of studies, tends to determine the questions that are pursued, the methodology used, and the form of the answers that are obtained. As an example, Wolfinger and Rosenstone's study of voter behavior, mentioned previously, was based on data collected by the U.S. Census Bureau. The factors analyzed were those for which the data were available. For example, the classification of occupation used in the study was that used by the Census Bureau. The same was true of definitions and categories of ethnicity,

---

Box 6.4

As an exercise, go to the library and look at the contents of issues of a major social science journal from the current year and from 1950. Do you see any evidence of the trends discussed in this section?

income, and other important factors. Whether these categories are relevant or important to social science theory was probably of no concern to the Census Bureau.

It is inevitable that the availability of data defines the questions that social scientists ask. Furthermore, it defines the methodology that is used and, as a consequence, the type of answers that will be found to the questions. There can be no doubt that the widespread availability of archival data, distributed by means of a computerized information network, will be tremendously beneficial to the social sciences. Nevertheless, it is also clear that the very form of these archives and data bases will shape the direction of inquiry. It remains to be seen whether or not this will limit the especially important findings that result from either serendipity or that special genius and insight that finds a relationship in apparently unrelated things. As a simple example, one can speculate whether a researcher using computerized data bases to search for a cure for smallpox would have been likely to find any reference to milking cows that would lead to discovering the relationship between cowpox and smallpox immunity.

FOR THE FUTURE

Computerization has had a significant effect on the social sciences over the past quarter-century. This change is by no means complete. Whereas the most significant aspect of the computer's impact to date has been in its capacity for reducing computational costs, the coming impact will be related to its capacity for accessing and distributing information. The changing nature of libraries, archives, and communication will change the nature of the social sciences most significantly.

The beginning of the changes that will occur in libraries is shown in the computerized search of *Psychological Abstracts* in the experiment we discussed above. Large amounts of computer-accessible bibliographic data are being made accessible for computer search. So far, references to books, journals, and articles are primarily being made accessible in this way. However, it is quite likely, perhaps even certain, that in the near future the very nature of publication of books and articles will change. With the widespread availability of high-speed computer terminals, there will probably be no need to actually duplicate printed copies of works that are "published." Publication will be accomplished by depositing a computer-readable form of the work in either a centralized computer-based library or a regional computer-based library connected to others by a high-speed data communication network.

Users of this new "distributed, computerized library" will be able to search and browse through a tremendous collection of resources and will be able to obtain copies of whatever references are needed. This will be a revolutionary breakthrough, as it will provide to scholars everywhere the even better resources than are now available to researchers at major centers of learning. Every community college student will have access to the same sources as the foremost scholars. Furthermore, all these resources will be continually available, because items will never be "checked out," but merely copied by multiple users.

Along with this machine-readable distributed collection, sophisticated search systems will develop that will make it possible to locate relevant works by subject, related subject, and so forth. The availability of this information and the data base searching system that will accompany it will probably cause a great increase in scholarship, which will make even more items available in the system.

Not only will books and articles be made readily available, but the actual data collected by investigators might also be deposited in computer-accessible archives. This will make it immensely easier for researchers to do their work. Although the idea of the "national data bank" which was proposed in the late 1960s was abandoned, expected developments in computer communication technology can make access to available data universally easy, with all the advantages and risks that such universal access implies. It is quite possible that any community college student will be able to construct and test hypotheses by using vast resources of experimental, survey, archival, and government data.

It is entirely possible that the nature of "publication" may change and that results will not be presented in the same form as they are today. Some predict that changes in information technology will change the form of the presentation of ideas, just as the transition from oratory to the written word changed it in the past. The new "document" might be structured in "layers," more like an extended outline than a sequential article. A reader could begin with a short summary of the publication, and request and examine further detail and explanation whenever desired, perhaps examining the raw data if desired. A single publication, then, could be accessible to lay readers, beginning students, advanced students, professionals, and specialists in the area of research. Coupled with computerized indexing and searching, this new form of information presentation has the potential of removing much of the tedium from research and opening up the possibility of productive, interesting research to a much larger population.

chapter *7*

Observation

Observation is probably one of the most basic and fundamental forms of data gathering in all of the sciences. And yet, it is too often taken for granted and so its value and potential have been far from fully realized. In addition, it should be emphasized that the importance of objective observation contributes to reaching more valid conclusions and decisions in our everyday living. In some sense, observation underlies *all* other data-gathering techniques. The ways in which observations are made are what differ.

In this chapter we will examine some of the major views on how observation should be conducted, the types of events that are most observable, differences between subjective and objective observations, and the importance of recording what is observed. We will also consider an overview of variables, the gestalt of observation, and present some examples of data collected through observation. We will encourage the uniform application of certain recommended techniques for social scientists and laypeople as well. Observation is the one data-gathering technique that is most readily capable of being used by all of us to obtain objective data that can lead to solutions to both personal and societal problems.

One major view of the observation technique comes from Weick (1968), who believes that the method has been impeded by the assumption that naturalness and control are mutually exclusive. He favors having the observation method more closely resemble the experimental method, especially when it comes to allowing and encouraging the observer to manipulate the natural setting almost as if it were an experiment. For Weick, observers need not remain docile and passive. Weick defines the observational method as "the selection, provocation, recording, and encoding of that set of behaviors and settings concerning organisms 'in situ' which is consistent with empirical aims." Weick's view differs from ours in that we classify situations where observers manipulate as being experimental and/or field research techniques.

The views of Webb et al. (1981) are much closer to our own. They discuss observational research where the observer is unobserved and in settings where the investigator has no part in structuring the situation. They point out that such a method makes it possible for the observed not to be aware of the observation—which in turn precludes possible concomitant role playing. This method also prevents the measurement (that which is being observed) from becoming an agent of change and, of course, the observer effects are not an issue. Webb et al. recognize the value of observation as a source of firsthand data as well as an "opportunistic sampling of important phenomena." They report that simple observational data do not offer the "why" but simply establish a relationship.

Webb et al. also point out some limitations of this method, such as the possibility that the observer may vary in observing because of changes in attention, increase in boredom, or being less conscientious. They refer to the work of Turner (1974), who concludes that good observers simply "see more to see" and, for whatever reasons, tend to be female, introverted, and nearsighted. Along different lines, they also indicate that caution should be employed in generalizing from research that gathered observations at one time in one place. To minimize this problem, it is suggested that time and location sampling should be employed in obtaining observational data.

Selltiz et al. (see Kidder, 1981) indicate that observation becomes a scientific technique when it serves a formulated research purpose, is planned and recorded systematically, and is subject to the controls of reliability and validity. They suggest that (perhaps) observation's greatest asset is that it can record behavior as it occurs. They recognize that observation serves a variety of research purposes, among which are gaining insights to be tested later and obtaining supplementary data or primary data. Since observing everything is an unachievable goal, it is helpful to narrow the range of situations to be observed. It is helpful to have two or more people observe the same event as a means of increasing both the reliability and the validity of observation.

Kidder (1981) refers to systematic observation as "the selection, recording, and encoding of a set of natural behaviors usually but not necessarily in their natural setting for the purpose of uncovering meaningful relationships." He lists six steps in conducting such observations: (1) choosing a natural behavior, (2) selecting an appropriate observational setting, (3) deciding on the mode of recording observation, (4) determining the sampling strategy, (5) training observers, and (6) analyzing the data.

Boice (1983) views observation somewhat differently from his predecessors. He posits that certain positions have led to misunderstanding and lack of progress in advancing observation as a psychological technique. Among them are: "good observers are born, not made," "good observers are identifiable in terms of personality traits," and "persistent methodological difficulties."

However, on a more positive note he suggests that emerging solutions can stem from research in such areas as nonverbal communications, social skills, and therapist training. In other words, these three areas lead to more fruitful results and the legitimizing of the study of observation in psychology. Boice believes this is achieved by specifying the skills of good observers, the situational factors that facilitate observation, and the formulation of training programs in observational skills. Boice points out that observers vary greatly in performance and that such differences can and should be reduced by training. It should be clear that some observer training is almost always required. One must learn to avoid making inferences and including them as observation. Making inferences comes later after all observations are collected. For example, a naive observer might report that "while waiting for a traffic light, the man driving became angry and began blowing his horn." A trained observer would report all of the same, except for the "became angry" inference. After all, becoming angry was not observed but inferred from what was, in fact, observed.

Boice also accepts findings that reveal differences in ability to observe. Among those mentioned are females and introverts, who are reported to be better observers. He subscribes to the view that "what an observer reports tells us something about the observed action and something about the observer." He states:

> Surely psychologists who devise experiments, who teach, who do therapy, and who apply psychology to real life problems can benefit from research on the measurement and improvement of observational skills. The question, then, is why we choose to leave this sort of training to the luncheon talks of business people and ignore it in our own curricula and laboratories? (Boice, 1983 p. 24)

WHAT IS OBSERVABLE

Although observation is pervasive, it can become quite specific and utilitarian when it is harnessed in accordance with the purpose of the observer. An observer's purpose is to define, describe, and, to a degree, quantify the actions or interactions of organisms, environments, or both.

A first step toward understanding the uses of observation as a data-gathering technique occurs as one examines what is observable. Figure 7.1 illustrates observables. Places, things, events, or situations exist or occur in the environment. Most simply, a *place* can be a geographic location such as a city or a seat you choose in the classroom and then occupy for the semester. A *thing* is an object, be it a book, ring, chair, or item of clothing. An *event* is an occurrence such as a dance, a wedding, a holiday, or a ball game. Events also can occur in the atmosphere and so we have hurricanes, snow, rain, or heat waves. *Situations* primarily describe the time frame and interaction in which the event takes place. They could include negotiations, a riot at a specific time in one area, a traffic jam, or the interaction of people in a specific environment such as a love-fest. *Organisms* include all living plants (not primarily the concern of social scientists) and animals, including people. Observing people, as separate from the preceding four environmental concerns, may even be a prerequisite for observing people as they and the environment interact or do not interact.

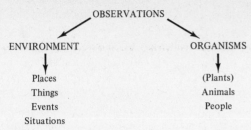

Figure 7.1 Observables.

This leads to Fig. 7.2, which recognizes the problems that not only are intrinsic in the act of observing, but also suggest the leads, direction, or purpose of that which is being observed.

The major problem of observation is to determine, define, and delimit that which is to be observed. Any thing, event, situation, or place as well as any person or group involved is generally likely to offer too much to be observed at one time or over a period of time. As a result, one needs guides or clues to what to observe. The first step in obtaining such clues requires one to determine the attributes or characteristics of the environment being observed and also the attributes of the person or persons being observed. Standing on a street corner, sitting in a classroom, walking in the park, or shopping in a mall, one must first determine the attributes or characteristics that describe the environment being observed. These may include the time, the day, the weather, or the temperature, to name a few characteristics that determine what is being observed. They might include sudden rain, a lecture or a visual aid demonstration, a special sale, or a live band. The extent to which the people are observed must also be defined by such characteristics as age, sex, manner of dress, hurried pace, being alone or with others, smiling or being without expression, and so forth.

It is necessary to recognize that attributes or characteristics differ in degree. Such differences require some classification system so that the observations can be categorized or measured. For example the characteristic of age may be classified as young, middle aged, or old. It also may be classified as under 21, 21 to 40, and 40+. Observing a shopper at a shopping mall might allow one to classify such shoppers as male or female or classify the shopper as being alone, with one other person, with two people, and so on. To be recognized is that several different

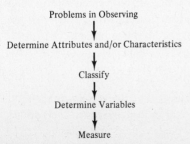

Figure 7.2 Problems in observing.

classification schemes are always possible. It is for the observer to decide which is most appropriate.

The next step is to determine the variables within the classification system, and herein lies the major difference between an experiment and an observation as a form of data gathering. In an experiment the experimenter manipulates one or more variables, but in an observation the observer is, and must be, an unobtrusive observer and must in no way manipulate the environment or the person(s) involved. It is recognized that others view observation differently (see Weick), but in science, and especially social science, difference rather than agreement is more often the rule.

Once the variables are known, they must be measured by using some system. It should be clear from the preceding discussion that any form of behavior or any environment is observable. Included at one level is any response or even a lack of response to stimuli impinging on our sensory mechanisms. More complex levels include the wide variety of individual behavioral manifestations that are socially or culturally acceptable or unacceptable. These include religiosity, homosexuality, abortion, and even being a little liberal or conservative. All of these and more involve not only individuals but also their interactions with other individuals and groups.

Another major problem in reporting observations is that the data stem from either subjective or objective procedures. The former are more frequently used by all of us and are casual in nature. This use may handicap the acceptance of objective observation as a scientific data-gathering system. To illustrate the difference between subjective and objective observations, the following example is offered. If an active child is suddenly inactive or if the child's face appears flushed, a worried parent may feel the child's forehead (subjective observation) to estimate whether the child has a fever. To be more objective, the parent would use a thermometer to determine more accurately not only if, but also how much of a fever is present (objective observation). Objective observations follow the measurement guidelines presented earlier (Chapter 2). The reliability and validity of objective observations can be checked; such checks are not made with subjective observations.

Because of the frequent lack of reliable and valid measuring instruments and the personal influences of observers, two or more people are quite likely to observe and report identical things, places, events, or situations differently. This results either in disagreement about what is reality, or in the belief that observations are unreliable descriptions of the reality. This is complicated by the belief of each individual that his or her report of the observation is the reality. All this can lead to the erroneous conclusion that reality is "in the mind" or "eye" of the beholder—just as beauty is. If beauty is objectively defined and its characteristics or attributes are determined and then measured, then beauty can be observed with reliability and validity.

Another major problem with observations is that there is so much to be observed that two or more people will hardly ever report the same observations, even though they both observed the same incident at the same time.

All of this may have stalled the research, development, and use of observations as a scientific technique. For this and other reasons, despite the availability of observation as a scientific technique, for some time it has lagged behind the other more "disciplined" forms of data gathering such as the experiment. As an early step it is necessary to identify two aspects of objective (scientific) observation. The *first* is to define the observation and the *second* is to measure its variables as determined by its attributes and characteristics.

For example, submissive behavior, a riot, a television set, or a tornado must be defined in terms of characteristics or attributes. Having done so, one then, with the use of a selected or constructed measuring instrument, measures or judges the extent or degree to which such characteristics exist. Our measurements must be reliable, valid, and replicable. They must correctly measure that which is being observed.

An observation is a report or record of an environment or of the characteristics or behavior of a person or persons as witnessed by observers with the aid of one or more measuring instruments. An observation may also be an observer's report or record of a thing or things, such as a picture in a home or a museum, a food, a label, or even a widget.

The person or thing being observed may be passive or active in many different environments. It is necessary that the observer or observers define and determine what is to be observed. Consider the observation of group behavior, for example. Different definitions as well as measuring instruments would be necessary to observe the shopping behavior of tourists or natives in different environments or to observe people at such events as a football game, an opera, a lecture, or a religious service.

When it comes to observing things, characteristics that differentiate within such items as furniture, clothing, automobiles, food, supermarkets, bars, or appliances, for instance, are included. In other words, *an observation is a report* of the behavior of an individual or individuals reacting to stimuli in an environment. In the environment are things or events, places or situations which in various ways can influence the individuals being observed.

SUBJECTIVE OBSERVATIONS

A subjective observation is the most common form of observation and must be differentiated and excluded from objective observations. It is casual and uncontrolled in that measuring instruments are not used and observations are hopelessly influenced by whether one likes or dislikes that person or those who resemble him or her in characteristics such as height, weight, and neatness. Observation is influenced by whether another person's behavior is or is not emotionally acceptable. An observation may also be influenced momentarily by the mental state of the observer. In addition, the observation is likely to be tinged by the attitude that one has toward a person or the group, be it black, red, yellow or white. Such attitudes can influence casual observation and predetermine such biased judgments as: "the person/group is noisy, aggressive, polite, or ignorant."

Since perceptions are the meanings we assign to stimuli impinging on us, we are subject to illusions that are the misinterpretations of stimuli. We judge people to be taller, heavier, or brighter, depending upon the stability of the stimuli and the environment. Stated another way, we may vary in determining the figure as differentiated from the ground. Whom do you see in Fig. 7.3?

The rationalisms described in Chapter 1 should not be overlooked. They are explanations of behavior based on a person's thinking, wishes, or perceived experiences rather than on the data. Rationalisms have a strong influence on data reporting as a result of subjective observations. The subjective observations are minimized, if not eliminated, when the observations are objective and the conclusion or decisions are based upon the data.

OBJECTIVE OBSERVATIONS

Whether in the laboratory or in the world, an *objective* observer is probably among the most reliable transmitters of reality. If the average person could be persuaded to give up subjective observations for objective ones, then it is likely that there would be less strife, conflict, and prejudice. As has been indicated, objective observation reduces the tricks that our emotions, prejudgments, attitudes, and even motives play on us as we try to ferret out reality from what we think it is. It is likely that an umpire on the yardline of a play may be more objective than a loyal graduate 50 yards away and 80 rows from the field.

A concept, instrument, or method approaches the standards of scientific criteria as it becomes measurable, reliable, and valid—and this is what objective observation is all about. Critical differences between objective and subjective observations include the number of observations, the number of observers, and the method used to obtain the data. Subjective observations tend to be the result of one observer making too few observations and without a clearly defined procedure.

Objectivity is enhanced by having more than one observer make repeated

Figure 7.3 An ambiguous figure that can be seen as a pretty woman or an ugly one. The observer's "set" helps determine which profile will be seen.

observations using a standard method. An exception occurs in the observation of price of a product when the price is clearly presented on the package or is clearly posted and can, thus, be independently checked.

The presence of two (or more) observers allows one to estimate the reliability of the observations made. For example, assume that observations are being made of individuals who use the elevator instead of walking up the stairs. Our list of observables includes weight, height, age, and sex of individuals. One observer reports seeing mostly young males of varying heights and weights using the stairs. Is this a reliable observation? If another observer is present, we can check the reliability by comparing the two sets of observations. If the other observer reports that an equal number of males and females used the stairs, we know immediately that the observations are not reliable. We do not know which observer (if either) is correct, but we do know that we should not trust the observations. On the other hand, if they agree on what they observed, then the observations are reliable and can be used. It is typical for social scientists to demand at least 80% agreement between observers before using the observations made as reliable data.

Regardless of whether the observation is of a person, thing, or event, the first need is to define what it is that is being observed (i.e., styles of walking, degrees of aggressiveness, art forms in a museum, people attending a concert, or a new model of refrigerator). Once the walking is defined and differentiated from running or jogging, then it is necessary to compile as thorough a list as possible of the attributes and characteristics of that which is being observed,as well as the variables differentiating each attribute or characteristic. For example, if walking is to be observed, then such characteristics or attributes of walking to be considered might be speed, stride, left foot movement, right foot movement, right leg movement, left leg movement, hand movement. (What others would you add?) As for variables, speed could be determined as fast, average, or slow depending upon the ground covered in a second or a minute, or, conversely, the time taken to cover a specified distance. Similarly, each additional attribute could be differentiated by its degree of variability. To offer an example of objective observation of a thing such as a refrigerator, the characteristics or attributes might include outer size, inner size, color, location of freezer, number of doors, special features, and price. Again, each of these would be variable. The color might be white, yellow, or green. The price, depending on inflation and features, might be $300 to $1800.

INSTRUMENTATION

In addition to defining that which we are observing and identifying, the attributes and characteristics of the person or thing, we need to record the observations. This is done either by taping or by having the observer record the observation as a result of using a measuring instrument. If it is the former, then the value is in replay either for further analysis or for transposition to the measuring instrument.

RECORDING OBSERVATIONS

To avoid redundancy, the reader is asked to refer to Chapter 5, on Measuring Instruments. However, in the context of this chapter it is necessary to point out that whether one continues to repeat the same observations over long periods of time, such as observing children at play, or observes people making telephone calls from a public phone, or people on a college campus or in a shopping mall, or people shopping in supermarkets with or without shopping lists, the basic need is to construct and use a measuring instrument that is reliable and valid and that will enable one to record the behavior as it takes place.

An important principle to consider in recording observations is *fractionization,* which is the degree of the detail to be observed. For example, instead of rating slow or fast, one might record such details as very fast, fast, average, slow, and very slow—all of which must be defined in a manner conducive to enhancing objective observation. Product appearance might be most meaningfully rated as excellent, good, fair, or poor, provided clear and defined differentiations are established. Teaching ability, which is defined as observed performance, might be rated as above average, average, or below average, or on a 10-point or 100-point scale. Probably as good an example as any is to rate observed student participation in class as either A—a great deal, B—somewhat, or C—not at all; or A, B, C, or D; or A+, A, A−, B+, B, B−, etc. One could even use double plus or double minus provided the minuteness does not introduce unreliability of rating an observation.

In other words, the measurability should reflect sensitivity, but not to such an inordinate extent that the rating really becomes insensitive because of its unreliability. For example, should we know a person's temperature by differences of degree, half of a degree, a quarter, or an eighth, or simply decide that the person has a temperature that is subnormal, normal, reflecting some fever, or critical?

The measuring instrument used to record the observation allows the observer to translate the behavior, thing, or event into some differentiable or quantifiable identity, be it nominal such as male-female or young-old, ordinal such as brightest-dumbest or tallest-shortest, or interval such as very much-somewhat-not at all. As mentioned in other chapters, gathering data should be followed by its collation, analysis, summation, and presentation. Here tallies, tables, charts, or graphs are the more frequently used.

VARIABLES

Once the characteristics of things, events, places, situations, or people have been identified, it is necessary to establish the variables contained within each of the characteristics. The term variables is used differently in the context of observation than when it is used in the context of an experiment. In the latter instance, it is a manipulated input provided by the experimenter, which in some way is intended to result in a differential response on the part of the subject(s).

Variable, when used in the context of an observation, is a measurable difference in any of the designated characteristics chosen to describe the thing, event, place, situation, or person being observed.

For things, the characteristic of price might include such measurable differences as: actual price, price range, sale price, or reduced price. In addition to these quantitative measures, there might be some qualitative measures such as the dimension—expensive, inexpensive, wholesale, retail, or lowest prices ever (as is typical of many furniture outlets). Similarly, size can be measured in waistline inches—28, 30, 32, 34, 36, etc.—or as large, medium, and small. In considering the features of a thing, the differentiations are endless and depend upon the almost infinite variety of things to be observed.

Situations involve such environment-people interactions as celebrations, funerals, and demonstrations, in which mores or customs influence behavior. In terms of people, the designated characteristics may be external physical characteristics. Examples would include height, weight, or hair style. Also, a number of expressive physical signs may be observed such as facial expression, which could include frowns, smiles, blinking, winking, nodding, or tics. A relatively unused emotional indicator rather easy to observe is nostril movement! The face also changes color and reddens, pales, or wrinkles. Tears may be silent or accompanied by sobs and screams. This leads into the category of language expression. Whether one understands the language or not, one can observe whispering, yelling, and talking fast or slowly. However, cultural differences may mean that the same sound is expressing a vastly different behavior. Add to this language observable body language such as hand movements, shrugging the shoulders, making a fist, folding one's arms, stamping, kicking, turning the head or body, standing close, or moving away. Clearly, there is much to observe.

It should be emphasized that all things can be *observed* without manipulation by the observer. The observation takes place in the setting in which the thing, event, or situation occurs or in which the person reacts to the environment.

In other words, we are able to observe things, events, places, situations, the environment, and people in a natural setting or an unfolding environment. Nothing artificial is created or manipulated. Determining the characteristics and the variables within each, be it something in the environment or in the person or the interaction that takes place, makes it possible to observe quite objectively and measure with a considerable degree of reliability—and that is observation.

A CHECKLIST

As an aid to gathering data based on observations, the following are recommended:

Determine and specify the purpose or objective to be achieved.

State it in the form of an hypothesis.

Conduct an informal observation to "guesstimate" the activities within the observation setting that are capable of being observed.

List the attributes, characteristics, and variables to be observed as they are revealed.

Define that which is being observed (only after the attributes are identifiable).

Determine the extent or degree to which the concept being observed varies.

Compare the findings based on differences in day of week, hour of day, weather, and so forth to determine whether the observations are specific or typical of the observation period or have more stability or generality.

Fully describe the situation, thing, event, and/or place in relation to the observations being made.

Fully describe the person's, persons', or group's behavior.

Relate the environment to the people aspect of the behavior.

Describe and note the various active or passive roles of those being observed.

Review the nature of the observation data to decide the aspects that are more or less germane in relation to objectives and analyze accordingly.

Construct the measuring instrument and then decide, if using rating scales, whether numbers, letters, or words can best differentiate the degrees of the characteristics or attributes being measured.

Consider the extent to which variables intrinsic to the observation affect the results.

Ascertain the possible influence of the antecedents on that which is being observed and either include them as part of the observation or start all over.

THE OBSERVATION GESTALT

The preceding sections presented an analytical description of the factors contributing to an observation. The danger is that one might consider observations to be separate, distinct, or discrete events, things, places, or situations in which a person or persons may or may not be involved. In reality, this is only partially accurate. Most often that which is being observed is part of a kaleidoscope. The observation must be defined, specified, and narrowed so that the observations that are recorded are valid and reliable indicators. This is the essence of the difference between the frequently used subjective observations and those that should be used, which are objective.

It is probably most appropriate to consider observations as a result of a modular approach in which the variables of the characteristics or attributes are estimated or measured as they take place or occur in that small part of the world being observed. To illustrate, two examples will be presented. The first indicates the influence on consumer behavior of posted gasoline prices. The second is a report of observations made at a hearing conducted by three government agencies concerned with the social/political issue of food labeling. This example is offered especially because it illustrates:

the thing   =   food labeling
the event   =   hearings
the place   =   two geographic locations
the people   =   citizens and groups who testify
the situation   =   the complex political atmosphere when business, government, and bureaucrats get together (or do they?)

Gail Helmkamp, an intern of the Consumer Affairs Institute at the time when Dade County in Florida was considering the passage of an ordinance requiring gas stations to post the price of the gasoline at their pumps, reported:

I observed 181 customers at eight gasoline stations with price signs prominently posted. In addition, I also observed 145 customers at eight gasoline stations with no such signs. I spent 45 minutes at each of the 16 stations. To collect data in an unbiased fashion, I visited four stations with signs and four stations without signs on two Mondays and also visited the same number of stations on two Fridays.

Based on observing eight gasoline stations with signs and eight stations without signs for a total of 12 hours and given equal time spent at both types of stations; the stations with signs posted served 11% more customers.

The customers spent an average of $12.64 at the stations with signs posted and at the stations without posted signs, the customers spent an average of $11.39. Gasoline stations with clearly posted price signs, on the average, sold gasoline for about 11¢ less per gallon than those stations without signs. This includes the variation of self and full service and the three types of gasoline (regular, unleaded and premium). The least price differential was 8.59¢ for unleaded, self service in the two types of stations.

To summarize, stations with prominent and clear price signs had more customers, sold more gasoline per customer and averaged a selling price of 11¢ less per gallon.

To the extent that the 16 stations were representative of gas stations in the county, then a generalizing of the findings is possible. Otherwise, the findings must be limited to the stations observed.

Observing meetings or hearings, provided the observers are objective and their reports accurately reflect what took place, can provide a data-gathering base that can add objectivity as one attempts to evaluate what took place and indicate the findings as well. The observation of a specific set of government hearings allows for the observation of places (two hearing sites), things (the consideration of changes in food labels), events (the combined efforts of three regulatory agencies), and situations (the possibility of setting mandatory standards for food labels). The hearings also allow for observation as people interact by representing themselves and in some instances representing various sectors of the population including consumers, business, and government. Also participating, in this instance, were educators, consumer groups, trade associations, farmers, and government officials. Since these hearings cannot be replicated in time or space, the observations can be considered as representative of that particular universe.

The Food Labeling Hearings conducted in Washington and Boston in 1978 by the Food and Drug Administration, the U.S. Department of Agriculture, and the Federal Trade Commission provided just such an opportunity. The observations in each city were made by two representatives of the Consumer Affairs Institute. One person attended both hearings and was joined by a different second observer in each city. The purpose of this design was to aid in establishing both the validity and reliability of the report.

The observations suggest that the various sectors came to the hearings with preformed judgments and left with the same judgments solidly in place. These specific hearings demonstrated that a big gap exists between business views on label changes and the views of other interested sectors, which intensifies the conflict about what exactly is in the best interest of the public.

Observation showed that the consumer representatives were the most numerous in offering testimony. They ranged widely in age and socioeconomic status. Sometimes they testified on behalf of an organization and sometimes as individuals. Their testimony favored changes as a means of obtaining more, better, and clearer information on matters related to food and health. The consumers who testified were sometimes one-issue people, reflecting their personal views or concerns. Others were more concerned with broader issues such as the role of the food label in providing more adequate information, allowing for better food purchase decisions.

The educators and professionally trained people testified in a precise and organized fashion. They were generally more informed about nutrition than the consumer group. Nevertheless, their recommendations were generally similar to those suggested by the consumer people.

The people employed on various government levels who testified more often reflected the views of consumers than those of business.

The views of business were presented primarily by trade association people. In a few instances "small businessmen" testified; in only one instance did a major food company offer testimony. Whatever the reasons for this, the question might be raised whether the position of major food companies was presented.

What is clear, based upon the testimony heard, is that business, through its trade associations, takes a very different stand on food label changes than do consumers. Business favors the status quo or, at most, voluntary change. It requests cost/value studies before any change becomes effective and unhesitatingly indicates that label changes will increase consumer costs as well as put small companies out of business.

The common denominator of the food label changes recommended was the preference for "the right to know and choose what one eats." These hearings obtained information on the direction and the nature of the general change, but did not spell out the best specific change.

The following changes suggested are not listed in any priority order since the hearings did not establish any.

- List ingredients by percentage or weight in order of predominance.
- Identify items presently considered hazardous to health, such as fat, salt, and sweeteners.
- U.S. RDAs (recommended daily allowances) may be unnecessary and misleading and, therefore, should be eliminated from the label.
- Fortification should be done only when it enhances the food and is economical and the reason for fortification should be so stated on the label.
- Imitation and substitute foods as well as such terms as "natural" and "pure" need clarification and should be considered in the context of food technological development. Imitation, substitute, natural, and pure should be justified on the label in terms of superior or inferior nutrient value.
- Consistent with "the right to know," an alphanumeric form of open date labeling is considered desirable and should be uniformly presented on labels. The problem is which of many different forms of open date labeling is most informative.
- The total food label needs to be more clear, readable, and understandable. Presenting ingredient and nutrient information in a graphic form was frequently suggested. In this connection, symbols communicating health hazards were also suggested.
- The concept of safe and suitable was accepted by all, but there was disagreement as to what elements were safe and suitable.

Additional observations were made as a result of the analysis and synthesis of the comments made by those who testified. First, if one is research-oriented and believes that research can be one of the considerations in setting public policy, then the hearings reveal a void. Practically no reference to the research of others was reported. Most of the subject matter offered was of the opinion or attitude variety. It is naïve to assume that attitudes can safely reflect the individual's behavior. Second, it is of concern that the hearing system obtains only the views of those willing to testify. Are such views typical of those who do not testify?

OBSERVATIONS OF A SECOND ORDER

The preceding example was essentially a report of observations made by double-teaming observers in two cities in which food labeling hearings were conducted. The findings are a result of the observation of proceedings and are therefore primary data. Research, however, should not only result in such direct findings but should also lead to interpretation and recommendation by the researcher. We choose to refer to these as observations of a second order. That these observations result from data rather than only thinking, or other forms of mental activity not based on data, should be emphasized. The point here is that they are different. The point also is not only to encourage obtaining data by using the observation

Box 7.1 A CRITIQUE OF FOOD LABELING HEARINGS

The Food Labeling Hearings to establish public policy are flawed because of procedural limitations and a lack of balanced evidence.

Establishing appropriate public policy requires fundamental changes in the hearing technique. Specifically, these include:

1. An improved hearing format to allow for an exchange of relevant information.
2. Participation by all concerned groups, guaranteeing a balanced expression of views.
3. An atmosphere that reduces adversary relationships among participants.
4. Training of examiners to conduct unbiased hearings as they solicit objective information.

These changes will lead to public policy that can isolate appropriate and relevant solutions to the food labeling problem. The current hearings, where ingredient labeling, nutrition labeling, open date labeling, etc., were discussed, generated more subjective opinions than scientific fact.

In dealing with the topics included in these hearings, business and consumer groups discussed very different issues and problems. The lack of common definition by these groups virtually precludes establishing public policy that will satisfy either group. As a result, greater conflicts and misunderstandings between these two groups were created. This places government in a "no-win" situation. An effective alternative would be to encourage equal participation by government, interested business people, and consumers in a peer relationship. This would generate a broader exchange of ideas where the first step would be to define the problems in a mutually acceptable manner.

What was learned from these hearings was limited to the attitudes and opinions of those who volunteered or were invited to testify. Whether these views are typical of the public at large is not known. Considering the questions raised, it is believed that when an examiner does not follow the rules set by the agencies, or when a serious conflict of interest is displayed by an examiner, or when a number of those who testify may not be sufficiently informed or qualified to contribute to the setting of public policy (even though they are entitled to state their own opinions), then the hearing evidence in no way can be justified as a basis for public policy formulation or change.

There is a need to have competent, qualified, and informed business and consumer people agree on issues related to health, safety, and nutritional information on food labels and then agree on the manner in which all citizens can best be informed so that the average consumer can be offered the healthiest diet at the least cost.

If the purpose of label changes is to provide information to promote nutrition, health, and safety, then one can question whether these particular hearings achieved this goal.

technique but also to encourage the researcher to interpret the data as well as to report it.

To illustrate, the material in Box 7.1. resulted from observation of the hearings. It goes beyond what was directly observed and is based upon interpretation of the data obtained. These recommendations were a direct result of the data.

PERSONAL APPLICATIONS

People who buy high-ticket items such as homes, cars, appliances, and home entertainment items can materially benefit by using the methods of observation described in this chapter. The first thing one might try is casual shopping where one merely observes in order to construct a checklist of items which includes the characteristics of the product that are personally important. For example, when purchasing a home one might construct a checklist that includes:

number of rooms	proximity to work
size of rooms	proximity to shopping
outdoor space	extra items that will be needed
privacy	price
proximity to schools	

This suggested checklist may need to be doubled, even quadrupled, in size. Whatever its length, observing and recording the attributes and variables of each house will be conducive to more valid judgments and even happy living.

In similar fashion, when purchasing a car one should do everything possible to minimize the role and influence of the salesperson and the car's appearance. Cost, mileage, safety, and quality should be of greater importance—especially in terms of the purchaser's need and use. For car purchasers, articles in magazines such as *Consumer Reports* can help in determining the list of characteristics that are important. Developing the list then aids the purchase decision in terms of dealer price, distance from home, service for the same make but for comparable models (consider weight, size) of different manufacturers. A separate section of the observation report should include the extras that are rated as essential, good to have, unimportant, or frivolous. Remember, observation is the one data-gathering technique that can be used by all in collecting objective data which can lead to solutions to personal and societal problems.

chapter 8

The Experimental Method: Basics

By definition, an experiment is conducted when some variable is *systematically manipulated* and the result(s) of that manipulation is/are measured. Systematic manipulation is a major characteristic of the experimental technique. It is one of the main distinguishing differences between an experiment and other data-gathering techniques. For example, the observation technique does not manipulate variables, and surveys do not manipulate variables systematically.

The basics or fundamentals of an experiment are quite simple. One systematically manipulates some variable(s), tries to control fluctuations in other variables, and measures the effects. Although the procedures involved in the systematic manipulation of a variable and the control of fluctuations in other variables can become quite complex, the essential components of an experiment are always the same. It is these basic components that have led some researchers to argue that the experiment is the most powerful methodology of science, since only in an experiment can a clear cause-and-effect conclusion be drawn. That is, only in an experiment can one establish the variable that actually produced an effect. This pointing or finding is a direct result of the control or elimination of other variables.

CAUSE AND EFFECT

The concept of causation is not simple. In fact, it is quite complex. Philosophers for many years have been troubled by and have wrestled with the nature of cause and effect. A clear-cut explanation still defies them. Recognizing this perplexity, we brazenly and simply suggest that a *cause* is the producer of an effect. Having said that, the difficulty is in deciding or determining what specific agent, force, or event has produced the effect that is observed.

Necessary and Sufficient

One pragmatic approach to this problem has been to distinguish between *necessary* and *sufficient* conditions. *A necessary condition is one that must occur or there will be no effect;* it is necessary to produce the effect. For example, one must turn the ignition key to start an auto. Turning the key is a necessary condition.

A sufficient condition is one that will always produce the effect; it is sufficient for the production of the effect. For example, diving into the ocean is a sufficient condition for getting wet. A cause can be attributed when it satisfies both conditions: necessary and sufficient. Using this as a paradigm, it cannot be claimed that turning an ignition key is the cause of starting an auto, since it is only a necessary and not a sufficient condition. All of us know only too well that a car will often fail to start even when the ignition key is turned. Similarly, it cannot be claimed that diving into the ocean is the cause of being wet since it is only a sufficient but not a necessary condition. One can get wet without ever seeing an ocean, simply by taking a shower or a bath.

Defining a cause as a condition that is both necessary and sufficient has, however, been frequently criticized and for a number of reasons. One reason is that the determination of necessary and sufficient is often decided by the experimenter. Since there is never an obvious set of necessary and sufficient conditions, one experimenter can accuse another of being arbitrary and having too high or too low a set of standards. Another problem with this approach is that it assumes a simpler universe than the one in which we live. Effects in our universe seem to be produced by a great many different conditions, acting at different times and in different ways.

This problem is not solved by altering the approach to say that necessary and sufficient conditions are two different kinds of causes. One might argue that there are no necessary or sufficient conditions for any effect. For example, one can start a car without using the key by "hot-wiring" the ignition. One can even avoid getting wet when diving into the ocean by wearing a wet suit. Since such arguments and counterarguments can go on *ad infinitum,* it is imperative to describe cause and effect in a different way.

Mill's Criteria

An early attempt to describe cause and effect that seems to have survived the test of time is that put forward by John Stuart Mill in 1874 (Boring, 1957; Cook and Campbell, 1979). Mill offered a number of canons that could be used to identify cause and effect. The canons sound remarkably like modern scientific method and basically require that three criteria be met before one reaches a conclusion regarding cause and effect.

The first criterion to be met is that the cause must precede the effect (in time). If A is a cause of B, then A must occur first.

Second, cause and effect must be related. When A is present, B should be present; when A is absent, B should be absent; when A changes value, B should change value.

Third, given that A and B are related, noncausal explanations of that relationship must be ruled out. Are A and B related because A produces B, or are they related because both are produced by condition C?

All of the data-gathering techniques used by researchers are able to meet some of these criteria some of the time. A well-designed experiment, however, is able to satisfy all three.

For example, consider that Tom reads the major newspaper headlines on a daily basis. He has just read that unemployment has risen to 11%. The next day he reads that the average price of a share of stock on the New York Stock Exchange declined. Can one conclude from these facts that the rise in unemployment (i.e., condition A) is the cause of the price decline (i.e., condition B)? Not really. Tom's observation indicates that the rise in unemployment came before the decline in the value of stocks, and thus meets the first criterion set forth by Mill. At the same time, it is, or should be, clear to Tom that a great many other conditions preceded the stock market decline. Among such events or conditions were that Tom mowed his lawn, Tom received a B on a sociology test, interest rates rose, and another war broke out in the Middle East. In reality, Tom cannot determine whether any of these prior events are related to the stock market decline. Only the first of Mill's criteria has been met.

About the same time, Phyllis, his friend, wants to know whether the violence shown on television is a cause of aggression in young children. With the permission of parents and a courageous school board she conducts a survey of all the third grade children in the local public school. The children are asked such questions as "Who picks fights?" and "Who is always quiet?" The results allow for a rating or score of aggressiveness or nonaggressiveness which is assigned to the various children named. She then asks the parents of these children to list the TV shows most frequently watched by their children. The data show that children with the highest aggressiveness ratings tend to watch more violent TV programs, while children with low aggressiveness ratings tend to watch less violent programs. The survey shows that television violence and aggression are related and, thus, Mill's second criterion is met. The survey does not, however, show which condition comes first. It may be that TV violence comes first *and* influences children who view it to become more aggressive than they were originally. On the other hand, it may be that children who are already demonstrating aggressive behavior patterns tend to select and watch more violent television programs. The simple study conducted by Phyllis does not (or should not) allow her to draw any cause-and-effect conclusion.

A more ingenious and sophisticated approach was used by Eron et al. (1972), who surveyed a group of third graders and then surveyed the same group again 10 years later. They found that violent TV was related to aggression. They then examined the relationships between the early TV habits and(10 years) later

105

aggression. They also compared early aggression and later TV viewing habits. While the latter relationship was virtually nonexistent, they found a fairly strong relationship between early TV viewing patterns and later aggressive behavior.

The Eron et al. study thus fulfills two of Mill's criteria by (1) establishing a relationship and (2) determining which condition precedes the other. Unfortunately, their research does not, by itself, show that TV violence *causes* aggression in children since other possible explanations of the relationship have not been ruled out. Other possibilities do exist. Perhaps the kinds of TV shows that children watch and the aggressiveness they display are both encouraged by parents. Aggressive parents may encourage their children to adopt aggressive models displayed on violent programs and children may later model the behaviors they see.

Meeting Mill's first two criteria is less difficult than satisfying the third criterion. Given that condition A comes before condition B and that these conditions are related, there may still be many possible explanations for that relation. To show that A causes B is the correct explanation, one must rule out all other possible explanations. The experimental method presents that possibility by its systematic manipulation of variables. To see why this is so, let us consider whether the kind of a test that one expects causes differences in test performance.

Foos and Clark (1983) attempted to answer this question. Students were told to expect either a multiple-choice or an essay test. All students, however, received the same test, which included *both* essay and multiple-choice questions. That is, the students were deceived. When we discussed deception earlier (Chapter 4), we said that deception should be used only when the methodological requirements of the research require it and no harm comes to any of the participants. That was the case in this study. Further, the experimenters explained the deception and the reasons for it to all participants when the experiment was over. Fortunately, none of the participants seemed troubled and the deception might be viewed as relatively mild since everyone did receive more or less the kind of test they were told to expect. The deception was that they *also* received other test items that they did not expect. The use of deception places a responsibility on the experimenter that should never be taken lightly.

If expected test and test performance are related, many possible explanations can be offered. For example, it may be that multiple-choice questions are less demanding and do not require as much knowledge and comprehension as essay questions. If this is so, then any relation between expected test and test performance might simply be due to test difficulty. This problem was controlled by giving all subjects the same material to study and also the same test consisting of multiple-choice and essay-type items.

Another possible explanation might be that brighter students prefer essay tests. They study harder than average students, who prefer multiple-choice tests. Further, any relation between expected test and test performance could be the result of the types of students placed in the two expected-test groups. The experiment avoided this difficulty by placing people in one or the other expected-test group by chance. This chance, or random, assignment makes it likely that the two groups will have approximately the same characteristics or be approximately equal. The experimenter treats the group expecting a multiple-choice test and the group expecting an essay test in exactly the same way and thereby attempts to rule out other possible explanations for any effects that are found. Foos and Clark found that those expecting a multiple-choice test did worse than those expecting an essay test, on both the essay and multiple-choice questions. People seemed to do better with multiple-choice tests when expecting essay tests.

Type of expected test does seem to cause differences in test performance. But why? Deese (1972) points out that causal connections are not isolated from other causal connections. When one finds a cause-and-effect relation, one looks at only a small part of a huge network of cause-and-effect relations. For example, there must be many other conditions that influence test performance. An example would be time spent studying. Another might be the student's anxiety level. Such combinations or networks are inferred and described in a number of relevant theories. The finding of Foos and Clark supports a theory that describes how information is stored for later retrieval (Anderson and Bower, 1974). People expecting an essay test are assumed to use a different strategy for remembering information than people expecting a multiple-choice test. Those expecting an essay test store items in memory very distinctively, while those expecting a multiple-choice test store items more broadly. That is why their test performance is influenced by their expectation. The Foos and Clark experiment is not perfect, but it seems to meet all of Mill's criteria.

OPERATIONAL DEFINITIONS AND VARIABLES

Variables are the changing conditions during an experiment. An experiment includes two kinds of variables. The variable that the researcher systematically manipulates is called an *independent variable*. The variable measuring the participant's response is called a *dependent variable*. In the experiment just described, the independent variable was the expected test and the dependent variable was the test performance.

Operational Definitions

Careful experimentation requires explicit descriptions of how an independent variable has been manipulated and how the dependent variable has been measured. This is usually accomplished by providing operational definitions of all variables. "An *operational* definition is one that defines a concept in terms of the operations used to measure that concept" (Matlin, 1979, p. 15). An example would be defining memory as the number of words recalled from a list of words. In the experiment just described, test performance was measured by counting the number of questions answered correctly.

It should be noted that there are many possible operational definitions for the same variable. Expected test, for example, might have been manipulated by giving a series of tests earlier to each group. Test performance could also have been measured differently. For example, time taken to complete the test, rather than number correct, could have been used. The important point is that an operational definition must be provided.

The fact that a single variable may have any of many operational definitions is troublesome and even anxiety-provoking, not only for the neophyte, but also for a most dedicated and experienced philosophical experimenter (Frank, 1956). The question that arises is, "Which one of the operational definitions should I use?" Several factors should be considered as an aid in answering this question. The first is that an operational definition requires a measurement. Accordingly, researchers should exercise caution and select a measure that is reliable and valid (see Chapter 2 for a discussion of reliability and validity). In addition, the research being conducted should be capable of being compared with previous research in the area. One way to ensure this is to use the same or similar operational definitions (not necessarily the same method) of variables previously used by others. A desirable step in selecting such an operational definition is a review of the literature to determine what has been previously acceptable. This enables one to select acceptable measures as well as to obtain some indication of the reliability and validity of those measures.

A third factor to keep in mind is that a direct measure is better than an indirect measure (see Chapter 5 for a discussion of direct and indirect measures). For example, test performance in the experiment described was measured by

---

Box 8.1 OPERATIONAL DEFINITIONS

A practical exercise in using *Psychological Abstracts* and in learning what kinds of measures are used to define a concept is to "take a concept" to the library and try to find an operational definition in the abstracts. You will never find an abstract that says "the operational definition of X is Z," where "X" is the concept and "Z" is the measuring operation. For this reason, the exercise becomes a challenge as you try to determine what the measuring operation actually was.

1. Select one of the concepts listed at the end of this box and look it up in the index to *Psychological Abstracts.*
2. Jot down the numbers of several abstracts so that you need not return to the index.
3. Read each abstract and find an operational definition for your concept.

Ask yourself whether the operational definition that you have selected is a measurement. Does it tell you *how* to measure that concept if you were to do it yourself? If the answer is "yes," then you have succeeded. If "no," then you should return to the abstracts.

Concepts: aggression, anxiety, competition, conformity, fear, habituation, hunger, obedience, reinforcement, schizophrenia, self-esteem, tolerance.

counting the number of correctly answered questions. This is a direct measure. An indirect measure might involve asking participants, after they looked at the test, how many answers they think they would answer correctly if they took the test. Both of these definitions are operational in that they tell how test performance was measured, but the direct measure is always to be preferred.

Should the researcher always examine the literature and select the most reliable, valid, standard, and direct measurement available? The answer is *yes*. Such a review might, however, indicate that a new measure is more desirable than those previously used. This might be the case when one attempts to extend the generality of some previous finding or needs to consider possible qualifications of it. For example, evidence exists that an expected test influences test performance when measured by the operational definition of correct responses. However, if one defined test performance as time taken to complete the test, one might be able to show that the effects of expected test generalize to speed as well as accuracy of performance, or that speed is not influenced in the same way as accuracy.

Expected test might also be defined differently depending on whether the researcher is attempting to extend the generality of the findings or explore possible qualifications of the findings. For example, instead of giving the series of tests mentioned previously, one might give a different kind of expected test such as a true-or-false examination. It should be emphasized that the selection of an operational definition must be made in relation to the objectives of the experiment and the sustaining or nulling of the experimental hypothesis.

Operational definitions are not always all-inclusive or complete. In fact, they are sometimes viewed as being rather incomplete. Consider anxiety as an example. Anxiety is frequently defined operationally as a score on a paper-and-pencil test (Taylor, 1953). However, it may also be operationalized as a change in level of heart rate and galvanic skin response or as an accumulation of free fatty acids in the bloodstream. None of these operational definitions can be considered as completely describing anxiety.

The terms used to refer to variables are usually quite global or extended. If we are experimenting on the effects of hunger or anxiety on learning or self-esteem, we cannot operationalize all the denotative, let alone connotative, aspects of these terms in a single operational definition. But operational definitions capture some aspect(s) of the total meaning of the term and, in so doing, remove ambiguity from communication among researchers. When hunger is defined as 24 hours without food, then one unambiguously knows what the researcher means by hunger. Similarly, when anxiety is defined as a certain level of free fatty acids in the bloodstream, then one knows how the researcher has measured anxiety. The reduction or elimination of ambiguity within scientific communication is the biggest advantage of using operational definitions.

Dependent Variables

Dependent variables or participants' responses are those which researchers measure, to determine the extent of change. Such variables are typically operationally defined as either behaviors or responses reflecting the states of an organism. For example, educators may be interested in conditions that influence reading ability. Responses may be either reading speed or comprehension. Nutritionists may be interested in conditions that influence blood pressure or cholesterol level or other physiological states.

It is typical for researchers to concentrate on a specific dependent variable and then describe their results in terms of the changes in that variable. One may be interested in studying aggression, for example, and then manipulate those variables which influence aggression. Such variables might be television, parents, socioeconomic level, neighborhood, or subculture. Such a researcher is likely to say "my area of investigation is aggression" rather than "my area is television" or "parents" and so on.

Independent Variables

Independent variables are those which the experimenter manipulates to see whether they produce an effect and, if they do, what kind and degree of effect they produce. An experiment must have at least one dependent variable and one independent variable. The independent variable must have at least two conditions. Without at least two conditions there is no basis for comparing and determining whether an effect has been produced.

The *conditions* of an independent variable are the qualitatively and/or quantitatively different values that are used in the experiment. For example, in the Foos and Clark experiment, the independent variable was the type of expected test. This variable had four conditions, although we have only mentioned the essay and multiple-choice conditions thus far. The additional two conditions involved telling some people to expect a memory test and telling others simply to expect a test without specifying what type. These four conditions are qualitatively different; they are different kinds of expected test. If the problem is whether or not study time influences test performance, then one might manipulate this independent variable by using quantitatively different conditions of study time, that is, different amounts.

Some independent variables have an already specified and limited number of conditions. For example, the variable sex has only two biological conditions: male and female. Most variables, however, have a virtually unlimited number of conditions. For example, there are many kinds of expected tests and amounts of study time. For these variables the experimenter must decide which and how many conditions to use.

Which Conditions to Use?   The first rule to consider is that the conditions of an independent variable that are used in an experiment should cover a range of values. By way of illustration, consider the problem of determining whether or not a person's anxiety while giving a speech is a function of the size of the audience. Audience size is then the independent variable and the experimenter must select the conditions to be used. If two audiences are selected and one is composed of 10 people and the other of 12, then the chances of finding an effect are diminished or limited. The difference between these two conditions is probably too small and not reflective of the extremes or range of audience size. It may also be the case that the effect of the audience size on anxiety is so small that it will be missed with conditions so similar or so close together. The extreme of a small audience is, of course, an audience of one. An audience of zero is no audience at all and can only be useful if one is interested in comparing audiences of different sizes with no audience at all. The extreme of a large audience is probably unlimited. It may be hundreds in a class or thousands at a conference. An practical approach to varying the size of the audience might include the conditions of 1-, 5-, 15-, and 30-person audiences. These conditions can readily be discriminated by students giving speeches, which increases the chances of detecting an effect if there is one.

The selection of extreme values is obviously subject to practical considerations. While the condition of zero or one person in an audience is easily attained, the upper extreme is not. It is impractical to use an audience of 10,000,000 persons unless national television is involved. One must select and decide upon an attainable upper condition when choosing extreme values of an independent variable.

Another factor that plays a role in the selection of conditions is the stage of the research project or program. In the early stages of manipulation, extreme conditions are used. In the later stages, when the effects produced by extreme conditions are known, one may manipulate conditions that are much closer to one another in an attempt to determine how much of a difference in the independent variable is needed to produce a measurable difference in the dependent variable.

How Many Conditions to Use?   How many conditions of an independent variable should be used? The answer is *more than two* whenever possible. Using more than two conditions provides several advantages. Suppose the research problem concerns improving memory. A number of memory improvement techniques could be compared with the use of no special technique. We might, for example, have one group memorize a list of words and another group memorize the same list by using the peg-word system (i.e., "one is a bun"; Cermak, 1975). This would be a simple two-group experiment.

We could also compare a group that uses no special technique with a group that has been trained to use imagery. Finally, we might conduct a third experiment to compare the peg-word and imagery techniques. In total, we will have used six groups in three experiments (two groups per experiment) to answer questions that might have been answered with one experiment having three groups. Using more than two conditions of the independent variable in the experiment would have saved time and work and would have required fewer participants.

Another advantage is that using more than two conditions increases the chances of detecting an effect if there is one. This is particularly true when the relation between independent and dependent variables is nonlinear. For example, consider the problem of establishing the relation between anxiety level and test performance. To conduct this experiment one might select two extreme groups, one very high on the measure of anxiety and one very low. After administering the test one might find no difference in test performance and falsely conclude that there is no relationship when, in fact, the true relationship is like that shown in Fig. 8.1. Too much and too little anxiety lead to poor performance, while a moderate level leads to better performance. By using the two extremes and a value midway between the extremes one would detect the effect, which would have been missed by using only the two extreme groups.

Finally, using more than two conditions allows one to more accurately and completely describe the relation between independent and dependent variables. If we had conducted our experiment on the effects of anxiety by using a group with very low anxiety and another group with a moderate amount of anxiety we would have obtained an effect. It would appear from these two groups that the more anxiety one has, the better one performs. However, adding the third group, which is high on the anxiety measure, gives us a more accurate portrayal of what the anxiety-test performance relation looks like. It is nonlinear. When deciding on the conditions of an independent variable one should strive to use reasonably considered extreme values and at least one value somewhere in between.

It must be emphasized and understood that the same variable can serve as a dependent variable in some experiments and as an independent variable in others. For example, anxiety was a dependent variable when we wished to see how it was influenced by the size of the audience. However, it was an independent variable when we wished to see how it influenced test performance. In principle, all variables are able to serve as either.

Internal-External Variables

The experimenter manipulating the independent variable in an experiment can do so by working with a myriad of conditions or stimuli. Each variable can be

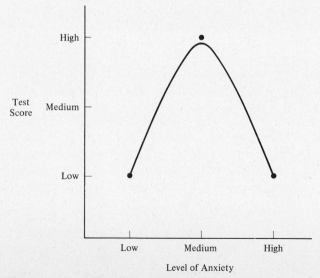

Figure 8.1 A relationship between anxiety and test performance.

labeled as either internal or external when the reference point is the participant(s) in the experiment. Figure 8.2 lists some examples from each category.

External variables are environmental conditions that can be used to serve as stimuli. They are not permanent conditions and generally can be changed quite readily. They are sometimes referred to as nonsubject or treatment variables (Wood, 1981). *Internal variables include any of many characteristics of and within an individual.* Such variables are intrinsic or indigenous as far as the individual is concerned. They are used to characterize or describe the individual. Included are sex, age, height, weight, and IQ, among others. By their nature they tend to be more fixed than changing. They are sometimes referred to as subject or classification variables.

To use internal variables as independent variables in an experiment, the experimenter must select individuals who already have those characteristics. To use an external variable as an independent variable, the experimenter creates or uses conditions in the environment and has them impinge on the individual. This is the main and most important distinction between internal and external variables.

INTERNAL VALIDITY

Previously we presented the various kinds of validity. Each one is intended to do the same thing, that is, to establish the degree or extent to which the method or

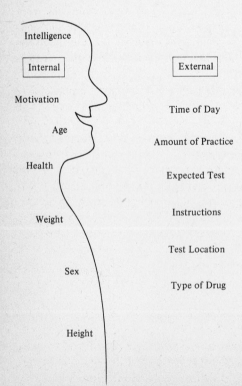

Figure 8.2 Some examples of internal and external variables.

measuring instrument measures what it purports to measure. For the experimental method an additional responsibility exists, since it is the one method that can establish causality. This leads us to a special consideration of internal validity.

As previously indicated, Mill's criteria for establishing a causal relationship include: (1) cause must come before the effect, (2) cause-and-effect conditions must be related, and (3) other and contrary explanations of the causal relationship must be ruled out. An experiment has internal validity when it meets this third criterion. *Internal validity refers to the ruling out of other explanations of the relation between independent and dependent variables.* The explanation not ruled out is that the change in conditions of the independent variable caused the measured changes in the dependent variable.

To illustrate the difficulties in establishing internal validity, we will examine a few of the many factors that threaten it (Campbell and Stanley, 1966). We will also examine the techniques used to control these threatening factors. At first, it may appear that the threats to internal validity are overwhelming and that one will never be able to achieve Mill's third criterion. Nothing could be farther from the truth. Researchers have been very creative at devising both simple and complex techniques of control.

Threats to Internal Validity

History   In this context the word history is used in a more narrow sense and refers to external events that take place during the data-gathering part of the experiment. For example, it would refer to the period between initial and later testing or more generally between the introduction of the independent variable and measurement of the dependent variable. Events may threaten internal validity by influencing the dependent variable or by altering the effect of the independent variable.

Suppose, for example, that we were interested in establishing the anxiety levels of Cuban refugees arriving at the time of the Mariel boatlift. To accomplish this, we might administer several anxiety scales to the first group of refugees arriving. As a second part of the experiment, and over a period of time, we might introduce an independent variable that consists of two different kinds of relaxation training (remember that an independent variable must have at least two conditions, although it is always desirable to have more than two). After 3 weeks of such training, the participants are again administered the anxiety scales. Assuming that no differences were found between the two training techniques, but that the anxiety levels were substantially reduced, can one conclude that relaxation training produced the reduction in anxiety that occurred between the initial (i.e., pre-) and later (i.e., post-) tests? The answer is no, at least not with any certainty. A number of historical events did occur between pre- and posttest which might easily explain or contribute to the observed reduction in anxiety. Imagine that you are a refugee leaving Cuba in a small boat, perhaps tossed upon stormy waters, and heading for a new country. On arrival you are "processed" and given some tests. Over the next several weeks you are fed, clothed, and housed by friends and/or relatives. They speak your language, care for you, and explain many things about living in southern Florida. It is conceivable that this reduces your anxiety, independent of the visits by the relaxation trainer. On the posttest, your anxiety score is much lower. Can one conclude that the reduction in anxiety was caused by the historical events? The answer is no. It is just as incorrect to attribute the reduction in anxiety to these events as it is to attribute it to the relaxation training. The point is that the historical events provide another possible explanation and, therefore, we cannot point to or establish the cause. The experiment as conducted does not have internal validity.

Maturation   Equally troublesome in establishing internal validity is maturation. It refers to internal events that take place between initial and later testing or between introduction of the independent variable and measurement of the dependent variable. Such events threaten internal validity just as history does. The difference between history and maturation factors is similar to the difference between external and internal variables. This usage of the term maturation is more broad than the typical dictionary definition, since it is intended to include such things as getting a cold, becoming tired, and feeling angry.

Let us consider another example. At a certain point in the development of civilization one may find that Disco Roller Skating is sweeping the country. As manager of the largest Disco Roller Skating rink in Topeka, and with an eye toward the next summer Olympics (after all, DRS may soon sweep the world), a researcher applies for and receives a grant to examine the effectiveness of two successful, but different, methods of two skating coaches. One coach is the well-known Ms. Speed Wheeler and the other is the popular Mr. Rock Roller. The study has each coach train a group of 10 youngsters who are 5 years old. The training goes on for 6 months with the objective of having them become "Olympic material." The skating ability of each of the 20 children was measured before coaching began and was found to be nonexistent. They all kept falling. At the end of the 6-month period, their skating ability was again measured and all had improved dramatically. The question is whether the coaching of Wheeler and Roller produced this improvement. Again, it is hard to say. It may be that the children simply became stronger and more coordinated over the 6-month period and became better skaters without the benefit of coaches Wheeler and Roller. Thus maturation may provide another possible explanation for the improved skating. Therefore, the experiment lacks internal validity.

Testing and Regression   Being measured or tested more often than once can also create problems. These problems are generally of two types, called testing and regression. *Testing* refers to any change in a test score the second time one takes the test; this is sometimes called a "carryover" effect. For example, your score on a test might be better the second time you took the test either because you had had some practice or because you knew the kinds of questions that would be asked. In any event, you are more familiar with the test situation.

Regression, in this context, refers to the tendency for extreme scores or measures reflecting human characteristics or abilities to revert to measures that are more reflective of average characteristics or abilities. Regression is a statistical artifact resulting from the imperfect reliability of tests or other measuring instruments. Sir Francis Galton (Boring, 1957) first noted regression when he observed an inverse relation between the intelligence of parents and their children.

By way of example, let us assume that the local school board wants to improve the reading scores of some students who are poor readers. By administering a reading test to all third graders, the lowest 15% are ascertained. These children are given special tutoring to improve their reading scores. After 8 weeks of tutoring this group is retested, with the result that all score higher than they did at the first testing. Their improved scores could be the result of either tutoring or regression (not to mention history, maturation, and testing). Accordingly, it would be erroneous to draw the conclusion that the tutoring caused the improved scores.

Instrument Change   The problem of *instrument change* occurs when the measuring instrument rather than the dependent variable itself has changed. For example, as instruments age or are damaged, they may lose reliability and give different readings. As observers, humans may improve as they gain more experience and, thus, provide different values while observing the same behavior. Accordingly, different scores for the same event may be a result of a change in the measuring instrument, the observer, or the behavior.

Biofeedback has proved to be a fairly useful tool for therapists (Danskin and Crow, 1981). For example, people with severe migraine headaches can be taught to raise the surface temperature of their hands and, in so doing, reduce their headache. A biofeedback researcher might decide to determine which of two forms of feedback is more effective. This could be done by recording the starting (i.e., with no feedback) temperatures of two groups of headache sufferers. Suppose that one group received auditory feedback (such as a tone that changes in pitch as temperature changes) and the other group received visual feedback (such as a bar that moves up and down as temperature changes). After several training sessions we find that the individuals receiving auditory feedback have recorded the greatest change from the starting temperature, but that the instrument measuring temperature is no longer correctly calibrated. Since we do not know when the error in calibration occurred (e.g., before or after the starting temperature) we cannot conclude that auditory feedback is better or even that any change from baseline has occurred. The differences in measured temperature might be due to the feedback, faulty calibration, or both. This experiment has also lost its internal validity.

Selection and Attrition   *Selection* refers to problems that can arise when individuals are chosen for an experiment. For example, suppose a researcher is concerned with the effects of audiovisual aids on learning. A possible approach would be to select two sections of the same course using the same textbook and hearing the same lectures and to give one of the sections a number of audiovisual aids such as movies and transparencies. One section has been scheduled during the day and the other at night. At the end of the term, the final exam scores for the two sections are compared and a difference is established. The evening section, which received the aids, did better than the day section, which did not. The problem with drawing a cause-effect conclusion here is that the two sections may have differed originally in other ways. For example, many of the night students have full-time employment. Accordingly, they may be described as both highly motivated and tired. This suggests that the two sections may differ not only because of the presence or absence of visual aids, but also in motivation and energy level. There is no way to determine which, if any, of these differences between the two sections produced the differences on the final exam. The experiment lacks internal validity because of the way the groups were selected (i.e., a day and a night section).

Attrition refers to the loss or withdrawal of participants from the experiment. When attrition is greater for some groups than others, it can create a problem that results in unintended differential selection—assuming that selection was equated originally.

Suppose the researcher is interested in the effects of reward and punishment on learning. Two groups of college students, assumed to have the same learning ability, are selected to participate. Each person is asked to solve a number of problems over several experimental sessions. Individuals in the reward group receive 25 cents for every problem correctly solved and nothing when an error is made. Individuals in the punishment group receive an electric shock for every error and nothing for correctly solved problems. After three sessions, all the remaining participants are given a number of test problems to solve. The 8 individuals, of the original 15, in the punishment group solve 85% of the test problems. The 14 individuals, of the original 15, in the reward group solve 65% of the test problems. The punishment group did better. To conclude that this result was due to reward and punishment could be an error. Everyone enjoys receiving quarters, while few enjoy receiving electric shocks. It is reasonable to believe that the individuals who were receiving the most shocks dropped out of the experiment. Those individuals were the ones who made the most errors and were the poorer performers. Those remaining in the punishment group can be assumed to have a greater ability to solve problems correctly. For the reward group, however, individuals with greater and lesser ability still remain. The two groups that were initially equal are no longer so because of differences in attrition.

Although there are very many other threats to internal validity, the preceding list (i.e., history, maturation, testing, regression, instrument change, selection, and attrition) should be sufficient to make the potential researcher aware of the problem as well as the seriousness and difficulty of conducting experiments with internal validity.

Control Techniques

An experiment that lacks internal validity is said to be *confounded*. Confounding occurs when another type of variable that is neither an independent nor a dependent variable influences the experimental procedure and/or results. A confounding variable has two properties. First, it influences the dependent variable or its measurement, and second, it is systematically related to the independent variable. A reexamination of some of the above examples illustrates these two properties.

In the relaxation training and anxiety example, a confounding occurred because of historical events. Everyone who received training also received help from friends and relatives. The variables are thus systematically related, and help from friends and relatives very probably reduced anxiety. In the example of tutoring to improve poor reading a confounding occurred because of regression. Regression affects test score and is systematically related. That is, everyone who received tutoring is also likely to have experienced regression.

The reader is invited to find these two properties in the other examples used (i.e., coaching roller skating; temperature and type of feedback; audiovisual aids to learning; reward, punishment, and problem solving). Spotting a confounding can be quite challenging. A collection of studies reported by Huck and Sandler (1979) is highly recommended to the serious reader. They ask their readers to determine whether or not Mill's third criterion has been met.

To establish internal validity in experiments one must find some way to eliminate confounding. *Control* is the term used when one attempts to eliminate a confounding. This is usually achieved by destroying or neutralizing any possible systematic relation between the independent variable and the unwanted confounding variable. When historical events are suspected of influencing the role of the independent variable it is usually not possible to eliminate those events or their effects. However, it is possible to add a group that experiences the historical events but does not experience the independent variable. For example, in our relaxation training experiment we might have used three groups: one that received training technique A, one that received training technique B, and one that received no training at all. If we now find that the groups that received training are less anxious than the group that did not, we can conclude that training did reduce anxiety. The differential reduction in anxiety cannot be attributed to historical events because all three groups experienced similar kinds of historical events. There is no longer a systematic relation between the confounding (i.e., history) and independent (i.e., training) variables.

Control Groups   *A group that receives a zero amount of the independent variable is called a control group.* Use of a control group is a highly recommended technique. It helps to reduce, if not eliminate, noncausal explanations due to history, maturation, testing, regression, and instrument change. Keep in mind that the control group experiences the same unwanted or confounding variables as the other groups and, as a result, when differences between these groups and the control group occur, they are likely to be due to the nonzero conditions of the independent variable that these other groups received. To clarify this, the following illustration is offered.

Many people report difficulty in remembering their dreams. Suppose that we have conducted a survey of several hundred individuals and have selected those who reported the greatest difficulty in remembering dreams. They remembered no dreams at all during the 2 weeks preceding the survey. We now divide these persons into two groups. One group is instructed in the use of a number of techniques designed to improve memory for dreams and the other group, the control group, receives no instruction. All individuals are then asked to keep a record of any dreams they remember over the next 2 weeks. At the end of this period, the participants report their dreams and we count how many each person had. These numbers are used to calculate means for each group and are shown in Table 8.1.

A number of factors could produce an increase in the number of dreams remembered. Since this number initially was zero, simple *regression* might make the number of remembered dreams greater than zero. (This assumes the true mean is greater than zero.) Being asked to keep a record of dreams, which is something people usually do not do, might increase the number remembered (i.e., *history*). Initially, people were asked how many dreams they remembered having had during the past 2 weeks. For the next 2 weeks they were told to keep a pad, pencil, and lamp at the bedside and write dreams down when they occurred. This is an *instrument change* and could also be a factor.

Similarly, *maturation* and *testing* could contribute to any change in number of remembered dreams between the first and last 2 weeks. All of these factors should operate equally for both of our groups. If our instructions had any effect, then the instructed group should remember more dreams than the control group. They did. While there may be other problems with this experiment, it should be clear that using a control group is an effective way to handle many of the threats to internal validity already discussed.

The control group is not a panacea since it does not eliminate problems brought about by *selection* and *attrition*. These threats require the use of somewhat more sophisticated techniques than simply adding a "no-treatment" control group. Selection problems are usually handled by equating all groups for internal variables such as motivation and energy level. This equivalence is achieved through the use of random assignment and special experimental designs. Differential attrition can also be handled by using special experimental designs such as matched groups or repeated measures on the same individual (Chapter 9).

When the independent variable in an experiment is an external variable one can always, in principle, achieve internal validity. This is so because the experimenter can select any of several techniques to make all of the groups equivalent except for the particular condition of the independent variable(s). The experimenter always strives to make all groups equivalent with respect to all non-manipulated external and internal variables. Equivalence allows, of course, for variation due to random fluctuations.

When the independent variable in an experiment is an internal variable, then internal validity cannot be achieved. Equivalence can be obtained when using external but not internal variables.

**Table 8.1 AVERAGE NUMBER OF
            REMEMBERED DREAMS**

Group	First 2 weeks	Last 2 weeks
Instructed	0.0	1.4
Control	0.0	0.8

The techniques that are used for creating equivalence on internal variables cannot be used when the independent variable is also an internal variable. Two examples should help to make this clear.

Each year, many people are killed or injured in auto accidents. Although many of these accidents are undoubtedly due to road conditions, weather, and the condition of the vehicle, many are also due to careless driving or other human factors. Using scores on a driving simulator as our dependent variable, let us plan two experiments to investigate the effects of two independent variables.

External Variable Experiment   In the first experiment we are interested in the effects produced by marijuana on driving performance. If marijuana produces poor driving scores on the simulator, we may be able to educate individuals to the dangers involved in driving under such influence. Assuming that we have obtained special legal permission to administer marijuana, we can consider it as an external, independent variable and give it to one group but not another.

To operationalize the quantity and quality of marijuana, a liquid form of the active ingredient, THC (tetrahydrocannabinol), is injected into each participant's arm. Three groups are used in the experiment; one receives 5 milligrams of THC, the second receives 10 milligrams, and the third receives no THC. The groups would not be equal if we injected the first two groups but failed to inject the control group, since any differences in performance on the simulator could then be due to the fact that some people received an injection and others did not. *All* groups must be given an injection. The control group receives a placebo substance. A *placebo,* in this experiment, is a pharmacologically inert substance (e.g., salt water) that should produce no changes in driving performance. There are a number of other external variables besides injection that we will also want to control.

Suppose we have two simulators available so that we can test two people at the same time. We would want to be sure that we do not test all of the control group on one simulator and all of the experimental groups on the other. We would control simulator differences by assigning half of the people in each of the three groups to one simulator and the other half to the other simulator. This type of control is called *balancing.* The conditions of simulator (i.e., the two simulators) are equal (i.e., balanced) across the conditions of the independent variable. We could do the same with sex of the participants by making sure that there are equal numbers of males and females in each of the three groups.

It would be a mistake to begin our experiment in the morning and test the 5-mg group at 8 A.M. and then test the 10-mg group in the afternoon and the control group in the evening. Scheduled time of test could very well influence performance. To control this we might test everyone in the afternoon on successive days. This would keep the time of testing the same for all three groups. This type of control is called *constancy* and involves using one condition of the variable to be controlled for all groups. When that one condition is zero the control is called *elimination.*

The decision to use balancing or constancy is up to the experimenter. Instead of balancing simulators or sex of participants we could have held them constant by using only one simulator and only one sex. Time of test could have been balanced rather than held constant. That is, we might have had one-third of the participants from the three groups tested in the morning, afternoon, and evening.

The control of external variables is not difficult because of lack of techniques. The difficulty is in finding all the external variables that need to be controlled. A search of the literature can be extremely helpful in identifying variables that influence the present dependent variable and in demonstrating the control techniques that others have used. The control of external variables demands a careful scrutiny of the materials and procedures to be used in the experiment. *The groups should be equivalent in all ways except for the conditions of the independent variable.*

When an internal variable can be readily identified, it can be controlled by balancing or constancy. The problem is that a number of internal variables are not so easily identified and yet may influence the dependent variable. For example, internal variables such as motivation, intelligence, age, anxiety level, and health status may influence performance. While one could attempt to measure all of these variables and then balance them or hold them constant, the task would be very difficult. Besides, there is always the possibility that some other important internal variable might be overlooked. A technique is needed that will help to control all internal variables at the same time. Randomization is such a technique.

Random assignment means that each participant has an equal chance of being placed in any of the groups in the experiment. When participants are placed in groups randomly it becomes extremely unlikely that any systematic relationship exists between the independent variable and some internal variable. Randomization thus controls all internal variables at once. Although it is unlikely that any systematic relationship might result from random assignment, it is not impossible. Realizing this, experimenters typically rely on replication to eliminate this possibility. If, for example, one has randomly placed all of the best drivers in the control group, then confounding has occurred. One would falsely conclude that THC produced lower driving scores when, in fact, driving ability might have produced the difference. When the experiment is replicated, the chance of again randomly assigning all of the best drivers to a single group and having that single group again be the control group is exceedingly small. If one obtains the same result, then the original conclusion seems sound. If one obtains a different result then further experimentation is necessary.

After we have randomly assigned persons to each of our three groups (i.e., 5 mg, 10 mg, and no THC), it is probable that average driving experience, drug experience, motivation, intelligence, age, anxiety level, health, and so on are similar for the three groups. If we have also carefully controlled the relevant external variables, we have achieved internal validity.

Internal Variable Experiment In a study of this type, we are interested in the internal variable sex. Males may claim, for example, that they are better drivers because they have greater spatial ability than females (but see Kail et al., 1979). Females may claim that they are better drivers because of superior verbal ability; males, for example, may have difficulty reading road signs. If there is a sex difference with one sex established as better drivers, then we may be able to concentrate driver education for _____ (fill in the name of the sex).

As in the previous experiment, we want to control the same external variables and use techniques such as balancing and constancy. The control of these external variables does not depend upon the type of independent variables that we have.

The control of internal variables is not possible. We cannot, for example, use random assignment to make the groups equivalent on all the known and unknown internal variables. We cannot have individuals come to the laboratory and flip a coin to decide whether they should be in the male or in the female group. Thus, while we could measure and balance some internal variables (see Chapter 9), we could never control all of them.

As a rule, internal validity can be achieved when the independent variable is an external variable but can never be completely achieved when the independent variable is an internal variable. This is so because external variables are relatively easy to control and can be controlled regardless of the type of independent variable used. Internal variables are difficult to control and can be controlled only when the independent variable is an external variable. Studies that use internal variables as independent variables are sometimes considered quasi-experiments rather than true experiments (see Chapter 11).

Finally, it is important to point out that one experimenter's confounding variable is another's independent variable. In the driving experiments just described, we controlled the external variable, time of test by holding it constant, and the internal variable, driving experience, by using random assignment. Another experimenter might manipulate time of test as an independent variable to see how it influences performance. Still another might manipulate driving experience to see how it influences performance.

BETWEEN-SUBJECTS DESIGN

The *design* of an experiment refers to the way(s) in which the conditions of the independent variable are distributed among participants. In a *between-subject design,* each condition of the independent variable is given to a different group of persons. When the independent variable is an internal variable, the type of between-subject design used is usually a *matched-groups* design (see Chapter 9).

When the independent variable is an external variable, the type of between-subject design used is usually a *randomized-groups* design, which simply means that individuals have been randomly assigned to the various conditions of the independent variable. Working through an experiment is intended to help clarify the details of between-subject, randomized-groups design and the reasons for the various decisions that always must be made.

Random Assignment

Table 8.2 is a table of random numbers that can be used to make random assignments. Random assignment is almost always achieved with the condition

Table 8.2 TABLE OF RANDOM NUMBERS

22 17 68 65 84	68 95 23 92 35	87 02 22 57 51	61 09 43 95 06	58 24 82 03 47
19 36 27 59 46	13 79 93 37 55	39 77 32 77 09	85 52 05 30 62	47 83 51 62 74
16 77 23 02 77	09 61 87 25 21	28 06 24 25 93	16 71 13 59 78	23 05 47 47 25
78 43 76 71 61	20 44 90 32 64	97 67 63 99 61	46 38 03 93 22	69 81 21 99 21
03 28 28 26 08	73 37 32 04 05	69 30 16 09 05	88 69 58 28 99	35 07 44 75 47
93 22 53 64 39	07 10 63 76 35	87 03 04 79 88	08 13 13 85 51	55 34 57 72 69
78 76 58 54 74	92 38 70 96 92	52 06 79 79 45	82 63 18 27 44	69 66 92 19 09
23 68 35 26 00	99 53 93 61 28	52 70 05 48 34	56 65 05 61 86	90 92 10 70 80
15 39 25 70 99	93 86 52 77 65	15 33 59 05 28	22 87 26 07 47	86 96 98 29 06
58 71 96 30 24	18 46 23 34 27	85 13 99 24 44	49 18 09 79 49	74 16 32 23 02
57 35 27 33 72	24 53 63 94 09	41 10 76 47 91	44 04 95 49 66	39 60 04 59 81
48 50 86 54 48	22 06 34 72 52	82 21 15 65 20	33 29 94 71 11	15 91 29 12 03
61 96 48 95 03	07 16 39 33 66	98 56 10 56 79	77 21 30 27 12	90 49 22 23 62
36 93 89 41 26	29 70 83 63 51	99 74 20 52 36	87 09 41 15 09	98 60 16 03 03
18 87 00 42 31	57 90 12 02 07	23 47 37 17 31	54 08 01 88 63	39 41 88 92 10
88 56 53 27 59	33 35 72 67 47	77 34 55 45 70	08 18 27 38 90	16 95 86 70 75
09 72 95 84 29	49 41 31 06 70	42 38 06 45 18	64 84 73 31 65	52 53 37 97 15
12 96 88 17 31	65 19 69 02 83	60 75 86 90 68	24 64 19 35 51	56 61 87 39 12
85 94 57 24 16	92 09 84 38 76	22 00 27 69 85	29 81 94 78 70	21 94 47 90 12
38 64 43 59 98	98 77 87 68 07	91 51 67 62 44	40 98 05 93 78	23 32 65 41 18
53 44 09 42 72	00 41 86 79 79	68 47 22 00 20	35 55 31 51 51	00 83 63 22 55
40 76 66 26 84	57 99 99 90 37	36 63 32 08 58	37 40 13 68 97	87 64 81 07 83
02 17 79 18 05	12 59 52 57 02	22 07 90 47 03	28 14 11 30 79	20 69 22 40 98
95 17 82 06 53	31 51 10 96 46	92 06 88 07 77	56 11 50 81 69	40 23 72 51 39
35 76 22 42 92	96 11 83 44 80	34 68 35 48 77	33 42 40 90 60	73 96 53 97 86

26 29 13 56 41	85 47 04 66 08	34 72 57 59 13	82 43 80 46 15	38 26 61 70 64
77 80 20 75 82	72 82 32 99 90	63 95 73 76 63	89 73 44 99 05	48 67 26 43 18
46 40 66 44 52	91 36 74 43 53	30 82 13 54 00	78 45 63 98 35	55 03 36 67 68
37 56 08 18 09	77 53 84 46 47	31 91 18 95 58	24 16 74 11 53	44 10 13 85 57
61 65 61 68 66	37 27 47 39 19	84 83 70 07 48	53 21 40 06 71	95 06 79 88 54
93 43 69 64 07	34 18 04 52 35	56 27 09 24 86	61 85 53 83 45	19 90 70 99 68
21 96 60 12 99	11 20 99 45 18	48 13 93 55 34	18 37 79 49 90	65 97 38 20 46
95 20 47 97 97	27 37 83 28 71	00 06 41 41 74	45 89 09 39 84	51 67 11 52 49
97 86 21 78 73	10 65 81 92 59	58 76 17 14 97	04 76 62 16 17	17 95 70 45 80
69 92 06 34 13	59 71 74 17 32	27 55 10 24 19	23 71 82 13 74	63 52 52 01 41
04 31 17 21 56	33 73 99 19 87	26 72 39 27 67	53 77 57 68 93	60 61 97 22 61
61 06 98 03 91	87 14 77 43 96	43 00 65 98 50	45 60 33 01 07	98 99 46 50 47
85 93 85 86 88	72 87 08 62 40	16 06 10 89 20	23 21 34 74 97	76 38 03 29 63
21 74 32 47 45	73 96 07 94 52	09 65 90 77 47	25 76 16 19 33	53 05 70 53 30
15 69 53 82 80	79 96 23 53 10	65 39 07 16 29	45 33 02 43 70	02 87 40 41 45
02 89 08 04 49	20 21 14 68 86	87 63 93 95 17	11 29 01 95 80	35 14 97 35 33
87 18 15 89 79	85 43 01 72 73	08 61 74 51 69	89 74 39 82 15	94 51 33 41 67
98 83 71 94 22	59 97 50 99 52	08 52 85 08 40	87 80 61 65 31	91 51 80 32 44
10 08 58 21 66	72 68 49 29 31	89 85 84 46 06	59 73 19 85 23	65 09 29 75 63
47 90 56 10 08	88 02 84 27 83	42 29 72 23 19	66 56 45 65 79	20 71 53 20 25
22 85 61 68 90	49 64 92 85 44	16 40 12 89 88	50 14 49 81 06	01 82 77 45 12
67 80 43 79 33	12 83 11 41 16	25 58 19 68 70	77 02 54 00 52	53 43 37 15 26
27 62 50 96 72	79 44 61 40 15	14 53 40 65 39	27 31 58 50 28	11 39 03 34 25
33 78 80 87 15	38 30 06 38 21	14 47 47 07 26	54 96 87 53 32	40 36 40 96 76
13 13 92 66 99	47 24 49 57 74	32 25 43 62 17	10 97 11 69 84	99 63 22 32 98

Source: This table is taken from Table XXXIII of Fisher and Yates, *Statistical Tables for Biological, Agricultural and Medical Research,* published by Longman Group Ltd., London (previously published by Oliver and Boyd, Ltd., Edinburgh), and by permission of the authors and publishers.

that there be the same number of participants in each group. In the present illustration, we are interested in replicating the finding of Foos and Clark (1983) by adding a new expected-test group. Foos and Clark originally found that students expecting an essay test did better than students expecting a multiple-choice test. We will use expected test as our independent variable and include three conditions: essay, multiple-choice, and true-false. Randomly assigned students will be told to expect *one* of these three kinds of tests. After they have all studied the same material, they will all receive the same test. The test will contain essay, multiple-choice, and true-false questions.

There are several possible ways to randomly assign participants to these three groups. Suppose we want to randomly assign 10 persons to each of the three groups. We could write each of the group names (essay, multiple-choice, true-false) on 10 slips of paper and place them all in a hat. When someone was ready to participate we would reach into the hat and assign that individual to whatever group name was drawn.

More typically, researchers use a table of random numbers to assign persons to groups. To do this, we must first number the groups, list them alphabetically, and number them accordingly. Thus, the essay group is 1, the multiple-choice group is 2, and the true-false group is 3. Second, we choose a starting point in the table. While there are rather elaborate procedures that can be used to select a starting point, researchers often simply shut their eyes and point a pencil to a number on the page. Third, we must decide in which direction to move by flipping a coin to determine whether to move the pencil to the left or right, or up or down. Let us assume that we are starting in the upper left-hand corner and moving from top to bottom. The first number is 2, which means that the first participant will be placed in the multiple-choice group. The next number is 1, so the next participant goes to the essay group. The next number is also 1, so that person also goes to the essay group. The next few numbers, -7, 0, 9, and 7, are skipped since they do not stand for any of our groups. The next number is 2, so that participant goes to the multiple-choice group. This procedure continues until the three groups have 10 people each. The crucial factor is that each person must have an equal chance of being assigned to each group.

Random assignment controls internal variables by minimizing the likelihood of any systematic relation between the independent variable and any internal variable. The control of external variables depends upon recognizing and identifying them and selecting an appropriate control technique such as balancing or constancy, as previously described. To understand how an appropriate technique is selected, one needs to consider the statistical analysis of data.

The statistical analysis of data is designed to tell the researcher how likely it is that the independent variable actually had an influence. Statistical analysis does this by telling the researcher how likely it is that his or her results are entirely due to chance. If (random) chance is unlikely, the researcher could conclude that the results were due to the manipulation of the independent variable. This suggests two strategies that researchers can use to increase the probability of detecting an effect of an independent upon a dependent variable. One strategy is to increase the impact of the independent variable and the other strategy is to minimize chance fluctuations.

Increasing Impact

One way to increase the impact of an independent variable is to select extreme conditions. Stated simply, if the independent variable influences the dependent variable, then large differences in the independent variable should produce large differences in the dependent variable. Recall, however, the effect produced by extreme conditions of anxiety (see Fig. 8.1). Only when a moderate condition was included could the effect be detected. Thus, a second way to increase impact is to use more than two conditions. One should use the two extreme conditions and at least one middle condition. As Aronson and Carlsmith (1968) pointed out, "It is the major objective of a laboratory experiment to have the greatest possible impact on a subject within the limits of ethical considerations and requirements of control."

Minimizing Chance Fluctuations

There are several ways to minimize chance fluctuations. First, the more reliable the measurement of the dependent variable, the greater the reduction in chance fluctuations. Second, there will be less chance fluctuation when the conditions of the experiment, apart from the independent variable, are constant. For this reason, constancy is often preferred over balancing as a way of controlling a possible confounding variable. At the same time, holding all possible confounding variables constant reduces the generality of the results. Thus, the decision to use constancy or balancing depends upon the size of the expected chance fluctuations and the intended generality of any results obtained. It should be obvious that a great deal of careful thought and decision making is involved in planning an experiment.

Sequence Effects

Unless all the participants in an experiment participate at approximately the same time, the experimenter must control for possible sequence effects. Scheduling individuals or groups at different times over a period of time may unknowingly produce a confounding in the form of a systematic relation between the conditions of the independent variable and the sequence in which those conditions are run. This can be unfortunate if, because of an historical event, another explanation of the obtained results is provided. It could also be the case that the observers were not well practiced for the first group but are for the later group(s) (a case of instrument change).

There is evidence to suggest that students who voluntarily participate early in the semester are different in a number of ways from those who voluntarily participate later in the semester (Evans and Donnerstein, 1974). As a rule, *participants from all groups must participate concurrently.*

SPECIAL PROBLEMS

There are a number of special problems or *artifacts* (Rosenthal and Rosnow, 1969) that the researcher must consider when planning an experiment. These artifacts exist for all kinds of experimental designs but are more likely to produce confounding in some situations than in others. A good discussion of these artifacts can be found in Jung (1982). Here we will focus on the three major artifacts presented by Jung: demand characteristics, evaluation apprehension, and experimenter bias.

Demand Characteristics

When an individual participates in an experiment it is unlikely that he or she passively receives the presented material. Individuals actively try to a greater or lesser extent to figure out what is going on and why the situation has been set up the way it has. Cues that individuals notice and that contribute to an interpretation of the experiment or hypotheses are called *demand characteristics* (Orne, 1962). Demand characteristics become a problem when the participant responds to these cues or his or her interpretation of the experiment rather than to the actual experimental situation or conditions of the independent variable.

In a classic demonstration of the power of demand characteristics, Orne and Scheibe (1964) exposed two groups to a sensory deprivation experiment. Both groups were isolated for 4 hours in a room that had a window and a paper and pencil on a table. One group was exposed to a number of cues. Before entering the room, they underwent a physical examination, signed a release form, were assured there was no real danger, and were told to press a "panic button" if they could not handle the situation anymore. The other group received none of these cues. Following the isolation, the "cued" group performed more poorly than the control group on a number of perceptual, cognitive, and motor skill tests. It appeared that the cued group responded to the cues and expected the isolation experience to be somewhat debilitating. They responded accordingly. This is not to say that sensory deprivation produces no effect (positive or negative), but that the effect can be altered by the presence of demand characteristics.

Demand characteristics are particularly threatening to the internal validity of an experiment when they differ from group to group. For example, in our expected test experiment we would not want the cues for one group to be different from those for another group. When we carefully balance or hold constant all the conditions of the experiment, we control that possibility. Several things can be done to detect the presence of demand characteristics and to minimize the effects. One useful procedure is to conduct an interview with the participant following the experiment. Although participants are frequently unwilling to reveal their interpretations, a carefully planned interview (see Chapter 15) often reveals the influence of different cues. Another useful procedure is the so-called nonexperiment in which a group of individuals are run through *all* the procedures and measurements used in the actual experiment except for the independent variable. This group can be considered a form of control group, which can be compared with the group(s) that receive the independent variable and thereby provide information on the effects of cues without any manipulation of the independent variable.

Demand characteristics can be minimized by using a between-subjects design. It is more difficult to guess what the experiment is all about when the participant received only one condition of the independent variable. It is also important to use *single-blind* procedures. These procedures prevent the participants from knowing whether they are in the control group or an experimental group. Giving everyone an injection so that they cannot tell who is receiving THC and who is receiving a placebo in the experiment described previously is an example of a single-blind procedure. A *double-blind* procedure prevents the experimenter from knowing which group a participant is in until after the experiment is completed. (This procedure will be discussed shortly.)

Demand characteristics are probably more of a problem when experiment participants are deceived about the true purpose of the experiment. Since deception is sometimes used in social psychology experiments, these experimenters must pay special attention to the measurement and/or elimination of demand characteristics. At the same time, demand characteristics are always a potential problem and the experimenter must carefully examine all materials and procedures for possible confoundings produced by different, often subtle, cues.

Evaluation Apprehension

Individuals who participate in an experiment may be apprehensive about being evaluated. They may be reluctant to reveal anything negative about themselves (Rosenberg, 1969). If some conditions of the experiment are perceived as more threatening than others, individuals experiencing those conditions may be far more cautious in responding to the manipulated independent variable. When this occurs, the experiment is confounded.

To avoid a confounding and the loss of internal validity due to different conditions of evaluation apprehension, one must again make all groups and the conditions they experience identical—except for the conditions of the independent variable. Carlston and Cohen (1980) suggest that evaluation apprehension may be fairly rare and not a serious problem for most experiments. On the other hand, some work by Christensen (1982) suggests that Carlston and Cohen's conclusion may not be correct. Whichever conclusion is correct, one should always strive to keep the conditions, internal and external, equivalent for all groups.

Experimenter Bias

Most experiments are set up with clear expectations concerning the effect that the independent variable will have on the dependent variable. This is generally referred to as an hypothesis. When these expectations influence the data collected, we have what is known as the experimenter bias effect (Rosenthal, 1966). Rosenthal and Fode (1963) demonstrated this effect by having student experimenters conduct an experiment with rats described as either "maze bright" or "maze dull." Although the rats were neither maze bright nor maze dull, the students who ran the "maze bright" rats presented data showing that their animals performed 50% better than the "maze dull" animals. This and other experiments conducted by Rosenthal suggest that the data one obtains can be influenced by the experimenter's expectations.

How do expectations influence data? Barber and Silver (1968) suggest that there are two general possibilities. One is that the experimenter *intentionally* influences the participant and/or alters the data. In the Rosenthal and Fode study, several student experimenters were observed prodding their "bright" rats through the maze. While such cheating is totally unacceptable it sometimes occurs.

We assume, or hope, that the vast majority of researchers are honest and do not intentionally alter data. Those who do may be detected as their results are not replicated. The other possibility is an *unintentional* influence exerted through nonverbal cues and reinforcements between experimenter and participant. While there is little evidence to indicate that such influences are widespread, the careful researcher must be aware of this possibility and take steps to avoid such effects. In general, confoundings produced by such effects are avoided by treating all participants in the same way, except for the condition of the independent variable that they receive.

Four procedures are typically recommended for eliminating experimenter bias effects. First, data collectors should *not* know what is expected. They should be unaware of the experimenter's hypothesis. The double-blind procedure, in which the data collector does not know which group (e.g., control or other) a participant is in, is recommended. Second, data collectors should be informed that their behavior will be monitored. Whether detailed monitoring actually takes place or not, the warning is often enough to make data collectors more conscientious. Third, tape-recorded instructions and automated data collection devices are highly recommended. This eliminates virtually all cueing that might otherwise take place between human experimenter and participant (human or not). Finally, Rosenthal has suggested using two groups of data collectors and giving the groups opposite expectations, as in the Rosenthal and Fode experiment. This seems a less satisfactory solution since it only reveals and neutralizes experimenter bias effects; it does not eliminate them.

In general, problems such as demand characteristics, evaluation apprehension, and experimenter expectancy are not threats to internal validity when the *only* difference between groups of participants is in the condition of the independent variable that they receive. Such problems may still, however, threaten the external validity or generality of results. For example, although evaluation apprehension may not threaten the internal validity of an experiment because all groups of participants were equally threatened and cautious in their responding, the result may not be generalized to people who are not apprehensive. External validity like internal validity, is a major concern for researchers and will be discussed in Chapter 10.

In spite of all the special problems involved in achieving internal validity, experiments do succeed. In Chapter 9 we will examine some special ways of controlling unwanted internal variables, and in Chapter 10 we will examine more sophisticated experiments that essentially build on the basics just introduced.

chapter *9*

The Experimental Method: Matched-Subjects, Within-Subjects, and Single-Subject Designs

In the preceding chapter we considered the basic characteristics of an experiment. The experimenter varies an independent variable(s) and measures its influence on a dependent variable, which is a participant's response(s).

At the same time, the experimenter attempts to control, eliminate, or neutralize all other potentially extraneous or confounding variables, of both the internal and external variety. External variables are controlled by holding them constant, balancing their conditions across the independent variable, or using them as additional independent variables (see Chapter 10).

A relatively simple way to balance internal variables (such as motivation, anxiety, or age) is to randomly assign participants to different groups. This control is used in a *between-subjects design,* in which each condition of the independent variable is given to a different group. Random assignment makes it very unlikely, but does not eliminate the possibility, that the groups in an experiment differ with respect to any important internal variables. Other ways to reduce this possibility and control internal variables include such experimental designs as *matched-subject designs, within-subject designs, and single-subject designs.*

These three designs exert strong control over possible confounding internal, variables such as motivation, age, or intelligence. In addition to becoming familiar with these three designs, it will be necessary to understand when and why they are used. Later (Chapter 10) we will compare and contrast all experimental designs covered in this and the preceding chapter.

MATCHED-SUBJECTS DESIGNS

A matched design is a special type of between-subjects design in which at least one potentially confounding internal variable is measured prior to the experiment and then all between-subjects conditions of the independent variable receive or are assigned the same value(s) of this internal variable. In this way, the internal variable that might have been controlled by random assignment is definitely controlled by matching. The following example is offered to clarify the distinction between random assignment and matching.

In the Foos and Clark (1983) experiment, internal variables such as motivation, intelligence, and age were controlled by randomly assigning people to a group expecting to receive an essay test and a group expecting to receive a multiple-choice test. When a difference in test performance was found for these two groups, it was not considered to be a result of some uncontrolled internal variable. However, Foos and Clark might have controlled one or more of these internal variables by matching instead of random assignment of subjects.

For example, they might have administered an intelligence test to the subjects before starting the experiment, or they might have decided that grade point average (GPA) was a valid measure of academic aptitude. Before starting the experiment, the researcher would then have obtained GPAs for all the participants. The group expecting an essay test and the group expecting a multiple-choice test would have been matched for GPA. Table 9.1 shows the GPAs for an imaginary sample of 10 participants. Matching involves finding individuals with the same score on the matching variable and then assigning one of them to each and every condition of the independent variable. In the present example persons A and J both have GPAs of 3.6, so one is *randomly* assigned to the essay group (person A) and the other to the multiple-choice group (person J). Persons D, F, G, and I all have GPAs of 3.0, so two of them are randomly assigned to one group and two to the other group. None of the remaining people have the same GPAs. Not to worry, we can still match. The average GPA for persons B and E (2.6 plus 2.4 divided by 2 is 2.5) and the average for persons C and H (2.9 plus 2.1 divided by 2 is also 2.5) are the same. We then randomly assign one pair to one group (B and E to the multiple-choice group) and the other pair to the other group (C and H to the essay group). Now our two groups are matched on GPA. We are certain that academic aptitude, as measured by GPA, has been controlled because the two groups have exactly the same average GPA (i.e., 2.92). With random assignments we would not have established this level of certainty, although it would have been probable that the two groups had the same average GPA.

Matching assures that an internal variable has been controlled; random assignment only makes such control highly probable. Therefore, one might ask why matching is not always used or why random assignment is ever used. A somewhat superficial reason is that matching takes extra time and effort, and random assignment is more convenient. Realistically, it is not possible to measure and then match all internal variables. There are just too many of them and, in addition, many cannot be measured with a meaningful degree of reliability and

Table 9.1   MATCHING ESSAY AND MULTIPLE-CHOICE GROUPS FOR GPA

Person	GPA	Essay	Group assigned to: multiple choice
A	3.6	X	
B	2.6		X
C	2.9	X	
D	3.0	X	
E	2.4		X
F	3.0	X	
G	3.0		X
H	2.1	X	
I	3.0		X
J	3.6		X
Average GPA		2.92	2.92

validity. Matching can only be used in certain situations when the purpose is to eliminate those known and measurable internal variables that are suspected of influencing or vitiating the results.

Reasons for Matching

In the preceding chapter we differentiated between *external* and *internal* variables. When a researcher uses an *external independent variable,* random assignment can be used to assume control of internal variables such as age, motivation, and intelligence. Matching is usually not used when the independent variable is external. One usually uses random assignment or a within-subjects design, which will be discussed later in this chapter.

When a researcher uses an internal independent variable, random assignment cannot be used. Under such circumstances, matching is the only technique available to control other confounding internal variables and is, therefore, highly desirable. There are two major reasons for matching. One is to form equivalent groups and the other is to minimize chance fluctuations.

Forming Equivalent Groups   Clearly, *one reason for matching is to make sure that all groups or conditions of the independent variable are the same with respect to the matching variable.* In the example shown in Table 9.1, we matched our two groups for GPA. Persons with the same GPA were randomly assigned to one of the two groups. Thus, academic aptitude (as measured by GPA) was controlled by matching, while other internal variables (e.g., motivation, age, weight) were controlled by random assignment.

Kahn (1976) provides an example of matching while using an internal independent variable. In his study, moderately retarded, mildly retarded, and normal individuals were compared with respect to measures of moral maturity and cognitive functioning. Before administering these measures, Kahn matched the three groups for mental age (MA), while allowing them to differ in chronological age (CA) and IQ. Many have assumed that the development of moral reasoning depends upon social experience as well as cognitive development. By matching his three groups for MA, Kahn succeeded in demonstrating the importance of experience as measured by CA. *Of course, matching for one variable does not control for other internal variables that may influence the results.* Kahn pointed out that, in his study, IQ and CA were confounded with etiology. That is, the participants with the highest CAs and the lowest IQs had organic abnormalities, whereas no organic abnormality was evident for the remaining participants. While this clearly is a problem, Kahn's matching for MA allowed him to rule out any alternative explanations of his results that are based on MA. In this study, matching did what it was designed to do; it made his three groups equivalent on MA.

Minimizing Chance Fluctuations   The preceding chapter reported that one would increase the probability of detecting the effect of an independent variable if one reduced chance fluctuation in the dependent measure. We suggested using reliable measures and instrument constancy as two ways to reduce chance fluctuations. Matching is a third way. *For matching to successfully reduce chance fluctuation, there must be a strong relationship between the matching variable and the dependent variable.* That is, they must be correlated. If the two are not correlated, then matching will have no effect on the chance fluctuations.

The variable on which groups are matched must be an internal variable that is correlated with the dependent variable. In this section we will examine the procedures involved in finding such a variable and measuring it, and will present two ways of matching groups.

Finding a Matching Variable   Leads to appropriate variables for matching are often obtained by reviewing the literature in the area under investigation. Such a review informs the researcher about the variables others have used for matching and also may reveal what variables are correlated with what dependent variables. In Kahn's (1976) study, it is clear that he matched MA to allow a wider range of CA in his three groups. Previous work had shown that MA influenced the measure of moral reasoning and he now wished to control MA while examining the influence of CA.

Measuring a Matching Variable   Once a matching variable has been selected there are two basic ways to measure it. One is to locate existing records. Examples might include school records (for matching on GPA), medical records, or varieties of public documents available under the Freedom of Information Act.

The other way to measure a matching variable is to test all potential participants. On the basis of such scores, participants can then be assigned to matched groups. Testing is usually preferable to using previously obtained information. It is quite possible that previously obtained information is no longer accurate. Although internal variables generally change rather slowly, they do change. One's level of anxiety, motivation, intelligence, or weight may or may not be the same as it was when previously recorded. Certainly, age is never the same.

Two Ways of Matching   One way to match groups is to determine that the groups have equal average scores on the matching variable (GPA). The other way is to match an individual with an individual. That is, each individual in the first group is matched with an individual in the second group who has *exactly* the same score or measurement on the matching variable. Matching individual by individual is more arduous but does offer the advantage of further reducing chance fluctuations.

Problems of Matching

There are a number of problems connected with experiments using a matched design. Two of these problems have been mentioned: matching takes considerable time and effort, and potential participants are lost because one is unable to match them with others on the matching variable. When the number of potential partici-pants for a research project is small, this problem can be critical and may force the researcher to choose a different type of experimental design.

Three additional problems must be considered before one decides whether to use a matched design. They are: the dependent variable match, the size of the dependent-matching variable correlation, and the inadvertent mismatch.

Dependent Variable Match   One variable that might be worth matching, as it is certainly correlated with the dependent variable, is the dependent variable itself. The problem with matching the dependent variable is that pretesting on that variable may introduce demand characteristics into the experiment. Two examples should clarify this problem.

In experiment A, the dependent variable is reaction time (RT) and the independent variable is alcohol consumption. Consider two alcohol groups (3 ounces and 6 ounces of alcohol) and a control group (no alcohol). We could, of course, randomly assign participants to one of these three groups and hope that this assignment leaves us with equivalent fast, medium, and slow responders in each group. Another way would be to measure RT before assigning individuals to groups. On the basis of these RTs, we would match the three groups so that they all have the same average RT. With RT measures, there is generally a "warm-up" or practice effect (Lachman et al., 1979) and we might, thus, expect all of the participants to be a little faster than they would have been without the pretest. This does not create a problem because everyone's RT changes in the same direction (all are a little faster). Matching our groups has not introduced any differential effects on the three conditions being manipulated.

In experiment B, the dependent variable is a questionnaire and our indepen-dent variable is fear of pain as a result of an administered electric shock. All participants are informed that they will receive a number of electric shocks; a high-fear group will be told that the shocks are very painful, while a low-fear group will be told that the shocks are like tickles. The questionnaire, administered after the information, asks individuals if they prefer to wait alone or with others while the shock apparatus is set up. (This example is based on an experiment by Schacter, 1959.) Since the preference for waiting alone versus waiting with others varies from individual to individual, we can assume that random assignment to the high-fear and low-fear conditions will neutralize individual preferences. Could we instead match the two groups by pretesting all the participants on their preference for waiting alone versus waiting with others? In this case, the answer is no. Responses on the pretest may influence responses on the dependent variable. Consider yourself as saying, when you took the pretest, that you prefer waiting alone. Now you have been exposed to the high-fear condition and would really like to wait with others. Your response on the dependent variable questionnaire may, however, be influenced by your prior response. You say that you would still rather wait alone, even though you would rather be with others, because you do not wish to appear inconsistent. Your response has been influenced by your response on the pretest.

For these two dependent variables (RT and preference for waiting alone) it is fairly easy to see why responding on a pretest may influence one (preference) but not the other (RT). For many dependent variables, however, it is not so easy to decide. *The researcher who considers using a pretest on the dependent variable, for the purpose of matching, must always carefully consider the potential influence of the pretest on the dependent variable.* While there is no simple rule to allow one to decide, it is generally true that measures of attitude are more likely to be influenced by a pretest.

Size of Correlation We have indicated that matching only reduces chance fluctuation on the dependent variable when the matching and dependent variables are correlated. The question is, how large must the correlation be in order to prefer a matched design to a randomized-group design? The answer is, as large as possible. The graph in Fig. 9.1 is from McGuigan (1968) and shows the minimum values for the correlation between matching and dependent variables for different sizes of matched groups needed to warrant the use of matching. For example, if each matched group has 5 participants (as in the example of Table 9.1), then the correlation between matching and dependent variables must be .53 or higher. If each matched group has 14 participants, then the correlation must be .14 or higher. As the size of the matched groups becomes larger, the size of the minimum correlation needed to warrant the use of a matched design becomes smaller.

Researchers considering a matched design should seek as many matched subjects as possible and should make certain that the correlation between matching and dependent variables is high enough to warrant matching.

An Inadvertent Mismatch One difficulty of the matched design is that matching groups for one internal variable may inadvertently produce a mismatch for another internal variable. If the mismatched variable is one that influences the dependent variable, then controlling the matched variable will have produced a confounding.

To illustrate this, suppose we are interested in comparing average annual incomes for people who have graduated from high school and those who have not. Since the independent variable is an internal variable it is important for us to match our groups so that we can rule out some alternative explanations for any results obtained. Doing this would enable us to reduce chance fluctuations in our dependent variables (i.e., income). One variable on which we might wish to match our two groups is *age,* since there is a rather complex relation between age and

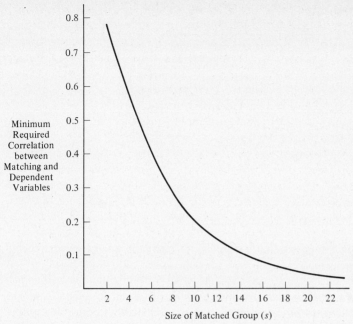

Figure 9.1 Minimum correlations needed for different sized matched groups. From F.J. McGuigan, *Experimental Psychology: A Methodological Approach,* © 1968, p. 187. Reprinted by permission of Prentice-Hall, Inc., Englewood Cliffs, N.J.

income (Schultz, 1976). Another variable we might wish to match is *intelligence*. Intelligence is also related to income (Duncan et al., 1972). Matching for age will probably not produce a mismatch on some other variable, but matching for intelligence may.

Table 9.2 shows the imaginary IQ scores (our measure of intelligence) for nine graduates matched with nine nongraduates. The IQ has now been controlled, and if we find any differences in income for graduates and nongraduates, those differences cannot be due to IQ. This matching for IQ, however, may have produced a mismatch for motivation, as the relationship between IQ and motivation is not a simple one (Weiner, 1972). For most of the participants in the two groups, we have no information that would allow us to estimate their level of motivation with any confidence. We might, therefore, assume that it is about average. We might assume that the high school graduates with lower IQs had quite high motivation and that this enabled them to finish high school in spite of having a low IQ. For nongraduates with high IQs, we might assume that motivation was quite low. In spite of their high IQ, a low level of motivation prevented them from completing school. There are, of course, many other possible reasons for finishing or not finishing high school, but if the above assumptions about motivation levels are at all reasonable, then it is quite possible that our matching for IQ has produced a mismatch for motivation. That is, our group of high school graduates appears to have average or high levels of motivation while our nongraduates have average or low levels of motivation. Any difference in income could, therefore, be due to differences in motivation.

TABLE 9.2   MATCHING AND MISMATCHING
GRADUATES AND NONGRADUATES

High school graduates		High school nongraduates	
IQ score	Assumed motivation	IQ score	Assumed motivation
70	High	70	Average
75	High	75	Average
80	High	80	Average
90	Average	90	Average
100	Average	100	Average
110	Average	110	Average
120	Average	120	Low
125	Average	125	Low
130	Average	130	Low

This example suggests that matching IQ might produce a mismatch for motivation. Of course, we might also have measured motivation levels to see whether they are different and, perhaps, matched for motivation as well as age and IQ. *The main problem in producing a mismatch is not in solving it but in detecting it in the first place.* Familiarity with the literature and careful planning must go into any decision to use a matched design.

Essentially, matched designs provide the researcher with an effective tool for controlling one internal variable at a time. Such control is very useful when the independent variable is an internal variable (e.g., Kahn's experiment, high school graduates versus nongraduates), but not when the independent variable is an external variable. When one manipulates an external variable there are simpler (e.g., random assignment) and more effective (e.g., within-subjects design) techniques available. The researcher considering a matched design should review the literature for information about the size of the correlation between matching and dependent variables. Also to be considered is the possible introduction of demand characteristics with any pretest, and the possible production of a mismatch on some other variable.

WITHIN-SUBJECTS DESIGNS

In a within-subjects design (sometimes referred to as a repeated-measures design) each and every condition of the independent variable is administered to every participant. Within-subjects designs have several advantages as well as limitations.

Advantages

Probably the greatest advantage of a within-subjects design is that all internal variables are controlled. The intelligence, motivation, age, anxiety level, physical health, height, weight, and so on of participants in one condition *are the same* as those of participants in every other condition, because they are the *same* participants. Each person is, in fact, a "self-control." Of course, it is possible that participation in one condition might change the individuals in some way so that they are not the same in the next condition as they were in the first. This potential problem is a limitation. Generally, a within-subjects design gives the researcher maximum control over unwanted internal variables.

A second advantage is that fewer participants are needed for a within-subjects than for a between-subjects design (whether groups are randomized or matched). In fact, if we allow K to stand for the number of conditions in an experiment, then a within-subjects design requires $1/K$ as many participants as a comparable between-subjects design. For example, if our experiment has three conditions and we would like to have 20 observations per condition, then a between design requires 60 participants (i.e., 20×3). A within design requires $\frac{1}{3}$ as many; that is, only 20 participants are required. While the number of participants is smaller, the amount of time that each participant spends in the experiment is, of course, greater (it is K times greater).

A third advantage is that the use of a within-subjects design reduces chance fluctuations of the dependent variable. That is, the chance fluctuations between person A in situation 1 and person A in situation 2 (the within design) are almost always smaller than those between person A in situation 1 and person B in situation 2 (the between design). Chance fluctuations within a single person tend to be smaller than those between different persons. Thus, within-subject designs are another way of reducing chance fluctuations.

Limitations

The advantages of a within-subjects design may seem, at first glance, to be quite worthy, and indeed the use of such designs has increased over the years in experimental psychology (Poulton, 1982). There are, however, a number of limitations that deserve consideration before such a design is selected. They include restricted use, demand characteristic problems, and the control of "time-related" variables.

Restricted Use It should be quite obvious that a within-subjects design cannot be used when the independent variable is an internal variable. Individuals cannot participate in all conditions of such variables. That is, they cannot be both male and female, first born and later born, or tall and short. *Within-subjects designs can be used only when the independent variable is an external variable.*

Even when the independent variable is external, there are a number of instances in which a within design should not be used. This is so when participation in one condition changes the individual so that he or she is no longer the same in other conditions.

For example, suppose we wish to compare two different feedback signals (e.g., audio versus visual) for learning to raise skin temperature in biofeedback training. If such an experiment is conducted as a within-subjects design, we could have individuals learn to raise temperature by using one signal and then learn again by using the other signal. However, once they have learned how to raise their temperatures by using one signal, they cannot return to their previous unlearned state and start all over again with the other signal. Participation in one condition (i.e., the first signal used) has changed the individuals, and so a within design is inappropriate in this situation. In such a case, a between-subjects design, using either randomized or matched groups, is needed.

Within-subjects designs cannot be used in many situations where it is appropriate to use a between-subjects design. There are a few cases, however, where a within design is more appropriate than a between design. An example is when the independent variable is practice. To determine the influence that practice has on a dependent variable, a within design is clearly more appropriate. Box 9.1 provides more examples of cases where a within design is preferable.

Demand Characteristics   As discussed in the preceding chapter, demand characteristics are a problem when a participant's responses are based on his or her interpretation of what the experiment is all about. These characteristics are generally more of a problem in a within-subjects than in a between-subjects design, because it is somewhat easier to develop a notion, correct or incorrect, of the researcher's hypothesis when one is exposed to all conditions than when one is exposed to only one condition. Demand characteristics should always be avoided, but when the selection of a within-subjects design is made, extra care must be exercised.

Time-Related Variables   Whether one uses a between-subjects or a within-subjects design, one must control a number of external and internal variables if one is to meet Mill's criteria. We have shown how the within-subjects design controls internal variables. In Chapter 8 we discussed the use of techniques such as constancy and balancing in a between-subjects design to control external variables. These techniques are also used when one selects a within-subjects design. However, with a within design there are additional variables that must be controlled. These additional variables are called time-related variables.

To illustrate, suppose we wish to compare memory for common or high-frequency words (time, chair, car, boy, etc.) with memory for less common, low-frequency words (muff, rib, ire, clove, etc.). Such words are selected from some objective count of word frequency (e.g., Kucera and Francis, 1967). It is known that frequency influences performance in a number of memory tasks (Gregg, 1976). In our experiment we will present a list of 20 low-frequency words (e.g., one word at a time for 1 second each) and then ask our participants to write down all the words they remembered). When all participants have completed this recall task, we will present a list of 20 high-frequency words (again one at a time for 1 second each) and again ask for immediate recall after the last word. Examining the data, we find that our participants recalled more high-frequency words than low-frequency words. Can we now conclude that the difference in recall was due to the frequency of the words presented?

The first answer might be that it depends on how well you have controlled all of the potentially confounding internal and external variables. Let us assume that all of the internal variables such as age, intelligence, motivation, birth order,

---

Box 9.1 THE CONSUMER CHALLENGE

With an internal independent variable only a between-subjects design can be used. With an external independent variable between- and within-subjects designs can be used. In the latter case, the choice of design depends upon a number of factors, one of which is the type of dependent variable.

In consumer and marketing research, a dependent variable of some interest is consumer preference. Do consumers like brand A more than (or less than) brand X? Can consumers tell the difference between the expensive product and its less expensive competitor? In such work, within-subjects designs are *always* preferable because the problem is related to how the products compare. The most direct way to answer that question is to allow the same participants to make the comparison. It would be an error to give brand A to one group and brand X to a different group of participants (i.e., a between-subjects design) and then compare ratings of the two brands in such a test. The ratings may be identical because, by themselves, the two brands seem fine. When consumers make a direct comparison, we have a better chance of finding a difference in preference, if in fact one does exist.

Another reason for preferring a within-subjects design in product comparison experiments is that it is often quite likely that participants will already have experience with one, or more, of the products (e.g., pop, soap, detergents). Thus, whether the experimenter likes it or not, the design is within-subjects even if it is intended to be between-subjects. That is, participants assigned to receive only one brand (a between-subjects design) have already experienced the other brand (thus, a within-subjects design).

Examples of within-subjects experiments, where two or more products are compared, abound. *Consumer Reports* (1978) compared Sizzlean with Swift Premium bacon (both made by Swift & Co.) and found that about half of the volunteer tasters preferred Sizzlean while the other half preferred Swift Premium. Cola beverages have been compared many times (e.g., Thumin, 1962), with results suggesting that consumers can differentiate between Coca Cola and Pepsi Cola. Other examples include picking out the expensive beer, discriminating butter from margarine, or comparing the ride in a Cadillac to that in a Lincoln.

---

and health have been controlled by our use of a within-subjects design. Let us further assume that we have held constant or balanced all of the external variables that could produce a confounding. That is, the two lists were of equal length, they were presented at the same rate, both contained only one-syllable words, the instructions were the same in both cases, the time given for recall was always the same, the room and experimenter were the same, and so on. In spite of all of these careful controls, the experiment is confounded because of time-related variables. Included in this category are practice, fatigue, boredom, interference, and transfer. Let us examine these variables one by one.

All of these time-related variables can be grouped under the general heading of practice. *Practice refers to any behavioral change that results from repetition or continuance of an activity regardless of the conditions under which the activity takes place.* Generally we think of practice as leading to improved performance, but there are other possible changes that fall under the heading practice as we have defined it. For example, participants may become tired (i.e., *fatigue*) or want to leave the experiment (i.e., *boredom*) after being there for a while.

Participating in some conditions may affect one's ability to do well in another and later condition. This is known as transfer. Learning how to do one thing (e.g., driving a Ford in Vermont) may *transfer* positively to some other tasks (e.g., driving a Chevrolet in North Carolina) but negatively to other tasks (e.g., driving on the left side of the road in England). It should be remembered that practice refers to *any change* resulting from repeated measures, whether behavior improves or declines.

In our memory experiment, word frequency and practice are confounded. Participants may have done better on the second list because it contained high-frequency words, or because their practice on the first list improved their performance, or for both of these reasons. *In a within-subjects design, the researcher must find a way to control for practice effects.*

Control Techniques

There are five basic techniques that researchers use to control practice effects. Since practice effects usually cannot be eliminated, most of these techniques involve neutralizing any systematic relationship between practice and the conditions of the independent variable. The particular technique selected depends on a number of considerations. (The reader should note that the technique used to control practice in a within-subjects design also controls variables such as history, maturation, testing, and regression, which are typically controlled by the use of a control group in a between-subjects design. In fact, the techniques are intended to control any variable that exacts its influence over time.)

A first consideration is the kind of practice effect. There are basically two kinds: linear and nonlinear. Figure 9.2 shows a linear practice effect. The change in performance from the first condition to the second is the same as that from the second to the third, third to fourth, and so on. *In a nonlinear practice effect, each additional condition does not produce the same incremental change in performance* (see Fig. 9.3). When the practice effect is linear, any of the techniques can be used, but when the practice effect is nonlinear, one must be selective.

The other considerations center on such things as the number of conditions of the independent variable, the type of conditions, and the possible presence of differential transfer between conditions. The five practice control techniques are: *random mix, within counterbalancing, complete counterbalancing, incomplete counterbalancing,* and *random order.*

Random Mix This control technique randomly mixes all of the conditions within a single presentation. Since all conditions are presented together, there is

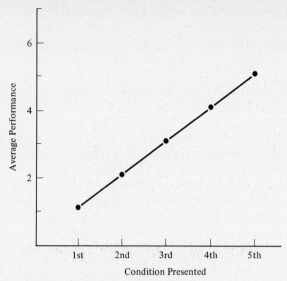

Figure 9.2   A linear practice effect.

no practice effect to influence performance on those conditions presented second, third, and so forth. Thus, it does not matter whether practice effects are linear or nonlinear. For our memory experiment we might use this technique and present only one list of words to our participants. The list would contain a random mix of high- and low-frequency items and the dependent variable (recall of presented items) would be measured only once. For further control a different random mix might be used for each participant.

Type of conditions is an important consideration with random mix, since many condition types cannot be randomly mixed into a single presentation. In most cases, it is fairly obvious whether conditions can or cannot be mixed. For

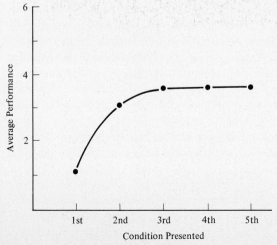

Figure 9.3   A nonlinear practic effect.

example, if the independent variable is the type of item presented to participants in a memory experiment (e.g., high- or low-frequency items, abstract or concrete words, once presented or twice presented items, one-syllable or multisyllable words), mixing is almost always possible. On the other hand, if the independent variable involves comparing the effects of different amounts of alcohol (or any drug), different kinds of teaching techniques, different instructions, different size groups, or the vast majority of independent variables that social scientists examine, mixing cannot be used.

Even when mixing can be used it may not be advisable. There is some evidence that when conditions are mixed in a single presentation, participants will often devote different amounts of effort to the different conditions (Underwood, 1983). For example, Duncan (1974) showed that low-frequency words were remembered better than high-frequency words when a random mix technique was used, but that exactly the opposite result was obtained when the two item types appeared in different lists. In the mixed list, participants seemed to be spending more time and effort on the low-frequency items. Most work shows that high-frequency items are recalled better (Gregg, 1976).

Within Counterbalancing   The next three techniques to be presented are forms of counterbalancing. In Chapter 8 we defined balancing as making the conditions of the confounding variable equal across the conditions of the independent variable. *Counterbalancing is the name given to the three balancing techniques used in a within-subjects design to control practice effects.* These three techniques make the conditions of practice equal across the conditions of the independent variable. For the *within counterbalancing technique, practice is equal across conditions for each participant.* To facilitate our discussion of this and the other counterbalancing techniques, we will label the conditions of this unspecified variable as A, B, C, D, and so forth.

The within counterbalancing technique is sometimes referred to as the ABBA technique. This is a very descriptive label since, with two conditions (i.e., A and B), A–B–B–A is the order in which participants would experience the two conditions. That is, they would receive condition A, followed by B, followed by B again, and finally A again. Some researchers give this sequence of conditions to a random half of the participants, while the others receive the sequence B–A–A–B. With three conditions, the sequence presented to participants would be A–B–C–C–B–A. *That is, all conditions are presented in one order and then again in the reverse order.* The data for each condition are averages of the values for its two presentations.

Within counterbalancing is a very good control because practice effects are equal across conditions for every participant. At the same time, the technique has limited use since practice effects must be linear. If one suspects or has evidence to show that practice effects are nonlinear, this technique should not be used. We refer to Figs. 9.2 and 9.3 to see why the type of practice effect is important. Assume that we have two conditions to present in the order A–B–B–A. Is the effect of practice equal for conditions A and B of our independent variable? If practice effects are linear, as in Fig. 9.2, the answer is yes. We can see that condition A picks up one unit of practice effect (i.e., average performance) when it is the first condition presented and four units when it is the fourth condition, for a total of five. Condition B picks up two units when presented second and three when presented third, also for a total of five. From this it is clear that the effects of practice are equal for the two conditions. If practice effects are nonlinear, as in Fig. 9.3, the answer is no. Here condition A picks up one unit when presented first and 3.5 units when presented fourth, for a total of 4.5. Condition B picks up three units when presented second and 3.5 when presented third, for a total of 6.5. Condition B benefits more from practice than condition A. Thus, practice and conditions are confounded. With a nonlinear practice effect, one must use a different technique.

Complete Counterbalancing   The two remaining counterbalancing techniques make practice equal for each condition but across, rather than within, participants. *In complete counterbalancing every possible order in which conditions can be presented is used.* The number of possible orders is equal to the number of conditions factorial (i.e., *K!*). The same number of different participants, or groups of participants, is randomly assigned to each different condition order.

To illustrate this technique, assume that we have three conditions, A, B, and C, and nonlinear practice effects (as in Fig. 9.3). Table 9.3 shows the six (3!) possible orders in which our three conditions can be presented. The same number of participants would be randomly assigned to each of these six orders. If practice effects are nonlinear, as in Fig. 9.3, practice is still balanced for the A, B, and C conditions *since each condition occurs in each position.* One can see this by adding the practice effects for the three conditions. Condition A picks up one unit each time it is presented first (i.e., two units), three units each time it is presented second (i.e., six units), and 3.5 units each time it is presented third (i.e., seven units), for a total of 15 units. The same is true for conditions B and C. (It may be helpful for the reader to take a few minutes and sum the effects of practice for condition B and C.) Thus, complete counterbalancing can be used with nonlinear, as well as linear, practice effects.

With this kind of counterbalancing, the number of conditions is a very important consideration. As the number of conditions increases, the number of possible orders quickly gets out of hand. For example, with four conditions (A, B, C, and D) there are 24 (4!) possible orders; with five conditions there are 120

Table 9.3   COMPLETE COUNTERBALANCING OF THREE CONDITIONS

Presentation order	Condition Presented		
	First	Second	Third
1	A	B	C
2	A	C	B
3	B	A	C
4	B	C	A
5	C	A	B
6	C	B	A

(5!) possible orders. Complete counterbalancing is usable only when one has a relatively small number of conditions. With a large number of conditions and a nonlinear practice effect, one should consider the techniques that follow.

Incomplete Counterbalancing   The technique of incomplete counterbalancing that is most frequently used is called Latin square (Underwood, 1957). In this case, the number of presentation orders is the same as the number of conditions *(K)* and each condition occurs once in each position (first, second, third, etc.). Looking at Table 9.3, one can see that practice effects could have been controlled by using only three of the six possible orders. For example, if we used orders 1, 4, and 5 (or 2, 3, and 6), each condition (A, B, and C) would occur once in each position (first, second, and third). If we now sum the effects of practice shown in Fig. 9.3, we obtain 7.5 for each condition. Practice has been controlled by using three, instead of all six, possible orders. *Latin square provides a way to randomly select a subset of all possible orders that meets the requirement that each condition occur once in each position.*

Table 9.4 illustrates a Latin square for four conditions. A Latin square is accomplished in three simple steps. First, one makes a systematic arrangement of the conditions, so that each occurs once in each position. While this arrangement would control practice, we wish to avoid any possible bias by randomly selecting the four presentation orders (out of 24) that we will use. To do this, we will randomize the systematic arrangement we have created. Thus, the second step shown in the table is to randomize the four rows of the first step. To do this, we will use the last row in Table 8.2, our table of random numbers. This row orders the rows 1, 2, 3, and 4 as 1, 3, 4, and 2. Thus, the first row remains the same, the third row becomes second, the fourth becomes third, and the second becomes fourth (the reader who is lost should reread the section in Chapter 8 on how to use a table of random numbers). The third step is to randomize the columns of the second step. Continuing in the last row in Table 8.2, the order of the four columns becomes 2, 4, 3, 1. That is, the second column in step two (i.e., B–D–A–C) is now the first column, the fourth is now second, and so on. We would now randomly assign the same number of participants to each of the four presentation orders shown in step three of Table 9.4. The reader should be aware that one could, of course, randomize columns as the second step and rows as the third. It only matters that *both* are done.

A Latin square technique is very useful when practice is nonlinear and the number of conditions is too large for complete counterbalancing. With a Latin square, however, one must carefully consider the possibility of differential transfer between conditions. *Differential transfer occurs when performance in one condition depends on the preceding condition(s) and different preceding conditions produce different performance.* If there is differential transfer, then incomplete counterbalancing does not control for it and the experiment is confounded. Look at condition A in step three of Table 9.4. In the first presentation order, A follows condition C; in the second order, A follows B; in the third order, A is first; and in the fourth order, A follows C again. Condition A never follows condition D. If performance in condition A depends upon whether it has followed B, C, or D,

Table 9.4 INCOMPLETE COUNTERBALANCING OF FOUR CONDITIONS[a]

Step	Presentation order	Condition presented			
		First	Second	Third	Fourth
1. A systematic arrangement	1	A	B	C	D
	2	B	C	D	A
	3	C	D	A	B
	4	D	A	B	C
2. Randomized rows	1	A	B	C	D
	2	C	D	A	B
	3	D	A	B	C
	4	B	C	D	A
3. Randomized rows and columns	1	B	D	C	A
	2	D	B	A	C
	3	A	C	B	D
	4	C	A	D	B

[a]This type of incomplete counterbalancing is called a Latin square (Underwood, 1957).

then we have uncontrolled differential transfer. To control differential transfer, we should use complete counterbalancing. In complete counterbalancing every condition precedes and follows every other condition.

Random Order *The fifth technique for controlling practice is to give each participant a different random order of conditions.* This is not the same as a random mix technique, where all conditions occur together in a single presentation and the dependent variable is measured only once. In the present case, conditions are not mixed, although they are presented in random order for each participant. For example, one participant might receive the four conditions in the randomly selected order C–D–B–A, another in the order B–D–C–A, and so on. The technique is based on the assumption that practice effects will balance out across conditions and participants. Of course, for one to have any confidence that such a balance has occurred there must be a fairly large number of random orders. Zimney (1961) recommends at least 60. Thus, if there are only four conditions, complete counterbalancing should be used. With complete counterbalancing there would be 24 orders and they would occur equally often. With more conditions (e.g., five or six), incomplete counterbalancing is to be preferred as long as there is no differential transfer. Counterbalancing is preferred because it controls practice effects, whereas a random order may or may not do so.

A Final Word One must control practice effects when one uses a within-subjects design. There are a number of available control techniques for doing this. To select the appropriate control, one must carefully consider the type of practice, type and number of conditions, and possible presence of differential transfer. For example, one should not use within counterbalancing when practice effects are nonlinear. One should not use within or incomplete counterbalancing when differential transfer is present. One should not use complete counterbalancing when the number of conditions is too large (of course, how large is too large is a judgment decision).

Each control technique is appropriate in some instances and not in others, but there are some situations where none are appropriate. Suppose we have six conditions that cannot be mixed, produce nonlinear practice effects, and indicate differential transfer. The random mix technique cannot be used because the conditions cannot be mixed. The within counterbalancing technique cannot be used because practice effects are nonlinear. In addition, complete counterbalancing cannot be used because the number of conditions is too large (i.e., 6! gives 720 possible orders). Further, incomplete counterbalancing cannot be used because of differential transfer. The only technique remaining is random order. We may justifiably be reluctant to trust this technique to balance practice and differential transfer over six conditions. What are we to do? For this type of situation, we could use a between-subjects design rather than a within-subjects design. A between-subjects design need not control practice or transfer, since each participant receives only one condition.

Finally, we should point out that although there are five available control techniques, some are better than others. For example, the random order technique makes it *likely* that practice is equivalent across the conditions of the independent variable, while counterbalancing (i.e., complete and incomplete) makes it *certain*. Within counterbalancing makes linear practice effects equal across conditions for each participant. Random mix eliminates the need to be concerned about practice effects since participation occurs only once. It is obvious that one must always carefully consider a number of factors when selecting an appropriate control technique.

SINGLE-SUBJECT DESIGNS

Single-subject designs are a special type of within-subjects design where there is only one participant. Since there is only one participant, such designs are often quite useful in an applied setting where the practicing professional may have neither the time nor the inclination to use large groups of participants, and yet is interested in reporting the results of her or his research. For example, Leitenberg (1973) showed how such designs can be used by clinicians in a therapeutic setting to answer questions about the effectiveness of different therapeutic techniques. LeBlanc et al. (1974) used a single-subject design in an examination of aggressive behavior in a 4-year-old child. Several other examples of the use of such designs in industry, advertising, and even litter control can be found in the book by Robinson and Foster (1979).

As a type of within-subjects design, the single-subject design has many of the advantages and limitations we have already discussed. That is, all internal variables are controlled across conditions since the single participant receives all conditions. Clearly, fewer participants are required and chance fluctuations also tend to be smaller. At the same time, the independent variable must be an external variable, and even some external variables cannot be used with a within-subjects design. One must take care to eliminate demand characteristics, and practice effects must, of course, be controlled.

With a single participant, one cannot use the techniques of complete or incomplete counterbalancing or random orders to control practice effects, since those techniques involve giving different condition orders to different participants. This leaves the random mix and within counterbalancing techniques. The former is limited since most conditions cannot be mixed and the latter is also limited since practice effects must be linear. Because of these difficulties, researchers using single-subject design have devised a number of additional control techniques. They include: *reversal designs, multiple-baseline designs,* and *random introduction designs.* Before examining these three designs, we will describe the basic single-subject procedure.

Basic Procedure

The basic procedure used in single-subject research is to measure carefully some behavior (i.e., the dependent variable) before the introduction of any experimental condition(s). This initial measurement of behavior is called the *baseline.* The researcher then introduces the condition(s) of the independent variable and measures the behavior again. The latter measure may be taken during or after presentation of the independent variable. If there are changes in behavior when this latter measure is compared to the baseline measure, those changes may be due to the experimental condition(s).

The problem in using this basic procedure is that one cannot be certain why behavior changed. This is so because of a number of confounding variables that fall under the broad and general heading of practice. That is, behavior may have changed as a result of history, maturation, regression, fatigue, transfer, and so forth. The three designs used by single-subject researchers are intended to control such confounding variables.

Reversal Design

The sequence A–B–A characterizes the simplest reversal design, where A stands for the conditions operating while the baseline is measured and B stands for the experimental condition(s). One measures behavior under the original conditions (A), under the experimental conditions (B), and then again under the restored, original conditions (A again). If the experimental condition is primarily responsible for the change in behavior, then behavior should return to its original baseline level when the experimental condition is removed. On the other hand, if practice effects are responsible, behavior should not return to the baseline level since restoration of the original condition does not eliminate the ongoing effects of practice.

The results shown in Fig. 9.4 are based on work by Sterman and Mac-Donald (1978) and illustrate the use of a reversal design in an investigation of the biofeedback treatment of epileptic seizures. A baseline measure of number of seizures was made and then the independent variable, electroencephalogram biofeedback training, was introduced. The participant was trained to produce high-frequency brain waves (12 to 15 cycles per second) during the first and third experimental sessions and low-frequency brain waves (6 to 9 cps) during the second and fourth experimental sessions. This design can be described as an A–B–C–B–C design. There is no return to baseline conditions (A) since the training cannot be erased and a large number of seizures is certainly not desirable. The reversals are over the two conditions (high- and low-frequency training) of the independent variable.

The data shown for patient 1 in Fig. 9.4 clearly indicate an effect of the conditions. The number of seizures is substantially reduced during high-frequency training. When such training is removed and replaced by low-frequency training, the number of seizures increases. The data shown for patient 2 indicate that seizure activity declines regardless of which condition is used and one can suspect that the decline may have nothing at all to do with the independent variable. That is, it may be some form of practice effect. In the study reported by Sterman and MacDonald (1978), the pattern shown by patient 1 occurred in three of their experiments while the pattern shown by patient 2 occurred in another three. The results are equivocal. They demonstrate that one experiment is not likely to be conclusive, and this is particularly true with single-subject designs.

Reversal designs can become even more complex. For example, with two conditions, a common design can be described as an A–B–A–C–A–BC–A design where one always returns to baseline conditions (A) preceding and following experimental conditions (B and C) and where each experimental condition occurs by itself and with the other conditions (BC). The many different types of reversal designs are described by Robinson and Foster (1979).

The major difficulty involved in the use of reversal designs is that the independent variable must have effects that can be removed. That is, the behavior must

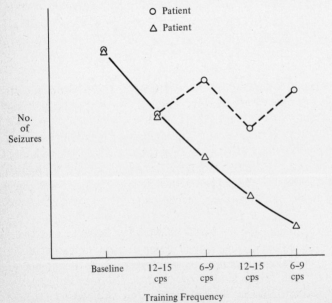

Figure 9.4 Effects of biofeedback on seizures.

be reversible. If the behavior is not reversible, one cannot be sure whether the measured change was due to the independent variable or to practice.

Multiple-Baseline Design

A second way of controlling practice effects in single-subject research is to use more than one baseline. The experimental condition is then introduced to the different baselines at different times. The basic design can be characterized as AA–AB–BB, where two baselines are measured (AA), the experimental condition is introduced to one but not the other (AB), and then the condition is introduced to the remaining baseline (BB). An example is shown in Fig. 9.5.

The example shown in Fig. 9.5 involves two baselines and one experimental condition. The baselines are average skin temperatures on the left and right palms of a participant. The experimental condition is biofeedback training for increasing skin temperature. If changes in the dependent variable are due to practice, then all baselines should change, since all are subject to the conditions of practice (history, maturation, fatigue, etc.). The results shown in Fig. 9.5 indicate that the change in temperature is not a practice effect. The change occurs only when the condition is introduced.

The major difficulty in the use of multiple baselines is that the baseline measures must be independent. If they are not, then when the independent variable is introduced to one, the other(s) will also change. In this case, the researcher will be unable to determine whether the change is due to the condition introduced or to practice.

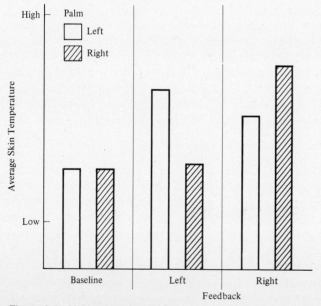

Figure 9.5 Multiple-baseline design.

Random Introduction Design

The random introduction design invokes a single baseline and a predetermined number of measurement stages. The condition is introduced during one of the middle stages (i.e., not the first or last), which has been selected randomly. The logic underlying this design is that practice is very unlikely to exert its influence at exactly the same, randomly selected, stage when the experimental condition is introduced. Thus, if the behavior changes at that stage it is probable that the change is due to the experimental condition.

Combination Designs

In practice, most single-subject researchers use some combination of the three designs we have just described. For example, a researcher might use more than one baseline, and restore baseline conditions to reverse the behaviors. Such combination designs exert the strongest control over practice effects.

Single-Subject versus Many-Subjects Designs

Experiments can be conducted with a single participant as well as with groups of participants. Both approaches have advantages and disadvantages that make them more or less appropriate in certain situations. Since there are many excellent and detailed comparisons of the two approaches (e.g., Neale and Liebert, 1973; Robinson and Foster, 1979; Sidman, 1960), we will focus on the major differences. These differences include breadth, artificiality of data, chance fluctuations, replication, and generality.

Breadth   *Breadth refers to the number and kind of situations in which a given experimental approach can be used. In terms of breadth, the many-subjects designs are far superior to the single-subject designs.* This is so because single-subject designs are exclusively within-subject designs, whereas designs using many subjects can be between as well as within. All internal and external variables can be examined with a many-subjects design, but only a subset of external variables can be examined with a single-subject (or any within-subject) design.

Artificiality of Data   An argument put forward in favor of the single-subject approach and against the many-subjects approach is that the latter results in "artificial" data. That is, performance under some condition(s) of the independent variable is based on group means and may or may not reflect the performance of individual participants. Figure 9.6 illustrates this view. It presents hypothetical data related to learning over time. The group data suggest that learning is incremental; each additional unit of time results in more learning. The individual learned nothing for a period of time (i.e., X), and then learned all. While arguments concerning incremental versus all-or-none learning are no longer of much interest (Horton and Turnage, 1976), the point is that group performance may tell the researcher nothing about the performance of specific individuals.

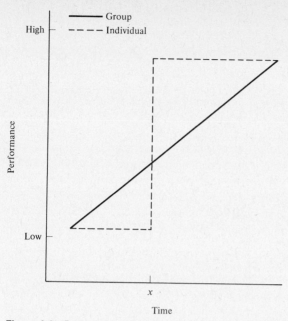

Figure 9.6 Performance of a group versus performance of an individual member of a group.

This problem is really an argument against between-subjects designs rather than against many-subjects designs. In a within-subject design, one can always examine the performance of individuals, whether there are many of them or only a single participant. The possible artificiality of group data leads to the argument that researchers should carefully examine the performance of individuals and should seek designs that make such examinations possible. Researchers are using within designs far more often (Poulton, 1982) and increasingly reporting the performance of individual group members (e.g., Foos, 1982). Single-subject-research always examines individual performance.

Chance Fluctuations   In Chapter 8 we said that one way of increasing the probability of detecting an effect of an independent upon a dependent variable is to minimize the chance fluctuations within a set of data. Since then, we have discussed several ways of doing this (e.g., using constant conditions, matching, using a within-subject design). In a many-subjects design, these unaccounted for, chance fluctuations are referred to as error variance (variance is the standard deviation squared and is another measure of fluctuations). Error simply means that we cannot account for this variance. This variance is probably a function of a number of internal or external factors that we have not measured or controlled. It is the inability to account for this variance that many advocates of the single-subject approach find unsatisfactory.

These advocates argue that social science rests, in part, on the assumption that behaviors are determined and it is the task of researchers to track down the determiner. Variance in behavior is not an intrinsic property of behavior itself. They argue that it is imposed by experimental conditions. To treat variance as error tells us nothing about the source or the determiners of that variance. We must establish the source, and then be able to eliminate it through experimental manipulations. This is done by focusing on the behavior of a single subject and attempting to relate *all* variance to changes in internal and external factors. Rather than having large, or even small, amounts of error variance, the single-subject researcher attempts to have none at all. All variance should ultimately be accounted for by experimental manipulations.

This is, indeed, an admirable goal and one shared by the vast majority of researchers. The single-subject approach offers an opportunity to account for all variance in the dependent variable for a particular participant. At the same time, some variance must be determined by internal factors or complex interactions that cannot be examined in single-subject experiments. We cannot conclude that the single-subject approach is the only method that will allow one to account for variance. It is, of course, an extremely useful approach, but so is the many-subjects approach.

Replication   Experimental findings must be capable of being replicated. In order to be taken seriously, one experiment never really confirms or disconfirms an hypothesis. To replicate an experiment with many subjects, one typically conducts another experiment with many subjects. To replicate a single-subject experiment, another single subject is needed. *Replications are thus quicker and easier for single-subject experiments.* In fact, when a single-subject experiment is published, its replications are usually published with it. Ease of replicability is an advantage of single-subject research.

Generality   *Generality, also referred to as external validity, involves the extrapolation of experimental findings to other situations.* Do the effects of this independent variable hold true for other participants and/or other dependent variables?

Other participants   The ability to generalize to a population is increased as the size of a randomly selected sample from that population is increased. It might, thus, appear that the many-subjects approach has a strong advantage. The problem is that this larger sample may not have been randomly selected. Simply increasing sample size does not automatically increase the probability of generality.

Other dependent variables   The more dependent variables sampled, or, perhaps more correctly stated, the more operational definitions sampled, the greater the possibility of generality. However, the number of variables sampled does not distinguish many-subjects from single-subject approaches and, thus, cannot be used to differentiate them in terms of generality.

Perhaps the real test of generality is to examine how well the findings of the two approaches have held up over time. Have the findings been replicated by other researchers using different participants and different dependent measures?

The answer is yes for both many-subjects and single-subject approaches. We would conclude that neither approach offers greater generality than the other.

This chapter has presented additional varieties of experimental designs. Included have been between-subjects designs with randomized or with matched groups, and within-subjects designs with many participants or with a single participant. In the next chapter we will combine some of these basic designs as we examine more complex experimental designs.

chapter *10*

The Experimental Method: Complex Designs

The preceding two chapters presented the various basic experimental designs as well as the control techniques used to neutralize potential confoundings. Figure 10.1 depicts the basic principle underlying the experimental method. In an ideal experiment, one attempts to isolate the influence of an independent on a dependent variable by controlling *all* other variables. This is done so that the researcher will be able to reach, with some certainty, a cause-effect conclusion. The hope of an experimenter is to be able to say that a change in the dependent variable behavior has been caused by the changes in the independent variable manipulated by the experimenter.

The problem is, as Deese (1972) points out, that cause-effect relations are rarely simple. It is naive to assume that a given independent variable *always* influences a given dependent variable and influences it in the same way. The effect probably depends upon what the situation is, what other variables are present or absent, who the participants are, and so on. To appropriately investigate such involved situations, an experimenter must manipulate more than one independent variable at a time.

We will now examine designs where more than one independent variable is manipulated, designs where the concept of experimental interaction exists, and the myriad of factors to be considered when selecting an appropriate experimental design. Finally, we will discuss the advantages and limitations of the experimental method of data collection.

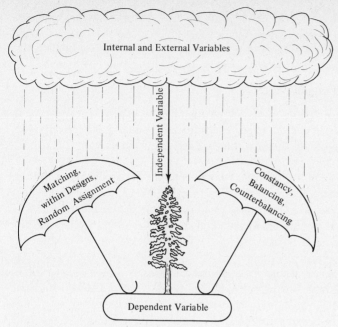

Figure 10.1 It never rains but it pours.

FACTORIAL DESIGNS

A factorial design occurs when more than one independent variable is manipulated and when many (if not all) combinations of the conditions of these variables are considered. Let us consider a simple example in which there are two independent variables, each with two conditions. In common parlance this would be referred to as a 2 × 2 factorial design. That is, two conditions of one independent variable are crossed with two conditions of another independent variable. If one of our variables had three conditions the design would be a 2 × 3 factorial design.

As an example, we will refer to an experiment by Clark (1983) with children 12 to 14 months old. She was interested in children's ability to seek, explore, and find hidden objects. Apparently, the ability to find hidden objects goes through several stages and develops over the first year or two of life. The experimental design included one independent variable labeled "type of object." It was either animate (a person) or inanimate (a toy). The second independent variable was "familiarity" and included a familiar and an unfamiliar object. In this 2 × 2 design, then, there are four combinations of conditions:

1. A familiar, animate object (e.g., mother)
2. A familiar, inanimate object (e.g., a favorite toy from home)
3. An unfamiliar, animate object (e.g., a female stranger)
4. An unfamiliar, inanimate object (e.g., a new, to the infant, toy)

This combination of conditions leads to four factorial designs, namely: completely between-subjects, completely within-subjects, and two types of mixed designs.

Types of Factorial Designs

Completely Between-Subjects   One way to conduct this experiment would be to place different infants in each of the four groups. We could do this by random assignment or by matching on some internal variable such as age.

Completely Within-Subjects   Another way to conduct the experiment would be to have each and every infant participate in each and every combination of conditions. In this case, we would have to control for practice effects, probably by using some form of counterbalancing. This design was used by Clark (1983). She used incomplete counterbalancing of the four combinations of conditions.

Mixed designs   A mixed design [also called a split-plot design (Kirk, 1968)] occurs when one variable (or more) is manipulated between subjects and one variable (or more) is manipulated within subjects. In the present example there are two possible mixed designs. One could assign some infants to animate objects and different infants to inanimate objects and then let *both* of these groups experience familiar and unfamiliar objects. That is, some infants would be exposed to mother and a female stranger (animate objects) while other infants would be exposed to a favorite toy from home and a new toy (inanimate objects). We would, of course, have to control practice for the two within-subjects conditions.

The other possibility is to assign some infants to familiar objects and different infants to unfamiliar objects and then let both of these groups experience animate and inanimate objects. That is, some infants would be exposed to mother and a favorite toy from home (familiar objects), while others would be exposed to a female stranger and a new toy (unfamiliar objects).

How one decides which of these possible designs to use is a complex and difficult question. It should be recognized that the number of possible factorial designs is quite large when all independent variables are external variables. If, on the other hand, at least one independent variable is an internal variable, a completely within design cannot be used, and if all independent variables are internal, then only a completely between design is possible. Incidentally, Clark (1983) found that familiar objects, whether animate or inanimate, were found more easily than unfamiliar objects.

Why Use Factorial Designs?

Factorial designs are used because they allow researchers to examine the influence of an independent variable under several different situations. Take, for example, the influence of alcohol consumption on driving performance. In a simple experiment we might test driving performance by using a simulator and administer different quantities of alcohol as the conditions of the independent variable. Presumably the more alcohol an individual imbibes, the lower the score on the simulator. But is this always the case? Does the same amount of alcohol lower driving performance a little in some situations and a great deal in others? That is, are the effects of alcohol qualified by other variables that may operate in real-life situations?

For a moment, ponder all the internal variables that might alter the effect of alcohol on driving performance. For example, is the effect the same for experienced and inexperienced drivers, or is the effect somewhat less for experienced drivers? What about experienced and inexperienced drinkers? Does the effect of alcohol depend on the age, weight, and/or health of the individual? In addition, a number of external variables might alter the effect of alcohol on driving performance. For example, does it matter whether the individual has eaten recently or not? Does it depend on weather conditions? Is the effect of alcohol greater when driving on a wet, slippery, unfamiliar road at night rather than on a dry, familiar road during the day? Does the effect of alcohol depend on the time interval between drinks and between drinking and driving?

Clearly, there are a number of variables that might or might not alter any effect that alcohol has on driving performance. The same can be said for the effect of any independent variable on any dependent variable. Factorial designs enable us to investigate these potential qualifications. Table 10.1, for example, shows a $2 \times 3 \times 3$ factorial design for investigating driving experience (less than a year versus more than a year), amount of alcohol (0, 3, and 6 ounces), and the interval between drinking and driving (5, 30, and 60 minutes). In this case there are 18 conditions ($2 \times 3 \times 3$) and several possible designs that are completely between or mixed. Since driving experience is an internal variable, a within design cannot be used. As an exercise, see if you can determine the total number of mixed designs that could be used in this case (the answer will be given below).

In short, factorial designs allow us to examine possible qualifications of the effect produced by an independent variable. It is very important to examine these qualifications, since in real life many different variables always operate at the same time. By the way, in the example of Table 10.1 there are three possible mixed designs. They are (1) experience between and amount of alcohol and drinking-

Table 10.1 A $2 \times 3 \times 3$ (18 CONDITIONS) FACTORIAL DESIGN

Driving experience	Amount of alcohol imbibed (ounces)	Drinking-driving interval (minutes)		
		5	30	60
Less than a year	0	1	2	3
	3	4	5	6
	6	7	8	9
More than a year	0	10	11	12
	3	13	14	15
	6	16	17	18

driving interval within; (2) experience and amount between, and interval within; and (3) experience and interval between, and amount within. The only other possibility is the completely between design.

Factorial designs also offer the advantage of allowing the experimenter to test several different hypotheses at the same time. For example, in the experiment referred to in Table 10.1, one can test hypotheses concerning the effects of driving experience (e.g., persons who have been driving for more than a year should do better), alcohol (e.g., more alcohol consumption leads to poorer performance), and time (e.g., the longer the interval, the less the decline in performance because of alcohol).

Finally, factorial designs offer the experimenter another way of controlling potentially confounding variables (see Chapter 8). This is accomplished by treating the confounding variable as an independent variable. For example, in the experiment outlined in Table 10.1, driving experience may have been a potential confounding variable that would be controlled by random assignment, matching, or the use of a within-subjects design. The advantage of turning it into an independent variable, as in Table 10.1, is not only that it is controlled but also that one can examine its effect on the dependent variable. For all these reasons, factorial designs are used far more frequently than designs with only a single independent variable. Box 10.1 summarizes the use of different kinds of designs in experimental psychology.

Experimental Interaction

When the effect of one independent variable depends on the condition of another independent variable we have an experimental interaction. For example, if the effect of alcohol on driving performance *depends* on the individual's driving experience, we would say that there is an interaction between amount of alcohol consumed and driving experience. Interactions occur between independent variables and not between conditions. When there is no interaction between indepen-

---

Box 10.1   DESIGNS USED

Weber and Foos (1983) examined one year (1982) of articles published in the *Journal of Experimental Psychology: Animal Behavior Processes, JEP: Human Perceptions and Performance,* and *JEP: Learning, Memory and Cognition.* Across these three journals they found that 37% of the articles used a single independent variable, while 63% used more than one. For the single-variable experiments, half used a between-subjects and half used a within-subjects design.

For the factorial experiments ($N = 413$), 23% were completely between, 46% completely within, and 31% mixed. These results coincide with Poulton's (1982) finding that the within-subjects design has become the first choice (i.e., 46%) among experimental psychologists.

dent variables we say that the effects are *additive*. That is, the effect of an independent variable is the same for each condition of another independent variable. For example, alcohol might add the same deficit to driving performance for experienced and inexperienced drivers.

The best way to gain an understanding of interactions is to examine the types of questions that can be raised in factorial experiments and to practice answering them. There are basically two types of questions and several types of answers.

Main-Effect Questions   Questions about main effects ask whether or not a single independent variable influences the dependent variable. All other independent variables must be ignored while answering a main-effect question. The number of main-effect questions is, of course, equal to the number of independent variables.

Interaction Questions   Interaction questions ask whether or not the effect of a single independent variable depends on the conditions of other independent variables. One asks, for example, Is the effect of independent variable A the same for every condition of independent variable B? When the answer is no, one has an interaction.

To practice answering these questions, we will use the fictitious data presented in Tables 10.2, 10.3, and 10.4. These data are means from a simple 2 × 2 factorial experiment. We have investigated the effects of type of task (a verbal and a spatial task) and sex (males and females) on test performance.

In Table 10.2, we might first ask whether there is a main effect of type of task. To answer this question we must ignore any differences between males and females and focus *only* on the overall means for the task conditions. Doing this, we find no main effect of task; the overall means are identical (i.e., 11). Is there a main effect of sex? We must now ignore any task differences and focus

Table 10.2   MEAN SCORES FOR MALES AND FEMALES ON VERBAL AND SPATIAL TASKS

Sex	Task Verbal	Spatial	Row mean
Male	10	6	8
Female	12	16	14
Column mean	11	11	

Table 10.3   MEAN SCORES FOR MALES AND FEMALES ON VERBAL AND SPATIAL TASKS

Sex	Task Verbal	Spatial	Row mean
Male	16	12	14
Female	10	6	8
Column mean	13	9	

**Table 10.4   MEAN SCORES FOR MALES AND FEMALES
ON VERBAL AND SPATIAL TASKS**

| | Task | | Row |
Sex	Verbal	Spatial	mean
Male	8	12	10
Female	12	8	10
Column mean	10	10	

only on the overall means for the two sexes. Doing this, we find that there is a main effect of sex; females scored higher than males. Is there an interaction between sex and type of task? To answer this question, look at the effect of task for males. For males, the verbal task provided *higher* scores (a mean of 10) than the spatial task (a mean of 6). Is the effect of task the same for females? The answer is no; for females the verbal task produced *lower* scores (a mean of 12) than the spatial task (a mean of 16).

Three things should be noted about the Table 10.2 example. First, when one has a main effect(s) *and* an interaction, it is the interaction that usually should be emphasized. Although there is a main effect of sex, it is clear that the effect *depends* on the other independent variable and that is the important finding.

Second, there is always more than one way to describe an interaction. The Table 10.2 interaction could be described by focusing on sex, rather than on type of task. That is, one could say the performance of females was a *little* higher than that of males on the verbal task but a *lot* higher on the spatial task. The description used depends upon the hypothesis(es) offered and the purpose of the experiment.

Third, when the interaction is one where the effect of an independent variable is in the same direction under all conditions of the other independent variable(s) (as is the sex difference), it may simply be a measurement problem. In the present example, it could be that the scores on the verbal and spatial tasks are really not equivalent and that a score of 10 on the verbal task is equivalent to or possibly lower than a score of 6 on the spatial task. If this is so, and a verbal score of 12 is equivalent to a spatial score of 16, then there is no real interaction between sex and type of task. The apparent interaction may simply be due to the fact that different measures were used but these differences were overlooked.

In Table 10.3 we have a different set of means. Is there a main effect of task? Yes, the mean for the verbal task (13) is higher than the mean for the spatial task (9). Is there a main effect of sex? Yes, the mean for males (14) is higher than the mean for females (8). Is there an interaction? For males, performance on the verbal task is better (by an average of four points) than performance on the spatial task. For females, exactly the same effect is observed. That is, verbal scores are higher than spatial scores for both sexes. The effects are additive; there is no interaction.

Table 10.4 presents our last set of means. In this case, there is no main effect of task (both means are 10) or sex (both means are 10). Is there an interaction? Yes, indeed. Males scored higher on the spatial task while females scored higher

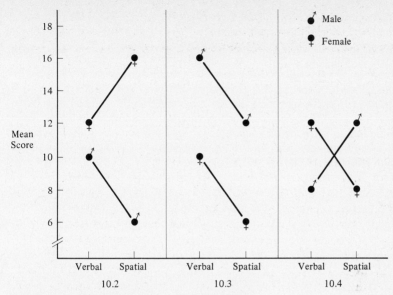

Figure 10.2   Data from Tables 10.2, 10.3, and 10.4.

on the verbal task. The effect of task depends on the sex of the participant (or, conversely, the effect of sex depends on the type of task). In a case like this, where the effects of both independent variables go in one direction (e.g., verbal better than spatial) for one condition of the other independent variable and in the other direction (e.g., spatial better than verbal) for another condition, we have what is called a *crossover interaction.* This is the most powerful type of interaction since we can be very sure that it is not a result of problems in measurement.

The data from all three experiments are shown graphically in Fig. 10.2. Here one can clearly see why the data from Table 10.4 are referred to as a crossover interaction. The two lines cross. When there is no interaction, the lines will be parallel (with the exception of random error). The reader should be aware that *all* combinations of main effects and interactions are possible. Knowing that there is or is not one main effect tells the researcher nothing about other main effects or interactions.

Sometimes interactions are welcomed by the experimenter and considered interesting. Welcome interactions are generally those predicted by the researcher's hypothesis. Whenever one expects the effect of some independent variable to depend on the condition(s) of some other variable, one expects an interaction. Examples of such expected interactions abound and can be found in many diverse areas. To illustrate:

1. *Is music processed in the right or left hemisphere?* It depends. Musicians seem to use the left hemisphere for melody while nonmusicians use the right (Bever and Chiarello, 1974).
2. *Who responds faster, men or women?* It depends. Women seem to have a faster decision time, while men seem to have a faster movement time when responding to stimulus lights (Landauer et al., 1980).

3. *Do cartoons seem less real than human-fantasy television for young children?* It depends on how old the child is; cartoons are less real for five- but not for four-year-olds (Skeen et al., 1982).
4. *Does the presence of others facilitate performance?* It depends. It seems to facilitate the performance of a well-learned task but slow the performance of an unfamiliar task (Markus, 1978).
5. *How many milk shakes can a person consume?* It depends on how many one has already consumed and on dieting. Nondieters consume fewer milk shakes after already having two than after none at all. Dieters do just the opposite (consume *more* after already having two) (Hibscher and Herman, 1977).

One can find example after example of situations where the effect of one variable depends on the particular condition of another variable.

Other Designs

We have discussed randomized groups, matched groups, and between-subject designs. We have also discussed within-subjects and single-subject designs as well as factorial designs. Although there are other designs (e.g., incomplete, fractional, nested), they are considered beyond the scope of this text. The interested reader should consult Kirk (1968) and/or Lindman (1974).

DESIGN SELECTION

Many things must be considered prior to the decision to use a particular kind of experimental design. Experience and the insights gained are helpful as experimenters decide on the use of a particular design for a particular situation. The factors that influence such decisions have been discussed (Chapters 8 and 9) and we will summarize what has already been presented. In addition, we will present factors that have not yet been discussed and offer some comments.

Practical Considerations

Several practical considerations can aid in the selection of an experimental design. Included are variables, participants, and validity considerations.

Type of Independent Variable When one has an internal independent variable, only between-subjects designs are possible. In this case, matching is highly recommended since it allows one to control at least some (those that groups are matched on) of the potentially confounding internal variables.

When one has an external independent variable, any kind of design can be used but some designs may be preferable. For example, a within-subjects design is preferred when one investigates the effects of practice. A between-subjects design is usually preferred when some form of deception on the part of the experimenter is part of the procedure.

Type of Dependent Variable   Sometimes the dependent variable dictates the type of design that can be used. For example, when the dependent variable is learning (e.g., learning French, learning to lower blood pressure, learning about experiments), it is most difficult to use a within-subjects design. This is so because once the individual has learned under one condition, he or she cannot return to his or her original state and start learning all over again under another condition. In such a situation, a between-subjects design is needed.

On the other hand, when the dependent variable is something like personal preference (e.g., for skim or whole milk; see Box 9.1), a within-subjects design is called for.

Number of Available Participants   Although this is rarely the most important factor, it certainly contributes to any design decision that must be made. Within-subjects designs require fewer participants. In an applied setting (e.g., a clinic), the practicing professional interested in doing some experimental research may be forced to adopt a single-subject design simply because there are so few participants available.

Validity Considerations

Several factors that can influence design selection fall under this general heading as they relate to preserving the internal validity or maintaining the external validity of the experiment.

Demand Characteristics   As discussed previously, all experimenters wish to eliminate demand characteristics. We do not want individuals simply responding to being in an experiment and guessing (rightly or wrongly) what is going on. Demand characteristics are generally more of a problem in a within-subjects than in a between-subjects design. That is, it is easier to form notions about what the experimenter's hypothesis is when one is exposed to all of the conditions then when one is exposed only to a single condition (or combination of conditions).

Control   While the control of potentially confounding external variables does not depend on the design selected, the control of potentially confounding internal variables does. A within-subjects design offers the best control over such variables. Matching effectively controls the internal variable on which groups are matched and is thus very useful when there is a particular internal variable that *must* be controlled in a between-subjects design.

One should not infer that this discussion implies that random assignment is a poor choice. It is not. Random assignment makes it very probable that all internal variables have been balanced.

Confounding by Design   One problem that experimenters must be aware of is that, in some cases, different experimental designs will result in different findings for the same independent and dependent variables. In the preceding chapter we saw an example of this in the recall of high- and low-frequency words. High-frequency words were recalled better when they were not in the same list as low-frequency words, but worse when they were in the same list (Duncan, 1974). When the two word types were mixed together in the same list, participants seemed to devote more time and effort to memorizing the low-frequency words.

Generally, the problem is one of within- versus between-subjects designs. As Grice (1966) states, "The nature of an observed relationship between variables is dependent upon the nature of the particular experimental design used to observe the relationship" (p. 488). The problem in the within-subjects design is not one of practice, which can be controlled, but one of exposure to more than one condition. Such exposure may change the participant so that he or she is no longer the same when exposed to other conditions.

Poulton (1982) points out that the change in the participant is usually one of learning a strategy in one condition and then continuing to use that strategy, where it is not appropriate, in other conditions. This results in a kind of differential transfer and introduces a systematic bias in the results. Such a problem is most likely to occur when the conditions of the independent variable demand different strategies, when strategies are unobtrusive, and when the conditions are mixed (e.g., in a random mix such as that used by Duncan, 1974).

The solution is to be both careful and eclectic. Within-subjects designs are very useful and should not be abandoned simply because a bias is sometimes introduced. Such designs offer benefits as well as problems (Greenwald, 1976). Of course, no one is certain how often this bias occurs, so one should vary the design used when investigating a particular problem. If the same findings are obtained regardless of the design used, then it is unlikely that any systematic bias, resulting from the within design, is present.

Replication

We have said that, to be taken seriously, experimental results must be capable of being replicated. Researchers are aware of the many problems and biases that can influence an experimental result and, in principle, favor replication. In reality, researchers rarely duplicate the research of others merely to establish replication. Variables are typically modified to establish generality.

With respect to design selection, a valuable replication is one that uses a different design. If a certain result has been obtained with a within-subjects design, a better replication of the findings would be to use a between-subjects design rather than another within-subjects design.

Unfortunately, many researchers tend to use the same basic design in all of their research endeavors. Although this makes life easier, it is probably not very wise. Designs should be intentionally varied to allow detection of any systematic bias resulting from a particular design.

Individual Performance

If one's intention is to determine whether or not groups of people (e.g., old versus young; first born versus later born) or types of conditions (e.g., essay expecters versus multiple-choice expecters) differ *overall*, then either between or within designs may be appropriate. If, however, the intention is to know whether and how conditions affect individuals, then a within-subjects design is the only choice. One way to determine which design is most appropriate is to ask whether individuals in real life are likely to be exposed to all or only one of the conditions of the independent variable. In the former case, a within-subjects design is most appropriate.

Error Variance

Reducing error variance affords one a better chance of detecting an effect of an independent variable if there is one. On the other hand, such reduction may be unnecessary when a very large effect is expected (e.g., reading comprehension as a function of illumination when a lighted room and a dark room are independent variable conditions).

Error variance is reduced by matching and by the use of a within-subjects design. When a small effect is expected, a within design is highly recommended.

No Simple Rule

There are many considerations that can sometimes play a role in design selection. The point is that there is no simple rule that will allow one to easily select the most appropriate design. Each design has advantages and disadvantages that must be carefully weighed in light of the problem under investigation.

Internal Validity

An experiment is considered to have internal validity when it establishes a cause-effect relationship between the independent and the dependent variable. Internal validity refers to the ruling out of any alternative explanations for an obtained result. This is accomplished by controlling any and all potentially confounding variables and is absolutely essential if one is to reach a cause-effect conclusion. While there is some debate about the ability of other data-gathering techniques to achieve internal validity, there seems to be no debate at all about the experimental method. *The greatest advantage of the experiment is that internal validity is achievable* if the experiment has been well planned and conducted with precision.

Of course, after reading about the experimental method and different design and control techniques, the reader is probably aware that, although internal validity is achievable, it may not always be achieved. Beveridge (1957) has said that no one believes an hypothesis except the originator, *but everyone believes an experiment except the experimenter.* Only the experimenter is close enough to see through all the sophisticated techniques and spot the flaw that prevents drawing a clear cause-effect conclusion. Most experimental researchers seem to experience many more failures than successes. Still they continue doing experiments because the technique is potentially so powerful.

Sometimes researchers are not particularly interested in establishing a cause-effect relation. Simply knowing that two (or more) variables are related may be sufficient to allow the researcher to apply the results to a real-world problem. Most social scientists, however, would probably regard such findings as limited. Experimental research allows us to focus on possible causes. For most researchers, this is far more satisfying than simply uncovering unexplained relationships.

External Validity

External validity refers to the generality of results. Can the findings be applied to other people and other situations? We must, however, distinguish this from *ecological validity,* which refers to how well the research situation represents real-life situations. Let us deal with ecological validity first.

Ecological Validity   It is typical to criticize laboratory experiments for artificiality (e.g., Harre and Secord, 1972; Neisser, 1982). One form of this criticism says that laboratory situations are very different from real-life situations (and, thus, artificial). That is, laboratories lack ecological validity (Brunswick, 1955). As Babbie (1975) states, "The greatest weakness of laboratory experiments lies in their artificiality. Social processes observed to occur within a laboratory setting might not necessarily occur within more natural social settings" (p. 254). Another way of saying this is that experiments have strived for experimental, rather than mundane, realism (Carlsmith et al., 1976). Experimental realism refers to the techniques involved in achieving internal validity (i.e., control techniques), while mundane realism refers to the resemblance between laboratory and real-world situations. Many experiments possess little mundane realism. Is this a worthy criticism of experimental methods?

Carlsmith et al., (1976) point out that "one cannot guarantee generality simply by providing an experiment that has a higher degree of mundane realism. This does not increase our confidence in our ability to generalize from the results, for in the final analysis the question is an empirical one" (p. 86). Berkowitz and Donnerstein (1982) also point out that it is not the ecological validity of the setting *per se* that determines generality, it is the meaning that is assigned to the situation by the participants. It is, thus, extremely naive to assume that an experiment with a high degree of ecological validity will produce more generalizable results than one with a low degree of ecological validity.

While it is true that experiments very often score quite low in terms of ecological validity, it is not true that this necessarily hinders the generalizability of the results obtained. Generalizability is an empirical question that is answered by further investigation.

Generalizability   Perhaps a more pointed criticism of experiments can be found in an examination of their generalizability or external validity. Are the results of experiments conducted in artificial settings (i.e., lacking ecological validity) and using restricted samples of participants (college students) generalizable to real-life situations and general populations?

Generality and utility of experimental findings may not be obvious for years or decades after the original work has been done (Snow, 1963). At the same time, experimenters who wish to generalize their results to real-life situations must be very concerned about the need for representative settings and samples. Such representativeness does not guarantee generality but does increase a researcher's confidence when generalizing.

Mook (1983) points out that external validity must be carefully considered when one wishes to generalize experimental findings but that, very often, experimenters are not interested in doing this. *It is frequently the theoretical conclusions, rather than the specific findings, that one wishes to generalize.* As an example, he presents the case of Harlow's well-known work with infant monkeys (e.g., Harlow, 1971). In some of the work, infant monkeys were exposed to wire-mothers and cloth-mothers. He found that the contact comfort of the cloth-mother had a powerful influence on attachment even when nutrition came from the wire-mother. Clearly, this work has little, if any, ecological validity. No wire- or cloth-mother can be found to exist except in the experiment. External validity for the finding—that is, that cloth-mothers are preferred to wire-mothers—is also lacking. There are no real-life situations to generalize to. The theoretical conclusions, however, had enormous generality. They revealed the flaws in drive-reduction theories of motivation, and it is exactly this kind of finding that makes the experiment so worthwhile.

External validity essentially raises an empirical question that must be taken seriously when one wishes to generalize findings. In experiments, however, it is often the case that the researcher has no interest in generalizing particular findings. Quite often experiments are conducted to test theoretical conclusions. It is from these conclusions that one may generalize.

Limitations of Usage

A cogent criticism of the experimental method is that there are a great many situations where it simply cannot be used. For example, one cannot or should not expose experiment participants to pain, fear, danger, or any other unpleasant state that may, in fact, occur in real life. To investigate such variables, one can only attempt to find persons who are already in such a state, study them, and then make every attempt to relieve the discomfort.

The experimental method demands careful attention to design and control and, thus, works best with relatively small problems. Using the experimental method to answer a large or comprehensive problem can easily result in a loss of important control over unwanted variables.

To sum up, the experimental method is the best data-gathering technique available for achieving internal validity and, thus, revealing cause-effect relationships. Experiments do achieve external validity but the researcher does not always strive for external validity. The experimental method is limited in use. In fact, all methods are limited and can be used appropriately in some situations and not in others.

chapter *11*

The Field

When comparing certain physical-biological sciences with the social sciences, one finds that the former make greater use of the laboratory in conducting experiments as a basis for data gathering.* The social sciences primarily gather data where they find it, which very often is in the field. Their use of the laboratory is much less. For sociology, anthropology, economics, and many branches of psychology, the data exist in the field and are most appropriately studied there. Psychology tends to bridge the gap and gathers data in *both* the laboratory and the field. Probably it does so to a greater extent than any of the other sciences.

A laboratory is a place or space where the experimenter(s) can do certain well-defined and specific things in a prearranged systematic fashion. That which the experimenter manipulates is known as the independent variable(s). The response or responses of the subjects as a result of the manipulations by the experimenter(s) are known as the dependent variable or variables.

In the laboratory, the environment, place, or space is confined and controlled so that any variables that might occur or might interfere with, obscure, or mask the otherwise "true" responses of the subjects are either eliminated, neutralized, or controlled.

Succinctly, the major advantage of the laboratory is that it facilitates experimentation. Although one can conduct experiments in the field, it is easier to do so in a laboratory. The major disadvantage is that the laboratory results may differ from those in life situations that occur in the field. There is a more or less

*There are exceptions, such as astronomy and geology.

continuing debate about whether and when laboratory findings can be extended, applied, or generalized to the real world (see Chapter 10).

The field is the place, space, or environment where that aspect of life that is to be studied or researched ordinarily takes place. The researcher primarily and unobtrusively observes (see Chapter 7) but is not generally able to control the subjects' responses by manipulating variables. The researcher can only decide and designate the specific scenarios or areas to be studied, usually by recording observations in a systematic fashion. The observations may refer to demographic differences, physical or ecological differences, or differences in varieties of behavior, all of which exist. A major consideration is that in the field, the independent variable is not readily manipulated by the researcher. For example, it may be changes in weather, time, or any environmental factor. The responses are the dependent variables and they may or may not occur as a result of the changes in the environment.

A legitimate question is whether data gathered in the field are as reliable and valid as those gathered in the laboratory. This question may be purely academic, since the problem confronting the researcher is to select the form of data gathering that most parsimoniously and appropriately leads to conclusions that solve the problem under investigation.

If the problem is to study the reduction of conflicts in the ghetto, then the field in which such conflicts exist is more appropriate than the laboratory, where such conflicts would be created by the experimenter. On the other hand, if the problem is to determine whether conflicts produce aggression or frustration, the laboratory may be more appropriate, since the experimenter can manipulate the independent variable and measure the responses. We think that both of the problems mentioned are researchable, and whether the field or the laboratory is the place used to gather data is determined by the training and experience of the researcher and his or her statement of the problem. Both places are equally good, but different. It is extremely important that the most appropriate data-gathering method be chosen and used. To use an inappropriate data-gathering method can create more problems than can be solved.

THE LEWIN POINT OF VIEW

When considering field research, one should not overlook the field theory proposed by Kurt Lewin. Briefly, Lewin (1936) considered and applied certain principles of physics as he evolved the concept of *life space.* Rather than consider the field as a place or space, Lewin perceived that life space includes all events that influence a person. His view was that life space portrays the needs of individuals interacting with the psychological environment.

Lewin was a most creative and influential psychologist, and his background in gestalt psychology led him to a qualitative rather than a quantitative analysis and explanation of the interaction between the individual and the environment. He was, for example, concerned with mapping (diagrammatically) the life space of an individual to reveal all possible goals and routes to such goals. In his schema, he borrowed from physics such concepts as valence and vector. The former refers to the positive or negative value of objects within the individual's life space. The latter refers to the directions of movement toward the goal. Lewin postulated that when the person and his or her environment are not in equilibrium, there is a tension (motive or need) to move in a direction to relieve (remove) the tension. For Lewin, the field consisted of the individual or the group in the environment and was the basis for study.

Lewin's concept of life space has been involved in such related activities as group dynamics, action research, and sensitivity training. All encompass the individual-environment interaction—*in the field.* For example, Lewinian *group dynamics* dealt with individuals or groups in terms of their tensions and movements. The concept of *action research* involved the study of various social groups as they intermingled or interacted to create the social climate. This in turn led to identifying the social problems, which in turn could lead to the possibility of change in the field. For Lewin, the field was the laboratory and the laboratory was the field.

From Lewin's point of view, it is necessary to see the individual or group in all of life's situations, and this includes the past, the present, and the changing situation as it will occur in the future. This type of theoretical structure enables the study, in the field, of individuals or groups in relation to problems of minorities, poverty, housing, or crime.

THE QUASI-EXPERIMENTAL POINT OF VIEW

To further understand the field as a space or place in which to gather data in a scientific manner, we will consider some of the work of Campbell, Stanley, and Cook. They are exponents of quasi-experimental design, which refers to "many natural settings in which the research person can introduce something like experimental design into his scheduling of data collection procedures even though he lacks the full control over the scheduling of experimental stimuli which makes a true experiment possible" (Campbell and Stanley, 1966, p. 34). They consider and describe 10 different designs that they classify as quasi-experimental, "lacking optional control but worth undertaking where better designs are impossible" (p. 71). Two of these designs are the time series and the equivalent materials design.

Briefly, the time series design is the use of periodic measurement. That is, one makes a measurement(s) several times before and after some event has occurred. Consider, for example, the effect of wage/price controls on inflation. If one measures inflation once before and once after the initiation of such controls and finds a change in the rate of inflation, can one attribute the change to the wage/price controls? The answer is, of course, no. Not controlled or even considered are all the factors discussed in Chapter 8: history, regression, instrument change, and so forth. The experimental method solves such problems by introducing a control group. One cannot do that here. There is not another United States that can be used for comparison. By using a time series design, however, one can determine whether it is likely that wage/price controls influenced the rate of inflation.

Figure 11.1 illustrates this situation. In each of the three panels we have a different possible, but fictional, set of measures. Four measures were taken of inflation before controls were begun and four measures were taken after. In Fig. 11.1A we can see that wage/price controls had no real effect on the inflation rate, which appeared to fluctuate considerably. Notice that if the measure had been made only *immediately* before and *immediately* after controls, we might have reached the false conclusion that controls lowered inflation. In Fig. 11.1B it appears, again, that controls were ineffective; inflation was already, and still is, declining. In Fig. 11.1C it appears that controls did make a difference. Did they *cause* the decline? We cannot say for certain, but we are confident that this is a tenable hypothesis and we can search for other possible causes that occurred between the rise and fall (e.g., a war, an assassination, a change in interest rates). Time series allows one to look at a broad range of measures and determine whether or not it is likely that some event influenced the measures taken.

In equivalent materials design, the same materials are presented, for example, to two different groups, such as classes or shoppers in a mall. Everything that can be held the same (constancy) or balance is controlled. Of course, not everything is controlled, particularly internal variables, and thus this procedure does not qualify as a "true" experiment. These procedures qualify for the designation of quasi-experiments in field research. Later in this chapter we will illustrate this

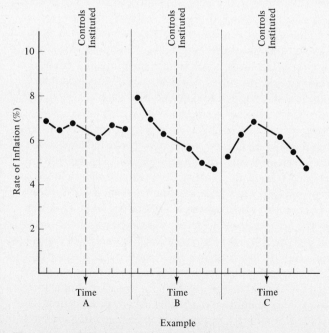

Figure 11.1 Three examples of time series design.

technique. The point we are emphasizing is the preference of the researcher to introduce into the data-gathering system in the field variations on the designs, plans, and systems capable of being used in the laboratory. Our chapters on experiments (Chapters 8, 9, and 10) might be reviewed at this point, not in the context of the laboratory, but in the context of applying such procedures for data gathering in the field to improve the reliability and validity of the results obtained as a result of considering the quasi-experimental technique. Cook and Campbell (1976), in a veritable tome, present a thorough and definitive discussion of the design and conduct of quasi-experiments.

The major point to be recognized in considering quasi-experimental designs is that they are primarily extensions or modifications of experimental designs intended originally for laboratory use and now recommended for field studies. As Box 11.1 illustrates, field studies have become the favored techniques in some areas of research.

Box 11.1 ENVIRONMENTAL PSYCHOLOGY

Since the early 1950s the methods that make up field research have broadened and grown. These techniques can be considered the backbone of a separate branch of psychology known as environmental psychology (see Fisher et al., 1984). The emphasis in environmental psychology is on the environment as an influential determiner of behavior. Researchers take their techniques to the environment, the field, and study behavior there. The techniques include time series designs, equivalent materials designs, and a number of other techniques (e.g., surveys, observations) used in the field.

The field that environmental psychologists study includes the effects of weather, space, architectural design, pollution, crowding, and environmental disasters on human behavior. Even this short list should explain why it is easier to take the research techniques to the field than to bring the relevant aspect of the field (e.g., the weather) to the laboratory.

A good example of field research in environmental psychology is provided by Baum et al. (1983). This research has examined some of the short- and long-range effects of living near Three Mile Island (TMI) during the March 1979 accident. Baum and colleagues examined physiological, behavioral, and survey measures of stress resulting from the near disaster. A control group (see Chapter 8) living more than 80 miles from TMI was used for comparison. On all measures the stress was greater in those living near TMI. For example, their levels of physiological arousal (determined by analysis of urine samples) were higher than those of control group participants, they performed worse on a number of tasks, and they reported more somatic distress. Stress was particularly high for those without a good social support network (e.g., family and friends). Such work cannot be carried out in a standard laboratory setting, and it demands that refined techniques (e.g., use of a control group) be brought to the field.

A FIELD STUDY

To serve as an illustration of a field study as a data-gathering technique, we have selected *Family Behavior, Attitudes and Possessions* by Blum and Candee (1944). We will refer to it in depth so that the reader will become aware of the care and concern involved in planning a field study, will understand the need for the development of measuring instruments to obtain reasonably objective data, and will learn from the data something about family living in terms of the use of space to perform some specific functions. Another reason for selecting this study is its interdisciplinary scope. The data and their application are of interest to architects, home economists, psychologists, and sociologists, among others.

The primary purpose of this study was to relate family possessions to space needs in the bedroom and bathroom. Although at the time of this study the "scientific kitchen" had received considerable attention, little, if any, research had been conducted in relation to space needs for such functions as sleeping, dressing, washing, and other grooming activities as well as bodily functions. This meant that the study was to concentrate primarily on the bedroom and bathroom and the activities that take place in this space.

Planning, prior to gathering data, was crucial in reaching decisions pertaining to the sample or participants, such as the size of the sample, type and size of the dwellings to be included, who would gather the data, and, most important, how the most meaningful and accurate data could be gathered. To a degree, it was hypothecated that satisfaction or dissatisfaction with living in a dwelling was related to the space needs, physical requirements, and inventory of possessions of the family occupying the space. Based on the assumption that different socio-economic levels would reflect different space needs and life styles, it was decided to limit this study to lower cost housing. That is, socioeconomic level was controlled by holding it constant. It was assumed that in areas of less rather than more space, more critical problems would exist.

The next matter for decision was to identify the location of low-cost housing that would allow for comparisons by holding rather constant the size of the living area, age of the dwelling, and family income. While attempting to hold such variables constant, it was still necessary to decide whether the study should sample families living in multiple dwellings or in one-family homes. It was preferred to include families living in both types of dwelling, provided the size of the living area, rent or maintenance, and family income were reasonably constant. As the study reported, most of these problems were dealt with. The sample of families included in the field study consisted of two groups. One lived in a multiple-dwelling housing project and the other lived in a tract of one-family homes.

The number of rooms in the dwelling, the monthly cost (which was either rent or maintenance), and the approximate size of the living space were equated in the two groups. Each home had approximately 800 square feet of living space with the option of add-ons in the unfinished attic.

To help in having families agree to participate, a letter was sent in advance of the first visit, informing the families that an interviewer would contact them.

The data were gathered by using four guided interviews, three "logs" (chronological records of sleeping, bathroom, and dressing activities), and three observation forms completed by the data gatherer. This quantitative phase was conducted during the course of five visits to the household by the same interviewer. The data collected were confined to two specific rooms, the bedroom and bathroom, and included the activities taking place in each as well as the family possessions in these living space areas.

The sample included 65 families in the apartment-type dwelling (group A) and 65 families in the homeowner group (group H). The families in each group were reasonably equivalent. For example, the average rent paid by group A was $52, and this included maintenance (remember that this study took place in the 1940s). For group H it was $43, but this did not include repairs and care inside and outside the home. When this consideration was added, both costs were quite similar. Educational background for both groups was, for all purposes, comparable. Thirty-three husbands in group A and 30 husbands in group H were either high school graduates or had college training. The wives in both groups had an average of 2½ years of high school; 9 wives in group A and 11 in group H were college-trained. The average age of the couples in group A was 31 years and in group H was 34 years.

As a crude socioeconomic indicator an inventory of such appliances as toasters, vacuum cleaners, radios, and washing machines was made. Group A had a total of 322 and group H had 319 such items.

The average family income in group A was $2596 per annum. Group H had an average income of $2566. The only statistically significant difference between the two groups of families was related to religious affiliation and parental nativity. In group A 54% of the families were Jewish, 26% were Catholic, 9% were Protestant, and the remainder were mixed. Group H consisted of 54% Protestant, 24% Catholic, and the remainder included families with other religious affiliations.

In terms of the findings, few, if any, differences between groups A and H were observed. This suggests that when equating for living space, family income, education, and socioeconomic level, differences in religious affiliation and type of dwelling (apartment versus house) have no bearing on the behavior, attitudes, and possessions of families with reference to such basic living functions as sleeping, washing, dressing, and bathroom activities. Whether one might or might not expect such differences might pertain to stereotypes or prejudice. In this study no differences were found.

The findings in this phase of the study are quite specific. They are presented to illustrate the worth of this type of data gathering. The implication is that carefully planned field studies can have considerable value.

Box 11.2 lists some of the findings obtained. Whenever the findings for the two groups were similar, they were combined. As an example,

Many items are kept out on various pieces of the bedroom furniture for display, utilitarian or esthetic purposes. Lamps, clocks, pictures, and perfume bottles are found most frequently of the 13 items listed.

Box 11.2   SOME FINDINGS FROM THE STUDY OF FAMILY BEHAVIOR, ATTITUDES, AND POSSESSIONS

1. All families have bedroom doors. Fifteen percent keep them closed at night and 11% keep them closed during the day. Thirty-six percent of the women report closing the bedroom door while dressing (p. 29).
2. In 67% of the cases group H reports that their neighbors can see into their bedroom. In group A this occurs in 47%. However, a greater percentage of those in group A mind this than in group H. Consistently, group A reports a desire for increased privacy from neighbors more than group H does. This may be an aspect of apartment living (p. 33).
3. On the average husbands go to bed at 11:20 on a weekday and 12:03 on Saturday. They spend 19 minutes in bed before "turning out the lights" on a weekday and 14 minutes on Saturday. Seventy-six percent sleep right through the night on a weekday and 83% do so on Saturday. They average 7⅓ hours sleep on a weekday and slightly less than an additional hour's sleep on Saturday. When the night's-sleep is not regarded as normal the most commonly stated cause is "to bed too late." Twelve percent of the men nap on Sunday (p. 38).
4. Wives get to bed at 11:13 on a weekday and 12:00 on Saturday. They spend 14 minutes in bed before "turning out the lights" on a weekday and 9 minutes on Saturday. Fifty-eight percent sleep through the night on a weekday and 65% do so on Saturday. On a weekday they average 7¾ hours sleep while on Saturday they sleep 8 hours. When a night's sleep is not normal the most common reason is "to bed too late." Eighteen percent nap on weekdays and 14% do so on Sunday (p. 39).
5. Falling out of bed was reported by three wives and three husbands (p. 51).
6. A tendency exists for those in group H to do laundering to a greater extent than those in group A (p. 69).
7. Toothbrushes are kept in a wall holder (p. 87).
8. Only 14% consider the storage space in the bathroom as adequate (p. 87).

When the groups differed to a statistically significant degree, the findings were reported separately. For example,

> Twenty-one percent in Group A report that the bedroom is drafty. Only 2% report this in Group H. Through ventilation is the most commonly stated reason.

Whether the various items reported are considered findings, results, or conclusions is a matter of semantics as well as an indication of whether a researcher perceives sample sizes of 65 and 66 to be adequate or inadequate. As leads or guides (especially when data are otherwise lacking), such data can be useful to home planners, home economists, architects, psychologists, sociologists, and others. For example,

... eighty-seven percent of husbands and wives sleep together in a double bed. While five percent of the wives express dissatisfaction with this sleeping arrangement, forty-two percent believe that twin beds would offer the ideal arrangement.

Given this information what speculations can be offered? We could (but will not) suggest quite a few.

To reiterate, the findings just sampled are intended to serve as an illustration of intensive and specific data gathering in the field. Before conducting this study it was necessary to be able to locate, within the limits of practicality, two rather equivalent groups with the independent variable that members of one group reside in a multiple dwelling and members of the other group in a one-family or private home. The two groups were needed because these are the two major types of domiciles in which families live and a study of one would not necessarily furnish data about the other. Fortunately, the selection of these two locations proved to be quite satisfactory because of the similarities in family characteristics with regard to income, family space, socioeconomic indicator, and educational background. However, a clear-cut difference was the fact that the religious affiliations of the two groups varied. The findings reported indicate that such religious differences do not result in appreciable differences with respect to behavior, attitude, and possessions when one studies such family living functions as sleeping, dressing, grooming, and bathroom activities.

Another objective of this study was to learn more about family living than is ordinarily obtained with such types of measuring instruments as guided interviews, questionnaires, and inventories of possessions. To achieve this, after the data already reported were gathered, two additional inquiries were made. They were both representative of the projective type of data gathering. In this process, the opportunity is presented to the respondent to introduce his or her own perceptions, motives, and aspects of personality as the answer, rather than to obtain more factual or objective responses. Examples of projective techniques include finger painting, sentence completions, word association, drawing figures, and the Rorschach inkblot test. Unfortunately, such techniques are often unacceptable measures in terms of the usual definitions of reliability and validity.

Two types of projective techniques were used. The first was an interview in which the questions were open-ended and the answers were likely to reveal the preferences, wishes, and concerns of the respondent as information was offered about plans to buy a house or what the ideal dwelling should be like, for example.

The second technique involved use of a number of differently shaped blocks representing various items of furniture that might be placed in "your ideal bedroom." The responses were analyzed and interpreted by reading the protocols and searching for repeated themes or other indications of the respondents' motives and perceptions. The researcher might then, in considering the question of differences between reality or fantasy, construct a scale on which discernible gradients indicate the degrees of reality over fantasy (or the other way around) in one's attempt to define the "ideal bedroom."

The purpose of using two rather different data-gathering methods (objective and projective) in the same field study is to determine in what ways these methods agree with, supplement, or disagree with each other. The results would suggest whether one or both methods might be used in future studies related to housing.

Blum and Candee (1944) state:

> Whereas the first method is usually considered as a better one in arriving at specificities, the second is likely to give more meaningful results when freer situations of a more complex pattern are to be investigated. Projective techniques follow a principle essentially opposite to that of questionnaires. Where the latter try to get information as specific and factual as possible and to eliminate subjective interpretations on the part of either interviewer or the person being questioned, a projective technique deliberately sets up a situation which can be interpreted in a variety of ways and then evaluates rather less the exact content of the answer than the particular way in which the individual interprets the situation and how he goes about handling it. This is based upon the principle that if anyone is given material which has no clearly defined form or meaning of its own, the particular one of all possible things he does with it will be determined by his own personality and will therefore give valuable clues about the basic guiding trends and values determining his specific attitudes and actions.

The data and findings reported suggest that the two groups studied were more alike than they were different. This second phase attempted to explore why certain families live in multiple dwellings while their counterparts choose to buy homes. The nature of the projective technique also allows for inquiry into areas of information that might be considered more dynamic than descriptive. A random sampling of families in each group accepted the invitation to participate in this phase of the study.

As for the type of findings obtained in the second phase, they should be considered as clues, hints to understanding, hypothesis formulators, and speculative. The findings nevertheless have value. They allow for a comparison between the quantitative and qualitative methods when the same area of family living is being researched.

As stated, the quantitative phase of this field study indicated that the two groups were certainly more similar than dissimilar with regard to attitudes, possessions, and behavior. Nevertheless, it did leave some unanswered questions. In the qualitative phase, it was decided to create two subgroups of group A and compare a sampling of the Jewish and non-Jewish families. A question to be answered was whether the characteristics of the apartment dwellers were influenced by differences (if any) between the Jewish and non-Jewish families.

Based on the protocols, using the projective interviewing technique, it was possible to construct such concepts as: family organization, the reality of the ideal dwelling, the emotional meaning of this ideal dwelling, and the probability of buying a (or another) house.

The projective technique phase of this study was conducted by Candee and without her knowledge of the results of the more objective or quantitative phase.

Here we can claim to have a situation in which validity is established by using two different methods of data gathering, using a subsample and a sample when investigating the same problem.

In summary, this chapter has been concerned with considering the field as a place or space in which to gather data. Whereas the laboratory enables the experimenter to have greater control over the independent variables, the field permits explorations in the natural or actual setting in which the scenario takes place. The field as a place for data gathering lends itself to various research designs so that different groups can be studied and different procedures used to enhance the reliability and validity of certain findings—with the exception of establishing causality.

The quasi-experiment is the favorite of experimentalists who work in the field and is one way of gathering field data. Quasi-experimental designs are contrived so that the field conforms more to the procedural designs used in the laboratory, and in this light the Blum-Candee study was planned.

The Blum-Candee study compared two groups of families who were found to be rather equivalent in the family living area investigated, even though one group lived in multiple dwellings and the other lived in private homes. In this field study, two different types of data gathering were used. One was more conventional in the measuring instruments used to gather the data. With this technique, it was found that with regard to attitudes, possessions, and behavior in such basic family living functions as sleeping, dressing, and grooming centered around the bedroom and bathroom, there were very few differences. The only background type of difference between the two groups was religious affiliation. Data-gathering techniques showed that differences in religion did not contribute to major differences between the two groups in their attitudes and possessions.

chapter *12*

Archives

An archive is defined by Webster's New Collegiate Dictionary (1956) as a place for keeping public records. It is also defined more broadly as, "documents or records relating to the activities, rights, claims, treaties, constitution, etc. of a family, corporation, community, nation, or historical figure or a place where public records or other historical documents are kept" (Random House Dictionary, 1966).

Although word of mouth reflects the folklore of a people, the progress of civilization is evidenced by the manner in which it is recorded. Thus we have seen the manner of recording change from stone carving to the printing press to the computer.

Much more important, though, is the need to recognize that these recordings or archives are as varied in content as they are reflective of what people and society choose to record.

Some archives are undoubtedly quite accurate and objective; others may well be subjective, either because of the event's lack of clarity or because of the recorder's interpretation. It can be expected that public records will vary in both completeness and accuracy and often will reflect not only the recorder's purpose or objective but also the complexity of what is being recorded. Certain public records are both accurate and simple. They are not subject to factual interpretation. Examples are dates of birth, marriage, and death. Other public records can be disputed as to fact. An example might be the legal record as a result of a decision that a traffic violation occurred when in fact it did not—or the reverse. More serious is the decision that someone did or did not commit a murder.

Factual or not, objective or not, archives are the social as well as historical records of what society regards as worthy of recording. They are the essence of and the basis for what we do when we review, compare, and interpret "then and now." Such archives reveal trends and changes over time, and in that respect they are at once dynamic and static.

Ordinarily, one can assume and believe that archives reflect both accuracy as to content and completeness. At times, however, one should determine and take into account the place and sponsor of the archive. Bear in mind that archives are not impersonal, because an archivist has gathered and stored the data. Considering the variety of depositories sponsored by universities, the Library of Congress, the National Safety Council, and single-issue and activist groups representing business or consumer associations, it should be obvious that some archives may be "more equal than others." Equally important is the fact that archives reflect all segments of society. The researcher's task is to seek the sources that are most appropriate.

Probably the greatest value of archives is their existence as a source for data gathering for historians, archeologists, architects, investigative reporters, and, of course, the varieties of social scientists. In addition, they are equally available to anyone in need of existing and specific kinds of data.

Archives, whether computerized or not, can be regarded as data bases that enable all of us to attempt to explain the past, understand the present, and even predict the future. Some researchers, however, make less valid use of archives than they might. This problem, along with the varying quality of the existing archives, must be considered when one incorporates the archives into acceptable scientific findings.

A frustrating problem for anyone who attempts to use existing archives occurs when one discovers that the archives were gathered for a purpose that is different from that of the researcher as a secondary user. For example, the archives reveal that accidents increase on the highways at the time of certain holidays. Two examples might be July 4 and January 1. Comparing accident totals may or may not be appropriate unless the archives also record road conditions, alcohol consumption, and age of drivers on the road. More significantly, one state may set age groups in such categories as less than 18, 18–21, and so forth; another may set age groups as less than 20, 20–24, and so on; and still another may use chronological year. In other words, categories of age, strictness of police enforcement, police attitude toward younger or older drivers—all of these and other factors mask the data.

Let us ponder the question of whether automobile accident fatalities are more frequent in January–February or in July–August. It is likely that your present answer is a rationalism. But later in this chapter you will learn that archives exist to answer the question and you may or may not have "guessed" correctly.

A major theme of this chapter is that archives, as a data-gathering mechanism, are or can become formidable evidence of what took place. Archives can describe or explain who a person was, or what a society encouraged or discouraged. Archives have a dual role. First, they record the inscriptions of the original archivist, and second, their very existence generates a "second opinion" based on what the researcher chooses to report and interpret from that which already exists. This is not to suggest unreliable subjectivity; rather it is to say that archives are factual as well as pliable.

Another way to look at this consideration of archival value is to recognize that archives do not lend themselves to manipulating an independent variable, which is the cornerstone of the experiment. In many respects the data reported by archivists are similar to the dependent variable, the responses. These responses, usually occurring in a natural or uncontrolled environment, may be based on observation, interviews, forms of rating scales, or a variety of measures of performance. It is characteristic of archives that they record, describe, and possibly explain, but never (or hardly ever) exercise control over the events they record.

USES OF ARCHIVES

Generally speaking, there are two primary uses of archival data. One is correlational, where two different forms of records are compared or related in some form of statistical context. For example, data on temperature variations are correlated with kinds and/or frequency of crime. One must be (repeatedly) alerted that in reporting such data it is a serious error to attribute a cause-and-effect relationship. Temperatures may or may not be associated (or correlated) with crime. If they are, it never means that one caused the other. Correlations do not establish cause and effect; they only establish relationships or the lack thereof.

Another major use of archival data, beyond merely reporting, is interpretative. In such instances, the archivist searches the record and determines the extent to which consistencies or inconsistencies exist. The archives may be about a president of the United States or any other office holder, a foreign policy, a movement such as that supporting an equal rights amendment (ERA), the status of a minority group, public housing, drug addiction, or anything, as we said before, that the archivist chooses to record.

It is the interpretation of the archives that indicates, reveals, or suggests that a policy led to war or peace, recession or recovery, or that someone was an overly ambitious and power-driven person or a benefactor of mankind, a genius or a fool. A problem with such findings or interpretations centers around whether the record was completely reported and, further, whether the archivist analyzed all or part of the information that was available.

A keen issue that arises as a result of the existence of archives is whether history is written in the past or the present. Archives that record events such as the New Deal of President Roosevelt can either be a record of what took place in the 1930s or interpreted in the context of the 1950s or 1980s or the twenty-first or twenty-second century.

Similarly, the data encoded in archives may be based on information obtained directly from the person involved, from that person's associates, or from observers. One biography may differ from another biography based on the same data. Further, laws and ordinances previously passed or about to be passed will turn out to be correct according to some archivists and incorrect according to others. The fact that archival data can be used by others with purposes quite different from those of the original creators of the record was mentioned earlier as a potentially frustrating problem.

A good example is the Nixon tapes, which were planned and recorded by Richard Nixon and then used by others to answer the question: "What did Nixon know and when?" Could Nixon have planned for the tapes to lead to the abrupt ending of his career as the president of the United States? To answer yes indicates belief in something comparable to a "death wish." The point is that the tapes can reveal much about what went on as well as much about the kind of person Nixon was. Undoubtedly, scholars or researchers will interpret the tapes differently, but then, in reality, do we not all interpret differently? At least as far as the Nixon tapes are concerned, posterity will have them.

BUT IS ARCHIVAL RESEARCH SCIENTIFIC?

Based on the material just presented, the question is: Can archives be accepted as scientific? Our answer is, yes.

When reading any article published in a professional or scientific journal or book, one will practically always find many references to the works of others. These works are generally referenced in such a way that the reader can locate them and determine whether the author is correctly quoting, or paraphrasing, the original. Assuming correctness, then one does have a form of reliability—that is, two or more independent findings that are similar. Further, if the referenced material includes multiple sources all reporting the same finding, such agreement or reinforcement can be considered evidence of validity. In addition, the data in the archives can indicate findings that are directional in nature. This is tantamount to measurement. Accordingly, if one inspects the archives and the secondary use of those archives and finds that the three important criteria of scientific data are present (measurement, reliability, and validity), then one is justified in concluding that the archives have standards similar to those imposed by science.

A more direct type of answer is furnished by Simonton (1981). He takes the position that the term scientific cannot be restricted to experimental inquiries. By this he means the manipulation of independent variables. In this case, then oceanography, and geology, as well as other branches of knowledge, would qualify as experimental sciences provided one recognized a more liberal definition of an independent variable.

Simonton limits his archival reviews of research in personality and social psychology to studies of general laws with groups (nomothetic) and quantitative techniques, while excluding case studies of a psychohistorical or cross-cultural format. Examples of material included are reviews of research relating intelligence to eminence as reported by Cox (1926) and the work of Zuckerman (1977) on the relation between creativity and productivity.

Simonton's conclusion is that "there is no scientific justification for rejecting the exploitation of archival data in personality and social psychology." He further states, "The reliability of coefficients calculated for content, analytical, biographical, and historical data are [in] the same league as those of more traditional methods." He refers to such methods as survey questionnaires and interviews and personality and intellectual tests. Simonton also states, "Archival studies can often tap the timewise sequencing of events, whether longitudinal or transhistorical, archival analyses can frequently excel most other correlational methodologies in internal validity" (p. 234). In addition, he believes that in external validity or the ability to generalize to the real world, archival studies are equal to if not able to surpass laboratory studies in researching many substantial issues.

We believe that Simonton has taken a small step forward, when he might have taken a giant step. With persistence, psychohistorical or cross-cultural material can be treated as scientifically valid data, especially when archives exist and can be examined by others and when measurements, whether qualitative or quantitative, are developed to evaluate their content. Our position is that anything that exists can be measured as long as appropriate measurements are devised. Archives can become a rich source of scientific data, provided a basis exists for evaluation.

ARCHIVAL SOURCES

In this section we present some examples of the wide and varied sources that are repositories of archives. Deciding which to select has been difficult because archives exist in superabundance, but we have tried to present a panoramic picture in the broadest of strokes.

Contemplating the major categories of sources, we judge the federal government to be the largest source, as well as resource, of archives. Considering other categories, we have selected organizations with special interests or with a penchant for promoting a single issue which they consider of paramount importance. Our third category includes foundations and universities, where the emphasis is as much on the accumulation of knowledge as on the preservation of the archives. A fourth category includes business and trade associations. Although those in the fourth category tend to be similar to the single-issue groups insofar as they promote the issue of business in general or an industry in particular, they differ in that their records are not readily (if at all) available for public inspection. The last category includes authors of books on topics or persons they believe should be subject to investigative reporting.

Before referring to examples from each of these categories, it is necessary to remind the reader of two types of repositories that are likely to be geographically convenient wherever you are as you read these pages. The first is the neighborhood library. What distinguishes this repository is not so much the books, but the librarian. Librarians are the one source professionally trained to know where to find information. As a profession they are extremely dedicated to service. They may best be described as the "social workers" of the world of information. Whenever anyone needs any sort of information that is likely to be stored in an archive, the first place to go is to a library and seek out the librarian or even request information by phone.

Of course, libraries vary in size, funding, and the variety of archives they

Box 12.1 **CONTRIBUTORS TO** *REFLECTIONS OF AMERICA*

Introduction to the Statistical
Abstract Centennial
Daniel Patrick Moynihan

AGRICULTURE

Agriculture: America's Number 1
Industry
Sylvan H. Wittwer

ARTS

The Arts, Their Growth and
Health
Charles D. Champlin

ATTITUDES

America—A Storehouse of Public
Opinion
*Ben J. Wattenberg and David
Gergen*

BUSINESS

Business Enterprise and Industrial
Development
Alexander B. Trowbridge, Jr.

CITIES

The Moving City
William Marlin

CLASSES

The Emergence of the Upper
American
Eric F. Goldman

COMMUNICATIONS

Communications by the Numbers
Ben H. Bagdikian

CONSERVATION

Use and Conservation of Natural
Resources
Marion Clawson

CRIME

What Do We Know About Crime?
Albert J. Reiss, Jr.

ECONOMY

The National Accounts: Arrival
and Impact
John Kenneth Galbraith

Economic Policy for Inflation:
Shadow, Substance, and Statistics
Walter W. Heller

EDUCATION

Education and Society: A
Complex Interaction
Roger W. Heyns

EMPLOYMENT AND INCOME

The Labor Market and the
Distribution of Income
Andrew F. Brimmer

HEALTH

Health as Ability To Function
René Dubos

HOUSING

Housing and Construction: The
Perspective of a Century
George Sternlieb

INTERNATIONAL
RELATIONS

Statistics and International
Relations
George Rathjens

INTERNATIONAL TRADE

A Case of International Trade
J. A. Livingston

MINORITIES

The Assimilation of Minorities in
America
Howard E. Mitchell

POPULATION

Population Change and
Distribution
Philip M. Hauser

POVERTY

Statistics and the Poor
Graciela Olivarez

QUALITY OF LIFE

The Quality of American Life and
the Statistical Abstract
James A. Michener

TRANSPORTATION

The Transportation Industry and
Its Changing Face
Isabel H. Benham

VOTING

Voters and Nonvoters
Richard G. Smolka

WOMEN

Women in the Seventies: Changing
Goals, Changing Roles
Jeane J. Kirkpatrick

The Future Role of Information in
American Life
Vincent P. Barabba

store. Librarians, however, are not very different, wherever they are stationed; they can either find the source for you or let you know where an expert can obtain the information for you. Another feature is that libraries have an interlibrary loan system, but to use it one needs time.

If the information sought is related more to laws, ordinances, regulations, or a variety of vital statistics, then contacting city or county headquarters is likely to be rewarding. Starting at the manager's office and working one's way down is likely to be more successful than contacting the information clerk at the information desk. Local government headquarters are of great value for obtaining archives that can form the basis of research in many fields such as environment, psychology, ecology, criminology, or life's vital statistics and demographics.

Before designating a variety of archival sources, we nominate two books as delightful means of becoming immersed in archives. The first is *Reflections of America* (1981), which was published to commemorate the centennial of the publication of *Statistical Abstracts*. The contributors, who are listed in Box 12.1, are undisputed experts on the topics about which they write. At the same time, the topics are probably as true and vivid a reflection as possible of the fabric of our society. What is more, they distinctly represent the areas that contain the essence of the social sciences. The book is published by the U.S. Government Printing Office and its price is $6.50.

The other book, also published by the Government Printing Office, is *Social Indicators III*. It includes 11 chapters describing social conditions and trends in the United States in the following major subject areas:

Population and the family

Health and nutrition

Housing and the environment

Transportation

Public safety

Education and training

Work

Social security and welfare

Income productivity

Social participation

Culture, leisure, and use of time

National Archives and Records Service

This archive repository can best be described as serving as the nation's memory. The National Archives spans two centuries. It stores billions of pages of textual material, 6 million photographs, 5 million maps and charts, 100,000 films, and 80,000 sound recordings.

Consultants are available to help clarify research objectives (something students and professional researchers can always use), arrange for staff interviews, and order the necessary records from the archives.

This service is administered by the General Services Administration and has its headquarters in the National Archives building in Washington, D.C. Also included, as part of the National Archives, are the six presidential libraries (plus a seventh to be the Gerald R. Ford Library). In addition, the National Archives has 11 branches in different geographic areas of the United States. More specific information can be acquired by obtaining the *Guide to the National Archives* (1974).

Bureau of the Census

The Census Bureau compiles the most complete data available on population and housing in the United States. Subject items included in the 1980 census are based on either the total population (as close as it is possible to attain) or a sampling of items, in which case they are generally based on one of every six housing units or households. Box 12.2 lists the subject items included as either complete-count items or sample items in the 1980 census.

Box 12.2 SUBJECT ITEMS INCLUDED IN THE 1980 CENSUS

Complete-Count Items

Population	Housing
Household relationship	Number of living quarters at address
Sex	Access to unit
Race	Complete plumbing facilities
Age	Number of rooms
Marital status	Tenure (whether unit is owned or
Spanish/Hispanic origin or descent	rented)
	Condominium identification
	Acreage and presence of commercial establishment or medical office
	Value of home (owner-occupied units and condominiums)
	Contract rent (renter-occupied units)
	Vacant for rent, for sale, etc., and duration of vacancy

Sample Items[1]

Population	Housing
School enrollment	Housing
Years of school completed	Type of unit and units in structure
State or foreign country of birth	Stories in building and presence of elevator
Citizenship and year of immigration	
Language spoken at home and ability to speak English	Year structure built
	Year householder moved into unit
Ancestry	Acreage and crop sales
Residence in 1975	Source of water
Activity in 1975	Sewage disposal
Veteran status and period of service	Heating equipment
Work disability and public transportation disability	Fuels used for house heating, water heating, and cooking
Children ever born	Costs of utilities and fuels
Marital history	Complete kitchen facilities
Labor force status	Number of bedrooms
Hours worked	Number of bathrooms
Place of work	Telephone
Travel time to work	Air-conditioning
Means of transportation to work	Number of automobiles
Private vehicle occupancy	Number of light trucks and vans
Year last worked	Homeowner shelter costs for mortgage, real estate taxes, and hazard insurance
Industry	
Occupation	
Class of worker	
Number of weeks worked in 1979	
Usual hours worked per week in 1979	
Unemployment in 1979	
Income in 1979 by source	
Poverty status in 1979	

Note: Censuses similar in subject content to that of the United States were also taken in Puerto Rico, Virgin Islands of the United States, American Samoa, Guam, Northern Mariana Islands, and the remainder of the Trust Territory of the Pacific Islands. Subjects were added or deleted as necessary to make the census content appropriate to the area. The questionnaire for Puerto Rico had complete-count items and sample items, but in the other areas all questions were complete-count items.

[1]For most areas of the country in 1980, one out of every six housing units or households received the sample from which included all complete-count questions as well as sample questions. Incorporated places and minor civil divisions estimated to contain fewer than 2,500 persons in 1980 had a three-out-of-every-six sampling rate, which is designed to provide satisfactory levels of sampling reliability in the statistics needed for participation in certain Federal programs.

From such data stem not only the allocation of the number of congressmen for each of the states but many funding allocations for education, federal assistance, and so forth. The Census Bureau also issues reports based on data obtained from census counts. An example is offered in the report on "Changing Family Composition" (Bureau of the Census, 1982). A topic as sensitive as this one deserves much thought. Segments of the report have been excerpted as follows:

> Between 1971 and 1981, families maintained by women increased from 31 to 42 percent for blacks and from 9 to 12 percent for whites. These trends are associated with lower overall family income levels and higher poverty rates because families maintained by women tend to be a relatively low-income group. How did this large increase in families maintained by women come about? First of all, the percent of women who are divorced or separated has been increasing dramatically over time. The number of divorces per 1,000 persons married with spouse present increased for blacks from 92 in March, 1971 to 233 in March, 1981; for whites, the comparable increase was from 48 to 100. The number of separated persons per 1,000 married persons with spouse present increased for blacks from 172 in March, 1971 to 225 in March, 1981; the comparable increase for whites was from 21 to 29.

> Increases in families maintained by women are also explained by dramatic increases in the percent of births out-of-wedlock. For whites, the percentage of births to unmarried women went from 7 percent in 1971 to about 9 percent in 1979; the comparable percentages for blacks were 41 and 55 percent.

As one aspect of these data, the Census Bureau asks:

> How much have these changes in family composition affected income and poverty statistics? The Bureau has been working on ways to address this question for the past several years. It is a difficult question to answer because the social scientist cannot recreate history or develop control groups as the physical scientist can, unless the experiment is planned in advance.

This report raises questions that are at the very core of our society if one accepts the belief that the family unit of wife-husband-child(ren) is the basic unit of our society. As the number of one-parent homes increases, what changes can be expected? One-parent families generally mean more households maintained by women, rather than women and men. How does this affect society and its problems now, and how will it affect them in the future? What impact does this have on people who have less money, moderate sums, or great wealth? We do not know the answers and we do not choose to propose any. We do propose that such records or archives that reveal differences and trends will present a basis for studying or perhaps trying to solve the ever increasing problems that confront our society.

The essence of this chapter is that records or archives are data that can be studied, analyzed, and interpreted. Such data are extremely useful for suggesting hypotheses. More attention should be paid to them and less to the rationalism our "favorite prejudice" tends to offer.

Library of Congress

The Library of Congress is the nation's library. Its collection includes almost 80 million items in formats varying from papyrus to microfilm. Its materials stretch along 532 miles of shelves and are acquired at the rate of 10 items a minute. Its staff answers more than 30,000 inquiries a year and consists of about 850 trained experts in such diverse fields as Soviet rocketry and labor arbitration. The Copyright Office is part of the library and it maintains about 16 million copyright registrations.

The vast resources of the library are available to the public. Included among its treasures, in addition to those items usually found in libraries, are one of the three remaining copies of the Gutenberg Bible printed on vellum, flutes from throughout the world, and Stradivarius instruments with Tourte bows.

For those who cannot use the library in person, its interlibrary loan program is available to librarians across the country. A staff also handles written requests for reference material by suggesting specific organizations likely to provide answers.

The library's priority is to satisfy requests from Congress. It declines requests for compilation of bibliographies as well as research into family history.

National Technical Information Service (NTIS)

The basic product of NTIS is federal research and technical information. It is an agency within the Department of Commerce. Its collection includes a topical sampling of more than a million research reports and it grows at a rate of about 70,000 titles a year. Included are such diverse areas as industrial engineering, game theory, cancer, behavior and society, and aging.

The National Technical Information Service conducts and publishes more than 3500 searches, each of which provides from 100 to 200 complete archival summaries. Examples include the international literature on all matters concerned with research and development in food science and technology, and papers presented at regional, national, and international meetings (100,000 papers each year) on such topics as engineering, life sciences, or the physical sciences.

Reviewing some of the titles of government-sponsored research impresses one with its wide range. Such research is organized into 39 major subject categories and these are divided into 325 subcategories. It is quite likely that the government will either have sponsored research on most any researchable topic or have a bibliography available through NTIS. Information may be obtained from NTIS at 5285 Port Royal Road, Springfield, VA 22161.

Consumer's Resource Handbook

This archival source is useful primarily for personal information in solving one's consumer problems. It is also a sourcebook for locating federal, state, county, and city offices involved in handling consumer problems. In addition, it lists trade associations, state banking and insurance regulations, and public utility commissions. Also listed are the Better Business Bureaus and some 400 corporations that have consumer contact or consumer relations departments. Sample copies of the *Consumer Resource Handbook* (1982) are available at no charge from the Consumer Information Center, Pueblo, CO 81009.

ERIC

Educational Resources Information Center (ERIC) is sponsored by the National Institute of Education of the U.S. Department of Education. Essentially it is an information data base in the field of education, which serves as an archive for significant documents in the field. There are 16 clearinghouses in the ERIC network. These include counselling and personnel services; handicapped and gifted children; reading and communication skills; social studies/science education.

The social studies/science education clearinghouse is known as ERIC/ChESS. It invites submission of documents. To be considered, a document must meet at least one of four stated criteria:

1. It should be relevant, answering current problems, needs, and interests of users.
2. It should contribute to new knowledge.
3. It should be creative or innovative.
4. It should be timely and reflective of current educational trends.

If a document is accepted, announcement is made to the approximately 5000 organizations that receive the abstract journal titled *Resources in Education* (RIE). The accepted document is also reproduced on microfiche and distributed to 700 subscribers to the microfiche service. All this takes place at ERIC/ChESS, 855 Broadway, Boulder, CO 80302.

Criminal Justice

Before presenting the archival material from this source, two relevant questions are appropriate. The first is whether we will be hopelessly inundated with statistics from records as computers develop the capacity to gather more of it and to do it faster. The other question is whether the increase in data bases begets more of the same. The answer to both questions is very probably yes, but we must hasten to add that this is not necessarily good or bad. Our society, as well as others, accumulates information as events take place and this produces more archives.

In this context, the archives on criminal justice are a good example. Different states have different rules and laws concerning mandatory prison terms, determinate sentencing, and what is known as good time policies (a statute that allows for reducing a sentence on the basis of the prisoner's behavior in prison). Because of the differences between states, it is exceedingly difficult to compare probation and parole from state to state. Further complicating or confounding the statistics is the fact that the terms probation and parole have become very similar in practice, although they meant rather different things in earlier years.

The point is that *researchers must be familiar with and evaluate the original sources of information that become the archives.* Secondary use of existing data is acceptable. One must, however, understand the limitations that determined the archival data.

Figure 12.1 shows an example of a datum that has been compiled by the Bureau of Justice. The Bureau of Justice works closely with the Criminal Justice Archive and Information Network (CJAIN), whose principal task is the acquisition, processing, and dissemination of major contemporary criminal justice data. CJAIN, in turn, is part of ICPSR or the Inter-University Consortium for Political and Social Research. This consortium is a membership-based organization comprising over 250 colleges and universities. The goal of ICPSR is:

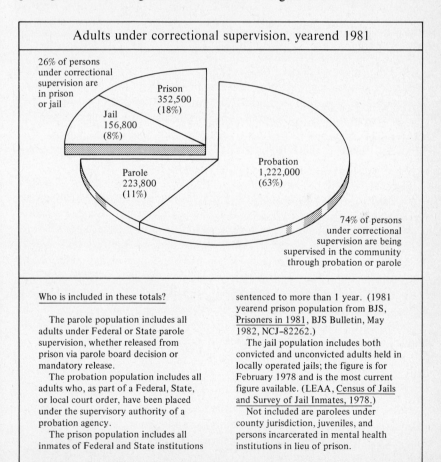

Adults under correctional supervision, yearend 1981

26% of persons under correctional supervision are in prison or jail

Prison 352,500 (18%)

Jail 156,800 (8%)

Parole 223,800 (11%)

Probation 1,222,000 (63%)

74% of persons under correctional supervision are being supervised in the community through probation or parole

Who is included in these totals?

The parole population includes all adults under Federal or State parole supervision, whether released from prison via parole board decision or mandatory release.

The probation population includes all adults who, as part of a Federal, State, or local court order, have been placed under the supervisory authority of a probation agency.

The prison population includes all inmates of Federal and State institutions sentenced to more than 1 year. (1981 yearend prison population from BJS, Prisoners in 1981, BJS Bulletin, May 1982, NCJ-82262.)

The jail population includes both convicted and unconvicted adults held in locally operated jails; the figure is for February 1978 and is the most current figure available. (LEAA, Census of Jails and Survey of Jail Inmates, 1978.)

Not included are parolees under county jurisdiction, juveniles, and persons incarcerated in mental health institutions in lieu of prison.

Figure 12.1 Adults under correctional supervision, year end 1981. (*Source:* Bureau of Justice, *Statistics Bulletin, NCJ83647,* August 1982.)

... to contribute to the advancement of social scientific research and instruction by providing three basic services: a central data archive and dissemination service for computer-readable social science data, training programs in basic and advanced techniques of quantitative analysis, and consultation on available computer technology and software resources.

Further information regarding ICPSR and its membership, policies, and services can be obtained by contacting the ICPSR staff at: ICPSR, University of Michigan, Post Office Box 1248, Ann Arbor, MI 48106.

SPECIAL-INTEREST GROUPS

National Gerontology Resource Center

The National Retired Teachers Association–American Association of Retired Persons (NRTA-AARP) operates this resource center as a library and reference facility. It is open to researchers and students as well as the general population. It is located in Washington, D.C.

The major responsibility of this center is to identify, acquire, and maintain all substantive publications related to the area of social gerontology. In addition, the center maintains on-line search facilities for many computerized data bases such as Psychological Abstracts, Sociological Abstracts, the Congressional Record, and ERIC.

Closely related is the NRTA-AARP Research and Data Resource Unit, which periodically conducts telephone interviews that are nationally representative of persons 55 years of age or older. These surveys obtain such information as employment-retirement status, attitudes and feelings about government spending, budget cuts, inflation, and other issues of primary importance to senior citizens. The value of such surveys is that they offer data indicating what older people do and think. The findings probably have higher reliability and validity than most of the more publicized surveys, in that the sample size of older people in these surveys is much larger than the sample size of older people included in a nationally projectable survey of people of all ages.

The need for records about elders will increase as people live longer. The projections suggest that the percentage of older people in the total population will increase and so will the problems related to aging.

Parent-Teacher Association

The national Parent-Teacher Association (PTA) with its 25,000 local units and its membership in the millions may be classified as a lobbying group. The national body takes a definite stand against tuition tax credits, which it considers the greatest threat to public education.

Concerning the subject matter of this chapter, a problem with such organizations as the PTA is whether they can be considered an archival repository in the sense that their primary function is to gather and store data. In this sense, they are not. However, if one takes a more lenient view and recognizes that such organizations as PTA and the National Organization for Women (NOW), to name only two, reflect societal issues and take an activist stand, then it is necessary that they be included in the archives of our society.

Consumer Activist Groups

Closely akin to the one-issue groups just presented are the specialized consumer activist groups. A network of organizations serving as advocates and activists on a variety of public consumer issues does exist. This network is structured as a loosely federated organization, although each member organization is a separate entity and concentrates its attention on issues clearly identified by its name. In certain respects this network can be considered the "house that Ralph Nader built." Box 12.3 lists the names and addresses of these organizations. The listing in Box 12.3 suggests the types of areas that concern each one and the types of data each gathers as it prepares to take its stand. It is characteristic of the organizations listed that they consider and then take a legal approach to an attempted solution. Usually they differ with an industry position, but with some frequency the government is also their target.

National Safety Council

This organization serves as a clearinghouse for research and reporting done by safety professionals in industry, government, and academe. Its principal publication is *Accident Facts.* All varieties of accidents are reported, but special attention is given to motor vehicles. Bear in mind the fact that from the age of 1 to 44 years, the leading cause of death is motor vehicle accidents. From the age of 45 to 64 years, motor vehicle accidents rank fourth as the cause of death. Heart disease, cancer, and stroke are the more frequent causes in the latter age group. Tables 12.1 and 12.2, reprinted from *Accident Facts,* indicate the hourly distribution of accidents by day of the week and month of the year.

As Table 12.1 shows, during the hour from 1 A.M. to 2 A.M. the greatest number of fatal accidents occur, and Saturday is the day with the greatest number of fatal accidents.

Table 12.2 suggests fatal motor vehicle accidents have been rather constant from 1978 through 1981. Motor vehicle deaths are at their lowest levels in January and February* and their highest levels in July and August, and this pattern continued through the decade of the 1970s.

Business Sources

Business, known as the private sector, tends to be restrictive about and less willing to allow access to its archives and the records it accumulates. This applies equally to specifics or areas where broader health and social implications may be in-

*Did you guess correctly?

Box 12.3   CONSUMER ACTIVIST GROUPS

Public Citizen Groups
Joan Claybrook, President

Public Citizen Administration P.O. Box 19404, Washington, D.C. 20036

Congress Watch (Nancy Drabble, Director) 215 Pennsylvania Avenue SE., Washington, D.C. 20003

Critical Mass Energy Project (Anna Gyorgy, Director) P.O. Box 1538, Washington, D.C. 20013

Health Research Group (Sidney Wolfe, M.D., Director) 2000 P Street NW., #708, Washington, D.C. 20036

Litigation Group (Alan Morrison, Director) 2000 P Street NW., #700, Washington, D.C. 20036

Tax Reform Research Group 215 Pennsylvania Avenue SE., Washington. D.C. 20003

Ralph Nader Groups

Center for Study of Responsive Law (Sheila Harty, Administrator) P.O. Box 19367, Washington, D.C. 20036

Corporate Accountability Research Group Public Interest Research Group 1346 Connecticut Avenue NW., #415, Washington, D.C. 20036

Telecommunications Research and Action Center (Sam Simon, Director) (formerly, N.C.C.B.) P.O. Box 12038, Washington, D.C. 20005

Colleague Public Interest Groups

Aviation Consumer Action Project (Mimi Cutler, Director) P.O. Box 19029, Washington, D.C. 20036

Center for Auto Safety (Clarence Ditlow, Director) 1346 Connecticut Avenue NW., #1223, Washington, D.C. 20036

Center for Science in the Public Interest (Dr. M. Jacobson, Director) 1755 S Street NW., Washington, D.C. 20009

Clean Water Action Project (David Zwick, Director) 1341 G Street NW., #205, Washington, D.C. 20005

Disability Rights Center (Evan Kemp, Director) 1346 Connecticut Avenue NW., #1124, Washington, D.C. 20036

National Insurance Consumer Organization (Robert Hunter, Director) 344 Commerce Street, Alexandria, Virginia 22314

Pension Rights Center (Karen Ferguson, Director) 1346 Connecticut Avenue NW., #1019, Washington, D.C. 20036

Table 12.1 HOURLY DISTRIBUTION OF ACCIDENTS BY DAY OF WEEK, 1981

Hour beginning	Fatal accidents					All accidents				
	Total	Mon.–Thurs.	Fri.	Sat.	Sun.	Total	Mon.–Thurs.	Fri.	Sat.	Sun.
All Hours	*100.0%*	*45.9%*	*16.2%*	*21.3%*	*16.6%*	*100.0%*	*54.3%*	*17.4%*	*16.4%*	*11.9%*
Total	100.0%	100.0%	100.0%	100.0%	100.0%	100.0%	100.0%	100.0%	100.0%	100.0%
Midnight	6.6	5.1	5.3	8.8	9.5	3.3	2.2	2.4	5.6	6.6
1:00 A.M.	7.0	4.6	4.7	10.0	12.1	3.2	1.9	2.1	5.5	7.5
2:00 A.M.	6.0	4.6	4.7	8.3	8.4	2.8	1.5	1.8	5.2	6.4
3:00 A.M.	3.7	2.2	2.8	4.9	7.3	1.6	0.9	1.0	3.0	4.2
4:00 A.M.	2.6	1.5	2.1	4.2	4.2	1.1	0.7	0.7	2.1	2.8
5:00 A.M.	2.1	1.8	1.7	2.2	2.8	1.0	0.7	0.7	1.3	1.8
6:00 A.M.	2.5	3.0	2.3	2.1	1.9	1.8	2.1	1.6	1.3	1.4
7:00 A.M.	2.5	3.2	2.4	1.7	1.4	4.1	5.5	4.1	1.5	1.4
8:00 A.M.	2.0	2.6	2.2	1.1	1.4	4.3	5.6	4.3	2.1	1.5
9:00 A.M.	2.1	2.6	2.0	1.9	1.0	3.5	4.0	3.2	2.9	2.3
10:00 A.M.	2.1	2.6	2.2	1.4	1.5	3.8	4.1	3.5	3.9	2.9
11:00 A.M.	2.7	3.4	2.1	2.3	1.7	4.7	4.9	4.5	4.9	3.4
Noon	2.5	2.9	1.9	2.4	2.3	5.4	5.7	5.2	5.1	4.6
1:00 P.M.	3.0	3.6	2.5	2.5	2.7	5.2	5.4	5.0	5.2	4.8
2:00 P.M.	3.7	4.5	3.5	2.7	3.2	5.8	6.1	5.6	5.2	5.3
3:00 P.M.	4.4	5.1	4.5	2.9	4.0	7.3	8.2	7.4	5.5	5.6
4:00 P.M.	4.4	5.3	4.2	3.5	3.5	7.8	8.8	8.2	5.5	5.6
5:00 P.M.	5.1	5.5	5.0	4.4	4.9	7.6	8.4	8.1	5.3	5.9
6:00 P.M.	5.6	6.1	6.3	4.5	4.7	5.6	5.6	5.9	5.3	5.6
7:00 P.M.	5.4	6.0	5.4	4.9	4.4	4.7	4.4	5.1	4.9	5.0
8:00 P.M.	5.3	5.5	6.1	5.0	4.2	3.9	3.6	4.3	4.3	4.4
9:00 P.M.	6.1	6.3	7.1	6.1	4.9	3.9	3.5	4.6	4.5	4.1
10:00 P.M.	6.3	6.0	9.5	5.6	4.6	3.8	3.2	5.1	4.6	3.7
11:00 P.M.	6.3	6.0	9.5	6.6	3.4	3.8	3.0	5.6	5.3	3.2

Source: Based on reports from 10 state traffic authorities. Reprinted from *Accident Facts* (National Safety Council, Chicago, 1982).

Table 12.2 MOTOR VEHICLE DEATHS BY MONTH, 1972–1981

Month	Deaths									
	1972	1973	1974	1975	1976	1977	1978	1979	1980	1981
Total	56,278	55,511	46,402	45,853	47,038	49,510	52,411	52,800	52,600	50,800
January	4,058	3,932	3,020	3,191	3,172	2,909	2,952	3,290	3,640	3,830
February	3,604	3,559	2,699	2,949	3,047	2,973	2,767	3,210	3,340	3,460
March	4,158	4,429	3,311	3,405	3,321	3,600	3,617	4,160	3,740	3,710
April	4,354	4,492	3,425	3,412	3,684	3,873	4,057	4,190	3,780	4,030
May	4,876	4,963	3,678	4,145	4,234	4,270	4,622	4,600	4,660	4,380
June	4,752	5,150	4,243	4,190	4,147	4,457	4,813	4,630	5,040	4,430
July	5,392	5,228	4,401	4,437	4,763	5,075	5,218	4,830	4,980	4,970
August	5,316	5,260	4,718	4,460	4,509	4,759	5,185	4,860	5,560	5,070
September	4,966	4,960	4,256	4,059	4,141	4,417	4,941	4,840	4,610	4,350
October	5,244	5,167	4,465	4,016	4,304	4,728	4,972	4,830	4,460	4,370
November	4,786	4,453	4,273	3,896	3,691	4,240	4,622	4,560	4,470	4,140
December	4,772	3,918	3,913	3,693	4,025	4,209	4,645	4,800	4,320	4,060

Source: 1972–78 deaths from National Center for Health Statistics. 1979, 1980, and 1981 (preliminary) deaths are National Safety Council estimates. Reprinted from *Accident Facts* (National Safety Council, 1982), p. 51.

volved. Lead in paint, asbestos, and certain pesticides are only a few examples of subjects for which data may not be readily available. An additional reason for not making archives available to the public is related to competition and unwillingness to reveal "trade secrets" such as special ingredients in a syrup. Some other situations that discourage the open sharing of archives might be those in which question arise such as, When did _____ (name of automobile manufacturer) know that its _____ (model name) had self-loosening bolts, or unprotected gas tanks, or brakes that fail? Such questions are especially difficult to answer when the archives do not exist or are not available.

Another part of the private sector does, with some frequency, make archives readily available when information is intended to present the position of an industry. Such groups are the trade associations. Trade associations, such as those representing food distributors, funeral directors, or truckers, present archives to support their positions.

National Association of Manufacturers

This group has a membership of about 12,000 companies. It testifies in or otherwise communicates with Congress. For example, it did so more than 300 times during the 96th Congress.

The NAM has proposed a program to revitalize U.S. industry. Its six points include:

Controlling federal spending

Making money available for investment

Sensible federal regulations

Using natural resources effectively

Competing more profitably with foreign manufacturers

Improving productivity

Examples of NAM publications are:

Industry's Agenda for the 97th Congress (1982). A 30-page booklet detailing specific legislative and regulatory recommendations necessary to achieve NAM's goal of revitalization.

Regulatory Failure: A Documentary of the Overregulation of Business by Federal Regulatory Agencies (1980). Primarily a collection of quotations from economists, lawmakers, and businessmen, with original sources indicated where possible.

Voting Records: U.S. Senate and House of Representatives, January–December 1980. A compilation of specific congressional floor votes, selected on the basis of their importance to industry, legislative significance, and relation to a specific NAM position.

Supreme Court Decisions Affecting Manufacturers, 1982–83 Term. A 44-page report summarizing 24 Supreme Court cases and decisions likely to have an impact on manufacturers.

Corporate Reports

Archives of the business sector that are not private are the financial reports of corporations that are "public" in the sense that they are traded on any of the stock exchanges and that anyone with money and a willingness to buy stocks becomes an "owner."

Forbes, a business/financial magazine, publishes an annual issue entitled "Report on American Industry." The list for the 1008 largest public companies presents their profitability and growth. The record is clear and enables comparisons within industry and between industries. As an illustration, the profitability of electric utilities is reported and compared with that of the tire and rubber industry. Our only reason for choosing the tire and rubber industry is that it was the one listed immediately after the electric utilities (pp. 92, 102). A logical question is how the profitability of the electric utilities compares with that of industry in general. (What do you think?) A major variable is that utilities are regulated by state public service commissions and they can and do petition for rate increases. This is not so with nonregulated industries. For example, the first electric utility group listed by *Forbes,* which was Northeast (see Table 12.3), was followed by tire and rubber (see Table 12.4). Comparing the profitability of these two groups reveals that the Northeast electric utilities do better on all measures than tire and rubber companies. One hypothesis is that the former has better management. Another is that the former has a regulated rate.

The fact is that for all industry the median net profit margin is 3.5% and for the electric utility industry it is 12.1%.

Ford Foundation

This foundation administers a program focused on six areas: urban poverty; rural poverty and resources; human rights and social justice; governance and public policy; education and culture; and international affairs. According to the foundation, "Running through all these program areas is a special concern for the needs of the severely disadvantaged, including racial and ethnic minorities, low-income women, and refugees and migrants."

In the publication *Ford Foundation Current Interests* (1983), the foundation indicates that because of reductions in health services funds it is interested in sponsoring programs that can become self-supporting. The foundation is concerned with the struggle to protect human rights and promote political liberty in this country and abroad.

Grants awarded by the Ford Foundation include the following areas, among many others:

Attempts to overcome racial discrimination in housing

Awards and scholarships

Building an alternative to commercial television

International studies

Table 12.3 ELECTRIC UTILITIES; YARDSTICKS OF MANAGEMENT PERFORMANCE

Company	Profitability								Growth			
	Return on equity			debt/ equity ratio	Return on total capital			net profit margin	Sales		Earnings per share	
	5-year rank	5-year average	latest 12 months		5-year rank	5-year average	latest 12 months		5-year rank	5-year average	5-year rank	5-year average
Northeast												
United Illuminating	1	15.4%	18.7%	0.9	2	8.8%	10.0%	17.7%	2	14.7%	9	4.7%
New England Electric	2	15.4	18.3	0.8	9	7.3	8.3	10.1	15	10.6	1	9.8
Commonwealth Energy	3	14.1	19.1	0.7	12	6.8	8.3	6.0	14	11.3	5	6.5
NY State Elec & Gas	4	13.8	14.3	0.9	3	8.3	8.5	16.6	8	13.3	7	5.7
Long Island Lighting	5	13.7	15.0	0.6	1	9.1	9.7	20.6	3	14.7	15	1.8
Niagara Mohawk Power	6	13.5	15.6	0.8	4	8.0	8.9	11.7	5	14.1	8	5.3
Orange & Rockland	7	13.3	14.1	0.6	7	7.4	7.9	7.0	12	12.5	4	6.6
Consolidated Edison	8	13.3	15.3	0.6	6	7.6	8.9	10.1	17	10.1	2	9.6
Rochester Gas & Elec	9	12.6	14.9	0.8	5	7.8	8.8	11.0	4	14.3	6	6.4
Penn Power & Light	10	12.5	12.6	0.9	11	6.9	6.7	25.3	16	10.4	16	1.2
Delmarva Power & Lt	11	12.5	15.2	0.9	8	7.3	8.2	13.0	9	12.9	10	3.8
Atlantic City Elec	12	12.0	14.9	0.8	10	7.1	8.0	12.6	6	13.7	14	2.2
Boston Edison	13	12.0	12.2	0.8	16	5.8	6.0	6.8	13	11.7	3	7.5
Northeast Utilities	13	12.0	17.3	1.2	12	6.8	8.4	11.1	1	14.9	13	2.8
Phila Electric	15	11.8	13.8	1.0	15	6.6	7.2	14.8	10	12.8	11	3.3
Pub Svc Elec & Gas	16	11.8	13.0	0.7	14	6.7	7.3	9.8	11	12.6	12	3.0
General Public Utils	17	3.1	3.2	0.9	17	3.8	3.8	1.9	7	13.5	17	−20.7
Medians		12.6	14.9	0.8		7.3	8.3	11.1		12.9		4.7

Source: Forbes, January 2, 1984, p. 90.

Table 12.4 AUTO SUPPLIERS; YARDSTICKS OF MANAGEMENT PERFORMANCE

| | Profitability | | | | | | | | Growth | | | |
| | Return on equity | | | | Return on total capital | | | | Sales | | Earnings per share | |
Company	5-year rank	5-year average	latest 12 months	debt/ equity ratio	5-year rank	5-year average	latest 12 months	net profit margin	5-year rank	5-year average	5-year rank	5-year average
Tire and rubber												
Goodyear	1	8.8%	7.0%	0.4	1	7.3%	7.0%	2.3%	3	7.4%	1	2.9%
Armstrong Rubber	2	6.4	13.1	0.5	2	6.3	10.0	3.0	1	9.3	2	−2.0
Genl Tire & Rubber	3	6.4	6.0	0.2	3	5.5	5.5	2.8	4	2.0	4	−7.8
B F Goodrich	4	3.7	def	0.6	4	4.8	2.3	def	2	7.5	3	−7.8
Firestone	5	2.8	7.3	0.3	5	3.1	5.7	2.4	5	1.4	5	−11.4
Uniroyal	6	def	4.8	0.8	6	1.8	4.7	1.6	6	−1.8	6	P-D
Medians		5.1	6.5	0.5		5.2	5.6	2.4		4.7		7.8

Source: Forbes, January 2, 1984.

Community development

Improvement in education and community life in low-income neighborhoods

Legal defense of civil rights

Energy policy studies

Family planning

Professional training for minorities

Clearly, the Ford Foundation, with its resources, is the creator of the wherewithal for research, including action research. Its product then becomes part of the archives that enable scholars to evaluate the research, plan further research, and attempt to offer solutions for the present and the future.

Institute for Social Research

Selecting one foundation to illustrate the archives that foundations generate was exceedingly difficult, and selecting a facility at a university was even more difficult. At best, each illustration is merely intended to call to the reader's attention the archival role.

Considering the realm of social science research, we chose as our example the University of Michigan. Its Institute for Social Research consists of four centers. They are the Survey Research Center, the Research Center for Group Dynamics, the Center for Research on Utilization of Scientific Knowledge, and the Center for Political Studies.

Related to and an outgrowth of the four centers is the Inter-University Consortium for Political and Social Research (ICPSR), which serves social scientists around the world by providing a central repository and dissemination service for machine-readable social science data; training facilities in basic and advanced techniques of quantitative social analysis; and resources for facilitating the use of advanced computer technology by social scientists. ICPSR is organized as a partnership between more than 260 universities and colleges in the United States and abroad.

Some of the major data collections include:

American National Election Studies, 1948–1980

Census of Population and Housing, 1960, 1970, and 1980

General Social Survey, 1972–1982

National Crime Surveys, 1973–1980

National Longitudinal Surveys of Labor Market Experience

Panel Study of Income Dynamics, 1968–1980

Survey of Consumer Attitudes and Behavior, 1953–1976

The depth and scope of the archives gathered by the ICPSR is gleaned from the publication *Guide to Resources and Services 1983–1984*. This book of 479 pages is organized into 17 major classifications, including conflict, aggression, violence, élites and leadership, community and urban studies, health care and health facilities, mass political behavior and attitudes, organizational behavior, and social indicators. The extent of the coverage is indicated by the fact that the documentation and subject index takes up 139 pages, set in rather small print.

Geda (1978), in a paper on social service data archives, most succinctly emphasizes the purpose and importance of archives in the following statements:

> It is rare that the principal investigators of a survey or the original collector of data extract all of the research values from the data. . . .

> Use of these materials for secondary analysis becomes increasingly more critical with the rising cost incurred to conduct a well designed sample survey. . . .

> Replication of original research through retesting hypotheses formulated by the original investigator is feasible only if the raw data are available to other scholars and students of the social sciences.

Archives of a Different Order

In addition to the uses of the archives of the types already mentioned there is another one that should not be overlooked. It is important to recognize that social scientists are not the only developers and users of archives that are pertinent and relevant in describing, understanding, and explaining our social fabric. This additional source, which we consider of inestimable value, includes researchers with varied backgrounds who often are without formal training in the social sciences. These researchers are quite frequently labeled *investigative reporters.* Our usage of that term specifies a sphere more broad than that of the media reporter. It includes all who write books that are primarily dependent on data obtained in the archives.

These are people who are either researchers turned authors or authors turned researchers. The content or substance of their books is often very closely intertwined with some of the most complex problems confronting our society. What is more, these individuals are likely to approach problems or issues in a more general way than social scientists, who are more often encumbered by their methods and discipline. We are not implying that one is better than the other. The point is that they are different and that there is room for both approaches.

The choice of books illustrating the use of archives by investigative reporters is based on our judgment. Instead of the three books we have chosen, any of many hundreds of others would have been equally appropriate. We selected: *The Years of Lyndon Johnson. The Path To Power* (Caro, 1983); *The Politics of Heroin in Southeast Asia* (McCoy et al., 1972); and *Future Shock* (Toffler, 1970). Other books would have been equally appropriate to illustrate investigative reporting; we chose the ones we did because they answer the questions: "Who and what was Lyndon Johnson?" "How did United States foreign policy aid and abet the growth of drugs (especially heroin) since World War II?" and "What does the roaring impact of change have on our lives and the society in which we live?" The books we selected offer rather clear answers. Before discussing the content of the books, we should know a little about the authors' credentials.

Robert Caro's first book, *The Power Broker,* won both the 1975 Pulitzer Prize and the Francis Parkman Prize. He graduated from Princeton and was a reporter for *Newsday,* a New York newspaper. McCoy, Read, and Adams, at the time of publication of their book, were Ph.D. students in history at Yale, in ethnomusicology at Wesleyan, and in history at Yale, respectively. Toffler graduated from New York University and has accumulated a number of honorary doctoral degrees. He has been an editor, a reporter, and a visiting scholar at a few universities.

Since this chapter is about archives, we will make the briefest of references to the content of the books. In considering these books as by-products of archives, it is necessary to emphasize the thoroughly scholarly manner of "researching" used by the authors.

The Years of Lyndon Johnson   Caro spent seven years working on his volume. His resources included such libraries as the Lyndon B. Johnson, the Sam Rayburn, the Franklin D. Roosevelt, and the Austin (Texas) public library. Further, he interviewed many Texans who knew Johnson, among them politicians, friends, neighbors, classmates, associates, and members of Johnson's family. He had nine interviews with Mrs. Johnson. He referred to the Werner file (Werner was the Internal Revenue Service agent in charge of an investigation concerning political contributions to Johnson). Of course, a thorough search was conducted of all the papers, files, and recorded archives of Lyndon Johnson.

The selected bibliography of this volume lists almost 200 separate sources and more than 60 pages of carefully documented notes, all of which are verifiable. If the content of a book can be judged by its index, then it should be mentioned that its entries cover over 30 pages.

All of this is to say that this book meets all the requirements of any scholarly endeavor. The question always arises, for this book and anyone else's research, Are the findings valid? Of course, this question applies equally to experimental data and to archival data. It must be borne in mind concerning archival data that someone else obtained it. This is both an advantage and a disadvantage.

With reference to notes based on interviews, a question that arises is whether the person interviewed actually said what the interviewer reports. The answer may be yes or no, but laws against libel, slander, and defamation of character tend to keep authors and their publishers quite responsible.

Regarding the question of who and what Johnson was, by reading this book one learns much, and this applies to people who were adults during his tenure as well as those who were not yet born.

Information about Lyndon Johnson's childhood and youth indicates that he came from a family of meager, but not destitute, means. His relation with his mother was closer than that with his father. As for his work history and career, with minor exceptions his jobs were in the public sector, generally paying lower salaries, and yet when he became president his fortune was estimated at about $14 million.

Quite revealing about his character was his behavior at college. He flattered and catered to the faculty, dean, and president of the small local college he attended. Fellow students nicknamed him Bull (for bullshit). On the positive side, he was recognized in college as creative, in a political sense, and driven by personal ambition. This stayed with him and propelled him into the highest office in the land.

As a politician he was friendly with such important people as Sam Rayburn, John N. Garner, and Franklin D. Roosevelt (a Speaker of the House, a Vice President, and a President), but to them and others he does not appear to have extended the loyalty that he demanded from those who worked for him. As for his political ideology, he was successful in speaking both as a liberal and a conservative, and this depended primarily on the composition of his audience.

A quote from Caro sums it all up: "A hallmark of Johnson's career had been a lack of consistent idiology or principle, in fact of any moral foundation whatsoever—a willingness to march with any ally who would help his personal advancement" (p. 663).

After reading the Caro book, it is quite possible to believe in the cliché that anyone born in the United States can become president. What is needed is the ambition to become president.

The Politics of Heroin in Southeast Asia   This book is as well documented as it is amazing in its content. There are approximately 1300 bibliographic references as well as firsthand research in Asia and Europe, where the files of newspapers and periodicals serve as the archival sources.

As World War II drew to a close, the disruption of the shipping lanes caused by submarine warfare made it nearly impossible for traffickers to smuggle heroin, and as a result there were fewer than 20,000 addicts in the United States. But "within several years, in large part thanks to the nature of United States foreign policy, after World War II, the drug syndicates were back in business" (p. 6).

To restrict Soviet influence in Western Europe, the Office of Strategic Services (forerunner of the Central Intelligence Agency) formed an alliance with the Sicilian Mafia and Corsican gangsters to fight the local communists. These groups were to be the providers of most of the heroin smuggled into the United States for the next two decades. From this beginning grew the Luciano-Lansky empire that controlled the lucrative drug and prostitution rackets.

In a somewhat related theme, one finds the Office of Naval Intelligence (ONI), concerned with New York waterfront sabotage, engaging Lanzia in 1943 to arrange for an antisabotage surveillance, but this required contact with and help from Luciano, who, even though he was in jail, did help and somehow was then transferred to a lower security prison.

From this point the book thoroughly and painstakingly describes the 4500-mile stretch of land from Turkey through the Indian subcontinent to the mountains of Laos and reveals the people and their officials. With such large numbers of people on all levels dependent on making a living by growing and delivering the "stuff," the consequences of addiction and crime that accompany it naturally follow. The authors take a dim view. They state: "Mafia bosses played a key role in reorganizing the international traffic after World War II but now that the links between the United States and Southeast Asia's Golden Triangle are well established, their retirement could have relatively little impact on the narcotics traffic" (p. 357).

The authors further indicate that the middle-level distributors, retailers, and pushers often have their own habits to support and no amount of police pressure will eliminate this, especially when "most States and local narcotics police are rotten with corruption" (p. 357). They go on to say, "In South Vietnam almost every powerful political leader is somewhat implicated in the sale of heroin to American Soldiers" (p. 359). The last sentence of their book is chillingly penetrating: "American people will have to choose between supporting doggedly anti communist governments in Southeast Asia *or* getting heroin out of their high schools" (p. 362).

Future Shock   The bibliography of Alvin Toffler's book is a veritable anthology of the social sciences. It leads us to believe that Toffler is a true disciple of the interdisciplinary doctrine and without formal training in any of the disciplines. Either that or his prolific and catholic interests encouraged him to search. His bibliography is listed under special topics such as adaption/social, automation, family/sex, science/technology, future studies. The bibliography lists 359 books, monographs, and proceedings, all of which are outstanding in their own right.

In addition, Toffler lists almost 400 notes as part of his references. Again, his selection of authorities and references is both thorough and of high quality. This book is clearly the work of a person who is capable of evaluating and selecting authoritative sources.

We believe that the phenomenon of change has not been sufficiently studied or researched. Change must be recognized not only as directional but also as a consequence of short or long intervals of time. Such change affects individuals, not only from day to day but also over any other time span. Toffler has probably explored the phenomenon of change more than anyone else in a serious fashion, while not encumbered by the chains of a discipline. He believes that change is occurring at an intensifying pace, and as a result it can be overwhelming. His concept of *"future shock"* is used to describe the shattering stress and disorientation induced in individuals who are subjected to too much change in too short a time. Of course, Toffler has much more to offer, and his book is worth reading.

This chapter has emphasized the value of archives as both an existing source of data and a check on what has been reported, believed, or doubted. All of us should be aware of the sources that store archives, recognize the nature of the source, and then make secondary use of the data. Archives are for everyone. We have referred to three books to clearly illustrate that archives are for scholars, students, and laypeople.

One problem must be discussed before bringing this chapter to an end, and we shall refer to it as *chutzpah.*

Chutzpah

Chutzpah is a Yiddish word that is not easily translated. A heroic effort would describe it "as a special kind of boldness, brazenness, or nerve." We believe that those who receive federal funds (taxpayers' money) to conduct research—that is, to generate archives—and who then refuse to share their raw data can only be characterized as having an excessive amount of chutzpah.

Ceci and Walker (1983) review the problem of not sharing data and propose as a solution an open data bank. The problem is that there are researchers who receive federal funds and who regard their research products as private property. Many of those with that belief have a desire for and seek publication in professional journals, but without revealing or being willing to share their data. Such researchers offer many reasons for this belief, most of which sound like our concept of rationalism described in Chapter 1. We tend to accept the view that those who refuse to share their data are primarily concerned that the secondary user may discover procedural irregularities, computational errors, or worse.

Always bear in mind that research provides input for archives. Whatever the source of funding, we believe that science in all of its ramifications is dedicated to revealing or avoiding deception. This means the sharing of data, especially when the taxpayer is supporting the "scholar."

chapter 13

Case Histories

A case history (or case study) is a biographical or autobiographical study and report of an individual, group, or phenomenon. Such information can come from a number of different sources and may include one or more of a number of different data-gathering techniques. For example, one might search existing records, administer questionnaires, conduct interviews, make observations, and even experiment in gathering case history data. In fact, it is advisable to gather as much data as possible to provide as detailed a description of the case under investigation as is feasible.

Prior to about 1950, biographical data and case histories were used fairly extensively, in attempts to understand changes over the life span and responses to stressful events such as natural disasters (Wrightsman, 1981). Since then, and as emphasis on quantitative methods has increased, the use of case histories or studies has declined. Biographical data are often shunned because of the unsystematic and uncontrolled methods of data collection. Carlson (1971), for example, in a review of the major journals in personality and social psychology, did not find a single attempt to study personality development based on biographical data.

Nevertheless, case histories and studies can and do play an important role in the social sciences (e.g., Ross, 1963). In the present chapter we will examine a variety of situations where case histories are used, as well as consider the advantages and limitations of the case history technique. We will use the terms case history and case study interchangeably.

CASE HISTORY SITUATIONS

Case histories are used extensively by physicians and social workers. This is so because, in each case, there is a need for the professional to gather information about a particular client in order to understand the factors that accompany and may have contributed to the existing problem. These data are then used to aid the individual client. In medical work, the bulk of the information involves the results of laboratory tests and family and personal medical history. Such information helps in diagnosis and suggesting prescribed treatment(s). In social work, most of the information centers on the client's occupational and educational history, as well as the results of psychological tests.

Such case histories are routine and are generally used solely by the professional. Rarely are they shared or used by the scientific community. They are not written for public consumption; generally, they are not designed for educational purposes.

Case histories are also used by historians and journalists. In contrast to the case histories of physicians and social workers, the work of historians and journalists is often intended for public consumption and educational purposes. Theodore White's case studies of presidential elections in his *Making of the President* series (e.g., 1973) are outstanding examples of such use. In a certain sense, all history texts can be regarded as case histories written to describe an historical figure (e.g., *Mao: A Biography* by Terrill, 1980); a particular time period (e.g., *A Distant Mirror: The Calamitous 14th Century* by Tuchman, 1978); a certain event (e.g., *Waterloo: The Hundred Days* by Chandler, 1981); or the development of a city, nation, culture, or the entire world. Historical case histories are often prepared by many different authors over periods of time, but are about the same person or situation. For example, there is not just one case history on America, but several hundred. Many books have been written about Richard Nixon and Franklin D. Roosevelt.

In contrast to the "everyday" case histories of physicians and social workers and the work of historians and journalists are the spontaneous case histories written as a result of some sudden, unexpected event. An example is the study of "assembly line hysteria" by Smith et al. (1978). Assembly line hysteria is so named because it occurs in factories from time to time. The scenario is that a number of workers suddenly experience physical symptoms like headache, blurred vision, and nausea following the reporting of a strange odor. Mass fainting may also occur. An outbreak of such symptoms presented the opportunity for Smith et al. (1978) to conduct a case history. They interviewed workers and administered several psychological tests. Their findings suggested that stress in the workplace was the underlying reason for the outbreak of hysteria. Case histories are often the data-gathering technique used to study unexpected events and are, thus, often criticized for not being well planned in advance (McBurney, 1983).

Generally, case histories can be categorized in four different ways (Neale and Liebert, 1973). Some case histories, however, will fit into more than one of these categories. The categories are: behavior examples, method demonstrations, rare phenomena descriptions, and disconfirming evidence.

Behavior Examples

Case histories are frequently written to illustrate a particular *pattern of behavior*. Such case histories have considerable educational value, particularly for those who will eventually have to deal professionally with such behavior patterns.

Consider the student therapist who will eventually have to work with clients diagnosed as schizophrenic. Schizophrenia is a severe form of psychosis and can be described in a number of different ways. One way is to list the primary and secondary symptoms displayed by individuals diagnosed as schizophrenic. Primary symptoms include shallow and/or inappropriate affect, autism, and disorganized speech and thought. Secondary symptoms include delusions, hallucinations, and certain behavioral anomalies (e.g., peculiar gestures, repetitive motor acts). Such a description can be very useful and informative but still does not describe a schizophrenic. The therapist, who will work with individual clients and not with individual symptoms, needs to recognize and understand how these different symptoms are integrated. What is a typical pattern of symptoms and behaviors in schizophrenia? A case history description of a schizophrenic helps answer this question.

Those who have an interest in better understanding a particular pattern of behavior should refer to an appropriate case history. Case histories or case studies provide an excellent description of a total behavioral pattern. Of course, a single case history is not sufficient to give a student therapist a full understanding of schizophrenic behavior, because there is no single schizophrenic behavioral pattern. There are many different patterns. Not all schizophrenics display all symptoms, and the student therapist will find it best to read several case histories. Several are available. Bowers' (1965) case history of David F. illustrates a typical pattern for an acute schizophrenic episode. Green's autobiographical novel *I Never Promised You a Rose Garden* (1964) describes an adolescent schizophrenic. A typical paranoid schizophrenic behavior pattern can be found in Enders and Flinn (1962). Box 13.1 illustrates the case history style with excerpts from McNeil's (1967) case history of Sam P., a chronic schizophrenic.

McNeil (1967), the author of a number of case histories, has indicated that such histories are rarely true when truth is defined very rigorously (i.e., as an exact replication of reality). One reason is that some changes in content are made intentionally to protect the identity of the participant. Another is that clinically consistent events are often substitued for actual events. The resulting pattern is true for a typical schizophrenic although it may not be true for a particular schizophrenic. Some professionals object to this because they believe that it results in the "textbook" case that never occurs in real life. One should realize, however, that even if such case histories were exact copies of a real life, it would still be unlikely that such real cases would ever be replicated in real life. No two people, even when both are schizophrenic, are exactly alike. Case histories that

Box 13.1   THE CASE OF SAM P.

The case of Sam P. is McNeil's (1967) description of a chronic, undifferentiated schizophrenic. McNeil introduces the reader to Sam by discussing his occupation(s):

> Along the Canadian-American border the ease of emigration from one country to another is phenomenal. That's how Sam P. came to America. He turned left in Windsor, Canada, drove over the Ambassador Bridge, rented a furnished room in a suburb of Detroit, and listened intently for the knock of opportunity. The first few things he tried made good sense, but something always went wrong. Without any previous business experience, Sam involved himself in money-making schemes that had an air of optimism and grandeur that was unwarranted by knowledge of the real world.
>
>   . . . A tour of Sam's basement told the story of his business career. One saw the unassembled parts of "revolutionary" fishing reels and poles, a bulky machine that made cement blocks for chimneys, a collection of now illegal punchboards offering prizes for the puncher of the lucky number and, finally, the parts and wiring apparatus needed to install complete home fire-alarm systems. Sam himself pointed out that his judgment looked faulty now but that could have been said for the judgment of men who were now rich and famous for their inventive accomplishments. (p. 175)

Sam displays certain behavioral anomalies that are not unusual for schizophrenics. The behaviors are not exceptionally bizarre but only somewhat different from normal:

> As a person, Sam P. was at first not much more odd than many other people one might meet. He was somewhat intense in his speech and would now and again stare fixedly into space for a moment. Once in a while, he would grimace, stretch his neck muscles, and run his finger inside his collar as if his tie were too tight. After a while this grimace became unnoticeable and was ignored by onlookers. His gestural patterns always interested me because they differed in some puzzling way from the average. Then I discovered that whenever Sam gestured, he did so in what looked like slow motion. Some of his gestures seemed to become frozen in mid-air or to take an interminable time to be completed. I dismissed this as no more than a personal idiosyncrasy. Later I discovered it had deeper meaning. (pp. 175, 176)

Eventually, Sam's behavior deteriorated further, and is described by his wife, Doris:

> Sam P. began to talk about the devil, sin, death, and reincarnation. He stopped working and just sat around the house all day thinking. Doris reported that she would hear him speaking but she discovered he was always talking to himself and never answered her when she spoke. He wore his pajamas all day and began to ask her strange questions—"Would God care if I didn't eat breakfast?" About three weeks after Doris spoke to me about

her husband, he was arrested at 3 A.M. in a small town about 40 miles from where they lived. The police report said he was driving through town at nearly 85 miles an hour when stopped and that he told the arresting officers that he was trying to "get up escape velocity for a trip to Mars."

When Sam left the county jail he was escorted directly to the state hospital (pp. 177–178). In the hospital, Sam went through a period of catatonia, violence, and then became "supernormal in his behavior" (p. 179). While there:

Sam's attention was focused almost exclusively on the chorus of voices that he heard all day, every day.

The voices spoke to Sam about Truth, Wisdom, Justice, and the Meaning of Life. The voices told tales of a place and a way of life in which man's troubles and woes lived only as dim shades in a faulty memory. The voices invited him to relinquish pain and seek solace with them. Once convinced, Sam attempted to become one with them by committing suicide. All his attempts failed and Sam finally abandoned them. He still listens intently when they speak to him and sometimes he replies incoherently. But, the voices have become a commonplace part of his existence and, as such, are not responded to in behavior.

. . . Sam is quiet, does what he is told, and causes no trouble. His reaction times are slow, as are his movements, and he seems numb to the world about him. He is, psychologically, a walking dead man whose inner experience is a secret since he is unable to relate it to us meaningfully. (p. 179)

McNeil reports his own attempts to understand the origin of Sam's difficulties by examining his early life:

I made an attempt to unearth some explanation for Sam's progressive psychological breakdown by asking his wife to relate, in as much detail as she could recall, all he had told her of his early life. This means of studying another human being is only one approach, of course, because it rules out the possibility that Sam's problem was really an organically based difficulty produced by faulty metabolism, improper diet, or brain tumor. It was my belief that his early childhood experience would help us to understand him, so I looked to his early years to comprehend his ignominious end as an adult.

. . . Sam's mother and father had conducted a running battle of 20 years duration. They fought continuously and with whatever weapon was closest at hand. Sam, it turned out, was an only child and became, thus, the instrument of convenience in marital free-for-alls. Sam, for example, was regularly employed as a message-bearer when his parents were not speaking. When the parental argument reached a fever pitch and could not be resolved, each contestant would retreat within himself and brood. Sam was then used as a communication system between them. The scene was a classic one. In earshot of his mother, Sam's father would tell Sam to inform her that he would not be home for supper tomorrow. This message dutifully repeated to the mother

Box 13.1 *(Continued)*

would be acknowledged and a reply phrased such as, "tell him who cares?" His anguish in being asked to play the role of a youthful intermediary was appreciated by both parents, but each took Sam's suffering as evidence of what the other was doing to their son. He was too young to survive. In part, the desperation of his illegal immigration to the United States expressed a need to escape he had experienced for most of his growing life. (pp. 179, 180)

McNeil's conclusions are unhappy:

> Sam had experienced a stressful and perturbing childhood from which he probably emerged scarred and less than a whole person. He had fought his way into adult life trying desperately to be successful, but had failed. With each failure, a greater and greater part of his self had been whittled away. As he attempted to adjust psychologically, increasing stress pushed him to even more desperate psychological defenses. Finally, even these failed, and Sam was rendered helpless in the face of assaults too severe and too unremitting. A state mental hospital became the only kind of safe and protective environment in which he could survive and his existence within it is a minimal kind of life.
>
> ... It is unlikely that Sam will ever rejoin society in any productive role. He has twice been given the full course of electric shock treatments and once underwent insulin therapy. The gains from these therapies were minimal and short-lived. In the eyes of the therapeutic staff members of the hospital, Sam is a hopeless case. He will get cursory contact in the next decade with therapy as we know it today. If he is ever to rejoin society, it will be a consequence of his own efforts or nothing at all. (pp. 180, 181)

are written to provide examples of behavior patterns do just that; they provide outlines of *possible* patterns of behavior.

Finally, it should be noted that the real-life episodes most likely to be replaced by clinically consistent episodes are those that are bizarre or distorted aberrations of the behavior being illustrated. Again, this is done to provide a pattern of *typical* behavior and to demonstrate that even abnormal behavior is different in degree and not in kind.

Method Demonstrations

Case histories are also written to describe how something is done. Therapeutic techniques are often described in case histories, which double as examples of abnormal behavior patterns and demonstrations of new methods used to treat the particular behavior patterns. Virginia Axline's 1974 book *Dibs: In Search of Self** is an example of this approach. She describes the treatment of Dibs, a disturbed child, through the use of play therapy. The child's play reveals much about the troubled family situation, as in the following:

> I had borrowed a world test set and it was in the playroom when Dibs came in the following week. This material consists of many detailed miniature figures of people, animals, buildings, trees, hedges, cars, airplanes, and the like. . . .
>
> "You can build a world with it, if you want to," I said. "There is a sheet to spread out on the floor and those blue strips are for water."
> "Oh, I say! This is very interesting!" he exclaimed.
> "This can be a toy town. I can build it any way
> I want to build it."
> "Yes. You can." (p. 189)
>
> Dibs continues:
>
> "Now then. Where are the children? Oh here is one child. He is going down to the river alone. Poor little child so all alone. And the alligator swims in that river. And here is a big snake. Sometimes snakes live in the water. The boy goes down closer and closer to the river. Closer to the danger." . . .
>
> He placed another child beside the one already standing on the river shore.
>
> "This child is going after the boy," he explained. "The boy is wading in the river now and he doesn't know about the alligator and the snake. But the other boy was a friend and called a warning to him and told him to get in a boat. The boy did get into the boat. See? And the boat is safe. The two boys get in the boat together and they are friends."
>
> He placed the two boys in a boat. (p. 192)
> . . . Suddenly he picked up the fire engine and zoomed it down the street.
>
> "The fire truck is called because the house is on fire and the people are caught upstairs—the grown people. They scream and yell and they can't get out. But the fire truck comes and pours on water. They are as scared as they can be but they are safe."
>
> Dibs laughed softly to himself.
>
> "Why that was your father, Dibs. And that was your mother." (p. 193)

Dibs had built a well-organized world, full of people and action. His plan showed high intelligence, a grasp of the whole as well as the details of his concepts. There was purpose, integration, creativity in his design. The attractive miniature figures intrigued him. He had built a highly developed, meaningful world. There had been hostile feelings expressed directly at the mother and father concepts. There had been expressions of responsible awareness. Dibs was growing up. (p. 194)

Much of the work of the noted child psychologist Jean Piaget is written in case history style. Piaget (1965) describes the normal development of intelligence by carefully describing the methods used to study such developmental milestones as conservation:

The child is first given two cylindrical containers of equal dimensions (A1 and A2) and containing the same quantity of liquid (as is shown by the levels). The contents of A2 are then poured into two smaller containers of equal dimensions (B1 and B2) and the child is asked whether the quantity of liquid poured from A2 into (B1 + B2) is still equal to that in A1. If necessary, the liquid in B1 can then be poured into two smaller equal containers (C1 and C2), and in case of need, the liquid in B2 can be poured into two other containers C3 and C4 which are identical with C1 and C2. Questions are then put as to the equality between (C1 + C2) and B2, or between (C1 + C2 + C3 + C4) and A1, etc. In this way, the liquids are subdivided in a variety of ways, and each time the problem of conservation is put in the form of a question as to equality or nonequality with one of the original containers. Conversely, as a check on his answers, the child can be asked to pour into a glass of a different shape a quantity of liquid approximately the same as that in a given glass, but the main problem is still that of conservation as such. (p. 4)

He then goes on to describe how various children respond to the task and how those responses change over time. Piaget's methods have been used again and again in studies of cognitive development.

Even this book contains case history descriptions of methods. In our description of the group discussion technique (Chapter 14) you will find a case history example of how the technique is used.

Rare Phenomena Descriptions

Every now and then an unusual, unexpected, but significant event will occur and some researchers will decide to study and record it in case history form. We have already mentioned Smith et al.'s (1978) description of "assembly line hysteria." Because such events are rare, the case history is usually the only available technique for describing them. Even if one had the time and available participants to simulate the event, the resulting data, simply and realistically, could not duplicate the reality of such rare phenomena as when an electrical power failure strikes a wide area, or a bridge caves in, or a plane lands on a two-lane road. We can best describe such events and the people involved by constructing a case history of the event itself.

Another, but quite different, example includes descriptions of multiple personalities, which are also rare events. Examples include the famous Eve (Thigpen and Cleckley, 1957); Sybil (Schreiber, 1973); Evelyn (Osgood et al., 1976); and Jonah (Ludwig et al., 1972). Such histories are usually quite interesting and often result in popular novels and movies. The following excerpt is from Thigpen and Cleckley's (1957) description of Eve White:

After a tense moment of silence, her hands dropped. There was a quick, reckless smile and, in a bright voice that sparkled, she said, "Hi there, Doc." . . . There was in the newcomer a childishly daredevil air, an erotically mischievous glance, a face marvelously free from the habitual signs of care, seriousness, and underlying distress, so long familiar in her predecessor. This new and apparently carefree girl spoke casually of Eve White and her problems, always using *she* or *her* in every reference, always respecting the strict bounds of a separate identity. When asked her own name she immediately replied, "Oh, I'm Eve Black."

Looking at the books in the psychology section of a typical bookstore, one might easily get the false impression that multiple personality disorders occur all the time. They do not. In fact they are so rare that they almost always result in a published case history.

In case histories of unusual phenomena, clinically consistent events are not substituted for bizarre events. It is the unusual and bizarre events that are of primary interest in such case histories. Furthermore, there are generally so few cases that it would be a guess, at best, as to what events are or are not clinically consistent. Although changes are still sometimes introduced to protect the participant's identity, the changes are not introduced to replace bizarre incidents.

A case history of an unusual phenomenon that resulted in considerable research and theoretical work was Brenda Milner's (1966) description of the epileptic Mr. H. M. Mr. H. M. had both temporal lobes of his brain removed to treat his severe epileptic condition. The operation cured his epilepsy but resulted in a very strange memory defect; he lost the ability to store new verbal information in memory! All of his preoperation memories were intact, his intelligence did not suffer, his speech was normal, his social behavior and emotional responses were appropriate, but he could no longer remember new verbal information (e.g., a new name, a magazine article, an address, or a telephone number). The case generated a great deal of interest among memory researchers and later work showed that the source of the problem was the removal of the *hippocampus.* Mr. H. M. never did recover his ability to store verbal information in memory. Ten years after the operation the family moved, and after several years he had still not learned the new address. He reports, in Milner's work, wondering whether he has just said anything or wondering what has just happened. He says that it is like waking from a dream, all the time.

Disconfirming Evidence

In a few instances, case histories have provided disconfirming evidence for some supposedly universal aspect of a theoretical hypothesis. If a theory claims that "all X are Z", a case history of one X that is not Z would disconfirm the claim.

The classic example of this type of case history is the one provided by Lenneberg (1962). Lenneberg studied an 8-year-old boy who had a congenital disability for the acquisition of motor speech skills. Before the study many theorists, speculating on how children first learn language, assumed that infant babbling and the imitation/production of speech sounds were essential for language acquisition. Lenneberg's study, however, provided convincing evidence that, although the boy could not speak, he had acquired the grammatical skills necessary for a complete understanding of his language. The study disconfirmed the hypothesis that speech production was necessary for language acquisition.

Of course, many studies which qualify as case histories could be placed in more than one of these four categories. To illustrate, several years ago a husband and wife team raised a chimpanzee named Washoe in their home (Gardner and Gardner, 1969). They taught American sign language to the chimp and detailed their work in a case study. Their case study could be classified as a method demonstration, since prior to their work no one had attempted to teach sign language to a chimp. Their article describes how they did it. They always used sign language in Washoe's presence and they always interacted with her as one would with a deaf/mute child. At the same time, chimps using sign language certainly are an unusual phenomenon, and the case could be viewed as an account of this rare event. Finally, it could be argued that the history of Washoe disconfirms the hypothesis that only humans can acquire language. This latter point is much debated as researchers argue that Washoe never, in fact, learned language (e.g., see Limber, 1977). The point is that a single case history is frequently so rich in information that it can readily defy a simplistic categorization system.

ADVANTAGES

The case history technique of data gathering has a number of distinct advantages. These advantages are related to its exploratory nature, attention to detail, and great flexibility.

Exploratory Nature

When little is known about a phenomenon, the case history technique is often the first choice of interested investigators. Since little is known, the case history technique is ideal. It accepts anything and everything that describes and aids in understanding the phenomenon. This freedom or openness increases the potential for revealing new and important findings that might be missed with a technique having narrower focus.

When a phenomenon first comes under investigation it is frequently difficult to generate hypotheses about its causes or effects. *Case histories, because of their wealth of information, are excellent for generating hypotheses.* Nowhere is this better illustrated than in the work of Piaget. His hypotheses about cognitive development grew, in large part, out of his case studies of his own children. Those hypotheses could then be tested under more rigorous experimental conditions. Such postulations may never have occurred to Piaget without the insights gained from his careful case studies of individual children.

Attention to Detail

The case history provides a detailed examination of a single individual or group. This attention to detail can be quite important for understanding that individual. Individuals that we may be interested in understanding are usually those of some historical importance. For example, Fallows' (1979) work reveals much about the presidency of Jimmy Carter. Carter may have had no overall view of the relations between different positions or no established precedents. Fallows says:

> Values that others would find contradictory complement one another in his mind. During the Campaign he used to say that our nation was the first to provide "complete compatibility" between liberty and equality. This pained me more than anything else he said. I sent him notes and told him in person that these two terms were like city and country, heaven and hell; the tensions between them shape much of American society. But Carter continued to make the same statement, and I realized that it was not because he was vulgarizing his ideas for the crowd, but because he genuinely believed what he said. (p. 42)

It will be interesting to compare Fallows' observations with those of other historians as time goes by.

The work of Sears (1979) attempts to show how Mark Twain's letters and novels were influenced by his own early experiences. Sears matches Samuel Clemens' writings with important life events such as the death of a brother, sister, and father before puberty and the death of his first-born child. Biographies and autobiographies are, for all practical purposes, case histories of important individuals.

Flexibility

Case histories have great flexibility with respect to the choice of a dependent variable. Usually enough information is collected to allow one to examine several different dependent variables at the same time.

Luria's (1968) case history of the mnemonist S is rich in different dependent measures. S was a man with an exceptional memory. For example, after being presented with a list of 70 items, S could recall the entire list, in reverse order, and do this hours, weeks, and even years later. Luria measured S's memory for many different kinds of items, under many different conditions, and over many different time spans (i.e., different dependent variables). S also had an extreme form of *synesthesia*, which is the tendency for an experience in one sense modality (e.g., seeing the color red) to produce sensations in another modality (e.g., hearing music or feeling warm). This synesthesia aided his memory for events by making them "sensational" for him. Later examination of all the dependent measures collected on S revealed some interesting findings. For example, although he could easily remember long sequences of items for long periods of time, he had great difficulty in detecting fairly simple patterns among items. For S, sequence 1 and sequence 2 given below would be equally difficult and equally disorganized:

Sequence 1: A,B,C, B,C,D, C,D,E, D,E,F
Sequence 2: J,M,B, T,L,K, E,F,B, J,S,Y

For you and me, sequence 1 is far easier to remember because of the simple pattern, which involves triplets of letters. That is, the pattern is ABC, followed by BCD, and so on.

The great flexibility with respect to dependent variables allows the investigator to return again and again, often years later, to examine other possible relationships.

LIMITATIONS

The case history technique has some important limitations. They fall into three general categories: internal validity, reliability, and external validity.

Internal Validity

Although the case history technique is excellent for generating hypotheses, it is generally inadequate for testing them. An exception to this rule is the previously discussed situation where the case history provides disconfirming evidence for some hypothesis.

We have already discussed the criteria for establishing a cause-effect relationship between two or more events. The most difficult criterion to reach is the ruling out of alternative explanations for any relationship obtained. The case history technique, with an almost total lack of control over unplanned or unwanted variables, is never able to rule out all possible alternatives. There are essentially no unwanted variables since all information pertaining to the case may be valuable. Thus, it makes little sense to talk of control. *Case histories are not meant to determine possible causes, only to suggest them.*

In many case histories, the investigator will start in the present and search backward over time for *possible* causes, while understanding full well that no cause-effect conclusion can be reached because of the lack of control. Even this search, however, is fraught with danger. All investigators are bound to have certain biases as to what sort of past events may or may not qualify as possible causal sequences. As Freud (1955) noted:

> So long as we trace development from its final outcome backwards, the chain of events appears continuous, and we feel we have gained an insight which is completely satisfactory or even exhaustive. But if we proceed the reverse way, if we start from the premise inferred from the analysis and try to follow these up to the final result then we no longer get the impression of an inevitable sequence of events which could not have been otherwise determined. (p. 167)

The series of events included in the case history and suggesting a possible string of causes and effects may also differ from one investigator to another describing the same event. Different writers will emphasize different events and downplay or ignore other events. This is really quite presumptuous since, at present, no one is able to fully describe the childhood events that produce particular patterns of adult behavior.

Consider the following three cases and try to imagine what the adult person would be like:

Case A: Six-year-old boy. Large head at birth. Thought to have brain fever. Mother lost three other children before his birth and insists he is normal. Relatives and neighbors do not agree. In school, a teacher diagnosed the boy as mentally ill. This angered the mother, who withdrew the child, claiming she would teach him herself.

Case B: Sixteen-year-old girl. Given to grandmother's custody by mother who rejected the homely child. Alcoholic father was fond of her and is now deceased. She has been proven to lie and steal sweets. At age five she swallowed a penny to attract attention. Grandmother is strict with child because she fears she has failed with her own children. Dresses child oddly, allows no playmates, uses braces to straighten child's back, and did not send her to grade school.

Case C: Boy in senior year of secondary school. Physician's certificate states he must leave school for six months due to nervous condition. He is not a good student, has no friends, is a problem for teachers, and was late to speak. He has little athletic ability, which shames father. He has odd mannerisms, chants to self, and made up his own religion.

Could you have correctly guessed that case A is Thomas Edison, case B is Eleanor Roosevelt, and case C is Albert Einstein (Goertzel and Goertzel, 1962)? Individual lives are full of all kinds of events and the writers of case histories tend to emphasize the events that seem most related to the end result. It is always possible that the events downplayed or ignored are the ones that are, in fact, most important.

Reliability

Much of the biographical information included in a case history is provided by the participant. It is to be emphasized that some events are more likely to be remembered and included than others. Some may even be intentionally suppressed. As Box 13.2 suggests, there can be real difficulties in remembering the events of one's life. In many cases, there is no simple way to check the accuracy or reliability of these memories of prior events.

Of course, some events can be compared with objective records. Examples are where an individual was born and when an individual graduated from college. It is also sometimes possible that other persons in the participant's life can be interviewed to check the participant's memory. For example, a participant's reported preference for team sports as a youngster might be checked by talking to parents and childhood friends, when they can be contacted.

Some claims are naturally easier to document than others. If a participant tells us that she had a lot of dolls as a child, lost them in a fire when she was eight years old, and secretly mourned their loss for the next five years, we can check

Box 13.2 MEMORY FOR REAL-LIFE EVENTS

Which came first, the Soviet invasion of Afghanistan or the launching of the first American space shuttle?

Most people have heard of both of these events and remember them, but are unable to tell (without looking it up) which came first. Such difficulties in recalling the events that occur in real life create problems for the author of a case history. For example, the participant may remember that she met her best friend at a sorority party and that her favorite teacher died in an auto accident, but be unable to recall which came first. Unless both events can be objectively dated there may be no way of finding out which came first. Linton (1975) has undertaken a study of real-world events in her own life. Every day she writes down two events on index cards and periodically tests her own memory. Her preliminary data suggest that errors in estimating the dates of events are small for events less than 16 days old and great for events more than 4 months old. The events to be recalled by the typical case history participant are almost always older than 4 months.

Other work, by Garmezy (1971), shows that parents also have great difficulty in remembering events in their children's lives. He reports that "the deficiency is particularly acute in spheres of behavior, such as emotions and affectively-tinged attitudes" (p. 105). These spheres are, of course, the ones that are usually most important for the author of a case history.

You can illustrate some of these difficulties for yourself by trying a little exercise. Write down what you would consider 10 important events in your life. Now see if you can put the 10 events in order from first to last. If the events are older than a few years you will probably have great difficulty in ordering all of them. Now ask your mother or father to do it for you. Do you think he or she can? Try to reconcile your listing and that of your parent(s). Who is right?

some of these claims but not others. For example, a major fire in the participant's house could be documented by a search of old newspapers or city records for the time and place in question. It might, thus, be quite easy to determine whether there was a fire. Parents and/or friends may be able to substantiate the claim that the participant had a "lot of dolls" as opposed to other sorts of toys. This can be slightly more difficult since parents and friends, unlike old newspapers, are not usually kept on file in libraries. If they can be found, they may be able to substantiate the claim that the dolls were lost in a fire.

The final claim seems virtually impossible to check. After all, if the mourning was secret, it is likely that no one but the participant knew about it. The problem is that this last claim may be the most important one for determining the participant's present behavior. It is the truly interesting claim but the one most difficult to check, which is, unfortunately, all too often the situation one encounters in interpreting and evaluating data obtained from case histories.

External Validity

The case history has several difficulties related to its generality or external validity. The first problem is simply one of representativeness. Case histories are not
randomly selected, and it is thus difficult to determine what sorts of individuals
the participant in a case history represents. Cases are selected for deliberate
reasons and often because of their unusual nature. Thus, some case histories are
initially selected because they do not represent any group of individuals at all;
they are unique.

A second problem relates back to the issue of internal validity. Many case
histories serve as behavior examples and method demonstrations at the same
time. For example, the history might describe an individual suffering from some
disorder such as acrophobia (fear of high places) and the treatment administered
to solve the problem (e.g., systematic desensitization). In the conclusion of the
case history, the author might point out that the acrophobia has disappeared and
might wish to generalize his or her belief that systematic desensitization is an
effective treatment for this disorder. Here is the problem. If there was "good"
evidence indicating that in this situation the treatment did relieve the disorder,
then generalizing would be possible. One might still be cautious in generalizing
from a single case, but would have at least some confidence since the treatment
clearly worked in that case. That is not, however, the situation that the author
is in. There is no substantial evidence that the disorder disappeared as a result
of the treatment. It might have disappeared without any treatment at all because
of historical events, maturation, or a host of other confounding variables. One
cannot know with certainty that the treatment was effective in this single case and
one should not attempt to generalize such an unfounded conclusion to new cases.
What could be generalized in such a situation is that the disorder disappeared.
The case history suggests the hypothesis, not the conclusion, that systematic
desensitization is an effective treatment for acrophobia.

Generalizing is always a risky business and only later work can determine
whether or not generalizations will prevail. It should be clear, however, that
adequate generalizations can be made from single cases. In the case just discussed,
one may not be able to generalize the possible effects of treatment or the initial
reasons for the acrophobia, but the acrophobic behaviors themselves probably are
generalizable. Such a case history description of the behaviors associated with a
certain disorder has been used many times and with great generality. For example, Guilleminault and Dement (1977) have used case histories to describe the
"automatic behavior syndrome" experienced by persons with excessive daytime
sleepiness (distinct from narcolepsy). The individual begins to feel drowsy and
attempts to fight it off by becoming active. Performance continues to deteriorate
and the person is less and less aware of his or her actions. Finally, there is
complete amnesia lasting from a few minutes to hours. Following this, the individual is again fully awake and consciously aware. This general syndrome appears
to have great generality for individuals with this particular sleep disorder.

Both the advantages and limitations of the case history technique are related
to the fact that it is a rather comprehensive but often unsystematic examination

of an individual or situation. Everything and anything can be included and there are no adequate controls. Reliability in such a situation is difficult, and sometimes even impossible to determine. These factors make the case history an incredibly rich, but possibly risky, source of information. The detailed description can provide insights and suggest hypotheses that might otherwise have been missed. The writer of the case history must be a scientist with a very open mind and a very cautious approach if this data-gathering technique is to have credibility.

Finally, this chapter has referred to the case history as if it were primarily the endeavor of the scientist. Chapter 12 referred to the work of professionals we labeled investigative reporters. This group gathers data by using similar methods when reporting on individuals and/or events. Such work might well have been included in the present chapter.

chapter *14*

Group Discussions

The group discussion technique described and illustrated in this chapter has been one of the primary research and development endeavors of Blum since 1950. Its evolution has been slow and cautious, although Blum has conducted more than 300 projects using the technique to be described. Through the years, steps and elements in the method have been revised, added to, deleted, and improved. Critical self-evaluation and comments from research sponsors have resulted in changes and improvements.

The research projects conducted can be classified as applied research. This means that they were all conducted under contract or grant and with the limitations of time and budget that such contracts always require. The projects were conducted for business, government, and consumer groups. Some of the industry project sponsors have been General Electric, Time Inc., and Fisher Price. Research was also conducted for the U.S. Department of Commerce, the National Science Foundation, and Dade County in Florida. The Consumer Affairs Institute and the National Consumers League were some of the consumer groups for which studies were conducted.

The technique has had varied application and has been applied to a wide range of problems. Studies for industry have included leisure time activities, the future of stereophonic sound, the design and appearance of various appliances, the evolution of a black doll, and the analysis of games versus toys. These studies are not in the public domain and for obvious reasons are privileged communications. Government and consumer projects have included such topics as the development of a consumer research program, unit pricing, see-through meat tray packaging, posting of gasoline prices, standard setting for liquid crystal thermometers, and the marketing practices of funeral directors. All of these studies were concerned with obtaining data that reflect the attitudes and perceptions of small but well-identified samples of populations who are or may be involved as a consequence of proposed or actual new products or services or proposed or existing ordinances, standards, or laws.

This technique has also been used to research existing products and laws to estimate the extent to which changes and improvements might be considered to influence life-styles in particular and the quality of life in general. Although the technique thus far has been used predominantly for consumer and marketing research, it is by no means limited to such types of research. For example, as suggested in Chapter 4, it could be used to investigate class differences in attitude toward public welfare programs.

Blum previously described some of his work in *Psychology and Consumer Affairs* (1977). One chapter describes and illustrates the technique, which at that time was labeled "interactional workshops." Another chapter reports the results of an interactional workshop comprised of 11 consumer leaders who represented major national and local organizations in the United States. The findings revealed these leaders' goals and unfulfilled needs and methods were suggested to produce more successful leadership in their endeavors. This study also uncovered the problems these leaders were having as a result of limited communication among themselves because of the perceived need to protect one's "turf." An interesting experimental variation in this project was the addition of two persons who, by profession, were qualified to serve as observers throughout the session. The value of this modification was that it provided an immediate feedback to the participants in the form of a critical summary.

While the method is basically qualitative, those with a quantitative bias are especially invited to add quantitative evaluations to this qualitative technique. In the opinion of Blum, the concept phase of the group discussion technique has now been completed. The transition to phase two, the measurement stage, is now taking place. This indubitably means the application of quantitative techniques to further establish the reliability and validity of this form of group discussion.

This chapter's purpose is to report a particular form of data gathering known as group discussion. Of course, compared to other data-gathering techniques it has advantages as well as disadvantages. In addition, it has some known limitations. Some are attributable to certain frailties in the method and others may exist temporarily for the need of additional and more creative efforts.

This chapter defines and describes the method that has evolved. It is also intended to serve as a "how-to" discussion. It covers the role and training of the discussion leader as well as the rationale and steps in constructing the discussion guide, which both confines and encourages free discussion as well as interactions among the participants. Included are such technical aspects as tape-recording, the frame of reference questionnaire, and the role of the assistant. In addition, an illustration and example from a previous research project is offered.

CONCEPT DESCRIPTION

A group discussion is vastly different from a group of people talking. The former involves a limited number of people carefully recruited to satisfy a known set of characteristics and demographics; a trained discussion leader who is familiar with and follows a prescribed set of rules; and a discussion guide prepared with circumspection. The primary objective of a group discussion is to cover the subject matter being explored logically and comprehensively and in a manner that produces valid and replicable findings. The primary purpose of a group discussion is to gather data that contribute to information and problem solving.

The group discussion technique to be described in this chapter has its roots in group psychotherapy. A keen understanding of the operations involved in group dynamics helps. Just as many people believe they can offer counseling on almost any subject without training, so there are many who believe that without training they can conduct group discussions. This is simply not so. One who is interested in conducting a group discussion should first become acquainted with the basics of group dynamics as described in the work of Shaw (1981) and/or Steinger (1972).

A key aspect of the group discussion technique is that it is an outstanding example of qualitative research. In the opinion of the authors, the potential of valid qualitative research has been underused, underestimated, and undervalued. Quantitative research tends to be more readily accepted. Although some qualitative procedures are purely subjective and even frivolous, such negatives are not applicable to the group discussion technique presented in this chapter.

A most important characteristic of the group discussion data-gathering method is that it enables one to probe in depth to learn the reasons *why*. This is one of its advantages.

Quantitative research often reveals how many, rather than why. For example, knowing that 52% expect to vote for candidate X or Y is of value, but once one has that fact, the researcher can only guess why. Qualitative research reveals that among those who will vote for X, reason A or B is cited. Knowing the reasons does not merely satisfy curiosity, it provides the basis for understanding and offers the potential for application.

The evidence from Blum's work is that group discussions, when properly conducted, meet such basic scientific prerequisites as validity, reliability, and appropriate measurability. The same requirements apply to the group discussion technique as to any of the other techniques presented in this book.

It should be noted that there are a number of definitions or varieties of the concepts of reliability and validity (see Chapters 2 and 10). They all have in common that they have been developed to accommodate quantitative data and quantitative methods. It may well be that additional definitions of reliability and validity should be developed that are more appropriate and applicable when qualitative data and qualitative methods are used. For example, the validity of a group discussion can be established when the findings reported conform to the reality that unfolds with time. Reliability can be established by conducting two or more group studies using the same inquiry and participants with similar characteristics and obtaining similar data or results.

Finally, by recognizing that whatever exists is measurable, it is possible to construct the inquiry or discussion guide in a manner that will give an indication of the general intent or direction of the findings, which either support or null the hypotheses being investigated. Sometimes findings are not clear-cut and decisive, but this must be recognized as reflecting the shades of gray or ambiguity that exist.

It is necessary to understand that the planning and conducting of group discussions resemble the planning and conducting of an experiment. The material presented in Chapters 8, 9, and 10 is most relevant and such background knowledge should be understood by anyone wishing to use the group discussion technique.

Briefly, this technique, as well as the experimental method, requires an awareness and identification of at least the independent and dependent variables so that one can readily determine the relationships, if any, between the experimenter's inputs and manipulations and the participants' responses. For group discussions, the independent variable is the discussion guide. The dependent variables are the participants' responses and interactions. Obviously, the output is determined by the input.

WHAT IS MEASURED

Group discussions primarily measure the attitudes, reactions, and interactions of the participants. All of these reflect both individual and group perceptions. Any research technique requires that appropriate degrees of measurement be obtained when measuring physical or psychological dimensions. Sometimes measurements in fractions of an inch are necessary; at other times miles are more meaningful. So it is with psychological measurements. One should not seek micro measures when macro scales are more meaningful and revealing. When minutely precise measurements are not needed, the findings and measurements as a result of group discussions are likely to be more understandable and valid. This seems to be especially so when such psychological concepts or dimensions as ideas, motives, opinions, views, perceptions, attitudes, images of persons or things, and sensory preferences are involved.

Probing for further information during group discussion elicits different results from those obtained when probing in individual interviews and therefore should not be neglected. In the latter instance it is sometimes merely a rationalization of the answer originally offered and rarely results in a shift or change of response. On the other hand, the probes in a group discussion obtain the reasons for the different views of the participants. This does sometimes lead to changes in attitudes and positions among some participants. Such changes can occur for a number of reasons and in cautious as well as risky shift directions (Hong, 1978). The possible reasons for such shifts can be sought by carefully examining the questionnaires and tapes of the group discussion. One thereby obtains a clearer understanding of the *whys* as well as the opportunity to evaluate the various whys in some priority ordering.

Such results lead to considerations of greater scope and on a more broad and comprehensive level. The reactions and interactions of the participants allow for the confirmation or rejection of hypotheses, as well as inferences leading to additional or different hypotheses. It might be recalled that hypotheses serve as tentative explanations of phenomena. The findings as a result of qualitative research, by their very nature, lead to speculations, inventions, and serendipities that are not ordinarily obtained from quantitative research. However, group discussions can serve as preliminary inputs for quantitative research. This is especially true in survey research, where the results of group discussions suggest questions and topics.

Group discussions can also lead to generalizations. Among many examples are perceptions of existing conditions such as the effects of inflation on society or some of its segments. Other examples would be attitudes toward nuclear energy or abortion. In many such controversial areas, knowing the characteristics or variables of the participants in the group discussion is more help in understanding their rationalism of the so-called facts they present than is the manifest content of the positions or statements offered.

Another type of finding can determine how various groups perceive themselves while at the same time showing how they perceive other groups. For example, if groups of leaders from business, consumers, and government were convened separately and each was asked to discuss the same series of issues and problems—such as "unemployment, its causes and cures" or "inflation, its causes and cures"—the results would reveal how each group perceives the causes and cures. They would also reveal how the group projects the other groups' perceptions of causes and cures. Considerable differences in perceptions would be found to exist. Similar exercises with reference to members of different religious groups, ethnic groups, or racial groups would be quite revealing of attitudes toward tolerance, prejudice, social beliefs, housing, busing, food stamps, and so forth.

This technique lends itself to discovering not only reasons for resistance to change but also the potential conditions or situation likely to produce change. Among those who prefer things the way they are, those who really do not care, and those who insist that things will be better as long as they are different, there are also those who, under certain conditions, change views during a group discussion.

Group discussions furnish data not only on the position one takes but also on the intensity of feelings. Attitudinal or behavioral changes (and they are not necessarily correlated or the same) are more or less predictable as a function of the intensity or lack of intensity of the feelings and involvement expressed (e.g., Freedman and Sears, 1965; Petty and Cacioppo, 1979). The greater the intensity, the less likely a change. Those with minimal or neutral feelings are more readily swayed. This applies generally, regardless of whether, for example, the issue is gun control, public rate increases, or divorce. There are those who wish and those who do, and those persons are on both sides of the issue being considered.

Still another and quite different use of group discussions results from the finding called *psychological pricing*, which is the "guesstimate" price of an item. Showing an item such as a proposed food, a toy, an appliance, or a wigwam, one can ask the group participants: "What are you willing to pay for this?" or "What is it worth?" or "What would you say this costs?" By asking people to indicate a price in dollars and cents as well as the reason(s) for the estimate, one can learn the extent to which there may or may not be price resistance or price flexibility between actual cost and the likely purchase. For example, if there were great gaps between actual selling price and psychological pricing for large-screen television, quadriphonic sound, or home computers, then one could predict limited purchases.

An ancillary question might be, "Who would be most likely to buy this?" Since the answer might be "I would," or "a rich person," or "someone who has everything," one can also estimate the likely success of the product. When the likely prospects are considered to be members of socially removed or distant groups, or are from groups that are deprecated, then the signs are negative. If the assignment is to "people like me," then success is more likely.

The key is whether such a product or service is perceived as filling a need. If it is, then it has greater potential than if it is referred to as a gimmick or is considered a passing fad. In summary, psychological pricing offers an estimated dollar and cents yardstick of the item's worth to the individual.

ROLE AND TRAINING OF DISCUSSION LEADER

Whether leaders in general are born or trained may not be clear, but group discussion leaders must be trained. They must know and follow a series of rules or guidelines. In practice, it appears as if a trained and experienced leader is doing nothing but reading a few questions. Nothing could be farther from the truth. Conducting a group discussion is an energy-draining, tiring, and tension-producing experience. Very many things are going on at the same time and all must be observed, manipulated, or controlled. This requires total concentration without a moment's relaxation.

One of the first and most important things that a group leader does is to develop rapport with the participants. This is started by encouraging a cordial feeling as each of the participants arrives for the group discussion. It is necessary to remove any uneasiness caused by the feeling of being a stranger in a strange setting. Exchanging names in a friendly fashion helps to break the ice. Conversing about the weather, distance, and travel conditions encountered on the way to the meeting place, as well as talking about the community, can be helpful in creating a setting to encourage optimal spontaneous participation in the discussion to follow. The group leader encourages talking about any subject, with the exception of the topic or theme of the group session.

To understand specifically what and how a group discussion leader performs requires complete familiarity with the following fourteen points.

1. *Never assume the role of an expert or even of being knowledgeable about the topic being discussed. Further, never be enticed or pushed into such a role by any participant.*

More often than not, participants will tell you what they think or guess you want to hear, and so quite a few will seek more direct structuring than has been deliberately offered. They tend to do this so that they can give you "correct" answers. It should be noted that the answers are correct only insofar as they reflect the participants' own views. Accordingly, it is important for the leader to avoid the "expert" role. This is accomplished by answering questions that seek further information by saying, "I'm sorry, I really don't know but I would like to hear what you think."

The leader should never act as if he or she is knowledgeable about the topic being discussed or even express a view. Authoritarian and "expert" leaders are less effective and seem to produce less productive groups than the more democratic leader conducting a group discussion (e.g., Lewin et al., 1939).

2. *Be passive and not active.*

If leaders in general are expected to be assertive, this surely does not apply to discussion leaders. It is necessary to get other people to talk and keep them talking. The best way to do this is to become a passive and somewhat spongelike person who listens attentively and encouragingly to all. The more the leader conveys the impression that he or she needs help to keep the discussion and interactions continuing, the more valuable will be the content offered. Such task-oriented but low-control leaders are known to produce more productive groups (e.g., Chemers et al., 1975). Participants should have the feeling that the person directing the discussion is pleasant and neutral and one who listens equally to all and equally to all views expressed.

3. *Read the guide.*

A carefully prepared guide must be followed exactly. Assuming that the study includes more than one group discussing the same topic, the guide must never be varied. The guide should be read with moderate expression and convey the impression that the reader is really interested in what is being presented. It must be understood that the guide has been prepared by a qualified technician who may know more about the construction of a guide than the discussion leader. The danger in allowing the discussion leader to modify the guide at his or her discretion is that it introduces variables, the consequences of which are unknown. A strong possibility exists that such variations can have a significant effect on the discussion and its content, which in turn may lead to different or even less valid conclusions.

4. *When questioned about the meaning of what has been read or when asked for clarification, the leader may only reread what has already been presented. The only other alternative is to ask someone in the group to offer his or her answer or comment.*

The leader must not elaborate, explain, or clarify. This tends to introduce information that may bias the discussion. Too often the questioner is either seeking more structure, seeking a clue as to what information is expected or desired, seeking attention, or even trying to establish that the leader is unclear or confused.

In a few instances, the questioner may truly not understand. Encouraging other participants to volunteer to clarify is the best way to handle this type of situation. Because of the need to meet the standards of research objectivity, the leader must perform in a consistent manner and cannot introduce variations in procedure that might vitiate the results.

5. *Be prepared to cope with and handle the wide variety of "oddballs."*

Not all sick people are in mental hospitals and some are likely to be recruited as participants in a group discussion. This type of individual can disrupt a group and wreak havoc with the proceedings. If possible, such people should be intercepted privately and before the session starts. Such a person should be told, in a tactful way, that unfortunately too many people are expected and it is necessary to excuse him or her as well as some others from the session, but that for arranging to attend the session, the full honorarium will be paid.

If the person has not been detected as a potential problem in advance of the session, then extra care must be used in controlling the number of times and the length of time that person speaks. Care must be taken by the leader to avoid any personal reaction to that individual, no matter what the provocation. The leader cannot allow such a person to win sympathy from the group. A way of controlling this type of situation might be to ask, "Can we hear some additional ideas from the rest of you?"

The leader must also be prepared for those who come to the group under the influence of alcohol or drugs. These people are generally easier to detect and intercept.

6. *Know how to handle the aberrants.*

All people are not alike or equal, and so in any group one encounters the brilliant one, the pseudo-brilliant one, the silent one, the shy one, the verbose one, the self-styled humorist, and the attention getter, among others. Fortunately, these characters do not all show up at the same time to constitute a group. But sometimes some do. The leader must be able to handle and control these "normal deviant." If possible, the leader tries to overlook the particular idiosyncrasy and deal with the aberrant as if all were normal. In so doing, the leader should concentrate on equal time for all. This will obtain maximal meaningful participation or contributions from the more normal people in the group. When this does not work, the leader must encourage greater participation from those who are less troublesome and even pretend not to see or not to hear the problem creator. Try to remember that all must be accomplished with tact. No participant should be made to feel rejected and all should be encouraged to participate.

7. *Keep on schedule.*

Experience has indicated that the optimal time frame for a group discussion is about 2 hours. In recruiting, emphasis must be placed on the importance of starting and ending on time as not only fair, but necessary. When people arrive late it means either postponing the scheduled start or starting on time and having a disruption because of a late arrival. Both are to be avoided. Both can be minimized by emphasizing this point when recruiting the participants.

Depending on the number of discussion areas and their relative importance, each may be scheduled for as little as 5 minutes to possibly 20 minutes. The easiest schedule plan is to have 12 discussion areas lasting 10 minutes each. Allocating minutes to each discussion area in advance is most practical. In addition, the leader should evolve a simple time-keeping scheme for starting each discussion area in order to run reasonably close to schedule. While one need not be obsessive or compulsive and one should not interupt an ongoing discussion if it is yielding rich results, it is nevertheless necessary for the leader to cover all discussion areas with reasonable fairness and completeness. Limited discussions with excessive crowding or rushing as one approaches the end of the scheduled time can be devastatingly harmful, especially since the last few discussion areas are likely to be more germane to some of the specific information needed than the discussion areas at the beginning of the session. All guides are developed by starting with the more broad and general areas and then becoming more specific in terms of the topics being researched. Accordingly, the early part of the discussion often provides background information and the end offers keys to the problem solutions. If one actually runs behind schedule, then the group should be informed that an additional 5 or 10 minutes are needed. Being told that the discussion is running behind because of the value of the information offered by the participants pleases most of them and they are cooperative. It is advisable to announce that if anyone must leave at once they may do so. Very few, if any, ever leave, and if they do it is often because of a hopeless inflexibility in their schedule.

8. *Know when and how to probe.* *

A probe is necessary when the discussion leader judges that a participant's answer could yield richer information, or needs clarification, or that additional information would shed considerable light on what has already been expressed. The skill in probing is to get the person to say much more (in meaningful terms) than has already been said. However, the probe is used to obtain this additional information without leading the respondent or in any way suggesting additional information that could be slanted, tilted, or inclined to support the leader's views. The best probe occurs when the leader does so with hardly a pause and almost immediately after the respondent has finished the sentence and stops talking. Among the appropriate probes are: "Why?", "Tell me more," "Please explain what you just said a little more," and "Because?"

When probing, the leader must never suggest possible answers. This is like putting words into the respondent's mouth. Equally inappropriate is leading the respondent by subtle, or not so subtle, clues submitted either verbally or behaviorally. Some verbal "no-no's" are: "That's great," "You are absolutely right," and "That's exactly what I wanted to hear."

Behavioral cues or leads are given when the leader makes a face, scowls, or uses hand gestures or even body movements that encourage or discourage what is being said.

The use of probes makes one a better listener. The more you listen to others, the fewer mistakes you make and the more you really learn about what the group is saying. Probing is valuable but should not be overdone. Probe when you believe the additional verbalization will add to the meaning of the content already revealed.

*This is probably the most important item on the list.

The "Because?" probe is most effective, especially when the leader has the respondent believe that his or her sentence may have been incomplete and the probe is perceived as a need to either finish the thought just expressed or add to it. A good prober always gets the person to say much more than might have been originally intended. A value of probing in the group discussion is that it encourages increased spontaneous interactions and leads others to talk or even ask each other questions.

9. *Differentiate between left field and serendipity.*

People do not always speak clearly, briefly, and concisely. Quite the contrary, people have wandering thoughts and are not always precise. Because of this, people also offer answers that are sometimes not related to the question but nevertheless reflect creative ideas. When the conversation among the participants gets off track, the leader must decide whether the respondent's comments are out in left field or are the beginning of a remark classifiable as a "rare gem." If it is the former, then the leader runs the risk of having a difficult time getting the group back on the topic. When that happens, the leader must cut in. One way of doing this would be for the leader to reread the original question at this time. However, the leader who is listening carefully might well decide that it is worth the risk to continue, even though the conversation may seem to be off the track. It is those risks that allow for the rare creative comment. Such a contribution can lead to the serendipity that fills the gap in knowledge and this may happen independently of the question asked or the discussion that was originally planned.

10. *Know what to do when challenged.*

At times, a participant may misinterpret the leader's passivity for weakness and decide that this person needs help. The help generally takes the form of attempting to take over the group discussion. At other times, an assertive and aggressive participant believes that he or she could handle the discussion in a better fashion and decides to do so. When this happens it is more serious than funny. In any event, the leader is challenged. The leader must avoid squelching the challenger on the one hand, or giving ground on the other. An appropriate way to handle the situation is to suggest to the individual that "the help offered is appreciated but it is important that equal time be given to all and I'm sure you understand why that is fair."

11. *Know when and how to use the "round-the-table" technique.*

While discussion and the order in which people speak must have maximum spontaneity, it sometimes happens early on that the group establishes a pattern for itself in which two or three people do most of the talking and the rest nod their heads (such nodding is never heard on the tape) in either agreement or disagreement. It is at such times that something has to be done. This is where the round-the-table technique comes to the rescue. It is introduced by the leader announcing, after reading the specific discussion guide item, "Let's discuss this by going around the table and let's begin with ——— on my right (or left)." The round-the-table technique may postpone interaction until all have spoken, but it reintroduces the concept of equal time for all, which is helpful in obtaining the participation of all in the group.

This technique may also be planned as part of the procedure in the guide simply as a change of pace. It is quite effective when "psychological pricing" items are discussed.

12. *Encourage interaction among participants.*

A considerable advantage of the group discussion as a data-gathering technique is that it creates a setting for people to interact. This also allows respondents to react to the ideas of others. As a result, either reinforcement or disagreement is evident.

When a group is interacting with maximum spontaneity, that is exactly when interpretation, understanding, and evaluation of findings are optimal. At these times, the researcher can determine which ideas or positions are more, rather than less, acceptable to others. Such interactions yield information leading to estimates of the likelihood of consensus or the possibility of one view prevailing over another.

There are times when an assembled group does not interact sufficiently and because of this the session becomes dull. Under such circumstances it is advisable for the leader to encourage discussion. One way is to ask whether there are "any other ways of looking at the view that has just been expressed," then pause, remain silent, and make eye contact with one or more people. If this does not encourage volunteers, then it is advisable to ask a participant directly, "What do you think?" It is then advisable to call on the participant whom you judge might be able to get things started.

13. *Always exercise control over the group.*

Once lively interaction takes place it can feed on itself and become excessive. Participants sometimes heatedly talk to and challenge each other and may unintentionally disregard the leader's attempt to regain order. It is equally important to control those who take issues personally and who may offend the feelings of others.

The leader must be prepared to stem, in a good-natured way, any overly intense interactions that might lead to excessive emotional expressions, insults, or unfortunate expressions of prejudice. On the other hand, it is also important for the leader to help the group break through the middle-class syndrome of passive politeness.

14. *Know how to start the group.* *

Once the group has assembled, all participants are invited to take a seat around the table, "because we will now have our discussion." First, and in a friendly conversational tone, all are thanked for attending, and then the leader states:

"We are going to be having a discussion and there are just a few simple rules. We want your candid, frank, and honest opinions. Please remember there is no such thing as a right answer or a wrong answer. It is your opinion that counts; therefore feel free to say what you think. In addition, feel free to disagree with any of the opinions already expressed. Just because someone expressed a view before you did does not mean that it is any more right than your view.

*This item is listed last because it is assumed that one cannot start a group without first knowing what to do.

"Because we are on tape (point to the microphone) and we will be analyzing the discussion at a later time, please talk one at a time. Also, would you please avoid whispering and private conversations with your neighbors. Talk loud enough for the group to hear you and for the tape to pick it up.

"Just one more thing, from time to time you will be filling in your answers on a questionnaire before discussing. Please do this according to the *way* you think."

A variation of these instructions is used when the group is more sophisticated and might interpret the former instructions as "talking down" to them. Its format is as follows:

"In conducting this session I will ask you to please observe a few rules:

"As you see, we are taping the session for analysis and report purposes, so please speak *one* at a time and *loud* enough for us to have your 'gems of wisdom' recorded.

"Avoid private and whispered conversations. We pick them up on the tape and sometimes hear what is not on the agenda.

"Try to cooperate by considering the other participants and allowing for equal time.

"Feel free to agree, disagree, change your mind, and register doubts, but please state your views in relation to the topic being discussed.

"Recognize that my job as discussion leader is to keep on track and on time, so state your points fully, but no speeches, please."

ROLE OF ASSISTANT TO GROUP LEADER

To reiterate, conducting a successful group discussion is a most difficult task—except for those who have never tried to conduct one. A factor contributing to the success of a group discussion is the recognition that a leader must have an assistant in attendance. The assistant is trained to become an objective observer as well as to perform specific tasks. Having a trainee serve as the assistant provides the advantage of training while doing. (Referring to relevant sections of Chapters 7 and 14 is helpful.)

The assistant runs the tape recorder, makes certain that it is recording, and changes tapes as necessary. He or she also takes notes of the highlights of the session as it evolves. These notes, which serve as summaries, allow for speculation or interpretation of the meaning of what was said exactly when it was said. The trained assistant also records his or her observations of the proceedings as they occur. in this respect the assistant is an invaluable aid to the leader, and both should immediately review what took place as soon as the participants leave. This should include further writing up of what took place and when. This adds flesh to the bones that the tape analysis provides and makes for a much richer and more humanistic report. Incidentally, among the effective ways to train a discussion leader is to have one person function as an assistant for quite a few sessions.

GROUP CHARACTERISTICS AND RECRUITING

The preferred number of participants in a group discussion is generally between eight and nine, but it is possible to gather meaningful data with as few as 6 or as many as 12 people. One should consider that there is a relation between the length, scope, and depth of the group discussion and the number of people in the group and their characteristics.

More than 12 may convert the group into a crowd. Fewer than 6 places too much responsibility on those people present and their interactions. If one person in a group of 10 is a severe problem, it is not as serious as if one such person appears in a group of 5 or 6.

More important than the number of people attending is need for the group members to have the characteristics assumed to be necessary to contribute to a meaningful discussion related to the problem under investigation. For example, if one wanted to learn about the characteristics necessary to create a highly desirable black doll, it could be an error to obtain suggestions solely from a group of white mothers. More meaningful and complete data would come from a group of black mothers. Or, for example, if one wanted to learn about the attitudes of the bereaved toward funeral directors, it would be advisable to convene a group who recently had direct contact with funeral directors rather than a group who had recently attended a funeral service.

The decision regarding the necessary characteristics of the people in a group depends first on the problem and then on the determination of a range or cross section of people with those characteristics.

When a study is concerned with a broad topic with which a very large segment of the population is involved, recruiting and selection are quite different from those for a problem of more narrow concern. If the study involves an almost universal type of problem such as food labeling or inflation or auto repairs, then purchasers/consumers of all ages and socioeconomic status are likely to be involved. To ensure coverage of that broad a range of people, the grid technique is most useful.

For example, to recruit people with a wide range of ages and incomes would require a grid with nine cells. One variable would include three age range categories and the other would include three income categories. The following grid is suggested.

	Income		
	Less $15,000	$15–29,999	Plus $30,000
Age 45+			
26–45			
25 or less			

Recruiting within this range for these two variables can guarantee three low-income people varying in age, three middle-income people varying in age, and three upper-income varying in age. This technique recruits nine people who represent a broad cross section of the population. On the other hand, the problem may require studying a more limited population. For example, it may be concerned with funeral costs in relation to funeral directors' practices. Recruiting on the basis of age and income might obtain very few individuals with actual experience. It would therefore be more appropriate to recruit people who in the last six months were responsible for arrangements and expenditures related to a relative's funeral. The variable might be to select people from low-income, middle-income, and upper-income neighborhoods. Another variable might be to select participants based upon differences in religious, ethnic, or racial groups.

Many cares and precautions must be exercised in the recruiting process since the person recruited must attend and not be a "no-show." If a prospect indicates hesitancy, the use of pressure in recruiting can be fatal. The person will say "yes" without really intending to attend. Sometimes as few as two "no-shows" can devastate a group discussion.

Recruiting is most effective when a chief recruiter works with three recruiters. Each one recruits from a different area within a geographic community that is known to reflect differences in age, income, ethnicity, and so forth. Each recruiter randomly contacts prospects either by phone or house-to-house visits in order to determine a person's interest and willingness to attend the discussion at a specific time, date, and place. Prior to confirmation the prospect is checked with the chief recruiter to see if the characteristics of the individual fit an open cell in the grid. When they do fit, either the recruiter or chief recruiter calls back to confirm the arrangements. Since people forget, change their minds, or other events arise, it is absolutely necessary to contact the potential participant a day or two before the session. If the arrangements are confirmed, then in all probability the person will attend. If an excuse is offered, then it is necessary to resort to a list of alternative prospects and make the necessary roster changes.

Participants must never be members of the same preformed group, such as a ladies auxiliary group of fire fighters, or a church choir, or any group where people know each other and have a "pecking order." The greatest degree of spontaneity occurs when people have not already made the judgments about friend or foe that probably exist in any preformed group.

People in a discussion group should generally not know each other, with one exception. It is permissible for one person to know one other person in the group. This practice encourages a more timid or shy person to attend, who might not otherwise attend.

Group discussions should preferably take place at a motel that is convenient to reach and has secure and safe car parking facilities. The motel represents a neutral meeting place and is more appropriate than an office, a home, or a college.

The seating of the participants must be considered. Most desirable is a round table large enough to seat a dozen people comfortably. The advantage of a round table is that it has no head or foot. All participants can easily see each other. Somehow circles promote group cohesion to a much greater degree than oblongs, rectangles, or squares. The cohesiveness also promotes more informality and relaxation than the other types of seating arrangements, which create distances from the leader, status positions, and other types of disadvantages for the flow of conversation. The final question to be considered is whether one does or does not pay the participants. Of course, one does. The view that paying participants at the end of a group discussion influences what they do or do not say is nonsense. Depending on the city, time of day or evening, average travel distance and cost to reach the meeting place, and likelihood that a participant may need a baby sitter, $15 to $20 in the early 1980s was surely a modest sum. Payment only acknowledges that in return for information the participants deserve a moderate material thank-you.

THE DISCUSSION GUIDE

The key to the value of the data obtained is care and planning in constructing the guide that forms the basis of the discussion. For a guide to have the greatest value and be most productive, a few simple principles must be observed.

Principle 1. A guide contains a series of discussion areas and not a number of narrow and specific questions of the type more typically used in survey research. The major purpose of a discussion area is to present the field being explored in a sufficiently unstructured or semistructured manner to elicit different interpretations as well as different points of view. Obtaining interactions that lead to better understanding of why, rather than direct answers to questions, is most important.

Principle 2. The researcher must clearly understand and define the problem. This is the primary step. It is a prerequisite to any procedural planning. In academic circles the researcher often invents or decides the problem to be researched. In the more practical and applied world, the researcher is commissioned to do the research. The client or research sponsor or grantor is frequently not adequately trained in data-gathering methods. The donor, who may or may not be emotionally involved, is quite likely to misstate the problem or confuse it. Worse, the research problem may be stated in terms of a preconceived solution, making the research itself an exercise in futility.

The researcher must therefore first and foremost restate to the client what the research problem is so that both understand and agree on the problem to be researched. Second, the researcher must decide whether the problem is researchable and, if so, which of the many data-gathering methods is to be considered and used. Once the problem has been adequately defined and the decision has been made that the group discussion technique is appropriate, the development of the discussion guide is planned.

The discussion should be planned to start with a coverage of the broader aspects of the problem and to encourage an orderly and logical flow of thoughts.

The guide and the discussion then proceed from the general to the specific. Figuratively speaking, a most successful guide is constructed to resemble an inverted pyramid. It starts with a broad-top and narrows to a pointed base.

Principle 3. Having defined the problem and the broader aspect of developing a guide that will result in data gathering, it is then necessary to construct the guide. In this respect, the first step is to develop an outline as well as a rationale that includes the points, topics, or areas that conceivably have a bearing on the problem. The second step requires the listing, arranging, and rearranging of the points to be covered in the discussion and in a logical order. This means that one aspect of the discussion will naturally lead to the next. While doing this, 10 or 12 (or fewer or more) major discussion areas must emerge which cover all aspects of the problem being investigated, from the most broad and general areas to the most specific and pointed areas directly related to the problem.

Principle 4. A frame of reference questionnaire which allows participants to respond individually and privately is a necessary accompaniment, if not an integral part of the discussion guide. A problem inherent in any group discussion is how to eliminate, neutralize, or hold constant the excessive effects that one or two participants may have on the group. Equally important is the need to preserve the objectivity of the discussion leader and the tape analyst in the data-gathering process and data analysis. They must not be swayed or biased by the rhetoric or position of the more vocal participants.

These are concerns of considerable significance, especially because the data and their analysis are based on information from small samples. Such difficulties are reduced, if not avoided, by the deft use of the frame of reference questionnaire.

At various times during the discussion, the leader reads from the specific discussion area, as it is worded in the guide, and requests the participants to write their answers on a frame or reference questionnaire before discussing them. This request might take the form of: "List the two most important reasons, in order of importance, on the questionnaire," or "Identify by letter which of these objects you prefer most," or "What would you pay for this, assuming you would be willing to buy it?"

This specific technique accomplishes at least three desirable and preferred results. First, it pins down an individual's initial response before it can be influenced by any other person's response. Second, it enables the leader to obtain independent data from *all* individuals and before any interactions can influence responses. Third, it crystalizes and identifies the factors that are capable of contributing to changes of views.

With some frequency, respondents will comment "I did not previously consider what has been mentioned and I wish to change my answer." The competent leader responds with, "Of course! What was your response, what do you want to change it to, and why?" A concomitant use of the frame of reference questionnaire is that it serves as a guide to the data-gathering analyst as well as to the report writer (who may or may not be the same person as the discussion leader). These data provide objectivity since they can serve as a guide in fairly reflecting the various points of view as well as the range of responses. They also have value in helping to resolve the problem of how many quotes should be used to represent which point of view. The questionnaire tallies—be they six for and three against; or three, three, and four for three different views; or eight undecideds and two against—can add objectivity to the omniscience of the report writer.

Furthermore, the questionnaire enables the leader to examine shifts in position in much the same way that others (e.g., Malamuth, 1975) have done. Such information is very useful in generating hypotheses about factors that produce changes in point of view.

AN ILLUSTRATION

The data gathered at a group discussion are based upon the rationale, discussion guide, and frame of reference questionnaire. Our illustration is taken from an unpublished study conducted in 1981 by the Consumer Affairs Institute (Blum, 1981). The study objectives were to obtain an indication of attitudes and reactions toward some samples of liquid crystal thermometers (LCTs) sold over the counter, and in comparison with other types of thermometers. Liquid crystal thermometers measure human forehead temperature as differentiated from oral or rectal measures.

The purpose of the study was to provide data to a committee that was considering whether it was propitious at this stage in the technological development of liquid crystal thermometers to recommend or not recommend the setting of voluntary or mandated standards and, if so, of what type.

As in many research problems, the time and budget limitations strongly influenced the decision about the kind and amount of data to be gathered. Faced with this reality, it was feasible to conduct two group discussions with subjects likely to yield the most meaningful results. Accordingly, a lay group and a professional group became the basis for the data gathering.

To obtain an optimal amount of information from the lay group, three population segments of frequent temperature takers were selected. These included mothers with at least one child younger than 1½ years of age and mothers with a child 5 years or older. The third segment included grandmothers. These ladies are frequently involved with their grandchildren's health care. In addition, they are an aging group and as such are more likely to have health problems and a need for temperature taking than younger adults.

The professional group included three segments. The first was comprised of three specialized medical doctors (an internist, a dermatologist, and a surgeon). The second segment included three nurses (hematology, geriatrics, and neontology), and three paramedics (licensed practical nurse, nurse's aide, and medical homemaker).

The rationale for developing the discussion guide is presented in Box 14.1.

Box 14.1   OUTLINE AND RATIONALE FOR DISCUSSION GUIDE ON LIQUID CRYSTAL THERMOMETER STUDY: LAY GROUP

The first discussion area was planned to have each of the participants discuss the last time they took their own or someone else's temperature. This was done by having them refer to a card that listed six items as follows:

Box 14.1 *(Continued)*

(a) Why you took the temperature
(b) What instrument you used
(c) How it was used
(d) Why that particular instrument was used
(e) Length of time lapse in taking temperature
(f) What the temperature reading was and, based on it, what you did

The rationale for starting the discussion in this manner was to have it serve as a warm-up to get people talking, to obtain information about the mechanics of temperature taking, and to learn about the human interest elements. The plan was to compare the similarities and differences among the discussants, especially with regard to motives, behavior, and attitudes toward temperature taking and their perceptions of normal temperature as compared to fever. Likes and dislikes of measuring instruments and usage can also be obtained from this discussion area.

The second area requested the participants to indicate whether they believed that the temperature, as indicated on the thermometers they used, was extremely accurate, rather accurate, or an approximation. The rationale was to determine the extent to which a thermometer is expected to be or considered to be a precision instrument.

The discussions were also expected to yield information about the degree of satisfaction or dissatisfaction with the thermometer as an indicator of temperature. It can be assumed that a thermometer judged to be imprecise or inaccurate could not be "trusted." The third area raised the problem of errors either as a result of the instrument itself or because the individual does not read the scale correctly. The rationale for this inquiry was to determine whether the probability of error was a disturbing factor. It is a further exploration into accuracy expectations and concern or anxiety about the accuracy of readings.

The next area presented the supposition of buying a thermometer and attempted to learn the relative importance of five potential influences or influencers in such a purchase. The five included clerk in store, doctor, personal experience, pharmacist, and printed material such as an insert or a display card.

The rationale recognized that any purchase decision is the result of many factors and this area covers the relative importance of five likely influences in the purchase of thermometers. Since LCTs are newer, it is assumed that they will be used to the extent that they have advantages over the mercury-type thermometer. Beyond satisfaction or dissatisfaction with the mercury thermometer, this area attempts to estimate the believability and acceptance of influences other than personal experience. By using a three-point rating scale, each item's relative strength can be estimated. The whys of the "very important" category are also expected to furnish leads as to problems related to standards.

The next area most simply attempted to ascertain the lay person's confidence in temperature readings and the extent to which the reading suggests contacting a doctor or taking certain personal action. In terms of rationale it is a further attempt to learn what people do after they obtain a thermometer reading and what reading is regarded as critical.

The discussion to this point gathered information on thermometer usage, expectation, satisfaction, and influences regarding usage, as well as the role of the doctor, among others. At this point, the planned discussion shifted to learn the extent, via recall, to which the participants were familiar with types of thermometers other than the one(s) they use. The rationale recognized the need to establish the extent to which thermometers, other than the one used by them, are known to the participants. This could also furnish leads as to reasons for not using these other thermometers.

Having an indication of the extent of familiarity with thermometers by using the technique of recall, the discussion shifted and was based on reactions to actual physical stimuli such as showing, demonstrating, and reading display material. The purpose was to provide further information about two different liquid crystal thermometers by obtaining reactions to them and in comparison with oral and rectal thermometers and a model of a battery-operated thermometer. This was planned to be accomplished in three stages. First, the five thermometers were shown one at a time. The thermometers included were: oral (Ballo), rectal (Ballo), LCT (E-Z Temp), LCT (Clinitemp), and battery-operated (L.G. Electronic). The participants were asked to indicate how familiar they were with each and to rate it as a temperature indicator. The rationale for this phase of showing was based upon reactions to the five samples to determine the differences, if any, in the recall or recognition of different types of thermometers, that is, talking about them or actually seeing them. When the thermometers are actually shown it can be expected that changes in performance expectations and perception will be more specifically a result of appearance. Such information furnishes leads on the basis that seeing can result in more concrete reactions than the reactions of a more general or abstract kind elicited by recall.

A further probing was obtained by demonstrating the three least familiar thermometers—the two LCTs and the battery-operated one—and asking for reactions. The rationale is most simple and direct. By demonstrating the three (assumed) less well known and less used thermometers, direct reactions can be obtained and compared with the reactions to the two more commonly used thermometers.

In the third stage, a more intensive exploration took place. The display material of each of the thermometers was duplicated so that each participant could read it in its entirety. Each was asked to react to one model at a time by stating what they thought about it and then suggesting improvements. The rationale was to learn how clear, confusing, effective, and so forth the written material was and, more important, to determine the degree to which the material provided relevant information about the performance of the instrument, how to use and care for it, and such other items that might be related to a problem definition.

Box 14.1 *(Continued)*

The next discussion area was assumed to be most critical for this aspect of the project. By immersing the participants in a concentration of thinking about the thermometer use and expectations, and by doing this on a step-by-step basis from general talk, to showing, to demonstrating, and to careful reading of the display material, one could assume that the participants could now react on a "best basis" of knowledge, encouraged by interactions, rather than superficial or even biased uninformed opinions. We believe that opinions expressed are more valid when they are offered as a result of providing information rather than assuming that a knowledgeable basis for the opinion exists.

The participants were then asked to indicate what should appear on a display card. The responses, it is expected, will highlight the information that is critical from a consumer viewpoint. The potential is to compare use and expectation with the intention of having them more closely aligned. Comparing this listing with the items on various display cards can clearly differentiate nonessential (from a consumer point of view) promotional material from that which the consumer has a right to know. It can also allow for determining similarities and differences between labels pointing to superior and inferior aspects. Further, it can serve as a basis for a set of guidelines for the "ideal" display card which might become the standard.

The last two areas discussed are related to psychological purchasing. The first requested the participants to indicate the models or types of thermometer they would most likely buy and least likely buy, first without knowledge of price and then with price information furnished. This is referred to as psychological purchasing because one cannot assume that asking a person to indicate what he or she is most likely to buy is equivalent to an actual purchase. It is psychological because it is based on appearance, preference, perception, and not on an actual purchase behavior. The rationale was to identify the most likely purchase and least likely purchase of the five thermometers discussed and, more important, to ascertain the reasons for the choices.

The last area introduced the variable of price to determine the relation between higher and lower costs and a thermometer's perceived cost/value. Further, it attempted to gather information about whether price/quality/accuracy is or is not related to price.

In summary, this discussion guide has been planned to provide inputs on problems definition as a guide to considering standards, by having a lay group, as realistically as possible, talk about problems and concerns of temperature taking in general and certain types of thermometers in particular.

The actual panel leader's guide and frame of reference questionnaire used in this study are presented in Box 14.2:

**Box 14.2   DISCUSSION GUIDE—LIQUID CRYSTAL THERMOMETER STUDY:
              LAY GROUP**

1. Tell me about the last time you took your or someone else's temperature.
   (SHOW CARD) Please refer to items on card as a guide.
   CARD 1.
   (a) Why you took the temperature
   (b) What instrument you used
   (c) How it was used
   (d) Why that particular instrument was used
   (e) Length of time lapse in taking temperature
   (f) What temperature reading was and, based on it, what you did
2. Talking generally about temperature taking, would you say that the
   measurement, reading, or indicator of degrees on the thermometer you
   use is extremely accurate, rather accurate (plus or minus 1°), or at best
   an approximation. On the questionnaire next to no. 2 and before discussing place an X next to the item that indicates your belief. What did you
   answer and why?
3. There can be two kinds of errors in temperature reading. One is that the
   instrument itself is inaccurate and the other is that the person does not
   read the scale correctly. Are either or both of these possible errors a
   problem for you? On the questionnaire next to no. 3 enter a yes or no
   next to instrument and/or reading error.
   (a) What did you answer and why—for instrument?
   (b) What did you answer and why—for reading error?
4. Suppose you were going to buy a thermometer tomorrow. In making
   your purchase would you say that each of the following would not be
   important, rather important, or very important. On the questionnaire
   next to no. 4, place an X in the appropriate place next to:
   Clerk in store
   Doctor
   Personal experience
   Pharmacist
   Printed material on insert or on display card (SHOW SAMPLE)
   (a) Which items did you indicate were very important and why?
   (b) Which items did you indicate were not really important and why?
5. What relation, if any, exists between temperature taking and contacting
   your doctor?
6. Are you familiar with types of thermometers other than the type you last
   used? On the questionnaire next to no. 6, list the type you last used next
   to (a) and next to (b) list the types you are also familiar with. Tell me
   about those mentioned in (b).
7. I now want to show you a display of five thermometers. Before I describe
   any let's talk about number 1. (SHOW ORAL) How familiar are you
   with it? On the questionnaire next to no. 7A #1 indicate not at all

Box 14.2 *(Continued)*

familiar, somewhat familiar, or very familiar. Would you say a ther-mometer of this type is poor, adequate, good, or excellent as a tempera-ture indicator? Enter either poor, adequate, good, or excellent next to no. 7B#1.

(a) How familiar are you with sample no. 1?

(b) How did you rate it as a temperature indicator?

Let's do the same for sample 2. (SHOW RECTAL) How familiar are you with it? On the questionnaire next to no. 7A#2 indicate not at all familiar, somethat familiar, or very familiar. Would you say a thermom-eter of this type is poor, adequate, good, or excellent as a temperature indicator? Enter next to no. 7B#2.

(a) How familiar are you with sample no. 2?

(b) How did you rate it as a temperature indicator?

Let's do the same for sample 3 (E-Z Temp). How familiar are you with it? On the questionnaire next to no. 7A#3 indicate not at all familiar, somewhat familiar, or very familiar. Would you say a thermometer of this type is poor, adequate, good, or excellent as a temperature indicator? Enter next to no. 7B#3.

(a) How familiar are you with sample 3?

(b) How did you rate it as a temperature indicator?

Let's do the same for sample 4 (Clinitemp). How familiar are you with it? On the questionnaire next to no. 7A#4 indicate not at all familiar, somewhat familiar, or very familiar. Would you say a thermometer of this type is poor, adequate, good, or excellent as a temperature indicator? Enter next to no. 7B#4.

(a) How familiar are you with sample 4?

(b) How did you rate it as a temperature indicator?

Let's do the same for sample 5 (battery-operated). How familiar are you with it? On the questionnaire next to no. 7A#5 indicate not at all familiar, somewhat familiar, or very familiar. Would you say a ther-mometer of this type is poor, adequate, good, or excellent as a tempera-ture indicator? Enter next to no. 7B#5.

(a) How familiar are you with sample no. 5?

(b) How did you rate it as a temperature indicator?

8. (a) I will now demonstrate sample no. 3.
       What do you think about it?

   (b) I will now demonstrate sample no. 4.
       What do you think about it?

   (c) I will now demonstrate sample no. 5.
       What do you think about it?

9. I now want to show you the description that appears on the back of the display card for:

   (a) Thermometer no. 1 (oral). Please read it. Will you tell me what you think of it? How would you improve upon it?

   (b) Let's do the same for no. 2 (rectal). Please read it. Will you tell me what you think of it? How would you improve upon it?

    (c) Let's do the same for no. 3. Please read it. Will you tell me what you think of it? How would you improve upon it?

    (d) Let's do the same for no. 4. Please read it. Will you tell me what you think of it? How would you improve upon it?

    (e) Let's do the same for no. 5. Please read it. Will you tell me what you think of it? How would you improve upon it?

10. What, in your opinion, should appear in the thermometer display card such as these (SHOW SAMPLES)

11. (a) Now that we have discussed each of the five would you enter the letter of the thermometer next to no. 11A that you would most likely buy the next time you purchase a thermometer? What was it and why did you select it?

    (b) Enter the letter of the thermometer next to no. 11B on the questionnaire that you would least likely buy and tell me why.

12. The actual prices of the thermometers in a drug store are:

Thermometer	Price ($)
A1	1.78
B2	1.78
C3	1.99
D4	1.98
E5	26.50

Next to no. 12A would you now enter the one you would most likely buy and why. If any of you changed your mind from your selection in 11A will you tell me what it was and why you changed your mind? Next to 12B enter the one that you would least likely buy. If you changed your mind from your selection in 11B will you tell me why?

ILLUSTRATION OF FRAME OF REFERENCE QUESTIONNAIRE

2. Extremely Accurate   ( )
   Rather Accurate   ( )
   At Best an Approximation ( )
3. Instrument Error   YES ( )   NO ( )
   Reading Error   YES ( )   NO ( )

4.

	NOT REALLY IMPORTANT	RATHER IMPORTANT	VERY IMPORTANT
Clerk in Store			
Doctor			
Personal Experience			
Pharmacist			
Printed Material on Display Card			

Box 14.2 (Continued)

6. a) ——————————————————————————
   b) ——————————————————————————
      ——————————————————————————
      ——————————————————————————

7A	NOT AT ALL	SOMEWHAT	VERY
#1			
#2			
#3			
#4			
#5			

7B.	POOR	ADEQUATE	GOOD	EXCELLENT
#1				
#2				
#3				
#4				
#5				

11A. ——————————————————————————
——————————————————————————

11B. ——————————————————————————
——————————————————————————

12A. ——————————————————————————
——————————————————————————

12B. ——————————————————————————

NAME ——————————————————————————

The rationale for the development of the discussion guide for the professional group is presented in Box 14.3.

Box 14.3 OUTLINE AND RATIONALE FOR DISCUSSION GUIDE—LIQUID CRYSTAL THERMOMETER STUDY: PROFESSIONAL GROUP

It is expected that the professional group will be more sophisticated in their attitudes toward and knowledge of temperature taking. Accordingly, the nature of the discussion guide must be quite different. Although the problem areas are hypothecated to be the same for both groups, the information obtained is expected to be different not only because the inquiries are different but also because their backgrounds are different and will reflect different experiences. In addition, it was planned to include some of the more critical findings of the lay group to determine the reactions of the professional group to the beliefs of the lay group.

The professional discussion group was started by inquiring into the way or manner, if any, in which they perceive their use of a thermometer as differing from the way a lay person uses one. The hypothesis suggests that if differences exist it might be advisable to propose different specifications or standards for thermometers (LCT especially) for each sector, professional or lay group. This discussion area also served as a warm-up for the session by emphasizing the participants' role as professionals.

The second area discussed was the same as that presented to the lay group. The rationale was to determine the expectations of this professional group regarding the accuracy and precision of the instruments used to measure temperature. By using the same inquiry it would be possible to compare the expectations of the groups.

The third area attempted to focus more specifically on how precise this group wants a thermometer reading to be. Are readings preferred by this group in fractions of a degree, a degree, or a two-degree range. Such information would point to whether the present method of scaling used with LCTs meets their needs or standards.

The next area asked the participants to list independently (via recall) important characteristics or specifications of a thermometer. It is assumed that discussing such lists helps to define problem areas that could be related to the project goal of determining needs related to setting standards.

At this point in the discussion the group was asked to indicate preference among oral, rectal, and skin surface thermometers. By learning why they do or do not prefer any of the three types, it is assumed that further information on instrument specification and characteristics as related to standards could be obtained.

For more than human interest and to learn what this group does "when the shoe is on the other foot" they were asked to indicate the type they personally use.

The seventh area discussed replicated the material presented to the lay group. The display cards for each of five thermometers were presented, one at a time, to each of the participants. After reading each card, the group was asked to discuss what was thought of it and how it could be improved. These data not only allowed for a comparison with the lay group but also could determine how they perceived the information offered and what could be done—from their professional point of view—to improve the display cards. This area is similar to the one asked of the lay group.

Further delving into this matter, the group was asked to suggest statements of caution, precaution, or warning. It was believed that obtaining such information would reflect the need to emphasize safety standards, if such were necessary.

In quite a different fashion from the lay group, the topic of standards

Box 14.3 *(Continued)*

was overtly raised. First the group was asked to express its views as to whether or not voluntary or regulatory standards for LCTs should be introduced. This was followed up with an attempt to learn from those who preferred standards, what standards they would propose.

The final discussion area was based on the presentation of a list of recommendations by the women. This group was asked to indicate what they thought of the list and to suggest items to be changed or added. This was done to compare the specifications on items of both groups and to determine whether a single and integrated list of recommendations would be possible.

The panel leader's guide and frame of reference questionnaire for the professional group is presented in Box 14.4.

Box 14.4   DISCUSSION GUIDE—LIQUID CRYSTAL THERMOMETER STUDY: PROFESSIONAL GROUP

1. In what way or ways, if any, would you say that the use of a thermometer by a professional differs from that of a lay person?
2. How accurately would you say that thermometers measure a person's temperature—extremely accurate, rather accurate (plus or minus 1°), or at best an approximation? Before discussing, on the questionnaire next to no. 2 place an X next to the item that indicates your belief. What did you answer and why?
3. How precise do you expect or want a thermometer scale to be?
4. What characteristics or specifications do you believe are necessary in a thermometer? On the questionnaire next to no. 4, please write, in your order of importance, the three, four, or five characteristics or specifications you believe to be most important.
   (a) What did you list as no. 1 and why?
   (b) What did you list as your second item and why?
5. Comparing oral, anal, and skin surface thermometers, which do you prefer to use and why? On the questionnaire next to no. 5 place a (1) next to the type you most prefer, then a (2), and finally a (3) next to the one that you least prefer.
   (a) Which do you prefer most and why?
   (b) Which do you prefer least and why?
6. When you have the need to take your own temperature, which type of thermometer do you use and why? Before discussing and on the questionnaire next to no. 6, indicate the type you use. What was the type you indicated and why?

7. I now want to show you the description that appears on the back of the display card:
   (a) Thermometer no. 1 (oral). Please read it. Will you tell me what you think of the description?
       How would you improve upon it?
   (b) Let's do the same for no. 2 (rectal). Please read it. Will you tell me what you think of it? How would you improve upon it?
   (c) Let's do the same for no. 3 (E-Z Temp). Please read it. Will you tell me what you think of it? How would you improve upon it?
   (d) Let's do the same for no. 4 (Clinitemp). Please read it. Will you tell me what you think of it? How would you improve upon it?
   (e) Let's do the same for no. 5 (battery-operated). Please read it. Will you tell me what you think of it? How would you improve upon it?

8. What, in your opinion, should appear in a thermometer display card such as these? (SHOW SAMPLES)

9. Should the directions include any statements of caution, precaution, or warning? If you believe they should, what would you suggest?

10. This discussion is being conducted as a preliminary to considering whether standards should be set for liquid crystal thermometers. On the questionnaire next to no. 10 indicate whether standards should be voluntary, regulated, or nonexistent. What did you answer and why?

11. For those who favor standards, be they voluntary or regulated, what standards would you propose?

12. We recently conducted a group discussion with a group of women. The topic was similar to what we have been discussing. When they were asked, "What in your opinion should appear on a thermometer display card?", they mentioned such items as those listed on the sheet I will give you.
    (a) What do you think of this list?
    (b) What item(s) would you change?
    (c) What item(s) would you add?

QUESTIONNAIRE

---

2. Extremely accurate   ( )
   Rather accurate   ( )
   At best an approximation ( )
4. 1. _____
   2. _____
   3. _____
   4. _____
   5. _____
5. Oral _____
   Rectal _____
   Skin _____

Box 14.4 *(Continued)*

6. _____

10. Voluntary   ( )
    Regulated   ( )
    Nonexistent   ( )

Name _____

In summary, one cannot overemphasize the importance of the discussion guide, since its content is analogous to the independent variable in an experiment. It is the vehicle that is used to obtain the responses known as the dependent variables. Adherence to the discussion guide enables one or more discussion leaders to communicate uniformly and objectively with the participants of different groups in the study. It is the source of the data that produce the findings and ultimately the conclusions. Constructing a valid and reliable guide to obtain objective information is most difficult. It requires much study and practice.

To recapitulate, a group discussion will be no better than its discussion guide. To obtain a good, objective, and meaningful guide requires:

1. An astute awareness of the problem
2. An outline of the problem's parameters
3. A rationale for each of the discussion areas included in the guide
4. The use of the inverted pyramid approach in developing the guide, the outline, and its rationale

Beyond the rules for the discussion guide construction as the instrument that obtains the data, there is a need for the group leader to read the guide exactly as it has been written. If a group leader varies from the guide, the responses will vary as a result of differing stimuli.

THE FINDINGS

An obvious question is, "What kind of findings are obtainable with the group discussion method?" The answer is a series of rather specific generalizations coupled with reasons why.

As already indicated, there is a great need for planning and carefully developing the instruments that gather the data as a result of group discussions. Despite the fact that this method is a form of qualitative research, the findings obtained can be summarized point by point, as well as generalized. Replaying the tapes allows for better understanding and for an accurate summary of each of the discussion areas, as well as the selection and use of virtually unedited quotes to serve as illustrations.

The summary of the specific findings of the liquid crystal thermometer study for the lay and professional groups is presented in Box 14.5. This illustra-

**Box 14.5   FINDINGS—LIQUID CRYSTAL THERMOMETER STUDY SUMMARY:
LAY GROUP**

The following items included in the summary are based on the analysis of
the tapes of the group discussions.

1. Temperature taking is a reasonably frequent activity in January.
2. With children two years of age or less, the rectal thermometer is used, otherwise and on through adulthood it is done orally.
3. The incident takes 2 or 3 minutes.
4. The thermometer used is easily and correctly read.
5. The thermometer used is considered accurate.
6. Unless the fever is 102°–103° or above and persists, the doctor is not called. The mother administers aspirin and retakes the temperature a few hours later.
7. Influencing the use of a thermometer is either the doctor, the pharmacist, or one's previous experience.
8. Display cards, especially for LCTs, can be read in supermarkets or be used to decide whether or not to purchase.
9. This group was generally unfamiliar with the LCTs.
10. Showing a sample, demonstrating it, or reading the display card generally results in judgments that the samples are ineffective and inaccurate and imprecise as temperature indicators.
11. Reading a precise measurement on a scaled indicator is regarded as more accurate than having an indication within a two-degree range.
12. Reaction to the E-Z display card was primarily related to concern about whether the instrument would be an accurate temperature indicator.
13. Reaction to the Clinitemp display card was that it was too general and that either it avoided mentioning LCT limitations and was misleading, or it was a better instrument than the E-Z one.
14. Use of temperature trend in the home is not particularly relevant based on the manner in which thermometers are used. Temperature measurements are considered discrete events and taken at timed intervals and not continuously.
15. Doctor-accepted, hospital-approved, or similar phrases are likely to be believed on face value. If such phrases are used, either evidence or caveats should be offered.
16. A list of 16 items was offered for consideration for inclusion on display cards.
17. E-Z Temp may be more a toy or a subterfuge than an accurate and precise instrument.

FINDINGS FOR PROFESSIONAL GROUP

1. The professional group perceived itself as different from lay people in the use of thermometry.

Box 14.5 *(Continued)*

2. This group recognized that it is better trained and capable of obtaining more accurate results in measuring temperature.
3. They believe that repeated measurements are more diagnostically accurate than a single reading.
4. They regard accuracy as a most important requirement of an instrument and expect the instruments they use to be extremely accurate to within two-tenths of a degree.
5. In addition to accuracy, an instrument should be easy to use, clean, and meet safety requirements.
6. The professionals differentiate between different thermometer types on the basis of function and practicality, more so than lay people do.
7. Axillary and skin surface thermometers are regarded as least accurate and of limited use.
8. LCTs are considered to be in their early stages of development. There is a need for more accuracy and greater precision than now exists.
9. The group was generally familiar with LCTs but did not consider them appropriate for either office or hospital use.
10. Some, condescendingly, thought there might be limited home use for an LCT with young children but not as an accurate indicator.
11. Display cards and their material in general were considered as possible for lay people but not for the professional group.
12. Concern was manifested about the illiterates who cannot read and the literates who do not read in relation to understanding and following directions.
13. They believe that directions should be more complete and explicit, especially in regard to safety, cleaning, and rectal use.
14. The LCTs are not taken seriously as accurate indications of temperature, at least not in their present stage of development.
15. Some might consider an LCT for use with a child but not for an adult.
16. Skin temperature can vary for many reasons related to skin condition, but it would be unwise to assume a correlation between skin temperature and body temperature.
17. Although this group acknowledged the marketing and sales use of display card material, they were nevertheless concerned that information on use, cleaning, accuracy, and safety should be detailed and complete.
18. This group generally favored setting standards but felt that LCTs should be made more accurate before setting standards. One cannot regulate accuracy for a known inaccurate instrument.

tion demonstrates how two different groups perceive temperature taking and shows a comparison of the uses of different instruments that record temperature.

This data-gathering process also lends itself to generalizations, implications, and interpretations. Again, to serve as an illustration, the following is offered.

Illustration of Implications/Interpretations

The perceptions of LCTs by both the professional and lay groups are generally more negative than positive. It is not considered either an accurate or precise instrument. Its scaling is too gross and does not come close to the 0.2° expected in temperature measurement. It is even considered by some to be a toy or gimmick.

Further research and development is needed to perfect the LCT as an accurate measuring device that would meet expected and acceptable standards. In its present state it has such advantages over mercury thermometers as rapid readings, convenience, ease of use, and avoidance of the problems of broken glass. However, it lacks what both groups perceive to be the most important characteristic and expectation of a thermometer, namely accuracy. Since LCTs are reasonably new, it appears that most people have not used them or are not familiar with them. Accordingly, instructions, directions, and so forth assume importance. Emphasis should be placed on directions for use of the thermometer, precautions to take to enhance the accuracy of the measurement, and the inclusion of disclaimers so that people know how the thermometers differ from mercury thermometers. Another point to consider is discouragement of the use of such statements as "doctor-tested," "used in hospitals," and so on. Such phrases would be misleading since they imply a state of the art that does not presently exist. The use of such statements implies either previous testing, recommendation, or testimonial. Such promotional techniques should be omitted because they are probably misleading, deceptive, or both.

After this report and other more technical data were presented to the committee, it was decided not to recommend standard setting for liquid crystal thermometers until further technological developments result in precise and accurate instruments.

The Quotations

The findings, interpretations, and implications are the result of the researcher's analysis and synthesis of the tapes. A good way to understand the human flavor of the data is to be familiar with the quotations from the participants. Such verbatim responses often suggest additional questions for further study. At times, the way in which something is said reveals more than the content of what is said. Verbatim responses must always be studied carefully.

In summary, the group discussion technique presented is recommended as a data-gathering method useful in obtaining information relevant to problem solving. Its use is appropriate in such diverse and yet related fields as consumer affairs, political science, the psychology of attitudes, explanations, and needs, as well as marketing strategy and executive decision.

The rules and guidelines that have emerged as a result of developing this technique require attention to the role of the leader, the selection of participants, the construction of the discussion guide, and the controls necessary to introduce objectivity in the gathering and analysis of data that are essentially qualitative in nature.

There are many values in using this technique. At one extreme it provides inputs and interactions from a group of people as they react to discussion areas posed by the researcher. In a sense, this can be considered helpful in the formation or testing of hypotheses. At the other extreme, it may offer a practical means of furnishing the reasons why people have attitudes, needs, or expectations as well as why they change them. Last, but surely not least, the technique provides data on the reasons why. This can be useful in evolving public policy, product use, political campaigns, and even the likelihood of accepting or rejecting change.

chapter 15

Surveys

The data-gathering technique known as survey research involves the presentation of oral and/or written questionnaires to a sample of chosen or designated respondents. The data gathered are generally verbally communicated, although sometimes included is the systematic observation of behavior. We prefer to separate observation of behavior from survey data. Accordingly, observation as a data-gathering technique has been presented in Chapter 7.

Survey data include responses that report or reflect the opinions, attitudes, beliefs, or intentions of the respondents as well as their perceptions of others. Such responses are generally anchored in the time frame of the present but they may also refer to the past (as perceived by the respondent) or the future, which is intended to indicate the respondent's expectations.

We subscribe to the position of Tull and Albaum (1973), who emphasize that the purpose of survey research is the understanding and/or prediction of some defined and delimited aspect of behavior. A simple example would be that of voting preference for the president of the United States when compared with actual voting. We hasten to add that responses obtained may or may not accurately reflect behavior. For example, even when past behavior is accurately recalled, individuals often lack insight into the underlying reasons (Nisbett and Wilson, 1977). The variables of time, learning, and forgetting, as well as the variables that change the social and physical environment, have a great influence on perceived reality.

We also agree with and like the title of a chapter in a book by Walizer and Wiener (1978). It is called "The Omnipresent Survey." It does appear that surveys (as a data-gathering technique) have become more a part of everyday living than the other scientific techniques. It might also be said that surveys are generally the most acceptable common core of data gathering among the various social sciences. When the media or mass communicators are considered, hardly a week or even a day goes by without someone reporting a survey on something.

Glock (1967) reflects this omnipresence in the book *Survey Research in the Social Sciences.* The book is a collaboration of 10 scholars, who contributed 9 chapters* on survey research from their perspective of the fields of sociology, political science, psychology, economics, sociocultural anthropology† education, social work, and public health/medicine. This book is a most worthy compendium of the uses and the various professional attitudes toward survey research in the social sciences. The authors present the advantages and limitations of survey usage in their respective fields and offer cogent examples of the wide range of survey topics in these fields. Despite the different identifications and training of the authorities writing the chapters, the similarities in survey purpose, problems, design, and usage are more evident than are the differences. In other words, the survey research data-gathering technique tends to have a common base or foundation, independent of the specific social science. It is almost as if the survey technique offers a common and unifying basis for the social sciences to work together. In some respects we think of this data-gathering technique as a sort of Esperanto, a common and universal language among the social sciences.

Requirements for acceptable survey research include a standardized and systematic sample, a standardized inquiry, and, as a result, a summary of findings that can be replicated by others independent of the identity of the specific branch of the social sciences.

According to Glock (1967), sociologists use surveys for description and/or explanation. An example of the former would be an enumeration of the characteristics of broken homes. Of course, by itself, a survey can only *suggest* the reasons for broken homes. A determination of causes depends on achieving a higher degree of internal validity than most surveys permit.

The basic survey design meets the criterion of collecting standardized information from a representative sampling of respondents. Generally, but not necessarily, surveys collect data within a defined time frame, regardless of whether references are made to attitudes, perceptions, events, or behavior in the present, the past, or the future. In some instances surveys may be repeated with a different sample at a later time. They are known as *trend studies* because they ostensibly reflect changes over a period of time. Surveys may also be repeated with the same respondents. Such surveys are classified as *panel studies* and are possibly more exacting reflections of changes over a time span. Whenever change is measured, be it through trend or panel techniques, the direction and degree of change allow for a "before and after" measure, whether it is about the popularity of a politician, the attitude toward the economy, or any of the many social issues that confront society.

In summary, data of interest to sociologists (as well as others) are collected

*One chapter was coauthored.
†This chapter has a coauthorship.

that lead to a description or explanation of the characteristics of people and their (supposed) reasons for feeling or behaving in a particular fashion, whether they are for or against any particular social issue. Surveys are intended to reflect attitudes and beliefs of the population related to minorities, voting intention, abortion, housing, the equal rights amendment, prayer in the schools, or nuclear energy, to name a few.

McClosky (in Glock, 1967) calls attention to the growing reliance on survey analysis in political science. Studies of surveys on political polling reveal that the act of voting is a complex phenomenon. Such surveys suggest that examining the responses of classes or groups more effectively reflects the success or failure of political candidates than does simply counting individuals. Since surveys gather information on demographics (age, sex, education, income, ethnicity, etc.) and attitudes, opinions, beliefs, and intentions, it is a rather simple task to relate these two types of data and infer associations *(not causes)* between, say, women and candidate preference or religious belief and candidate preference. The more ambitious surveys also seek information about the reasons for a stated preference. These, in turn, can then be compared and/or related to demographics, psychological dimensions, or both.

According to McClosky, most voters consult the media to strengthen voting intentions already formed. He also concludes that mass media communications are more likely to be received by the educated and articulate segments of the population. He indicates that the undecided voters, those whom the candidates most want to reach, are usually inaccessible. What is apparently overlooked by McClosky is the potency of "word of mouth." Blum, in his group discussion research (see Chapter 14), has found this factor to be very influential whether one is shopping for a cake mix in a supermarket or trying to estimate the perceived role and/or threat of the police in a ghetto or barrio.

Surveys not only serve as fact-gathering procedures but also contribute to the construction and testing of theory. This appears especially true as attempts are made to understand the factors that contribute to extremism. McClosky concludes that the political left and the political right, for example, are not in all respects the polarities they are perceived to be; indeed, the values of both are often embraced by the same individual.

Political polling and other types of surveys may not be as bland as the simple reporting of the findings might imply. The influence of the results of polls on both the population and the politicians, may be considerable. A variation on the chicken-and-egg problem is posed when it is asked whether polls, after they are reported, influence voters. Surely, the announcement of projected winners of national elections in our country, while the polling places may still be open on the Pacific Coast, might discourage California voters, whose voting places are open 3 hours after the voting is complete and projected in New York. An even more complicated issue is whether politicians are leaders or followers in paying attention or not paying attention to the results of polls. We have the "unscientific" opinion that candidates who win polls do consider and refer to them but candidates who lose polls do not pay attention—at least according to their news releases.

The critical issue, in our view, is not that of leadership versus "followship," but whether polls and the media influence leaders—or is it the other way around? We think it can work either way, but it is difficult to predict which is the antecedent or the presumed cause.

Katz (in Glock, 1967), reviewing survey methods in psychological research, designates two areas: a social psychological taxonomy of human behavior, and the study of complex social psychological problems. Included in the former area are four dimensions. The first is group involvement and social interaction with survey topics such as religious views and practices or participation in labor unions. The second is population statistics of personality types with topics such as adjustment to aging and retirement. The third is descriptive statistics of deviancy from social norms with topics such as juvenile delinquency or gang culture. The fourth is descriptive accounts of beliefs, attitudes, and values with topics such as bias toward minority outgroups.

With reference to the study of complex social psychological problems, Katz designates six dimensions. Included are: socialization and personality development with topics such as child-rearing practices; adult socialization process with topics such as socialization and the professions; nature and determinants of mental disorder with topics such as efficacy of various therapies; psychological basis of groups and organizations with topics such as perception of demands; individual involvement and organizational norms with topics such as the potency of involvement; and organizational typology with topics such as influences on performance.

Morgan (in Glock, 1967) emphasizes that in economics, surveys provide information about consumers, business people, and the forces that affect their economic behavior. An example might involve a survey on spending or saving behavior, the perceived reasons for it, and the consequences for business and the entire society.

It should be clear that Morgan, Katz, and Glock reveal not only an overlapping of interests in subject matter but also a strong commonality regarding survey elements and conduct. Stated somewhat more broadly, there appears to be a considerable overlapping of subject matter interest in sociology, psychology, and economics, and this is exemplified by the strong influence survey research has on the information obtained as well as the development of theory in the respective fields.

Morgan also points to the role of survey research in providing information for public policy decisions based on knowledge. Such surveys indicate the overlapping of economics and political science. Examples include unemployment, automobile insurance, social security, business bankruptcies, loans, interest rates, and purchases.

Economics is also concerned with changes in behavior. These changes are considered in the short run, the middle range (next 2 or 3 years), and the long run. Because of this, economic surveys must reflect snapshots of the present and also measure changes or trends over time.

Bennett and Thaiss (in Glock, 1967) present material on the applicability of survey research to sociocultural anthropology. Their views of surveys appears to be more temperate than those of the previously mentioned authors. They welcome surveys, but, as it were, through the back door. They prefer the role of the researcher to be that of an observer of subject-to-subject interactions or of "key members" of the group or population. At best, they accept the use of surveys when accompanied by other preferred methods (e.g., field research). They are accepting of holistic depictions rather than small samples. As examples of survey research, they refer primarily to studies conducted by sociologists or those conducted jointly with anthropologists. While Bennett and Thaiss recognize the need for a variety of approaches and methods in the social sciences, they state, "the human reality must be apprehended by a variety of viewpoints, not by one alone." We conclude that anthropologists like Bennett and Thaiss prefer observational data from a trained researcher about subjects, rather than survey data obtained directly from the subjects. It is sometimes difficult to separate one data-gathering technique from another; however, surveys and observations differ, not only from each other, but within each single technique. Not all surveys are equally reliable and valid, and neither are all observations.

Trow (in Glock, 1967) writes about survey research in educational sociology. He believes that students and teachers are, for the most part, the pollster's dream. Such surveys present relatively few problems in obtaining the sample of respondents. He considers the variety of questions for survey research as almost limitless. Among those mentioned are: recruitment to occupations, image of occupations, and the public and its educational and cultural sophistication.

Masarik (in Glock, 1967) presents a review of the status of survey research in social work. One of the topics is the recipient of the service, which he considers to be the favorite area of inquiry. The other topics include the needs of agencies and the services and practices offered by the profession. Here we see a most clear example of "know thyself." The social work field does surveys to know what it does, and by whom and to whom it is done.

The last chapter in Glock's book is, in certain respects, the best chapter. Suchman approaches his area of medicine and public health in a most comprehensive manner. He recognizes surveys as the data-gathering method that has been basic to the progress made in this field and also recognizes the value of clinical observation and laboratory experiments. He comments that recognizing the radical difference between communicable diseases and the chronic and addictive diseases has had great significance for survey research.

Topics where the survey approach has great relevance include: information and attitudes about health sources, health in relation to economic and social characteristics, the process of growth, development, and aging, specific diseases (especially the newer types such as Legionnaires' disease and acquired immune deficiency syndrome), nutrition, and harmful elements in the physical environment.

Obviously, for an individual and for society, surveys in the (public) health area are of critical importance. If a poll incorrectly predicts the next president, it is unimportant. But if a survey in the area of health is incorrect, the consequences may be not only severe, but vital. We are referring, for example, to surveys that (allegedly) do or do not find a relationship between cigarette smoking and cancer. Assuming the preponderance of evidence is that a relationship exists and recognizing that a warning appears on all cigarette packages and in advertisements, then the question is, Do people, especially young nonsmokers, stop or start smoking? Further, are they influenced by industry studies stating the opposite?

A problem of health-related surveys is whether people accept, believe, and follow the findings or recommendations. A more serious problem occurs when researchers, with possible conflicts of interest, conduct studies. For example, should universities or their professors conduct such studies and accept funds from tobacco interests?

Prior to interpreting or evaluating survey results, one should know who the sponsor is. Trade associations, whether they represent funeral directors or meat institutes or even government agencies, are unlikely to report that people spend more money on funerals than planned, or that ground meat contains more than meat, or that a particular government agency was anything less than fair or objective in recommending enforcement or nonenforcement in dumping toxic waste or concealing drug defects.

Because of the serious implications regarding life and death conveyed by the results of certain health surveys, it is incumbent upon us to list certain caveats regarding the limitations of such surveys. These include: the time the survey was conducted and whether the findings are still applicable; the need for a selection of comparison groups such as those with and those without the symptoms or illness; the problems related to the findings as a result of the characteristics of nonrespondents and dropouts; the need to define the disease under study; and *who* sponsors as well as *who* conducts the survey.

In summary, surveys using representative samples and unbiased inquiry can result in important findings that can benefit individuals and society. This occurs regardless of the discipline or educational background of the researcher who conducts the survey.

THE AJZEN-FISHBEIN THEORY

Now that we have discussed the widespread use of the survey as a method of gathering data, it is then necessary to clearly understand that surveys estimate and/or measure attitudes, beliefs, opinions, and intentions as well as inferred, actual, or predicted behavior.

Simply reporting that the attitudes of a population indicate benign tolerance toward people of all colors, religions, and even hair styles may or may not be valid because statements reflecting attitude may or may not predict either intent or behavior. The relationships between attitude, intent, expectation, and behavior must be studied. The theory of Ajzen and Fishbein (1980) appears at present to be the theory that most intensively and comprehensively *attempts* to relate attitude and behavior. One should remember that many surveys, measuring attitude and beliefs, assume that such measures are reflective of behavior. This assumption is not always correct.

The concepts that Ajzen and Fishbein use in presenting their theory are: beliefs, attitudes, intentions, and behavior. They indicate that their theory "is just

as applicable to buying behavior as it is to voting behavior or family planning."
They offer a series of assumptions such as: a person will usually act in accordance
with his or her intention.

According to their theory of "reasoned action," a person's intention is a
function of two basic determinants. One is personal in nature and the other
reflects social influence. The first is concerned with attitude toward behavior. It
is the individual's evaluation of performing the behavior—such as voting, buying
a product, or deciding to have a child—and this is the personal determinant.

The second is the person's perception of social pressures, which Ajzen and
Fishbein term the subjective norm. It is their view that an individual intends to
perform a behavior when he or she evaluates it positively and believes that
"important others" think it should be performed. However, they recognize that
for some intentions, attitudinal considerations may be more important than normative considerations, and vice versa. According to them, it is the relative weights
of these two determinants that indicate the intention.

Ajzen and Fishbein consider personality characteristics and demographics
as variables that can influence behavior. They believe, however, that there is no
necessary relation between any given variable and behavior.

They do draw clear distinctions between beliefs, attitudes, intentions, and
behaviors, but their thesis sometimes becomes a little blurred possibly because of
oversimplification. Their position, as we understand it, is that:

1. Information constitutes a person's belief.
2. People's information is often incomplete and at times also incorrect.
3. The two types of beliefs are behavioral and normative.
4. Systematic processes link these beliefs to behavior by way of attitude
   toward the behavior, subjective norms, and intentions.
5. There are likely to be some human behaviors that cannot be explained
   by a theory of reasoned action (pp. 244–255).

Azjen and Fishbein include examples of steps in the construction of a
standardized questionnaire in accordance with their theoretical constructs. The
first step is to define the behavior of interest. Behaviors are defined in terms of
action (e.g., voting), target (e.g., presidential election), and contract time (e.g.,
next election). One then *defines* and *measures* the behavioral intention (e.g., It
is likely/unlikely that I intend to vote), attitude (e.g., My voting is harmful/
beneficial), and subjective norm (e.g., Most people think I should/should not
vote). The survey would also attempt to measure behavioral beliefs (e.g., My
voting will help candidate X get elected), outcome evaluations (e.g., Helping
candidate X is good/bad), normative beliefs (e.g., My parents think I should
vote), and motivation to comply (e.g., How much do you want to do what your
parents think you should do?). Box 15.1 illustrates part of Ajzen and Fishbein's
sample questionnaire.

What is most interesting about the theory of reasoned action is that it not
only relates attitude and behavior, but also includes and considers beliefs as well
as intents. It is probably too soon to embrace, adopt, or reject the theory. The

Box 15.1   SOME SAMPLE QUESTIONNAIRE ITEMS

In this particular questionnaire we are mainly concerned with people's views toward the regulation of nuclear power plants and related facilities.

In addition to a few general questions, we would like to ask you about one of the statewide propositions that will appear on the November general election ballot, the Oregon Nuclear Safeguards Initiative—Ballot Measure No. 9, that "Regulates nuclear power plant construction approval."

Do you have any questions?

Intention

I intend to vote "Yes" on the Oregon Nuclear Safeguards Initiative—Ballot Measure No. 9

likely _____ : ____ : _____ : _____ : _____ : ____ :

      extremely quite slightly neither slightly quite

      _____ unlikely

      extremely

Attitude toward the behavior

My voting "Yes" on the Oregon Nuclear Safeguards Initiative—Ballot Measure No. 9

good _____ : ____ : _____ : _____ : _____ : ____ :

      extremely quite slightly neither slightly quite

      _____ bad

      extremely

Outcome evaluations

1. Requiring new tests of nuclear safety systems

   good _____ : ____ : _____ : _____ : _____ : ____ : _____ bad

      extremely quite slightly neither slightly quite extremely

Behavioral beliefs

1. My voting "Yes" on the Oregon Nuclear Safeguards Initiative—Ballot Measure No. 9, would require new tests of nuclear safety systems.

   likely _____ : ____ : _____ : _____ : _____ : ____ :

      extremely quite slightly neither slightly quite

      _____ unlikely

      extremely

Now we would like to know how you think other people would like you to vote.

Subjective norm

Most people who are important to me think I should vote "Yes" on the
Oregon Nuclear Safeguards Initiative—Ballot Measure No. 9.

likely _____ : ____ : _____   _____ : _____ : ____ :

         extremely quite slightly neither slightly quite

         _____ unlikely

         extremely

Normative beliefs

1. Most members of my family think I should vote "Yes" on the Oregon
    Nuclear Safeguards Legislative—Ballot Measure No. 9.

    likely _____ : ____ : _____ : _____ : _____ : ____ :

           extremely quite slightly neither slightly quite

           _____ unlikely

           extremely

Motivation to comply

1. Generally speaking, I want to do what most members of my family think
    I should do.

    likely _____ : ____ : _____ : _____ : _____ : ____ :

           extremely quite slightly neither slightly quite

           _____ unlikely

           extremely

theory can be considered either too simple or too complex and all-embracing.
What is clear is that the theory is built around and supported by survey data. The
theory attempts to predict behavior by using a limited number of concepts such
as attitude, belief, and intent. Whether it stands the test of time remains to be seen.

COMPONENTS OF A SURVEY

*The objective or purpose of gathering the data is the first requirement when plan-
ning to conduct a survey.* If the researcher is commissioned to do a survey, he or
she must establish whether the sponsor's stated purpose is the true purpose.
Sponsors are frequently not researchers and sometimes want a survey to prove
their position—for example, that theirs is the best dog food, or that it is necessary
to balance the federal budget by increasing taxes.

    What must be clear and certain is that a survey should gather data in an
honest and unbiased fashion, or the researcher is not meeting ethical standards.
*Having identified and defined the objective(s), the decisions regarding the sample
that furnishes the data must be made. Shortly thereafter, the inquiry form must
be constructed.* It may be a questionnaire, a rating scale, an unstructured interview, or some form of test. The respondent furnishes the responses to a data

gatherer, who generally is known as an interviewer. Since responses are some-times related to the interviewer's style, training, and briefing, the interviewer encourages standardization and stability as well as rapport. *The data gathered are then coded, analyzed, and summarized in the form of a report.*

A basic component of conducting a survey, which should not be overlooked, is the budget that is available. It determines, even predetermines, the nature and length of the inquiry, the sample and its size, the manner in which the data are gathered, and the time that can be allocated to conduct the study.

Purpose

The purpose of survey research is to obtain data that describe, offer understand-ing, and reveal attitudes, opinions, or beliefs of a selected sample of respondents. It is assumed that proper choice of the sample (see Chapter 4) results in responses that reflect the attitudes, opinions, or beliefs of the universe it represents. In addition, a survey may be planned to gather data that describe or predict behavior —either as a separate entity or as the varieties of behavior that are expected to be accompanied by certain attitudes, opinions, or beliefs.

When the client or research sponsor wants to know if the survey will support specific preconceived or anticipated conclusions, the researcher should recognize that such a survey is an exercise in futility and should not do the research. The researcher must first restate the research problem to the sponsor so that both understand and agree on the problem to be researched. In addition, the researcher must decide whether the problem is researchable and, if so, what data-gathering method or methods should be used. Once the problem has been adequately defined and the decision has been made that the survey technique is appropriate then further planning for the research takes place.

Surveys are helpful and useful in revealing associations or relationships between attitudes and demographics. An example might be the changes, with age, in the liberal-conservative dimension. Another might be the attitude toward the willingness of a particular group to work and the extent to which they benefit from some government financial aid program. While revealing relationships and associations, such data are not at all likely to reveal cause and effect. Simply stated, two things may be related without having one cause the other. It is hoped that our readers recognize the peculiar oddity of the "surveys" reported in television commercials. They are done in the form of good triumphing over evil. The sponsor's detergent, dog food, hamburger, or cereal always wins. In other words, there are surveys and there are "surveys," and commercials generally debase, rather than promote, the survey as a data-gathering technique.

The Sample

A survey requires that a sample be obtained that is representative of the universe from which it was selected (see Chapter 4). Public opinion surveys are generally summarized in the media. On television one is likely to hear one of two qualifiers as the findings are reported. One is that the probable error of these findings is ±3%. The other is that these findings are not a result of a scientific survey. Both of these comments can be, and probably are, misleading to the television audience.

The first comment implies that the results were obtained from a probability sample of a certain number of respondents. The ±3% means that with the size of the sample used and the percentages reported, the results reported, if replicated, would not be expected to vary by more than 3% in either direction of the reported result. The second comment implies that a probability sample was not used. It is never said, but it should be said, that these results (while not projectable to a universe) may nevertheless be accurate. For example, conducting 16 or 167 interviews with a specific inquiry at a defined location (e.g., outside a theater) can accurately show how many of the people who saw a movie cried, laughed, liked it, and so forth.

It is important to understand that there are a variety of ways to select a sample. Again, and to be practical, the sample selected often depends on the purpose of the survey (users of a product, or people who voted for candidate X in the last election) and the budget available. Generally, surveys reported in professional journals by professors are likely to have different purposes and budgets than those of advertising agencies or market research companies. Samples can be considered to project the total population, in which case they represent probability sampling. The other class is known as nonprobability sampling.

Let us first consider probability sampling. Generally, there are four kinds of samples: *random, systematic, stratified,* and *cluster* (Kish, 1965; Moser and Kalton, 1972). If the respondents are selected to have all the characteristics expected or known to exist in the population, then it is highly probable that the sample will resemble and be duplicative of the results that would be obtained from the entire population as defined in the survey. The sample might be from such populations as people in the country or county, or customers in a store, or freshmen, or union members.

Random selection has been discussed in Chapter 4. To review, a *random sample* includes people who have been selected from the population in such a manner, that all in the population had an equal and independent chance of being selected. Therefore, it is assumed that the sample has all the characteristics and ingredients of the total population. The safest way to select a random sample is to use a table of random numbers (see Kish, 1965). A *systematic sample* is a variation of the random sample. Instead of a table of random numbers, every Nth name is selected from an existing population such as a county telephone directory, an alphabetic listing of credit card holders at a retail outlet, or the senior class of a university.

A *stratified sample* divides the population into subpopulations known as strata. Examples of strata are product users and nonusers, older males and females, or groups representing almost any variable in the characteristics of a population. These strata are considered because one hopes to obtain data that lead to a solution to the problem being investigated, such as differences among owners of Japanese-manufactured cars and domestic cars or differences in attitudes of males and females over 70 years of age (Blum and Naylor, 1968).

The last type of probability sampling to be considered is *clustering*. It includes a sampling confined to a specific geographic region or a group with a specific and identifiable concentration, such as a sample from five cities, or 10 blocks in an area, or any defined and selected segment of a population (Hayes, 1963).

The other class of sampling is known as nonprobability sampling. The sample is selected and determined by the purpose of the survey. An example of a nonprobability sample is a quota sample. For any of many reasons, a study design might include equal numbers of people in four different age groups even though the age group 40–49 might be more numerous in the total population than, for example, 50–59, 60–69, or 70–79.

Another form of sampling is convenience sampling. These are the most easily obtained samples. They may include people at a shopping mall in a suburban area, or college students, for example. In reviewing psychology journals, one must wonder what would happen if the convenient use of college students as respondents was outlawed.

In discussing sampling, we must keep in mind that not all of the appropriate or eligible potential respondents do respond. Some may refuse to participate, some may not be at home at the time when the interviewer calls, and some may refuse to complete the interview after it has been started. A valid question is whether the demographics and responses of the respondents are similar to those of the three categories of nonrespondents just mentioned. Anyone with firsthand experience in conducting surveys knows that they are not similar, but the statistics to prove it are difficult to obtain. A method for correcting for this phenomenon is to compare the demographics of the respondents with census demographics and then make appropriate adjustments. Incidentally, very few studies report the refusals or the dropouts. Obviously, the fewer the nonrespondents there are, the more accurate the sample.

Sources of Information

Responses from participants are obtained in various ways. The most expensive method of obtaining responses is conducting face-to-face interviews. Obviously, obtaining the sample is best controlled by using this method, provided the interviewers are trained to conduct unbiased and standardized interviews, and provided they do not cheat. As a built-in precaution, it is usual to have an interviewing supervisor audit at least 10% of the interviews ostensibly conducted. This is done by either phoning or revisiting the respondent to verify that the interview did, in fact, take place. Face-to-face interviews have more or fewer nonrespondents, depending on two factors. One is the day and hour of the interview and the other is related to certain demographics and behavior patterns of the potential respondents. By behavior patterns we mean hours of shopping, work, sleep, or just not being at home.

Telephone interviews are less expensive than face-to-face interviews. Contacts can be made with greater frequency and call-backs are less time-consuming. Many telephone surveys are now computer-assisted. Box 15.2 describes some of the advantages and limitations of this new technology. Of course, not all people have telephones and so telephone interviewing is representative of people with listed phones and not of all people.

A mail survey offers the greatest number of sampling problems. It obtains only a small percentage of respondents and, in most instances, the respondents are those who choose to complete the questionnaire and take the trouble to mail back their response. Literacy as well as perceived value are factors to consider when offering premiums to respondents.

A variation of the mail survey is the questionnaire left in hotel rooms, restaurants, and airlines. One of the authors once completed a questionnaire for an airline. The question was, "Did anything on this flight displease you?" The answer was, "Yes!"—a passenger had taken off his shoes and revealed a hole in his sock. The suggestion is that these studies may be useless except to the person who is employed to print the questionnaires and maybe tally them. The possibility exists that respondents may not be the customers or the persons intended to respond to the survey; they may be employees or their friends.

The Inquiry

Most usually the instrument used to gather survey data is the questionnaire, which may be closed or open-ended. Closed means that the questionnaire includes the questions as well as a request to check off one of a number of provided

---

Box 15.2 COMPUTER-ASSISTED TELEPHONE INTERVIEWING

Computer-assisted telephone interviewing (CATI) typically involves a main computer that feeds information to and from screens and keyboards (Palit and Sharp, 1983). The interviewer reads the questions from the screen, to the respondent on the telephone, and keys in the respondent's answers on the keyboard. Such a system has been used in the past by Chilton Research Services (Fink, 1983) and may soon be used by the U.S. Census Bureau (Nicholls, 1983).

As Freeman (1983) points out, there are a number of advantages in using CATI. For example, "branching" becomes almost limitless with computer assistance. *Branching* occurs when different answers to a particular question lead to different follow-up questions. For example, a "yes" answer to the question "Have you ever been camping?" might lead to questions concerning where, when, how, and so on. A "no" answer might lead to questions about other vacation activities. With CATI, branches can build on branches built on branches; the computer will not lose its place in the interview. CATI can also use alternate wordings for different respondents and easily randomize sets of items if necessary. Data are immediately entered into the computer for analysis. Finally, the human interviewer can spend her or his time on obtaining responses and not on keeping place or readying questions. The main disadvantage may be that human interviewers will become bored with their work (Groves, 1983).

responses or ratings. Open-ended means that the response is offered in the respondent's own words. Occasionally, questions are of the rating or rating scale variety.
As an example of the closed-end/rating scale type of questionnaire, Box 15.3
illustrates a form that permits a quantitative evaluation of professors by students,
used in the psychology department at Florida International University.

An example of a questionnaire with the open-end type of question and
answer is offered in Box 15.4. It is the qualitative evaluation counterpart of the
preceding quantitative form.

Our experience is that this form leads to more insightful understanding of
the quality and effectiveness of the professor. Area 4 answers indicate the personal
reactions of the students and the impact that the professor had on the student.
If, for example, a professor receives a relatively low rating on the form shown in
Box 15.3. The reason(s) for that low rating remains unknown. The form shown
in Box 15.4 allows the student to clearly state specific reasons (e.g., the classroom
examples were boring) for any rating given the professor.

The Interviewer

Too often in survey research, too much emphasis is placed on the critical importance of the sampling technique and the key role of the interviewer is glossed over.
The interviewer is as much a data gatherer as is the questionnaire that the interviewer uses.

Since interviewers who conduct surveys are generally part-time workers
supervised by contractors in specific communities, problems can arise. In the
language of the field, these supervisors are sometimes referred to as "queen bees,"
an unflattering appellation which implies that getting the job done becomes more
important than paying attention to the critical details that researchers consider
essential. Interviewers who conduct surveys need training and briefing. Some
years ago, Blum hired interviewers in six key areas around the country. As a
psychologist, in addition to interviewing the applicants he administered a battery
of tests. Among the applicants were people who had previous survey interviewing
experience and people who had none. The data revealed that those with experience scored somewhat lower on a brief intelligence test and higher on an aggressive scale of a personality test. He decided to hire those without experience and
train them. Based on the criteria of tenure and interview completion rate, the
newly trained interviewers performed quite well.

Training interviewers should require emphasis on objectively recording the
answers, reading the questions exactly as they are written, and following the
directions to obtain the sample desired (Wood, 1981).

AN ILLUSTRATION

Consumerism at the Crossroads

While it is difficult to select one study that in style and substance represents "the
best of all possible worlds," we would, nevertheless, not hesitate to nominate

Box 15.3   **STUDENT EVALUATION OF THE INSTRUCTIONAL PROCESS**

General Instructions: This evaluation form is used together with an answer sheet that can be scored by a machine. Please make *no* marks on this booklet. Confine *all* your marks to the answer sheet. Another form is available for your free-response answers.

   Instructions for Identification: This evaluation is anonymous, do *not* put your name or ID number on the answer sheet. Please fill in only the number provided by your instructor in the course "Identification Number" box at the top of your answer sheet.

   Instructions for Marking the Items: The following statements reflect some of the ways teachers can be described. Mark the number which indicates the degree to which you feel each item is descriptive of your instructor. In some cases, the statement may not apply to this individual. In such cases, leave the item blank. The numbers 1, 2, 3, 4, 5 below correspond directly to the letters A, B, C, D, E after each item on the answer sheet. *Important note: On the answer sheet the item numbers go from left to right,* not directly down. Please note: This is a research evaluation form aimed at the development of the most effective possible teacher evaluation procedure. Your complete cooperation is very important and will be appreciated.

	Not at all Descriptive				Very Descriptive
1. Discusses recent developments in the field	1	2	3	4	5
2. Presents origins of ideas and concepts	1	2	3	4	5
3. Is well prepared	1	2	3	4	5
4. Gives lectures that are easy to outline	1	2	3	4	5
5. Summarizes major points	1	2	3	4	5
6. Encourages class discussion	1	2	3	4	5
7. Invites students to share their knowledge and experience	1	2	3	4	5
8. Has interest in and concern for the quality of his teaching	1	2	3	4	5
9. Recognizes and greets students outside of class	1	2	3	4	5
10. Is accessible to students out of class	1	2	3	4	5
11. Is a dynamic and energetic person	1	2	3	4	5
12. Seems to enjoy teaching	1	2	3	4	5
13. Seems to have self-confidence	1	2	3	4	5

Box 15.3 *(Continued)*

	Not at all Descriptive				Very Descriptive
14. Has command of the subject, presents materials in an analytic way contrast various points of view, discusses current developments.	1	2	3	4	5
15. Makes himself clear, states objectives, summarizes major points, presents material in an organized manner, and provides emphasis	1	2	3	4	5
16. Course content was difficult	1	2	3	4	5
17. Too much material was assigned	1	2	3	4	5
18. The major textbook(s) were at an appropriate level for the course and relevant and/or complementary to the material presented in lecture.	1	2	3	4	5
19. The instructor expected good work from everyone, including me	1	2	3	4	5
20. This course will be beneficial to my store of knowledge	1	2	3	4	5
21. This course will yield practical benefits for my daily living	1	2	3	4	5
22. On an overall basis was a good instructor	1	2	3	4	5

Consumerism at the Crossroads (1976). This study was sponsored by the Sentry Insurance Company. Professor Stephan A. Greyser, executive director of the Marketing Science Institute, Harvard University, developed the content of the study and was assisted by Dr. Steven Diamond. Louis Harris and Associates were responsible for the questionnaire, design, field work, analysis, and observations.

For the reader to obtain a thorough flavor of this study, a comprehensive review follows:

Sentry Insurance undertook the sponsorship of this study to try to learn how accurately the differing views of consumer activists, business executives, as well as of regulators and legislators reflected the views and aspirations of the public with respect to consumer-related issues.

Taken as a whole, this study was designed to achieve two overriding goals:

1. To serve as a national "report card" on the consumer movement to date.

2. To provide insights into future directions for the consumer movement.

Box 15.4   ANONYMOUS COURSE EVALUATION FORM, OPEN-ENDED ITEMS

Quarter: F W Sp S

Year: 19————   Name of Course ————————

Instructor's Name ———————— Number of Course ————————

Instructions: Please use the space below (and on back of this sheet if needed) to make written comments. Especially valuable are pro, con, and constructive suggestions and comments. These comments will not be seen by the instructor until *after* he/she has turned in all grades for this quarter.

Area 1:   The instructor (pro, con, constructive suggestions)

Area 2:   Course content in texts, readings, lectures, discussions, labs, etc. (pro, con, constructive suggestions)

Area 3:   Course administration such as assignments, exams, grading, etc. (pro, con, constructive suggestions)

Area 4:   Thoughts, feelings, reactions, experiences I have had related to this course.

The sample included a representative national cross section of adults, and also included six separate leadership groups. The details of the sample description given in the report are:

A total of 2,032 interviews were conducted in person for this study. Each interview lasted on the average 80 minutes.

The sample included:

- A representative national cross-section of 1,510 adults who were interviewed between November 27 and December 7, 1976.

  Moreover, the difference in meaning of the terms "consumerism" and "consumer movement" was explored in an additional cross-section of 1,459 adults between December 17 and December 30, 1976.

• Six leadership groups were interviewed between January 24 and February 10, 1977. These groups included:

—219 consumer activists
—85 government consumer affairs officials
—33 insurance regulators
—32 non-insurance regulators
—100 senior business executives
—53 consumer affairs specialists in business

This study also presents in detailed fashion the demographics of the sample by geographic region, age, education, sex, and income. Note that the unweighted and weighted percentages are furnished. Table 15.1 presents the data. Most often overlooked in the presentation of "nationally projectible" samples is the variance between the actual sample and the expected sample (i.e., how well the actual sample accurately portrays the reality as established by U.S. Census data). As can be seen, for most of the demographics the actual sample closely resembles the projectible national sample. In all instances, it is either exact or varies by 2%. The only exception is that 50% of those interviewed were men and 50% were women, whereas according to the census there are 53% women and 47% men in the United States.

To obtain the results:

Interviewers in the field were provided with detailed maps of the ultimate sampling units, and then they interviewed within the assigned respective areas. The national sample consisted of 200 such interviewing areas (sample points) throughout the country. At each sample point one respondent from each of 8 different households was interviewed. At each household the respondent was chosen by means of a random selection pattern geared to the number of adults of each sex living in that household.

As for the leadership samples, the respondents were systematically selected from lists from such sources as:

Consumer Activists
Capital Contacts in Consumerism
Consumer Federation of America list
HEW, Office of Consumer Affairs, State & Local Programs

HELP Useful Almanac, published by Consumer News
Council of Better Business Bureaus

Government Consumer Watchdogs
HEW, Office of Consumer Affairs, Washington Information Directory
Selected State Officials and Legislators, published by the Council on State Government
Government Manual 1976/77, General Administrative service
Selected State Manuals

Table 15.1 CHARACTERISTICS OF SAMPLE

	Number in Sample #	Unweighted Percentage %	Weighted Percentage[a] %
Total	1510	100	100
Region			
East	448	30	29
Midwest	449	30	30
South	349	23	24
West	264	17	18
Size of Places			
Cities: central cities in urbanized areas (generally 50,000 or more)	488	32	33
Suburbs: urbanized areas outside central cities	419	28	28
Towns: other urban areas (generally 2,500 to 40,000)	236	16	15
Rural: anything not included above	367	24	24
Age			
18–29 years	410	27	29
30–49 years	498	33	34
50 and over	595	39	37
Education			
8th grade or less	188	12	12
Some high school, high school graduate	742	49	50
Some college, college graduate	574	38	37
Type of Work			
Professional	283	19	18
Executive	198	13	13
Skilled labor	478	32	32
White collar	158	10	10
Sex			
Men	758	50	47
Women	752	50	53
Income (total household income for 1975)			
Under $5,000	202	13	14
$5,000–$9,999	372	25	24
$10,000–$14,999	351	23	23
$15,000 and over	529	35	35

[a]Based on national census figures.

Insurance Regulators
A list of all state insurance regulators

Non-Insurance Regulators
HEW, Office of Consumer Affairs, Washington Information Directory
Selected State Officials and Legislators
Government Manual, 1976/77
Selected State Manuals

Senior Business Managers
Randomly selected

Business Consumer Affairs Executives
The membership list of the Society of Consumer Affairs Professionals
(SOCAP), after eliminating all those not working for corporations.

The following data provide insight into the "fairness and lack of bias" of the
questions as well as the nature of the responses. For example Table 15.2 reports
the findings in response to the following question:

> I am going to read you a list of things which are of concern to some consumers.
> Please tell me, for each one, how much it has worried you personally—a great
> deal, somewhat, a little bit, or not at all. I want you to think about your own
> experiences as a consumer.

An addition or modification of the reported findings is our weighting or scoring
of the responses. By assigning (arbitrarily) a five to "great deal," a three to
"somewhat," and a one to "a little bit," we can see how the items do or do not
vary in rank depending on whether a scoring system is used to summarize the
answers, or each percentage is reported according to the answer given and in
decreasing frequency of the response "a great deal." As can be seen, not much
difference does exist, and often it is merely the preference of the researcher that
determines how the data are reported. Obviously, some forms of data reporting
are more clear and meaningful than others.

When the interviews were conducted in 1976 (November 27–December 7)
the first two most frequent consumer worries were the high prices of many
products and the high cost of medical and hospital care.

A valuable feature of this study is that it reports not only the views of a
national cross section but also the views of six different "leader" groups. The
differences in the answers among these seven different samples reveal the differences in perception among these groups. They raise serious questions such as:
"Who best speaks for the consumer?", "Do leaders represent the consumers or
their own viewpoints?", and "Are they "avant-garde"? To illustrate the differences, a sample of questions and answers from the Sentry Study is shown in Table
15.3.

The other side of the coin is reflected by Table 15.4, which shows some
perceptions of consumers. The reader might do well to compare the data from
Tables 15.3 and 15.4. It appears that there is some consistency in a variety of
attitudes, opinions, and beliefs, depending on the group you belong to or identify
with. At the same time it is necessary to ponder the questions: Who and what
are the leader groups?, Are they nominal or actual leaders? and To what extent
do various leader groups know or even care about the total population which can
be called "the citizenry"?

Consider for a moment the perceptions of advertising revealed in Table
15.5. The table suggests that a large percentage (46%) of a sample representing
a national population think that television advertising (i.e., all or most of it) is

Table 15.2 THINGS OF CONCERN TO CONSUMERS

(Sample size = 1,510)	A Great Deal %	Some-what %	A Little Bit %	Not At All %	Not Sure %	Score
The high prices of many products	77	17	5	1	*	441
The high cost of medical and hospital care	69	15	6	8	1	396
The poor quality of many products	48	33	13	6	*	352
The failure of many companies to live up to claims made in their advertising	44	32	16	7	1	332
The poor quality of after-sales service and repairs	38	31	14	15	2	297
The feeling that many manufacturers don't care about you	36	32	19	12	1	295
Too many products breaking or going wrong soon after you bring them home	35	29	20	15	1	282
Misleading packaging or labeling	34	29	20	15	2	277
Not being able to afford adequate health insurance	32	23	12	31	1	241
The feeling that it is a waste of time to complain about consumer problems because nothing substantial will be achieved	32	27	20	19	2	261
Not being able to get adequate insurance coverage against an accident or loss	30	23	14	30	3	233
Inadequate guarantees or warranties	30	31	17	21	2	260
Failure of companies to handle complaints properly	29	31	19	19	2	257
Too many products which are dangerous	26	27	22	22	2	233
The absence of reliable information about different products and services	26	33	22	18	2	251
Difficulty in getting insurance claims settled fairly	23	19	15	39	4	187
Not knowing what to do if something is wrong with a product you have bought	21	28	20	30	1	209
Difficulty in getting insurance claims paid promptly	20	20	17	39	4	177
The difficulty of choosing between so many products	11	23	25	41	1	149

Note: Totals may not add to 100% because of rounding.

Table 15.3 SOME PERCEPTIONS OF BUSINESS

I am going to read you a number of statements. Please tell me, for each one, which one of the phrases on this card (HAND RESPONDENT CARD) best describes how you feel about it—whether you agree very strongly, agree but not strongly, neither agree nor disagree, disagree but not strongly, or disagree very strongly.

					Leaders			
(Sample size)	Total Public (1510) %	Consumer Activist (218) %	Government Consumer Affairs (85) %	Non-Insurance Regulator (31) %	Insurance Regulator (33) %	Senior Business Manager (99) %	Business Consumer Affairs (53) %
If people have problems or complaints about things they buy and use, it is often very difficult for them to get them corrected							
Agree	65	89	81	77	73	43	53
Disagree	19	6	11	16	15	38	41
Most companies are so concerned about making a profit, they don't care about quality							
Agree	59	63	32	41	24	7	8
Disagree	25	25	51	48	69	88	83

Most companies do a good job of providing reasonable products at fair prices							
Agree	52	37	71	52	72	95	94
Disagree	26	40	16	16	15	1	2
Most manufacturers don't really care about giving consumers a fair deal							
Agree	46	45	23	16	9	3	—
Disagree	34	41	58	58	70	94	94
Business usually opposes efforts to protect consumers and give them a fair deal							
Agree	44	66	47	42	42	13	13
Disagree	30	23	37	42	45	72	76
Most stores don't really care about giving consumers a fair deal							
Agree	44	27	13	6	6	11	8
Disagree	36	52	63	81	76	81	89
If a company doesn't make a reasonable profit, it can't afford to be socially responsible							
Agree	NA	38	41	45	63	67	60
Disagree	NA	49	39	46	24	21	32

Table 15.4 SOME PERCEPTIONS OF CONSUMERS

I am going to read you a number of statements. Please tell me, for each one, which one of the phrases on this card (HAND RESPONDENT CARD) best describes how you feel about it—whether you agree very strongly, agree but not strongly, neither agree nor disagree, disagree but not strongly, or disagree very strongly.

(Sample size)	Total Public (1510) %	Consumer Activist (218) %	Government Consumer Affairs (85) %	Non-Insurance Regulator (31) %	Insurance Regulator (33) %	Senior Business Manager (99) %	Business Consumer Affairs (53) %
				Leaders			
Consumers can most effectively voice their discontent with products by not buying them							
Agree	75	59	66	61	72	88	81
Disagree	12	35	25	38	18	9	15
If people are careful and use good judgement, they can still get good value for their money today							
Agree	75	75	91	84	84	99	92
Disagree	14	15	6	9	9	—	4
Many of the mistakes consumers make are the result of their own carelessness							
Agree	69	56	76	71	72	86	83
Disagree	17	31	19	22	12	6	8

Most consumers do not use the information available about different products in order to decide to buy one of them							
Agree	65	67	84	77	78	81	91
Disagree	15	18	2	12	18	10	6
There is generally enough information available for consumers to make sensible buying decisions							
Agree	58	24	42	38	42	82	72
Disagree	27	71	50	55	48	13	23
Most peoples' problems as consumers are among the most nagging and annoying in everyday life							
Agree	53	76	69	83	51	32	53
Disagree	24	10	18	13	24	52	34
Most peoples' problems as consumers are relatively unimportant compared with other problems faced by the average family							
Agree	46	14	23	16	36	44	35
Disagree	30	69	59	68	45	37	53
Consumers don't need any help in looking after their own interests; they are quite able to do it themselves							
Agree	24	8	9	3	3	28	4
Disagree	58	90	87	93	91	57	92

Table 15.5 THE RELIABILITY OF ADVERTISING

How much, if any, TV advertising do you think is seriously misleading—all of it, most, some, not very much, or none at all?

(Sample size)	Total Public (1510) %	Consumer Activist (218) %	Government Consumer Affairs (85) %	Leaders Non-Insurance Regulator (31) %	Insurance Regulator (33) %	Senior Business Manager (99) %	Business Consumer Affairs (53) %
All of it	9	7	7	10	3	—	2
Most	37	60	32	47	30	12	8
Some	39	30	55	40	58	55	55
Not very much	11	2	4	3	3	32	30
None at all	2	*	—	—	—	1	2
Not sure	3	*	2	—	6	—	4

*Less than 0.5%

seriously misleading. The survey finds that consumer activists are often in disagreement with business interests. About two-thirds (67%) of consumer activists think TV advertising is seriously misleading, whereas only 10 to 12% of senior business managers or their consumer affairs executives think so.

Accepting these data as reliable, we nevertheless do not have a factual answer to the question whether or not such advertising is misleading. Business, which does the advertising, thinks it is not misleading. An important concern is to know who conducted the survey, who was the sponsor, and who were the respondents. It should be remembered that the independent variable (the survey sponsor or conductor) manipulates the responses, but it is equally true that the respondents may not be offering truthful responses. To return to Table 15.5, the conclusion *might* be that TV advertising is seriously misleading—more or less.

Survey research is a form of data gathering. When it is conducted with the standards expected in scientific research, its conclusions are as reliable and valid as those of other forms of data gathering and are assessed in the same way (see Chapter 2). It is very useful in measuring attitude, intent, expectation, recall, behavior, and the possible association between attitude and behavior.

Caution and attention must be given to sampling, the inquiry, the data gatherers, and the possible conflict of interest between the sponsor and the need for unbiased findings. The Ajzen-Fishbein theory was discussed and considered to be a worthy attempt to formulate underlying theory for survey research.

Consumerism at the Crossroads was referred to as an example of a survey study that might even serve as a prototype for future surveys.

chapter 16

Simulation

Simulation can take many forms but its primary characteristic is that it assumes the appearance of a reality. By reality we mean a thing, a person's behavior, the interrelations of people or groups, an event, or a situation.

Cherulnik (1983) defines simulation as "a means of recreating an important natural setting for behavior by physical props and instructions that represent its essential properties to subjects" (p. 363). An example would be the creation of a device that looks like a plane or its cockpit, sounds like a plane, flies (on the ground) like a plane, but is not a plane. A different example, illustrating the range and variety of simulation, might be a scenario that involves a person or persons following rules in the performance of such tasks as those of an executive or a production worker. The difference is that the executive or factory worker is not in the office or plant but is in a situation that requires reactions as if he or she were. Another example might involve a scenario where a husband and wife act out a marital problem.

The extent to which simulation is effective is the degree to which it has fidelity, that is, is as close to the real thing as possible but without the risks or dangers of the real thing. An accident in a simulation of a plane never has the fatal consequences of an actual plane crash.

A primary reason for including simulation as a chapter in this book is that it can obtain data in a practical and parsimonious manner. In fact, certain kinds of data cannot be gathered from the real world without excessive costs and time and also without danger to life and limb. Certain events or situations may occur too rarely, or be too dangerous, or need planning or preparation prior to the expected event, which may not occur. Hurricanes, earthquakes, and erupting volcanoes are some examples. Planning for a plane crash at or near a major airport is another example. Simulation can often be the only way to plan for such events.

In creating a simulation, the basic need is to create a thing or scenario that resembles the reality as closely as possible. The emphasis must be placed on reducing the aspects of artificiality in the simulation. Since simulation is called by many different names, we choose to classify it by designating two types, which we call A and B.

TYPE A AND B SIMULATIONS

Type A simulations rely on a variety of apparatus or instruments as they exist in the real world. People can be trained in a simulation of an aircraft so that they are able to fly the real aircraft. Even video games in arcades can be considered simulations. Although the apparatus is intended for entertainment rather than training, it creates a simulation of flying in space or participating in a space war.

Type B simulations include scenarios that primarily involve problems or conflicts of individuals or groups. In such instances, the simulation presents the problem and the participants are expected to plan, make decisions, or react as if it were the real thing (rather than a simulation). The diversity of such scenarios is vast and includes personal interrelations involving individuals and groups in any and all organizational structures in society. These include business and the public sector, as both are involved in training on the specific level or education on the more broad general level. Games that simulate the real thing, be they war games, traffic control operations, or inter-nation affairs, should not be overlooked as a segment of type B. Type A lends itself more readily to quantitative data gathering, while type B is essentially qualitative.

BLENDS

Most proposed typologies have problems with overlapping and gray areas. Sometimes this applies to our types A or B. The value of proposing types is to set some rules or standards for classification and understanding rather than to establish unique distinctions. To add to this lack of clear-cut separation is the fact that computers are integral parts of both type A and type B simulations. Whichever the type or combination, the simulation enables various behaviors to occur in safety, even though it creates the stresses that are found in the real situation. To differentiate types A and B, the former can be referred to as "hard" and the latter considered as "soft."

TYPE A ILLUSTRATED

A major purpose of constructing type A simulators is to achieve more effective training or retraining of those expected to perform a task that requires the use of machines or equipment.

According to Orlansky (1983), "The term 'simulation' covers a huge variety of applications: training, engineering design, test and evaluation, operational analysis and combat engagement, both in the field (e.g., aircraft vs. aircraft, soldiers against tank, . . .) and in large scale control centers (gaming and exercises)." On a nonmilitary level, an automobile driving simulator known as the Moving Road Scene Driver Test has been in existence for many years.

The apparatus allows for a simulation of a driver's behavior by measuring such functions as general motor aptitude, driver coordination, and speed of reaction, and can conduct and measure several activities that simulate driving conditions. Bork (1984) describes a simulation of a Boeing 759 built by the Link Flight Simulation Division of Singer Company. Incidentally, Link was the original developer of the Link trainer, the first aircraft simulator.

A question concerning a driving simulator (and all other type A simulators) is: How close to the real thing are the data obtained? That is, how valid is the simulation? This comparison may be made concurrently by observing an experienced driver under both conditions, or may be measured as the person is learning to drive and then later when the person actually drives under real road conditions. That is, one can assess criterion-related validity (see Chapter 2) for type A simulators. Reliability can be checked by using any of the techniques previously described (Chapter 2). For example, one could compare performance in the simulator for the same group of drivers driving on two different occasions (i.e., a form of test-retest reliability). In any simulation, it is important to assess reliability and validity as simulators are meant to replicate the actual performance of a craft, whether it is a helicopter "landing" on a pitching aircraft carrier, a tank driving in rough terrain, or a supertanker carrying petroleum navigating rough seas.

The complexities of simulators increase as computers are programmed to create replicas of the real conditions. In fact, the Federal Aviation Administration now allows simulator training to qualify a pilot for upgrading. These complexities include speed acceleration, scenes depicting what the pilot would actually be seeing, and the various stimuli that require responses to keep the craft from crashing.

Despite the glamor of the simulation, the problem for the research evaluator is related to the need to answer such questions as: Do simulators train? Are the skills learned in simulators transferable to the real thing? Are simulators worth what they cost in relation to the savings obtained? Such questions are important and are answerable.

Orlansky and Chatelier (1982) report that about one-fourth of all hours available to the Department of Defense are spent by trainees in designated schools. The cost of military training at such schools was $12.8 billion in fiscal year 1983. A further statistic indicating the magnitude of training and simulation is that the procurement of new simulators, including improvements to those already procured, averaged $275 million per year for the 8 years preceding 1983.

Orlansky reports that flight training simulators save about 50% of the time otherwise needed to train in aircraft and cost only 7% as much to use.

Another form of simulation studied by Orlansky is related to the effectiveness of maintenance simulators in comparison with actual equipment. He reports that maintenance simulators are as effective as training with the use of actual equipment, but require somewhat less time. In addition, the simulation acquisition cost, depending on the specific maintenance simulation, is between one-fifth and three-fifths as much as that for comparable actual equipment.

Orlansky and String (1977), in a paper on the effectiveness of flight simulators for military training, indicate that there are many ways to evaluate such simulators.

A favorite one is to have experienced pilots judge whether a simulator flies about the same way the comparable aircraft does. This is the test of *"fidelity of simulation"*. Since we were concerned with the use of flight simulators for flight training, we were particularly interested in whether skills learned in a simulator carry over to an airplane. That is called *'transfer of training'*, which we will define in a moment. Although simulators have been used for training almost since the airplane was invented (at least two flight simulators are known to have been available in 1910), many studies of training are concerned only with how well pilots perform in simulators. For our purposes, we wanted to know how well pilots trained in simulators perform the same tasks in the air and whether training in simulators saves any flight time.

(Italics are ours)

They conclude that pilots trained in simulators perform in aircraft as well as those trained only in aircraft on such tasks as cockpit checkout, flight procedures, instrument flying, takeoff and landing, acrobatic maneuvers, and air-to-ground gunnery.

Also reported are data from an airline indicating that in 1976, the cost of training was $6.8 million using simulators and aircraft. The airline that estimates training costs, if only aircraft were used, would have been $32.1 million. This means that with the use of simulators, training costs were 21% of what they would have been if only aircraft were used.

An advantage of maintenance simulation is that it can be designed and programmed to demonstrate a large variety of malfunctions because of computer input and, it is hoped, before the real thing breaks down.

In summary, brief reference has been made to three papers reported by the Institute for Defense Analysis not only to illustrate the use, cost, and savings of simulators in the type A class, but also to emphasize that in the search for reliability and validity it is necessary to develop and consider appropriate criteria. The value of a simulation in type A can be demonstrated when one considers its *fidelity* (similarity to the real thing) and its transfer of training. Transfer of training means that the learning as a result of the simulation is transferred to (or operates as if the learning took place with) the real thing.

TYPE B ILLUSTRATED

Type B simulation can most readily be differentiated from type A since it does not have machine or instrument emphasis, but is oriented toward personal interaction.

This type of simulation has a scenario and the people involved act/behave as if the scenario were the real thing. This means that the situation is simulated. The jargon includes such terminology as psychodrama, sociodrama, role playing, role practice, and games. The simulation occurs primarily in business and educational institutions and is used to develop or train people in such diverse skills as decision-making or interpersonal relations. Type B is most often found in the various social sciences, whereas type A is more often found in the military and engineering worlds. Both are useful when the schema involves research, development, and training.

Moreno's Contribution

Moreno, in our opinion, is justifiably recognized as the originator of type B simulation. His work *Who Shall Survive?* (1953) sets the stage (pun intended) for his concepts of sociometry, group psychotherapy, and sociodrama, but the major aspect of Moreno's group psychotherapy is the psychodrama.

Psychodrama, sociodrama, and the closely related role theory and practice concept are illustrations of type B simulation. In various forms of modification and use by others, they eventually led to the notion of games and gaming. The latter are extensions of the foundations offered by Moreno. (It should be noted that we present Moreno's concepts almost as if they were separate from his beliefs as evidenced in his writings. Accordingly, we overlook the mysticism, metaphysics, claims, and pretensions of Moreno.)

Moreno's psychodrama employs five "instruments." They are: stage, subject or patient, director, staff, and audience. According to Moreno, the stage provides the patient with living space that is more flexible than real-life space. The stage offers freedom from stress and freedom for expression. The patient is himself (herself) on the stage. The director has three functions: producer, therapist, and analyst. The staff function as auxiliary egos and portray roles required by the patient. The audience helps the patient by being a sounding board of public opinion.

And so, the psychodrama is a form of simulation in which the world, or at least the personal life of the patient, becomes a stage. Moreno (1946) states that "role is the functioning form the individual assumes in the specific moment he reacts to a specific situation in which other persons or objects are involved" (p. IV).

Whereas the psychodrama deals with interpersonal relations and private ideologies, the sociodrama deals with group relations and collective ideologies. The distinction is similar to the one between social psychology, where the focus is on an individual in a social setting, and sociology, where the focus is on a group or groups interacting. It should be obvious that the two overlap considerably and the dividing line is not very sharp.

Role Playing

Much that is written about simulation, role playing, and games gives little or no credit to or even makes reference to Moreno. An exception is *Role Playing in*

Business and Industry (1961). The authors, Corsini et al., dedicate their book to Moreno as "our mutual friend, counselor, and teacher."

They consider role playing to consist of four different concepts. One is theatrical, in which the actor functions. Another is sociological or people behavior in society. The third is dissimulative or playing roles with the intention to deceive, as in spying. The fourth is educational, wherein the purposes are diagnosis, information, or training.

For Corsini et al., role playing is useful as a technique for training and informing. It can also be considered a form of testing. In these respects, we can see the similarity of uses and functions of types A and B simulation.

Bear in mind that other researchers ascribe other names to role playing, such as "reality make believe," sensitivity training, and action learning. By whatever name, role playing has people make believe that what they are doing is real. Corsini et al. define role playing as providing "a simulated reality experience in which one can practice complex skills without hurting himself or anyone else through failure" (p. 2). They offer another definition of role playing as "a method of human interaction that involves realistic behavior in imaginary situations" (p. 8).

These definitions point to a major problem of this form of simulation. If the role player is realistic and serious and has sufficient information regarding the behavior of the role person (father, president, foreman, etc.), then this form of simulation may be appropriate and valid. The need to consider the criterion of fidelity, mentioned in reference to type A, is of paramount importance. Assuming that all role players are equally serious and informed is to make a grave error.

Similarly, the criterion of transfer of training must also be considered. Is there a transfer of what has been learned, while role playing, to the real thing, and for how long? Results of role playing are more often reported as illustrations. Evidence of the criteria against which the results must be measured is usually not presented.

To achieve some success, four steps should be considered: plan, develop, enact, and feedback. Just doing may not be enough. For example, in industry, role playing (by whatever name) is supposed to develop decision-making abilities by having the participants learn the correct decisions. Frankly, we have not seen any good evidence for this. We have seen many testimonies from the researchers and the participants.

An example, and one that we have some difficulty with, is the use of simulation in a study of inter-nation relations (Guetzkow, 1962). In this study, a "nation" had an "external decision maker" and an "internal decision maker." These decision makers were senior or graduate students majoring in political science. No matter how seriously a student plays the role of a nation's decision maker, do we really believe that we are simulating an inter-nation reality? This is not to imply that students cannot learn a great deal or even come up with better decisions than the decision makers. The point is, who knows? Simulation must simulate the real thing, but there must be a real thing to be simulated. For example, playing the role of a factory foreman is a simulation if one is familiar with what a factory foreman does. A factory worker probably can simulate such a role better and more realistically than a college student, who may never have been inside a factory.

Guetzkow states, "perhaps most exciting is the potential which simulation models hold for exploration of contemporary verbal theories about international relations" (p. 90). Based on data from college students, we have doubts and reservations.

Games

Another variety of type B simulation is known as *games*. Games are an extension of role playing but with an important modification. While the player(s) is an actor, such an actor(s) is given a set of rules by the "director/researcher/experimenter," who is responsible for the rules and the control of the game. In role playing, a scenario is provided and the rules are not as structured. In games, as a form of simulation, the rules have a purpose, especially in relation to the outcome of the game. According to Bowen (1978), the player is an actor in a game going on in a real world. The player receives the rules for making judgments and communicating. Simulator games have the director/experimenter/researcher inform the players of the rules, determine the influence that the players will have, and analyze the data, which are often decisions or judgments that need to be analyzed by the director. Guetzkow (1962) recognized that simulation permits the researcher to study the process as it may be unfolding and, because of this, such games are useful for training as well as research. Role playing emphasizes the role played by the self or as it is expected or perceived by another. In games, the emphasis shifts from the person to the situation and the decisions necessary to ameliorate, expedite, improve, or correct a situation.

An early form of a simulation game was known as the War Game. According to Corsini et al. (1961), its first application was in 1933 by Simoneit, a German psychologist. War games, or Kriegspiel, continue on land, sea, and air. Of course, much of Kriegspiel is type A, but it is also an example of the blending of types A and B. War games offer the opportunity for training. They are also exercises and practice. The simulation rather closely approaches the real thing, except that people are not expected to be killed and cities are not really destroyed. The crisis situation game evolved from the war games. Such games include simulated community disasters, fighting forest fires, and treating the injured in a plane crash.

Games require players to be either in competition or in opposition. Rules and conditions are also required. It is expected that the player will be able to exercise a sufficient influence to determine the outcome of the game. The game is a simulation of something that is or can be expected to happen in the real world.

In addition to the games that simulate a crisis, there are management-type games. These tend to be more sedentary in nature and supposedly train or improve one's ability to make decisions. Games of this variety, it seems to us, have been held on a plateau since the initial enthusiastic acceptance by some social scientists during the period 1950–1960.

In summary, type B simulation does have the appeal of entertainment while learning. To the extent that its participants are serious and know what the real thing is, one can expect it to produce data (e.g., scores on a simulator or observations of role playing) worthy of scientific analysis, which in turn can produce information and knowledge.

Simulation allows the collection of data in situations similar to reality. The reality simulated is typically one that would not easily allow data collection (e.g., a plane crash or a marital fight). In this way, simulations extend the reach of social scientists into problems that might otherwise go uninvestigated.

REFERENCES

Ajzen, I., and Fishbein, M. 1980. *Understanding attitudes and predicting social behavior.* Englewood Cliffs, N.J.: Prentice-Hall.

American Psychological Association. 1973. *Ethical principles in the conduct of research with human participants.* Washington, D.C.: Author.

Anastasi, A. 1982. *Psychological testing.* New York: Macmillan.

Anderson, J.R., and Bower, G.H. 1974. A propositional theory of recognition memory. *Memory and Cognition* 2: 406–412.

Angoff, W.H. 1971. Scales, norms, and equivalent scores. In R.L. Thorndike (ed.), *Educational measurement,* 2nd ed. Washington, D.C.: American Council on Education.

Aronson, E., and Carlsmith, J.M. 1968. Experimentation in social psychology. In G. Lindzey and E. Aronson (eds.), *The handbook of social psychology.* Reading, Mass.: Addison-Wesley.

Aserinsky, E., and Kleitman, N. 1953. Regularly occurring periods of eye motility and concomitant phenomena during sleep. *Science* 118: 273–274.

Asimov, I. 1960. *The Intelligent man's guide to science.* New York: Basic Books.

Axline, V.M. 1974. *Dibs: In search of self.* New York: Ballantine.

Babbie, E. R. 1975. *The practice of social research.* Belmont, Calif: Wadsworth.

Barber, T.X., and Silver, M.J. 1968. Fact, fiction, and the experimenter bias effect. *Psychological Bulletin Monograph Supplement* 70: 1–29.

Baum, A.; Fleming, R.; and Davidson, L.M. 1983. Natural disaster and technological catastrophe. *Environment & Behavior* 15: 333–354.

Bennett, E.L.; Rosenzweig, M.R.; and Diamond, M.C. 1969. Time courses of effects of differential experiences on brain measures and behavior of rats. In W.L. Byrne (ed.), *Molecular approaches to learning and memory.* New York: Academic Press.

Bent, A.E., and Rossum, R.A. 1976. *Police, criminal justice, and the community.* New York: Harper & Row.

Berkowitz, L., and Donnerstein, E. 1982. External validity is more than skin deep. *American Psychologist* 37: 245–257.

Bever, T., and Chiarello, R. 1974. Cerebral dominance in musicians and nonmusicians. *Science* 185: 537–539.

Beveridge, W.I.B. 1957. *The art of scientific investigation.* New York: Random House.

Blum, M.L. 1981. *Attitudes and reactions to two liquid crystal thermometers.* Miami: Consumer Affairs Institute.

Blum, M.L. 1979. *Industrial psychology,* p. 29. New York: Harper & Row.

Blum, M.L. 1977. *Psychology and consumer affairs.* New York: Harper & Row.

Blum, M.L., and Candee, B. 1944. *Family behavior, attitudes and possessions.* New York: John B. Pierce Foundation.

Blum, M.L., and Naylor, J.C. 1968. *Industrial psychology: Its theoretical and social foundations.* New York: Harper & Row.

Boice, R. 1983. Observational skills. *Psychological Bulletin* 93: 3–29.

Boring, E.G. 1957. *A history of experimental psychology.* New York: Appleton-Century-Crofts.

Bork, R.H., Jr. 1984. The technology of illusion. *Forbes* (February 27) 133 #5 158–165.

Bossard, J.H.S., and Boll, E. 1956. *The large family system.* Philadelphia: Univ. of Pennsylvania Press.

Bowen, K.C. 1978. *Research games.* London: Taylor & Francis.

Bowers, M., Jr. 1965. The onset of psychosis—A diary account. *Psychiatry* 28: 346–358.

Briggs, J.W. 1978. *An Italian passage: Immigrants to three American cities, 1890–1930.* New Haven, Conn.: Yale Univ. Press.

Broad, W.J. 1981. Science frauds. *Science* 212: 264–269.

Brown, B.B. 1977. *Stress and the art of biofeedback.* New York: Harper & Row.

Brunswick, E. 1955. Representative design and probabilistic theory in a functional psychology. *Psychological Review* 62: 193–217.

Bryden, M.P. 1965. Tachistoscopic recognition, handedness, and cerebral dominance. *Neuropsychologica* 3: 1–8.

Buros, O.K. (ed.) 1974. *Tests in print: II.* Highland Park, N.J.: Gryphon.

Buros, O.K. (ed.) 1978. *Eighth mental measurements yearbook.* Highland Park, N.J.: Gryphon.

Campbell, D.T. 1960. Recommendations for APA test standards regarding construct, trait, and discriminant validity. *American Psychologist* 15: 546–553.

Campbell, D.T., and Fiske, D.W. 1959. Convergent and discriminant validation by the multitrait-multimethod matrix. *Psychological Bulletin* 56: 81–105.

Campbell, D.T., and Stanley, J.C. 1966. *Experimental and quasi-experimental designs for research.* Chicago: Rand McNally.

Carlsmith, J.M.; Ellsworth, P.C.; and Aronson, E. 1976. *Methods of research in social psychology.* Reading, Mass.: Addison-Wesley.

Carlson, R. 1971. Where is the person in personality research? *Psychological Bulletin* 75: 203–219.

Carlston, D.E., and Cohen, J.L. 1980. A closer examination of subject roles. *Journal of Personality and Social Psychology* 38: 857–870.

Caro, R.A. 1983. *The years of Lyndon Johnson. The path to power.* New York: Knopf.

Ceci, S.J., and Walker, E. 1983. Private archives and public needs. *American Psychologist* 38: 414–423.

Cermak, L.S. 1975. *Improving your memory.* New York: McGraw-Hill.

Chandler, D. 1981. *Waterloo: The hundred days.* New York: Macmillan.

"Changing Family Composition." Bureau of the Census. *Department of Commerce News*, Sept. 22, 1982, C B 82-137, Washington, D.C.

Chemers, M.M.; Rice, R.W.; Sundstorm, E.; and Butler, W. 1975. Leader esteem for the least preferred co-worker score, training, and effectiveness: An experimental examination. *Journal of Personality and Social Psychology* 31: 401–409.

Cherulnik, P.D. 1983. *Behavioral research.* New York: Harper & Row.

Christensen, L. 1982. Examination of subject roles: A critique of Carlston and Cohen. *Personality and Social Psychology Bulletin* 8: 579–583.

Church, R.M. 1983. The influence of computers on psychological research: A case study. *Behavior Research Methods and Instrumentation* 15: 117–126.

Clark, M.C. 1983. The relationship between cognitive and affective behaviors in thirteen month old infants: A study of object-person permanence and quality of attachment. Master's thesis, Florida Atlantic University.

Clark, R.S. 1979. Police and the community. New York: New Viewpoints.

Clinard, M.B. 1970. *Slums and community development.* New York: Free Press.

Cohn, A.W., and Viano, E.C. 1976. *Police community relations: Images, Roles, realities.* New York: Lippincott.

Consumerism at the Crossroads. 1976. Boston: Sentry Insurance Company.

"Controlled drinkers" sue Sobells. 1982. *American Psychological Association Monitor,* September 11:6.

Cook, T.D., and Campbell, D.T. 1976. The design and conduct of quasi-experiments and true experiments in field settings. In M.D. Dunnette (ed.), *Handbook of industrial and organizational psychology.* Chicago: Rand McNally.

Cook, T., and Campbell, D.T. 1979. *Quasi-experimentation: Design and analysis issues for field settings.* Chicago: Rand McNally.

Corsini, R.J.; Shaw, M.C.; and Blake, R.R. 1961. *Role playing in business and industry.* New York: Free Press.

Cox, C. 1926. *The early mental traits of three hundred geniuses.* Stanford, Calif.: Stanford Univ. Press.

Craik, F.I.M., and Lockhart, R.S. 1972. Levels of processing: A framework for memory research. *Journal of Verbal Learning and Verbal Behavior* 11: 671–684.

Crano, W.D., and Mellon, P.M. 1978. Causal influence of teacher's expectations on children's academic performance: A cross-lagged panel analysis. *Journal of Educational Psychology* 70: 39–49.

Cronbach, L.J. 1984. *Essentials of psychological testing.* New York: Harper & Row.

Cvetkovich, G.; Baumgardner, S.R.; and Trimble, J.E. 1984. *Social psychology: Contemporary perspectives on people.* New York: Holt, Rinehart & Winston.

Danskin, D.G., and Crow, M.S. 1981. *Biofeedback: An introduction and guide.* Palo Alto, Calif.: Mayfield.

Deese, J. 1972. *Psychology as science and art.* New York: Harcourt Brace Jovanovich.

Detterman, D.K., and Sternberg, R.J. 1982. *How and how much can intelligence be increased?* Norwood, N.J.: Ablex.

Dolliver, R.H., and Will, J.A. 1977. Ten-year follow-up of the Tyler Vocational Card Sort and the Strong Vocational Interest Blank. *Journal of Counseling Psychology* 24: 48–54.

Doyle, A.C. 1930. *The complete Sherlock Holmes,* vol. 1, p. 163. Garden City, N.Y.: Doubleday.

Duncan, C.P. 1974. Retrieval of low-frequency words from mixed lists. *Bulletin of the Psychonomic Society* 4: 137–138.

Duncan, O.D.; Featherman, D.L.; and Duncan, B. 1972. *Socio-economic background and achievement.* New York: Seminar Press.

Enders, L.J., and Flinn, D.E. 1962. Clinical problems in aviation medicine: Schizophrenic reaction, paranoid type. *Aerospace Medicine* 33: 730–732.

Eron, L.D.; Lefkowitz, M.M.; Huesman, L.R.; and Walder, L.O. 1972. Does television violence cause aggressions? *American Psychologist* 27: 253–263.

Evans, R., and Donnerstein, E. 1974. Some implications for psychological research of early versus late term participation by college students. *Journal of Research in Personality* 8: 102–109.

Fallows, J. 1979. The passionless presidency. *Atlantic* (May) 243: #5 33–48.

Festinger, L. 1950. Informal social communication. *Psychological Review* 282–777.

Fink, J.C. 1983. CATI's first decade: The Chilton experience. *Sociological Methods & Research,* 12: 153–168.

Fisher, K. 1982. Report to Foundation supports the Sobells. *American Psychological Association Monitor* 13 (no. 12): 2.

Fisher, K. 1983. Debate Rages on 1973 Sobell study. *American Psychological Association Monitor* 13 (no. 11): 8–9.

Fisher, K. 1984. Incomplete reports clear Sobells. *American Psychological Association Monitor* 15: 2.

Fisher, J.D.; Bell, P.A.; and Baum, A. 1984. *Environmental Psychology.* New York: Holt, Rinehart & Winston,

Foos, P.W. 1980. Constructing cognitive maps from sentences. *Journal of Experimental Psychology: Human Learning and Memory.* 9: 371–377.

Foos, P.W. 1982. Searching memory for congruent or incongruent information. *Journal of Verbal Learning and Verbal Behavior* 21: 108–117.

Foos, P.W., and Clark, M.C. 1983. Learning from text: Effects of input order and expected test. *Human Learning: Journal of Practical Research and Applications* 2: 177–185.

Ford Foundation Current Interests 1982 and 1983. New York: Ford Foundation.

Frank, P.G., ed. 1956. *The validation of scientific theories,* Boston: Beacon.

Freedman, J.L., and Sears, D.O. 1965. Warning, distraction, and resistance to influence. *Journal of Personality and Social Psychology* 1: 262–266.

Freeman, H.E. 1983 Research opportunities related to CATI. *Sociological Methods & Research* 12: 143–152.

Freud, S. 1955. The psychogenesis of a case of homosexuality in a woman. In *The standard edition of the complete works of Sigmund Freud.* London: Hogarth.

Fried, M. 1969. Social differences in mental health. In J. Kosa, A. Antonovsky, and I.K. Zola (eds.), *Poverty and health: A sociological analysis.* Cambridge, Mass.: Harvard Univ. Press.

Garber, H., and Heber, R. 1982. Modification of predicted cognitive development in high-risk children through early intervention. In D.K. Detterman and R.J. Sternberg (eds.)., *How and how much can intelligence be increased?* Norwood, N.J.: Ablex.

Gardner, R.A., and Gardner, B.T. 1969. Teaching sign language to a chimpanzee. *Science* 165: 664–672.

Garment, S. 1980. Science academy cholesterol report spatters in capitol. *The Wall Street Journal* June 27. 201:21

Garmezy, N. 1971 Vulnerability research and the issue of primary prevention. *American Journal of Orthopsychiatry* 41: 101–116.

Geda, C.L. 1978. *Social science data archives.* Center for Political Studies, Ann Arbor, Michigan.

Glock, C.Y. 1967. *Survey research in the social sciences.* New York: Russell Sage Foundation.

Goertzel, V., and Goertzel, M. 1962. *Cradles of eminence,* Boston: Little, Brown.

Government and the consumer. 1976. New Jersey: Opinion Research Corporation.

Green, E., and Green, A. 1977. *Beyond biofeedback.* New York: Delat.

Green, H. 1964. *I never promised you a rose garden.* New York: Holt, Rinehart & Winston.

Greenwald, A.G. 1976. Within-subject design: To use or not to use? *Psychological Bulletin.* 83: 314–320.

Gregg, V. 1976. Word frequency, recognition, and recall. In J. Brown (ed.), *Recall and recognition.* New York: Wiley.

Grice, G.R. 1966. Dependence of empirical laws upon the source of experimental variation, *Psychological Bulletin* 66: 488–498.

Gronlund, N.E. 1981. *Measurement and evaluation in teaching.* New York: Macmillan,

Groves, R.M. 1983. Implications of CATI: Costs, errors, and organization of telephone survey research. *Sociological Methods & Research* 12: 199–215.

Guetzkow, H. (ed.) 1962. *Simulation in social science: Readings.* Englewood Cliffs, N.J.: Prentice-Hall.

Guide to the National Archives. 1974. Washington, D.C.: National Archives and Record Service, Stock no. 2203-00908.

Guide to resources and services 1983–1984. 1983. Ann Arbor, Mich.: Inter-University Consortium for Political and Social Research, University of Michigan.

Guilleminault, C., and Dement, W.C. 1977. Amneria and disorders of excessive daytime sleepiness. In R.R. Drucker Colin and J.L. McGaugh (eds.), *Neurobiology of sleep and memory.* New York: Academic Press.

Guion, R.M. 1965. *Personnel testing.* New York: McGraw-Hill.

Guthrie, R.V. 1976. *Even the rat was white: A historical view of psychology.* New York: Harper & Row.

Hagan, J., and Albonetti, C. 1982. Race, class, and the perception of criminal injustice in America. *American Journal of Sociology* 88: 329–355.

Harlow, H.F. 1971. *Learning to love.* San Francisco: Albion.

Harre, R. & Secord, P.F. 1972. *The explanation of social behavior.* Oxford: Blackwell.

Hays, W.L. *Statistics.* 1963. New York: Holt, Rinehart & Winston.

Hempel, C.G. 1966. *Philosophy of natural science.* Englewood Cliffs, N.J.: Prentice-Hall.

Hesse, M.B. 1966. *Models and analogies in science.* South Bend, Ind.: Univ. of Notre Dame Press.

Hibscher, J.A., and Herman, P.C. 1977, Obesity, dieting, and the expression of "obese" characteristics. *Journal of Comparative and Physiological Psychology* 91: 374–380.

Hillery, V.J. 1982. Stocks finish mixed in heavy day as industrials slide 8.19 to 1031.09. *Wall Street Journal* December 2.

Hong, L.K. 1978. Risky shift and cautious shift: Some direct evidence on the culture-value theory. *Social Psychology* 41: 342–346.

Horton, D.L., and Turnage, T.W. 1976. *Human learning.* Englewood Cliffs, N.J.: Prentice-Hall.

Hsieh, D. 1979. *Fiscal measures for poverty alleviation in the United States.* Geneva, Switzerland: International Labour Office.

Huck, S.W., and Sandler, H.M. 1979. *Rival hypotheses: Alternative interpretations of data based conclusions.* New York: Harper & Row.

Hull, C.L. 1920. Quantitative aspects of the evolution of concepts. *Psychological Monographs* 28: 123–129.

Hull, C.L. 1943. *Principles of behavior.* New York: Appleton-Century-Crofts.

Hull, C.L. 1953. Hypothetico-deductive method of theory construction. In L. Stolurow (ed.), *Readings in learning.* Englewood Cliffs, N.J.: Prentice-Hall.

Huttenlocher, J. 1968. Constructing spatial images: A strategy in reasoning. *Psychological Review* 75: 550–560.

If you like bacon, will you like "Sizzlean"? *Consumer Reports* 43: 124–125.

James, W.H. 1982. The IQ advantage of the heavier twin. *British Journal of Psychology* 73: 513–517.

Jessen, R.J. 1978. *Statistical survey techniques.* New York: Wiley.

Jung, J. 1982. *The experimenter's challenge: Methods and issues in psychological research.* New York: Macmillan.

Kahn, J.V. 1976. Moral and cognitive development of moderately retarded, mildly retarded, and non-retarded individuals. *American Journal of Mental Deficiency* 81: 209–214.

Kail, R.; Carter, P.; and Pellegrino, J. 1979. The locus of sex differences in spatial ability. *Perception and Psychophysics* 26: 182–186.

Kantowitz, B.H., and Roediger, H.L., III. 1978. *Experimental psychology: Understanding psychological research.* Chicago: Rand McNally.

Kaplan, A. 1964. *The conduct of inquiry.* New York: Harper & Row.

Katz, M. 1961. *Selecting an achievement test: Principles and procedures.* Princeton: Educational Testing Service.

Kelly, H.H. 1973. The process of causal attribution. *American Psychologist* 28: 107–128.

Kidder, L.H. 1981. *Research methods in social relations,* 4th ed. New York: Holt, Rinehart & Winston.

Kimble, G.A. 1984. Psychology's two cultures. *American Psychologist* 39: 833–839.

Kirk, R.E. 1968. *Experimental design procedures for the behavioral sciences.* Belmont, Calif.: Brooks/Cole.

Kish, L. 1965. *Survey sampling.* New York: Wiley.

Kress, G. 1979. *Marketing research.* Reston, Va.: Reston Publishing Co.

Kucera, H., and Francis, W.N. 1967. *Computational analysis of present-day American English.* Providence, R.I.: Brown Univ. Press.

Kuder, G.F., and Richardson, M.W. 1937. A theory of estimation of test reliability. *Psychometrika* 2: 151–160.

Kuhn, T.S. 1962. *The structure of scientific revolutions.* Chicago: Univ. of Chicago Press.

Lachman, R. 1960. The model in theory construction. *Psychological Review,* 67: 113–129.

Lachman, R.; Lachman, J.L.; and Butterfield, E.C. 1979. *Cognitive psychology and information processing: An introduction.* Hillsdale, N.J.: Lawrence Erlbaum.

Landauer, A.A.; Armstrong, S.; and Digwood, J. 1980. Sex differences in choice reaction time. *British Journal of Psychology* 71: 551–555.

Lauden, L. 1977. *Progress and its problems: Towards a theory of scientific growth.* Berkeley and Los Angeles: Univ. of California Press.

LeBlanc, J.M.; Busby, R.H.; and Thompson, C.L. 1974. The function of timeout for changing the aggressive behavior of a preschool child: A multiple baseline analyses. In R. Ulrich, T. Stachnik, and J. Mabry (eds.), *Control of human behavior,* Glenview, Ill.: Scott, Foresman.

Leitenberg, H. 1973. The use of single-care methodology in psychotherapy research. *Journal of Abnormal Psychology* 82: 87–101.

Lenneberg, E.H. 1962. Understanding language without ability to speak: A case report. *Journal of Abnormal and Social Psychology* 65: 419–425.

Lewin, K. 1936. *Principles of topological psychology,* translated by F. Heider and G. Heider. New York: McGraw-Hill.

Lewin, K.; Lippitt, R.; and White, R.K. 1939. Patterns of aggressive behavior in experimentally created "social" climates. *Journal of Social Psychology* 10: 271–299.

Lewis, A. 1964. *Gideon's trumpet.* New York: Vintage.

Limber, J. 1977. Language in child and chimp? *American Psychologist* 32: 280–295.

Lindman, H.R. 1974. *Analysis of variance in complex experimental design.* San Francisco: Freeman.

Linton, M. 1975. Memory for real-world events. In D.A. Norman and D.E. Rumelhart (eds.), *Explorations in cognition* San Francisco: Freeman.

Loeb, M. 1983. If the moon controls the tide, just think what it does to you. *Wall Street Journal* April 27, p. 1.

Ludwig, A.M.; Brandsma, J.M.; Wilbur, C.B.; Bendfeldt, F.; and Jameson, D.H. 1972. The objective study of a multiple personality, or, are four heads better than one? *Archives of General Psychiatry* 26: 298–310.

Luria, A.R. 1968. *The mind of a mnemonist.* New York: Basic Books.

Lynd, R.S., and Lynd, H.M. 1929. *Middletown, a study in contemporary American culture.* New York: Harcourt, Brace.

Malamuth, N.M. 1975. A systematic analysis of the relationship between shifts and characteristics of the choice dilemmas questionnaire. Ph.D. thesis, University of California, Los Angeles.

Markus, H. 1978. The effect of mere presence on social facilitation: An unobtrusive test. *Journal of Experimental Social Psychology* 14: 389–397.

Marx, M.H. (ed.) 1963. *Theories in contemporary psychology,* 2nd ed. New York: McGraw-Hill.

Maslow, A. 1970. *Motivation and personality,* 2nd ed. New York: Harper & Row.

Matlin, M.W. 1979. *Human experimental psychology.* Monterey, Calif.: Brooks/Cole.

McBurney, D.H. 1983. *Experimental psychology.* Belmont, Calif.: Wadsworth.

McCoy, A.W.; Read, C.B.; and Adams, L.P., II. 1972. *The politics of heroin in Southeast Asia.* New York: Harper & Row.

McGuigan, F.J. 1968. *Experimental psychology: A methodological approach.* Englewood Cliffs, N.J.: Prentice-Hall.

McNeil, E. 1967. *Quiet furies: Man and disorder.* Englewood Cliffs, N.J.: Prentice-Hall.

Mehrens, W.A., and Lehman, I.J. 1984. *Measurement and evaluation in education and psychology.* New York: Holt, Rinehart & Winston.

Michelotti, K. 1978. Educational attainment of workers, March 1977. Special Labor Force Report No. 209. Washington, D.C.: U.S. Department of Labor.

Milner, B. 1966. Amnesia following operation on the temporal lobes. In C.W.M. Whittey and O.L. Zangwill (eds.), *Amnesia.* London: Butterworth.

Mirowsky, J., and Ross, C.E. 1983. Paranoia and the structure of powerlessness. *American Sociological Review* 48: 228–239.

Mishkin, M., and Forgays, D.G. 1952. Word recognition as a function of retinal locus. *Journal of Experimental Psychology* 43: 43–48.

Mitroff, I., and Kilmann, R.H. 1975. On evaluating scientific research: The contribution of the psychology of science. *Technological Forecasting and Social Change* 8: 163–174.

Mook, D.G. 1983. In defense of external invalidity. *American Psychologist* 38: 379–387.

Moreno, J.L. 1946. *Psychodrama,* vol. 1. Beacon, N.Y.: Beacon House.

Moreno, J.L. 1953. *Who shall survive?* Beacon, N.Y.: Beacon House.

Morowitz, H.J. 1982. Rediscovering the mind. In D.R. Hobstadter and D.C. Dennett (eds.), *The mind's I.* Toronto: Bantam.

Moser, C.A., and Kalton, G. 1972. *Survey methods in social investigation.* New York: Basic Books.

Mynatt, C.R.; Doherty, M.E.; and Tweney, R.D. 1978. Consequences of confirmation and disconfirmation in a simulated research environment. *Quarterly Journal of Experimental Psychology* 30: 395–406.

Neale, J.M., and Liebert, R.M. 1973. *Science and behavior: An introduction to methods of research.* Englewood Cliffs, N.J.: Prentice-Hall.

Neisser, U. 1982. *Memory observed: Remembering in natural contexts.* San Francisco: Freeman.

Nicholls W.L., II. 1983. CATI research and development at the Census Bureau. *Sociological Methods & Research* 12: 191–197.

Nisbett, R.E., and Wilson, T.D. 1977. Telling more than we can know: Verbal reports on mental processes. *Psychological Review* 84: 231–259.

Nunnally, J. 1978. *Psychometric theory.* New York: McGraw-Hill.

Orlansky, J. 1983. Private correspondence with author. Institute for Defense Analysis, Alexandria, Va.

Orlansky, J., and Chatelier, P.R. 1982. The cost effectiveness of military training. Proceedings of the Fourth Interservice/Industry Training Equipment Conference, National Security Industrial Association, Vol. 1, pp. 97–109.

Orlansky, J., and String, J. 1977. Cost effectiveness of flight simulators for military training. I.D.A. paper P-1275. Arlington, Va.: Institute for Defense Analysis.

Orlansky, J., and String, J. 1981. Cost effectiveness of maintenance simulators for military training. I.D.A. paper P-1568. Arlington, Va.: Institute for Defense Analysis.

Orne, M.T. 1962. On the social psychology of the psychological experiment: With particular reference to demand characteristics and their implications. *American Psychologist* 17: 776–783.

Orne, M.T., and Scheibe, K.E. 1964. The contribution of nondeprivation factors in the production of sensory deprivation effects: The psychology of the "panic button." *Journal of Abnormal and Social Psychology* 68: 3–12.

Osgood, C.E.; Luria, Z.; Jeans, R.F.; and Smith, S.W. 1976. The three faces of Evelyn: A case report. *Journal of Abnormal Psychology* 85: 247–286.

Osgood, C.E.; Suci, G.J.; and Tannenbaum, P.H. 1957. *The measurement of meaning.* Urbana, Ill.: Univ. of Illinois Press.

Oxford English dictionary. 1971. New York: Oxford Univ. Press.

Palit, C., and Sharp, H. 1983. Microcomputer-assisted telephone interviewing. *Sociological Methods & Research* 12: 169–189.

Panning, W.H. Inequality, social comparison, and relative deprivation. *The American Political Science Review* 77: 323–329.

Peper, E. 1973. Frontiers of clinical biofeedback. In L. Birk (ed.), *Seminars in psychiatry.* New York: Grune & Stratton.

Petty, R.E., and Cacioppo, J.T. 1979. Issue involvement can increase or decrease persuasion by enhancing message-relevant cognitive responses. *Journal of Applied Social Psychology* 37: 1915–1926.

Piaget, J. 1965. *The child's conception of number.* New York: Norton.

Popper, K. 1981. Science, pseudo-science, and falsifiability. In R.D. Tweney, M.E. Doherty, and C.R. Mynatt (eds.), *On scientific thinking.* New York: Columbia Univ. Press.

Potts, G.R., and Scholz, K.W. 1975. The internal representation of a three-term series problem. *Journal of Verbal Learning and Verbal Behavior* 14: 439–452.

Poulton, E.C. 1982. Influential companions: Effects of one strategy on another in the within-subject designs of cognitive psychology. *Psychological Bulletin* 91: 673–690.

Radelet, L.A. 1980. *The police and the community.* Encino, Calif.: Glencoe.

Radner, D., and Radner, M. 1982. *Science and unreason.* Belmont, Calif.: Wadsworth.

Reference guide to the NTIS biographic data base, A. 1980. National Technical Information Service, NTIS-PR-253. Washington, D.C.: U.S. Department of Commerce.

Reflections of America. 1981. Washington, D.C.: U.S. Department of Commerce.

Reisman, D. 1950. *The lonely crowd: A study of the changing American character.* New Haven, Conn.: Yale Univ. Press.

Researcher's Guide To The National Archives, A. 1977. General Information Leaflet no. 25. Washington, D.C.: General Services Administration,

Robinson, P.W., and Foster, D.F. 1979. *Experimental psychology: A small-n approach.* New York: Harper & Row.

Rosenberg, M.J. 1969. The conditions and consequences of evaluation apprehension. In R. Rosenthal and R.L. Rosnow (eds.), *Artifact in behavioral research.* New York: Academic Press.

Rosenthal, R. 1966. *Experimenter bias in behavioral research.* New York: Appleton-Century-Crofts.

Rosenthal, R., and Fode, K.L. 1963. The effects of experimenter bias on the performance of the albino rat. *Behavioral Science* 8: 183–189.

Rosenthal, R., and Rosnow, R.L. (eds.) 1969. *Artifact in behavioral research.* New York: Academic Press.

Ross, A.O. 1963. Deviant case analysis: A neglected approach to behavior research. *Perceptual and Motor Skills* 16: 337–340.

Rossi, P.H. 1969. Practical, method, and theory in evaluating social-action programs. In J.L. Sundquist (ed.), *On fighting poverty: Perspectives from experience.* New York: Basic Books.

Sarason, S.B. 1978. The nature of problem solving in social action. *American Psychologist* 33: 370–380.

Sargent, J.D.; Green, E.E.; and Walters, E.D. 1972. The use of autogenic feedback training in a pilot study of migraine and tension headaches. *Headache* 12: 120–124.

Schacter, S. 1959. *The psychology of affiliation.* Stanford, Calif.: Stanford Univ. Press.

Scheirer, M.A. 1983. Household structure among welfare families: Correlates and consequences. *Journal of Marriage and the Family* 45: 761–771.

Schreiber, F.R. 1973. *Sybil.* Chicago: Regnery.

Schultz, J.H. 1976. *The economics of aging.* Belmont, Calif.: Wadsworth.

Scott, W.A., and Wertheimer, M. 1962. *Introduction to psychological research.* New York: Wiley.

Sears, R.R. 1979. Mark Twain's separation anxiety. *Psychology Today* 14: 100–104.

Shaw, M. 1981. *Group dynamics: The psychology of small group behavior.* New York: McGraw-Hill.

Sidman, M. 1960. *Tactics of scientific research: Evaluating experimental data in psychology.* New York: Basic Books.

Sidowski, J.B. 1966. *Experimental methods and instrumentation in psychology.* New York: McGraw-Hill.

Simonton, D.K. 1981. The library laboratory: Archival data in personality and social psychology. *Review of Personality and Social Psychology* 2: 217–243.

Skeen, P.; Brown, M.H.; and Osborn, D.K. 1982. Young children's perception of "real" and "pretend" on television. *Perceptual and Motor Skills* 54: 883–887.

Skinner, B.F. 1950. Are theories of learning necessary? *Psychological Review* 57: 193–216.

Smith, M.J.; Colligan, M.J.; and Hurrell, J.J., Jr. 1978. Three incidents of industrial mass psychogenic illness. *Journal of Occupational Medicine* 20: 399–400.

Snow, C.P. 1963. *The two cultures and a second look.* Cambridge, England: Cambridge Univ. Press.

Sobell experiment. CBS, *"60 Minutes,"* March 6, 1983.

Som, R.K. 1973. *A manual of sampling techniques.* London: Heinemann.

Sommer, R., and Sommer, B.A. 1983. Mystery in Milwaukee: Early intervention, IQ, and psychology textbooks. *American Psychologist* 38: 982–985.

Spence, K.W. 1956. *Behavior theory and conditioning.* New Haven, Conn.: Yale Univ. Press.

Springer, S.P., and Deutsch, G. 1981. *Left brain, right brain.* San Francisco: Freeman.

Srole, L. 1962. *Mental health in the metropolis.* New York: McGraw-Hill.

Steinger, I.D. 1972. *Group process and productivity.* New York: Academic Press.

Sterman, M.B., and Macdonad, L.R. 1978. Effects of central cortical EEG feedback training on seizure incidence in poorly controlled epilepsy. *Epilepsia* 19: 207–222.

Stevens, S.S. 1951. Mathematics, measurement, and psychophysics. In S.S. Stevens (ed.), *Handbook of experimental psychology.* New York: Wiley.

Taylor, J. 1953. A personality test for manifest anxiety. *Journal of Abnormal and Social Psychology* 48: 285–290.

Terrill, R. 1980. *Mao: A biography.* New York: Harper & Row.

Thigpen, C.H., and Cleckley, H.M. 1957. *Three faces of Eve.* New York: McGraw-Hill.

36th Annual Report on American industry. 1984. *Forbes,* January 2, 99–102

Thumin, F.J. 1962. Identification of cola beverages. *Journal of Applied Psychology* 46: 358–360.

Toffler, A. 1970. *Future shock.* New York: Random House.

Tuchman, B.W. 1978. *A distant mirror: The calamitous 14th century.* New York: Ballantine.

Tull, D.S., and Albaum, G.C. 1973. *Survey Research: A decisional Approach.* New York: Intex/Educational Publishers.

Turner, J.L. 1974. Powers of observation: The measurement and correlates of observational ability. *Dissertation Abstracts International* 35 (2-B): 1031–1032.

Underwood, B.J. 1957. *Psychological research.* New York: Appleton-Century-Crofts.

Underwood, B.J. 1975. Individual differences as a crucible in theory construction. *American Psychologist* 30: 128–134.

Underwood, B.J. 1983. *Attributes of memory.* Glenview, Ill.: Scott, Foresman.

Walizer, M.H. and Wiener, P.L. 1978. *Research methods: An analysis.* New York: Harper & Row.

Wason, P.C. 1968. Reasoning about a rule. *Quarterly Journal of Experimental Psychology* 20: 273–281.

Webb, E.J.; Campbell, D.T.; Schwartz, R.D.; Sichrest, L.; and Grove, J.B. 1981. *Nonreactive measures in the social sciences,* 2nd ed. Boston: Houghton Mifflin.

Weber, R., and Foos, P.W. 1983. The methods of experimental psychology. Unpublished manuscript.

Weick, K.E. 1968. Systematic observation methods. In G. Lindzey and Aronson (Eds.). *The handbook of social psychology,* Vol. II, *Research methods,* pp. 357–451. Reading, Mass.: Addison-Wesley.

Weiner, B. 1972. *Theories of motivation: From mechanism to cognition.* Chicago: Rand McNally.

We Work For You. 1982 Washington, D.C.: National Association of Manufacturers.

White, T.H. 1973. *The making of the president, 1972.* New York: Atheneum.

White, W.H. 1956. *The organization man.* New York: Simon & Schuster.

Wilson, E.O. 1975. *Sociobiology: The new synthesis.* Cambridge, Mass.: Harvard Univ. Press.

Winans, R.F. 1984. Wall Street ponders if bull market in '84 hinges on Redskins. *Wall Street Journal,* January 19, 205:47.

Wolfinger, R.E., and Rosenstone, S.J. 1980. *Who votes?* New Haven, Conn.: Yale Univ. Press.

Wood, G. 1981. *Fundamentals of psychological research.* Boston: Little, Brown.

Wrightsman, L.S. 1981. Personal documents as data in conceptualizing adult personality development. *Personality and Social Psychology Bulletin* 7: 367–385.

Yanis-McLaughlin, V. 1978. *Family and community: Italian immigrants in Buffalo, 1880–1930.* Ithaca, N.Y.: Cornell Univ. Press.

Yaremko, R.M.; Harari, H.; Harrison, R.C.; and Lynn, E. 1982. *Reference handbook of research and statistical methods in psychology.* New York: Harper & Row.

Yerkes, R.M., and Dodson, J.D. 1908. The relation of strength of stimulus to rapidity of habit formation. *Journal of Comparative and Neurological Psychology* 18: 459–482.

Zimney, G.H. 1961. *Method in experimental psychology.* New York: Ronald.

Zuckerman, H. 1977. *Scientific elite.* New York: Macmillan.

appendix

A Primer in Statistics*

Although we refrained from presenting statistics while considering the methods of data gathering, such a separation of statistics and methods is somewhat artificial. Researchers in all branches of social science use statistics to describe and interpret data. Statistics is an integral part of research and we recognize this. However we wanted to emphasize method in an uncluttered fashion. We reason that statistics are typically used after data have been gathered and so we have elected to consider them separately and in an appendix.

This appendix, stripped of methodology, covers basic statistical concepts such as "true" score, the role of variability or deviation, the null and research hypotheses, correlation, and analysis of variance. Each of these concepts has been briefly covered in the text but within the framework of methods. In this appendix they are presented from the viewpoint of a statistician. This appendix will not make a statistician out of the reader, but we hope that it will provide a basic understanding of how and why researchers rely on statistics in the description and interpretation of data.

Statistical techniques allow social scientists to make less ambiguous statements about their research hypotheses and literally to squeeze the maximum possible information from the available data. This Appendix will provide an overview of some of the available statistical techniques and indicate the rationale for their use and the information that can be abstracted from the data. The details necessary to carry out the statistical procedures are not included, since that is not possible in a single chapter but would require a separate text.

At issue is what should be done with the measurements that have been collected in order to be able to summarize the results and present conclusions in some manner which will clearly and objectively convey the information contained in the data. Statistics is a

*Guest author, Dr. Samuel S. Shapiro

branch of applied mathematics which has developed the techniques necessary for performing such an analysis. The material to be presented here will be limited to offering the rationale for the use of statistical procedures and the type of information that can be obtained. The objective will be to provide the reader with some insight into why statistical procedures are necessary and to provide some of the language and concepts used in the statistical analysis of data.

As a basis for our discussion an example will be used which illustrates the basic concepts. This example is typical of many data collection studies in which measurements are being made. We will discuss an observation which is a "quantitative" measurement that, theoretically, can take on any value. Such measurements would include height, weight, time, test scores, and blood pressure. In this example, let us assume that the researcher is interested in observing the intelligence of a subject. The information is collected by administering one of the standardized tests. Let us assume that the resulting score is 115. What does this mean? Does this score mean that the intelligence level of the individual *is* 115? Suppose the subject is given an equivalent test, different from the first, and now scores 119. Now what can be said about the correct or "true" score of this individual? Using the language of the scientist, it is possible to express the results of such tests in terms of a "model." A model is a mathematical statement which attempts to describe by a formula the object or phenomenon being examined. The above measurement, IQ level, might be described as follows:

$$\text{IQ}_i = A + e_i \qquad i = 1, 2, \ldots, n \tag{A.1}$$

where n is the number of tests taken; IQ_i is the score of the subject on the ith test; A is a constant or "parameter" which represents the true level of the individual; and e_i is the experimental error for the ith subject, which can be attributed to many effects such as environmental conditions at the time of each test, the emotional and physical conditions of the subject at the time of each test, the attitude and skills of the test administrator, and any intrinsic errors in the test as a measure of IQ level. Equation (A.1) indicates that in order to understand the measurement and make conclusions regarding the value of A it is necessary to understand and describe the properties of e_i.

The statistician uses what is called "descriptive statistics" in order to describe the properties of e_i. It is important to know about the long-term "average" of e_i. That is, if IQ tests were administered to the individual many, many times and if the values of e_i could be obtained for each test, what would be their arithmetic average (or mean)? (The arithmetic average is obtained by adding all the n values and dividing by n.) If the tests were constructed so that the measurement was unbiased this average should be zero. It will be assumed in this example that the measurements are unbiased. Thus, on any one measurement e_i might be positive or negative, but over a large number of tests the arithmetic average is zero. Examination of Eq. (A.1) shows the implication of the unbiased property; the long-term average of the IQ_i's will equal A, the true IQ level. The statistician would then suggest that if an "estimate" of A is desired the "sample mean" should be used. This estimate represents the best information from the data concerning the value of A. Since n is usually not a very large number, the sample mean will not equal A. Procedures which give information about the value of a parameter of the model are called "estimation" techniques.

Another property of e_i which is essential to understanding a measurement is its *variability*. It is important to have some information about the extent to which an individual value of e_i can vary from its average of zero. This is also the extent to which an individual IQ score can vary about its true value, A. The statistician gives the name "variance" to the average of the squares of the differences between each individual value and its mean and the name "standard deviation" to the square root of this quantity. The more the individual values of e_i depart from zero, its mean, the larger the value of the variance or standard deviation. These two quantities describe the spread or dispersion of the individual values about the average value. Generally, the standard deviation is used to describe this property. In any study it is desirable to have as small a standard deviation as possible, and this can be achieved in part through proper design. Chapters 8, 9, and 10 describe some experimental designs whose goal is to reduce this standard deviation. In the intelligence example a reduction in variability would be accomplished by controlling the environmental conditions, training the test administrator, and properly designing or selecting the measurement instruments.

A third property of the e_i which is of interest is how the values are spread out over the range of possible values. Are the values symmetrically spread around the mean? Are extreme positive values as likely as extreme negative values? Are the values highly concentrated about the mean or are they uniformly spread over the possible values? Such questions can be answered by knowing what statisticians call the "probability distribution" of the e_i. This concept is best illustrated with diagrams such as those given in Fig. A.1, a–c. In these diagrams three of the many possible shapes of probability distributions are illustrated. The curves show the relative concentration of the e_i values over the range of possible values. They represent the possible values of e_i if the same individual was given a very large number of tests. Figure A.1a represents a situation where any value of e_i within its range is equally likely. The values are "uniformly" distributed over the range. Figure A.1b indicates a situation where values of e_i close to its mean are more likely than those

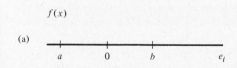

(a)

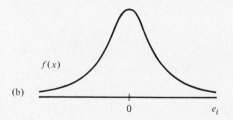

(b)

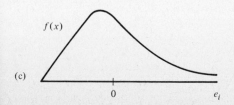

(c)

Figure A.1 Probability distributions. (a) Uniform distribution; all values of e_i between a and b are equally likely. (b) Symmetric distribution; values of e_i close to the mean of zero are more likely and the concentration falls off symmetrically in both directions. (c) Asymmetric distribution; high extreme values can occur but not very small values.

farther from the mean and the density or concentration of values falls off symmetrically in the positive and negative directions. The values are symmetrically distributed about the mean. Figure A.1c shows a situation where extremely high values (positive) are more likely than extremely low values (negative).

The concepts of mean, variance, and probability distribution are illustrated in Fig. A.2, which shows pictorially the effect of differences in means and variances.

Once the mean, variance, and probability distribution are known, the scientist knows everything the data can tell her/him about the IQ level of the subject. However, in almost all situations the number of observations is limited and hence we can only estimate these quantities. As stated previously, an estimate of A is obtained by using the average of the test scores. By using an estimate of the standard deviation, it is possible to describe a range of possible values of A. The variability in the estimates of A arises from the variability of the e_i and the fact that only a limited number of observations was available.

The statistician expresses this variability or uncertainty in terms of a "confidence interval." This interval consists of two numbers, an upper and a lower limit, which give a range of probable values for A. The width of the interval can be determined from the standard deviation of the e_i, the sample size, and the assurance or confidence with which one asserts that the value of A is within the limits. For example, if the upper and lower limits of a 95% confidence interval for A were 112 and 117, a confidence interval statement would assert that with 95% confidence the true value of IQ level lies between 112 and 117. (Formally, a statistician would state that in repeated samples of size n in 95% of the cases the computed upper and lower limits would contain the true value of A.) Thus the interval tells the researcher at a given confidence level the probable upper and lower bounds of A. The more confidence one desires (the higher the confidence level), the wider the interval must be. The higher the variance of e_i the wider the confidence interval; that is, the more variability in the measurement the wider the interval. The width of the confidence interval for a given confidence level can be reduced by increasing the sample size and/or reducing the measurement error. With more information, we can make more precise statements.

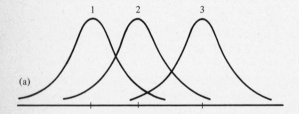

(a)

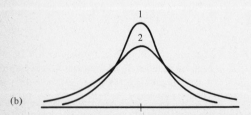

(b)

Figure A.2 Comparison of probability distributions. (a) Distributions with the same shape and variance but with different means. The mean of distribution 1 is the lowest and the mean of distribution 3 is the highest. (b) Distributions with the same shape and mean but with different variances. The variance of distribution 2 is higher than that of distribution 1.

This simple model can be extended without change to more complex situations. Suppose the scientist wishes to study the intelligence level of a group of 10-year-old children from Boston who come from affluent families. In this study a single test is administered to a group of n students. The model for this study is identical to that given in Eq. (A.1) except that IQ_i represents the test score for the ith child, A is the true average IQ level for the group, and e_i is made up of all the factors previously mentioned plus the inherent differences among individuals in the group. The statistical analysis would proceed as above and the conclusions would include an estimate of A with a corresponding confidence interval.

Let us now consider an even more complex situation which will allow the introduction of additional statistical concepts. Suppose the researcher was interested in studying the effect of fathers' occupation on the IQ level of 10-year-old males from Boston, with occupations grouped into two categories: professional and nonprofessional. The objective of the study is to investigate the hypothesis that a child whose father is in a professional occupation has an average intelligence level different from that of a child whose father is in a nonprofessional occupation. The IQ scores are collected for n 10-year-olds in each category. In order to analyze this information it is necessary to expand the previous model to include a factor that corresponds to the "research hypothesis." One possibility is

$$IQ_{ij} = A + P_i + e_{ij} \qquad i = 1, 2 \quad j = 1, 2, \ldots, n \qquad \text{(A.2)}$$

In this model IQ_{ij} is the test score for individual j in group i, where $i = 1$ is the group with professional fathers and $i = 2$ is the group whose fathers do not have professional occupations. The constant A represents the overall IQ level of the two groups averaged over occupation, P_i is the difference in IQ level due to being in the ith group, and e_{ij} is the measurement error for the jth individual in the ith group. The e_{ij} are made up of factors similar to e_i in the previous model, and it is assumed that the mean of the e_{ij} is zero and the variance of the e_{1j} equals the variance of the e_{2j}. The constants A, P_1, and P_2 have been defined so that P_1 and P_2 represent the incremental difference in the IQ levels for the two occupational groups, with $P_1 + P_2 = 0$. Setting up the model in this fashion will allow the researcher to assess whether P_1 and P_2 are different or, in the words of the statistician, "test the hypothesis of whether occupation (professional or nonprofessional) is related to the IQ level of the child." The main objective of the analysis is to assess whether $P_1 = P_2 = 0$. This procedure is called "a statistical test of a hypothesis" and in this case a "two-sample test of independent means." While it is not our purpose to describe how to carry out this test, it is important to understand the underlying rationale of the procedure so that the reader can use and interpret the results of such procedures.

In such an analysis the statistician starts with a statement called the "null hypothesis." This is a statement which is the opposite of the "research hypothesis." In this example it would be that occupational group has no relationship to IQ level, that is, $P_1 = P_2 = 0$. The research hypothesis is that there is a relationship i.e., $P_1 \neq P_2 \neq 0$. The test procedure is based on the assumption that the null hypothesis is true; it proceeds as follows:

1. A "test statistic" is computed from the data via a simple formula. In this case the formula is called a "Student t" statistic for two sample means, which is described in most elementary statistical texts.
2. Assuming that the null hypothesis is true, the chance or probability of getting a value of the test statistic at least as extreme as that calculated is obtained. The probability is based on the properties of the e_{ij}.
3. If this probability is small [less than 5 in a hundred (.05) or perhaps 1 in a hundred (.01)], the statistician would state that the result is improbable and the

assumed null hypothesis is not correct. This would result in the "rejection of the null hypothesis" and the assertion that occupational category of the father had a "statistically significant" effect on IQ level.

4. If the probability is not small (greater than .05 or .01), the statistician would state that there is no evidence to substantiate the research hypothesis because the null hypothesis has not been rejected. Thus, there is no evidence that occupational category of the father is related to IQ level of the son.

Inherent in the four steps above describing the test procedure is the possible occurrence of two types of errors. The first, called a "type I error," occurs when the null hypothesis is rejected when, in fact, it should not have been. The null hypothesis is rejected when the probability of getting as extreme a value as the observed test statistic is small. Assume that this probability was .04. The .04 value indicates that there are only 4 chances in 100 that a value as extreme as the observed value of the test statistic could have occurred by chance if the null hypothesis was correct. In rejecting the null hypothesis and stating that it is false, the researcher takes a .04 chance that it is true. Thus the rejection of the null hypothesis is accompanied by a risk of making an error. In this case the probability of a type I error is .04. A type I error is denoted by the Greek letter α. In carrying out a statistical test a minimum value of α is set prior to the analysis, and the null hypothesis is rejected when the oberved value of α is less than this preset value. Typical values used are .10, .05, and .01; the actual choice depends on the consequences of making a type I error.

The reader might ask why not make α very small, perhaps zero. This cannot be done because of the existence of another error, called the "type II error," which is also important. A type II error occurs when the null hypothesis is *not* rejected when it is false. It occurs when we state that there is no evidence that P_1 and P_2 are different when, in fact, they are. Unfortunately, the smaller we set the probability of a type I error, the larger we make the type II error. The probability of a type II error is denoted by the Greek letter β. The goal of a good experiment is to choose reasonable values of α and β and then determine how many observations are needed to achieve these goals. That is the subject of the statistical design of experiments, which is a topic beyond the scope of this appendix. When data are collected without a prior design, then the analyst has no choice but to preset α and accept whatever value of β is inherent in the analysis. Thus the type II error is ignored.

Let us now further extend the model so that it can be used to compare more than two means. Suppose that instead of considering the occupational groups as professional and nonprofessional we consider a group of r categories which include occupations such as farmer, laborer, and manager. The model which describes the IQ measurements of n individuals in each category is

$$IQ_{ij} = A + P_i + e_{ij} \qquad i = 1, 2, \ldots, r \quad j = 1, 2, \ldots, n \qquad (A.3)$$

This formulation is similar to Eq. (A.2) except that r different occupations are included instead of two. Again, A and the P_i's are defined so that $P_1 + P_2 + \cdots + P_r = 0$ and the P_i's represent the incremental effect of a particular occupational group on IQ level (the difference of each group's average from the overall average A). The null hypothesis in this case is that $P_1 = p_2 = \cdots = p_r = 0$; that is, there is no relationship between the fathers' occupational category and the IQ level of the child. The statistical technique for analyzing this type of model is called the "analysis of variance" or ANOVA, and for this particular case a "one-way ANOVA" would be used. The same test rationale described above is used to assess this hypothesis, except that the test statistic has a different form. The ANOVA can also be used in more complex cases, two of which will be described in the following examples.

Let us now assume that the researcher believes that there is also a sex difference between the IQ levels of 10-year-old Boston children and that the effect on IQ level is additive. The additive assumption means that the effect of sex, if any, is independent of the effect of occupational category of the father. The model for IQ score would be

$$IQ_{ijk} = A + P_i + S_j + e_{ijk}$$
$$i = 1, 2, \ldots, r \quad j = 1, 2 \quad k = 1, 2, \ldots, n \tag{A.4}$$

where n measurements have been taken on each sex for each occupational group. Here A and P_i have the same meanings as before, S_1 is the incremental effect on IQ level of being male, and S_2 is the effect of being female. Again, the symbols are defined so that $P_1 + P_2 + \cdots + P_r = 0$ and $S_1 + S_2 = 0$. The e_{ijk} represent the random experimental error associated with the kth subject in occupational category i and sex j. The analysis of variance technique enables the researcher to assess independently the null hypotheses that $P_1 = P_2 = \cdots = P_r = 0$ and $S_1 = S_2 = 0$. In this example two null hypotheses are being evaluated, and the prior test rationale applies to both. The ANOVA technique allows one to add as many factors (such as occupation and sex) as desired and, provided there are sufficient numbers of subjects and sufficient resources to measure them, it enables each hypothesis to be independently evaluated.

Another level of complexity which is easily handled by the ANOVA technique is the case where the effect due to a level of one factor depends on the level of another factor. Consider Eq. (A.4). Suppose the occupational category effect on IQ level depends on the sex of the child. Thus the effect on IQ level for the category "sex" depends on the father's occupation. An interaction would occur if the female children of farmers have a higher IQ level than the males but the opposite is true for children whose fathers are doctors. A statistician would state that these factors interact and an "interaction" term must be added. The model becomes

$$IQ_{ijk} = A + P_1 + S_j + C_{ij} + e_{ijk}$$
$$i = 1, 2, \ldots, r \quad j = 1, 2 \quad k = 1, 2, \ldots, n \tag{A.5}$$

where C_{ij} represents the incremental effect of the combination of the ith occupational group and the jth sex. Here the additional null hypothesis that $C_{11} = C_{12} = \cdots = C_{r2} = 0$ is added to the analysis; that is, there is no relationship to IQ level due to the interaction of sex and occupation.

In order to illustrate another data analysis concept let us consider a different situation. An economist has a research hypothesis that an individual's income is related to the number of years of schooling received. Furthermore, the hypothesis states that this relationship is linear; for each additional year of schooling the income level increases by a constant amount. This relationship can be expressed as $I = A + BX$, where I is the income level of an individual, A is the income level for those with no schooling, B is the constant increase in income for each year of schooling, and X is the number of years of schooling. The approach to analyzing this research hypothesis is similar to that in the previous examples. The first step is to construct a model representing a measurement, in this case the annual salary of a responding subject. Again we must include in the model the constants which will allow for the evaluation of the hypothesis. The model is

$$I_i = A + BX_i + e_i \quad i = 1, 2, \ldots, n \tag{A.6}$$

where I_i = income of the ith individual
$\quad\quad A$ = true average income of an individual with no schooling

B = constant rate of increase in average yearly income attributed to an additional year of schooling

X_i = number of years of schooling for the ith subject

e_i = measurement error for the ith individual

n = number of subjects included in the study

This model is similar to the simple measurement model given by Eq. (A.1) except that the true response is $A + BX_i$, which depends on the number of years of schooling, rather than just the constant A. The measurement error e_i represents variability due to all factors not accounted for. These would include differential in subjects' abilities, environmental factors, nonlinearity in the relationship, differing occupations, and so forth. The general technique used to analyze this model is called "regression analysis," and for this particular case it is called "simple linear regression." A basic assumption of this analysis technique is that the X_i's are known without measurement error. Thus, in this example one must assume that the subjects accurately know their number of years of schooling. The results of the regression analysis give the researcher the following information:

1. Estimates of the values of A and B. This allows the researcher to predict the income level of an individual, given the number of years of schooling, i.e., predict the value of $A + BX_i$.
2. Confidence intervals for A, B, and $A + BX_i$.
3. A test of the research hypothesis that there is a linear relationship between income level and years of schooling. This is done by examining the null hypothesis that $B = 0$. [Note that if $B = 0$ the model given in Eq. (A.6) is identical to the model of Eq. (A.1), and one can then state that there is no evidence of a relationship between I and X.] The test of this hypothesis is carried out in a similar fashion to that explained previously.
4. An estimate of the variability of the e_i's.
5. A statement that indicates how well the data fit the linear model. There is a statistic denoted R^2 which indicates what percentage of the total variability in the I_i's (income) is due to the differences (variability) in years of schooling. This measure will be discussed in more detail in conjunction with the coefficient of correlation.

Equation (A.6) is known as a "regression model"; it can be expanded to include higher order terms (for example, the relationship might be quadratic: $I = A + BX + CX^2$) or to include other factors such as occupation, IQ level, and area of the country. When there is more than one factor (on the right-hand side of the equation), it is called a "multiple regression" model. The addition of more factors increases the complexity of the calculations, but with the availability of high-speed computers and general statistical programs this is no longer a problem. However, as the number of factors increases the complexity of the interpretation also grows, and a thorough understanding of the subject of regression is required in order to avoid errors.

One basic assumption is that the values of X_i (also of any additional factors) must be known without error; the only measurement error is associated with I_i. If this is not so, then a different formulation must be used.

Consider the research hypothesis that there is a linear relationship between the weight of a cow and its girth measurement at its center. In this case both weight and girth measurements are subject to error. Each variable might individually be represented by Eq. (A.1) except that this would omit the linear relationship between these two factors. A more appropriate expression is

$$\begin{pmatrix} Y_i \\ X_i \end{pmatrix} = \begin{pmatrix} A \\ B \end{pmatrix} + \begin{pmatrix} e_i \\ f_i \end{pmatrix} \qquad i = 1, 2, \ldots, n \qquad\qquad (A.7)$$

where the parentheses indicate a pair of observations, each with different means and measurement errors, and

Y_i = weight of the ith cow
X_i = girth in the center of the ith cow
A = true weight of a cow
B = true girth at the center of a cow
e_i, f_i = measurement errors associated with Y_i, X_i
n = number of cows in the study

The information concerning the relationship of X_i and Y_i is contained in the e_i and f_i. Again we assume that the means of e_i and f_i are zero; however, we must now learn about the variances of these two quantities and the "correlation" between them. The constant that expresses the linear relationship between the two, and hence between Y_i and X_i, is called the "coefficient of correlation" and is denoted by the Greek letter ρ. This constant can have values between -1.0 and $+1.0$. The farther ρ is from zero the stronger is the relationship. The sign associated with ρ indicates whether there is a direct relationship (a plus sign) or an inverse relationship (a minus sign). A direct relationship indicates that increasing values of Y_i are associated with increasing values of X_i. An inverse relationship would indicate that increases in Y_i are associated with decreases in X_i. The estimate of ρ is denoted by r. The objectives of a correlation analysis are as follows:

1. Estimate ρ by calculating r.
2. Obtain confidence intervals for ρ.
3. Test whether there is a relationship between Y and X. This is done by considering the null hypothesis that $\rho = 0$. When $\rho = 0$ there is no linear relationship between the factors. This is similar to the previously described test of a hypothesis.
4. Indicate what percentage of the variability in one factor is due to the variability in the other factor. The "coefficient of determination," which is the square of the estimate of the coefficient of correlation, r^2, gives the information on the strength of the relationship between the factors. That is, it indicates what percentage of the total variability of the weight of the cows is due to the fact that they have different girths. The closer the percentage is to 100, the stronger the relationship. The value $\rho^2 = 0$ indicates that there is no relationship. (Suppose 20 cows were measured for girth. The cows will all have different weights. Some of the differences in weight will be due to the fact that the girths of the cows vary; the bigger the girth the heavier the cow. Some of the differences will be due to other factors such as differences in density and height. Suppose $r^2 = .75$. This would indicate that 75% of the variability in cow weight is due to differences in the girth of the cow and 25% is due to other factors.)

There are other statistical techniques which are used with more complex models; however, discussion of these is beyond the scope of this text. A word of caution is in order at this time. Most of the statistical calculations discussed are easy to perform, especially with the widespread availability of computers and statistical analysis packages. However, it is one thing to obtain the calculations from a statistical analysis and another to *make the proper interpretation of the results*. There is a common belief that one can prove anything with statistics, and "there are liars, damn liars and even worse, statisticians." The results of a statistical analysis are only as valid as the model used to describe the observations and the accuracy and relevance of the data collected. If the data collected are inaccurate, the statistical analysis can be misleading.

Up to this point the discussion has covered only those models used in conjunction with measurements, i.e., interval or ratio scale responses such as length, time, weight, and test score. However, in many instances in the social sciences the observation is a "count" or a "ranking." For example, in a study of income an economist might count the number of households in the sample in which income was below the poverty level. In this case the observation is a number, in fact, an integer which gives the number of such families in a sample size of n families. A ranking observation would result in a study where the participants were assigned ordered numbers according to some characteristic of each individual. For example, in a psychological experiment an observer might rank from 1 to n the n subjects at a meeting according to his/her assessment of their leadership abilities. In this example a "1" would be assigned to the individual judged to have the highest ability and an "n" assigned to the person with the lowest ability. It is necessary to consider different types of models in order to analyze data resulting in counts or rankings. These observations are nominal or ordinal scale, as opposed to the interval or ratio measurements discussed previously.

The first of these models, called the "binomial" model, is used to describe an experiment where there are only two possible responses for each subject and the observation is the number of occurrences of one of the responses in the n subjects. Thus, experiments in which the only possible responses from a subject are pass or fail, yes or no, live or die, above or below a limit, etc. would fit the binomial situation. This model is used if the probability of a yes response (one of the two responses) is the same for all subjects, one subject's response is not dependent on the response of any other subject (a statistician would state that the responses are "independent"), and the researcher is interested in learning about the probability of a yes response. The binomial model and the associated statistical procedures give the following information:

1. An estimate of the probability of a yes response
2. Confidence interval estimates for this probability
3. A test of hypothesis concerning possible values of the probability of yes; or, in the case of two groups of subjects, tests concerning whether or not the probability of a yes response is the same for both groups.

An example of the use of a binomial model is given by the following illustration. A doctor claims to have found a method for predicting the sex of an unborn child which, while not being perfect, is a better technique than simply guessing. In order to demonstrate the merits of this technique a study is run with n pregnant women. The research hypothesis is that the probability of a correct sex determination using the new method is greater than ½, while the null hypothesis is that the probability of a correct determination equals ½, i.e., the doctor is just guessing. Using the binomial model and a test of hypothesis similar to that described previously, it is possible to assess whether the doctor's predictions are better than chance and, if so, to obtain an estimate and confidence limits for this probability.

An immediate extension of this illustration is the case where one has several groups and the binomial model is appropriate for each group. In such a case the investigator is interested in whether the probability of a response (say a yes) is the same for each group. For example, there are three different methods of assembling an electronic component. Each method is taught to a different group of persons. Each individual is then asked to assemble n components and the good assemblies are counted. The researcher wishes to know whether there are differences in the probability of a good unit for the three methods. A technique known as a "chi-square" test can be used to test the null hypothesis that the probability of a good assembly is the same for each method. The binomial can also be extended to cover the case where there are more than two possible responses for each subject. The extension is then called the "multinomial"; the same types of analyses can be performed as in the binomial case except that one is now dealing with several probabilities of responses, one for each type. For example, in a study of possible hair color for a given ethnic group there are several possible observations for any individual—blonde, black, red, and brown—and thus the multinomial would be the appropriate model. Each of the probabilities can be estimated and a variety of tests of hypotheses can be performed, for example, whether a given color of hair is equally probable for members of the ethnic group.

The multinomial model is also useful when one has two or more factors and the researcher is interested in determining whether there is a relationship between these factors. Each factor can have two or more responses. Examples of this situation are: Is there a relationship between smoking and cancer? and, Is there a relationship between severity of sentencing in district criminal courts and ethnic background of the criminal? The data consist of a count of the number in each cross-classified category, that is, the number of nonsmokers who contracted cancer, the number of nonsmokers who did not contract cancer, the number of smokers who contracted cancer, and so forth. The research hypothesis would be that there is a relationship between these factors and the null hypothesis would be that there is none. The statistical technique used to evaluate this relationship is called "contingency table" analysis, and a chi-square test is used to assess the null hypothesis.

Another model used with responses that are counts is the "Poisson" model. This is an appropriate model when one is observing a study in which an event occurs from time to time and the observation is the number of such occurrences in some period of time. It is assumed that the occurrence of one event is not dependent on the occurrence of any other event and that the rate of occurrence is constant over time. In a study of behavior, the number of times a subject gives a response during a 1-hour observation period would be described by the Poisson model. The Poisson is also appropriate for describing events which occur in a given area or volume, where the number of occurrences per unit area or volume is counted. The number of defects in a roll of carpeting and the number of defects in a television set are other examples. A Poisson analysis will provide the following information:

1. An estimate of the rate of occurrence
2. Confidence intervals for the rate
3. A test of hypothesis concerning the rate

An example of the use of the Poisson model is as follows. The number of phone calls between the hours of 5 and 7 P.M. is used as a criterion in evaluating an advertising campaign for a restaurant which delivers meals ordered by phone customers. If one assumes that calls from individual customers are independent, that the rate of calls is constant over the time period, and that the rate is a function only of the advertising campaign, then the Poisson model and the associated statistical procedures can be used to estimate the call rate for each type of advertising campaign and can be used to compare the rates for different campaigns.

The analysis of data which consists of rankings is performed by using a group of techniques known as "nonparametric statistics." The model used here is that the data are the first n integers, i.e., the numbers 1, 2, 3, ..., n. For example, a political survey of a group of Democrats asked each subject to rank in order of preference the candidates who are vying for the presidential nomination. Assuming that there are seven candidates and ties are not allowed, the data collected from each subject are the numbers 1 to 7. Several techniques can be used to analyze these responses, including the Mann-Whitney U test, the Friedman test, and the Kruskal-Wallace test. Such procedures can be used to determine whether there is a preferred candidate. Since it is possible to turn interval scale measurements into rankings, these techniques can also be used with such observations. This is often done when the distribution of e_i of the measurement is not known.

The above discussion has given the reader a brief glimpse into the discipline of statistics. The objective has been to describe situations where statistical analysis must be used. The concept of a statistical model has been introduced and the role it plays in the analyses of data has been indicated. The common statistical techniques of estimation of means, confidence intervals, tests of hypothesis, regression analyses, chi-square tests, and nonparametric procedures have been introduced so that the reader will have some familiarity with these terms. This material should provide an introduction to the subject of statistics.

Name Index

Adams, L. P., II, 203
Ajzen, I., 260–261, 281
Albaum, G. C., 255
Albonetti, C., 60
Alsabti, E. A. K., 5
Anastasi, A., 25, 30, 71
Anderson, J. R., 106
Angoff, W. H., 54
Aronson, E., 125
Aserinsky, E., 40
Asimov, I., 19
Axline, V. M., 212

Babbie, E. R., 166
Bagdikian, B. H., 184
Barabba, V. P., 185
Barber, T. X., 128
Baum, A., 172
Benham, I. H., 185
Bennett, E. L., 52, 56, 58
Bent, A. E., 18
Berk, T., 77
Berkowitz, L., 166
Bever, T., 161
Beveridge, W. I. B., 165
Blum, M. L., 5, 29–30, 32, 173, 177–178,
    223–225, 239–257, 265, 268
Boice, R., 87–88
Boring, E. G., 103, 115
Bork, R. H., Jr., 284
Bowen, K. C., 288
Bower, G. H., 106
Bowers, M., Jr., 209
Briggs, J. W., 58
Brimmer, A. F., 184
Broad, W. J., 5–6
Brown, B. B., 69

Brunswick, E., 166
Bryden, M. P., 68
Buros, O. K., 71
Burt, C., 6

Cacioppo, J. T., 227
Campbell, D. T., 31, 103, 170,
    172
Candee, B., 173, 177–178
Carlsmith, J. M., 125, 166
Carlson, R., 207
Carlston, D. E., 127
Caro, R. A., 202–203
Ceci, S. J., 206
Cermak, L. S., 110
Champlin, C. D., 184
Chandler, D., 208
Chatelier, P. R., 284
Chemers, M. M., 229
Cherulnik, P. D., 282
Chiarello, R., 161
Christensen, L., 127
Church, R. M., 77, 79, 80
Clark, M. C., 105–106, 109, 124, 130,
    155–156
Clark, R. S., 18
Clawson, M., 184
Cleckley, H. M., 214
Clinard, M. B., 54–55
Cohen, J. L., 127
Cohn, A. W., 18
Cook, T. D., 103, 170, 172
Corsini, R. J., 287–288
Cox, C., 182
Craik, F. I. M., 44
Crano, W. D., 31
Cronbach, L. J., 30

Crow, M. S., 115
Cvetkovich, G., 74

Danskin, D. G., 115
Deese, J., 106, 154
Dement, W. C., 221
Detterman, D. K., 72
Deutsch, G., 68
Diamond, S., 270
Dodson, J. D., 47
Dolliver, R. H., 73
Donnerstein, E., 125, 166
Doyle, A. C., 41
Dubos, R., 184
Duncan, C. P., 142, 164
Duncan, O. D., 135

Enders, L. J., 209
Eron, L. D., 104
Evans, R., 125

Fallows, J., 217
Fink, J. C., 267
Fishbein, M., 260–261, 281
Fisher, J. D., 172
Fisher, K., 6–7
Fisher, R., 38
Fiske, D. W., 31
Flinn, D. E., 209
Fode, K. L., 127–128
Foos, P. W., 42–43, 72, 105–106, 109,
      124, 130, 151, 158
Forgays, D. G., 68
Foster, D. F., 146, 148, 150
Francis, W. N., 138
Frank, P. G., 107
Freedman, J. L., 227
Freeman, H. E., 267
Freud, S., 45, 83, 218
Fried, M., 52, 59

Galbraith, J. K., 184
Galton, F., 115
Garber, H., 72
Gardner, B. T., 216
Gardner, R. A., 216
Garment, S., 6
Garmezy, N., 220
Geda, C. L., 202
Gergen, D., 184

Geyser, S. A., 270
Gideon, C. E., 59–60
Glock, C. Y., 256–259
Goertzel, M., 219
Goertzel, V., 219
Goldman, E. F., 184
Green, A., 69
Green, E., 69
Green, H., 209
Greenwald, A. G., 164
Gregg, V., 138, 142
Grice, G. R., 164
Gronlund, N. E., 74
Groves, R. M., 267
Guetzkow, H., 287–288
Guilleminault, C., 221
Guion, R. M., 30
Guthrie, R. V., 67

Hagan, J., 60
Harlow, H. F., 167
Harre, R., 166
Harris, L., 270
Hauser, P. M., 185
Hays, W. L., 23, 266
Heber, R., 72
Heller, W. W., 184
Helmkamp, G., 97
Hempel, C. G., 36–37, 40
Herman, P. C., 162
Hesse, M. B., 44
Heyns, R. W., 184
Hibscher, J. A., 162
Hillery, V. J., 3
Hong, L. K., 226
Horton, D. L., 150
Hsieh, D., 55
Huck, S. W., 117
Hull, C. L., 19, 41
Huttenlocher, J., 42–43

Jessen, R. J., 56
Jung, J., 126

Kahn, J. V., 131–132, 136
Kail, R., 120
Kalton, G., 55, 265
Kantowitz, B. H., 44
Kaplan, A., 14
Katz, M., 258

Kelly, H. H., 40
Kidder, L. H., 87
Kilmann, R. H., 42
Kimble, G. A., 61
Kirk, R. E., 156, 162
Kirkpatrick, J. J., 185
Kish, L., 265
Kleitman, N., 40
Kress, G., 56
Kucera, H., 138
Kuder, G. F., 26
Kuhn, T. S., 34, 36–37

Lachman, R., 44, 133
Landauer, A. A., 161
Lauden, L., 36
LeBlanc, J. M., 146
Lehman, I. J., 54, 71
Leitenberg, H., 146
Lenneberg, E. H., 215
Lewin, K., 169–170, 229
Lewis, A., 59–60
Liebert, R. M., 150, 208
Limber, J., 216
Lindman, H. R., 162
Linton, M., 220
Livingston, J. A., 185
Lockhart, R. S., 44
Loeb, M., 10
Long, J., 5
Ludwig, A. M., 214
Luria, A. R., 217
Lynd, H. M., 83
Lynd, R. S., 83

McBurney, D. H., 39, 208
McCoy, A. W., 202–203
MacDonald, J. R., 147–148
McGuigan, F. J., 134–135
McNeil, E., 209–212
Malamuth, N. M., 239
Maltzman, I., 7
Markus, H., 162
Marlin, W., 184
Marx, M. H., 40, 42
Matlin, M. W., 106
Meck, W., 77, 80
Mehrens, W. A., 54, 71
Mellon, P. M., 31
Michelotti, K., 52, 59

Michener, J. A., 185
Mill, J. S., 103–106, 113, 117, 138
Milner, B., 215
Mirowsky, J., 60
Mishkin, M., 68
Mitchell, H. E., 185
Mitroff, I., 42
Mook, D. G., 167
Moreno, J. L., 286–287
Morowitz, H. J., 39
Moser, C. A., 55, 265
Moynihan, D. P., 184
Mynatt, C. R., 45

Nader, R., 193
Naylor, J. C., 29–30, 32, 265
Neale, J. M., 150, 208
Neisser, U., 166
Nicholls, W. L., II, 267
Nisbett, R. E., 255
Nunnally, J., 30

Olivarez, G., 185
Orlansky, J., 283–285
Orne, M. T., 126
Osgood, C. E., 75–76, 214

Palit, C., 267
Panning, W. H., 60
Pendery, M., 7–9
Peper, E., 69
Petty, R. E., 227
Piaget, J., 213–214, 216
Popper, K., 45
Potts, G. R., 42–43
Poulton, E. C., 137, 151, 158, 164

Radelet, L. A., 18
Radner, D., 4
Radner, M., 4
Rathjens, G., 185
Read, C. B., 203
Reasoner, H., 7–8
Reiss, A. J., Jr., 184
Richardson, M. W., 26
Riesman, D., 83
Robinson, P. W., 146, 148, 150
Roediger, H. L., III, 44
Rosenberg, M. J., 127
Rosenstone, S. J., 81, 83

Rosenthal, R., 125, 127–128
Rosnow, R. L., 125
Ross, A. O., 207
Ross, C. E., 60
Rossi, P. H., 53
Rossum, R. A., 18

Sandler, H. M., 117
Sarason, S. B., 12–14
Sargent, J. D., 69
Schacter, S., 133
Scheibe, K. E., 126
Scheirer, M. A., 59
Scholz, K. W., 42–43
Schreiber, F. R., 214
Schultz, J. H., 135
Scott, W. A., 63
Sears, D. O., 227
Sears, R. R., 217
Secord, P. F., 166
Sharp, H., 267
Shaw, M., 225
Sidman, M., 41, 150
Sidowski, J. B., 67, 70
Silver, M. J., 128
Simonton, D. K., 182–183
Skeen, P., 162
Skinner, B. F., 41
Smith, M. J., 208, 214
Smolka, R. G., 185
Snow, C. P., 166
Sobell, L., 6–9
Sobell, M., 6–9
Som, R. K., 56
Soman, V., 5
Sommer, B. A., 73
Sommer, R., 73
Spence, K. W., 41
Springer, S. P., 68
Srole, L., 52
Stanley, J. C., 170
Steinger, I. D., 225
Sterman, M. B., 147–148
Sternberg, R. J., 7
Sternlieb, G., 184
Stevens, S. S., 19

Straus, M., 5
String, J., 285

Taylor, J., 108
Terrill, R., 208
Thigpen, C. H., 214
Thumin, F. J., 139
Tkacz, S., 70
Toffler, A., 202–203, 205
Trowbridge, A. B., Jr., 184
Tuchman, B. W., 208
Tull, D. S., 255
Turnage, T. W., 150
Turner, J. L., 87

Underwood, B. J., 37, 47, 142, 144–145

Viano, E. C., 18

Walizer, M. H., 255
Walker, E., 206
Wason, P. C., 45
Wattenberg, B. J., 184
Webb, E. J., 87
Weber, R., 72, 158
Weick, K. E., 86, 90
Weiner, B., 135
Wertheimer, M., 63
West, J., 7
White, T. H., 208
White, W. H., 83
Wiener, P. L., 255
Will, J. A., 73
Wilson, E. O., 39
Wilson, T. D., 255
Winans, R. F., 10
Wittwer, S. H., 184
Wolfinger, R. E., 81, 83
Wood, G., 112, 268
Wrightsman, L. S., 207

Yanis-McLaughlin, V., 58
Yaremko, R. M., 63
Yerkes, R. M., 47

Zimney, G. H., 145
Zuckerman, H., 182

Subject Index

Achievement tests. *See* Standardized tests
Action research, 170, 201
Aggression
  in children, 47
  and violent TV, 47
Alcoholism, 6–9
American Psychological Association, 7,
  9, 56, 289
Anthropology. *See* Science, social
Aptitude tests. *See* Standardized tests
Archives, 1, 12, 49–50, 61, 84–85, 132,
  179–207
  sources of 183–202
Artifacts, 125–126
Attribution, 40
Assembly line hysteria, 208, 214
Automatic behavior syndrome, 221

Baseline, 147–150. *See also* Experimental
  design, single-subject
Biofeedback, 48, 68–70, 115, 137, 147,
  149
Boredom, 139–140, 267
Branching, 267

Case history, 1, 12, 49–50, 59–61, 182,
  207–222
  as behavior example, 209–212, 221
  as disconfirming evidence, 209,
    215–216, 218
  as method demonstration, 209,
    212–214, 216, 221
  as rare phenomenon description, 209,
    214–216
Case study. *See* Case history
Cause
  and effect, 3, 10–11, 102–106, 113, 116,
    154, 165–167, 171, 178, 181, 216,
    218, 256, 264

  necessary, 103
  sufficient, 103
Census Bureau, 55, 81–84, 186–188, 267,
  272
Chance fluctuations, 124–125, 131–134,
  137, 146, 150–151
Chutzpah, 205–206
Computers, 63, 72, 77–85, 190, 201,
  266–267, 283–285
Conditions, 109–111, 113, 125. *See also*
  Variables, independent
Confounding. *See* Variables, confounding
Conservation, 213–214
Consumer activist groups, 193–194
Consumer Affairs Institute, 97–98, 223,
  239
Consumerism at the Crossroads, 268,
  270–281
Consumer Reports, 101, 139
Consumer's Resource Handbook,
  189–190
Control, 34–36, 48–49, 102, 124–125,
  129, 132, 136–137, 140, 158, 163,
  165, 168–169, 181, 218. *See also*
  Counterbalancing; Experimental
  designs; Random assignment
  balancing, 119–121, 124–126, 129,
    138–139, 142, 155, 171
  constancy, 119–121, 124–126, 129,
    138–139, 151, 155, 171, 173
  double-blind, 127–128
  elimination, 119
  group, 117–118, 126–127, 140, 170,
    172, 260
  random mix, 140–142, 145–146, 164
  random order, 140, 145–147
  single-blind, 127
  techniques, 116–121, 140–150, 154,
    165–166

Correlation, 10–11, 24–26, 28–32, 47, 66, 132–136, 181, 183, 227
Counterbalancing, 155–156
  complete, 140, 143–147
  incomplete, 140, 144–147, 156
  within, 140, 142–143, 145–146
Criminal Justice Archives and Information Network, 191–192

Data, 15, 17, 33
  analysis, 2, 58. *See also* Statistics
  gathering, 1–4, 11, 15, 18, 35–37, 44, 86, 90, 102, 154, 168–169, 178, 180, 264
  methods of collection, 49–61
  organization of, 39–40, 44
  qualitative, 11, 177, 224–225, 227, 250, 268, 283
  quantitative, 11, 177, 207, 224–225, 227, 268, 283
  sharing, 206
  snooping, 82
Deception, 56–58, 105, 127, 162, 206
Deduction. *See* Theory, deductive
Demand characteristics, 126–128, 133, 136–138, 146, 163
Dependent variable. *See* Variables, dependent
Description, 34–36, 49–50, 88
Differential transfer, 140, 144–146, 164. *See also* Transfer
Direct response measures, 71, 76
Discovery, 34–36, 49

Economics. *See* Science, social
Educational Resources Information Center, 190, 192
Effect, 109–110. *See also* Cause; Interaction
  additive, 159–160
  main, 159–161
Empiricist school, 83
Equivalent materials design, 170–172, 176. *See also* Quasi-experiments
Error. *See also* Chance fluctuations
  random, 161, 264
  variance, 151–152, 165. *See also* Statistics, standard deviation
ESP, 48
Ethics, 56–58, 125, 263

Evaluation apprehension, 126–128
Experience, 4, 162, 169
Experimental design, 121
  between-subjects, 121–124, 126, 129–130, 137–140, 151, 153, 156–158, 162–164
  and confounding, 163–164
  factorial, 155–159, 162
  fractional, 162
  incomplete, 162
  many subject, 150–153
  matched group, 118, 121, 155–156, 158, 162–163, 165
  matched subject, 129–138, 151, 153
  mixed, 156–158
  multiple baseline, 147, 149–150
  nested, 162
  random introduction, 147, 150
  randomized groups, 121–124, 134, 137–138, 153, 162
  reversal, 147–150
  selection, 162–165
  single subject, 129, 146–153, 162–163
  within-subject, 129, 131, 136–153, 155–158, 162–165
Experimenter bias, 126–128
Experiments, 1–2, 12, 49–51, 56, 58–60, 85–87, 90–91, 181, 207, 216, 226, 259
Explanation, 3, 5, 34–49, 256. *See also* Models; Theory
  as restatement, 38

Facts, 15–18. *See also* Data
Falsifiability, 44–45
Fatigue, 139–140, 147, 149
Federal Aviation Administration, 284
Field research, 1, 12, 49–50, 59–60, 87, 168–178, 259, 270
Food and Nutrition Board, 6
Food labeling, 97–100
Forbes, 198–200
Ford Foundatio, 198, 201
Fractionization, 94
Fraud. *See* Science, and misrepresentation

Games, 283, 286, 288. *See also* Simulation, type B

Generality, 108, 125, 128, 150, 152, 164, 166–167, 169, 183, 227, 250. *See also* Validity, external
Gideon's Trumpet, 60
Goals of science, 34. *See also* Control; Description; Discovery; Explanation; Prediction
Graduate Record Examination (GRE), 73
Group discussion, 1–2, 12, 49, 51, 60–61, 223–254, 257
  frame of reference questionnaire, 238
  guide, 229, 237–239, 250, 253
  leader, 228–234, 250, 253
  probes, 231–232
  recruiting, 235–237, 253
Group dynamics, 170, 225

History, 113–114, 117–118, 125, 140, 147, 149, 170, 221
Hypothesis, 16–18, 34–35, 39, 58, 82, 95, 108, 126–128, 138, 152, 158, 160–162, 165, 171, 177, 188, 198, 202, 215–216, 218, 221–222, 226–227, 254

Independent variable. *See* Variables, independent
Individual differences, 47. *See also* Variables, internal
Induction. *See* Theory, inductive
Institute for Social Research, 201
Instrumentation. *See* Measuring instruments
Intelligence, 22–23, 27–28, 31. *See also* Standardized tests
Interaction, 154, 158–161. *See also* Effect, additive; Effect, main; Experimental design, factorial crossover 161
Interactional workshop, 224. *See also* Group discussion
Interest tests. *See* Standardized tests
Interference, 139
Interviews, 1–2, 50, 126, 174–176, 181, 183, 192, 203, 207, 226, 263–264, 266–268, 272. *See also* Surveys by telephone 266–267
Investigative reporters, 202, 222

Journal of Experimental Psychology: Animal Behavior Processes, 72, 158
Journal of Experimental Psychology: Human Perception and Performance, 72, 158
Journal of Experimental Psychology: Learning, Memory, and Cognition, 72, 158
Journal of Parapsychology, 4

Kuder Preference Record, 73

Latin square, 144–145. *See also* Counterbalancing, incomplete
Law of the instrument, 14
Laws, 34–36, 39–40, 46, 48. *See also* Theory
Library, 183, 185, 203. *See also* Literature review
Library of Congress, 180, 189
Life space, 169–170
Literature review, 107–108, 120, 132, 136
Locus of control, 60

Maturation, 114, 117–118, 140, 147, 149, 221
Measurement, 2, 11–12, 32–34, 92, 102, 106–108, 110, 114, 127, 160–161, 182, 225–226, 261. *See also* Direct response measures; Measuring instruments; Rating scales; Standardized tests; Testing; Tests
  direct, 66, 107–108
  error, 24, 63. *See also* Error
  independent, 30–31
  interval scale, 20–23, 75, 94
  labels, 17–20
  macro-, 51–53, 65, 226
  micro-, 51–53, 65, 226
  nominal scale, 19, 21–22, 94
  ordinal scale, 19–23, 74, 94
  periodic, 170
  qualitative, 17–20, 51–53, 95, 183
  quantitative, 17–20, 51–53, 83, 95, 183
  ratio scale, 21–23
  repeated 118. *See also* Experimental design, within-subject

Measuring instruments, 62–76, 90–91, 93, 96, 113, 132, 173, 176, 178. *See also* Direct response measures; Measurement; Rating scales; Standardized tests; Testing; Tests
  brass, 67
  change of, 115, 117–118, 125, 170
  electronic, 67–70
  and error, 63–64
  selection of, 66–67
  standardized, 63, 108
  uses of, 64–65
Memory
  for dreams, 117–118
  exceptional, 217
  improvement, 110
  for life events, 219–220
  organization, 40
  in rats, 77
  search, 43
  storage, 106, 215
  for time intervals, 77
  and word frequency, 138–142, 163–164
Methods of data collection, 49–61
  selection factors 50–53
Metropolitan Achievement Test, 73
Minnesota Multiphasic Personality Inventory (MMPI), 27
Mismatch, 134–136. *See also* Experimental design, matched groups; Experimental design, matched subject
Models, 34–36, 40, 43–44. *See also* Theory

National Academy of Sciences, 6
National Archives and Records Service, 186
National Association of Manufacturers, 197
National Gerontology Resource Center, 192
National Organization for Women, 193
National Safety Council, 180, 193
National Technical Information Service, 189
Nature, 47, 72
Nurture, 47, 72

Object permanence, 155–156
Observation, 1–2, 12, 16–17, 49–50, 58, 60, 86–102, 115, 172, 181, 207, 224, 234, 255, 259, 270, 289
  charts, 11
  of events, 88–90, 93–94, 97
  fractionization, 94
  objective, 90–96
  of organisms, 88–89, 93–94, 96–97
  of places, 88–90, 94–97
  reliability of, 26, 87, 93. *See also* Reliability
  second order, 99–101
  of situations, 88–89, 93–94, 96–97
  subjective, 90–92, 96
  of things, 88–90, 93–97
  unobtrusive, 58, 90, 169
Operational definitions, 46, 106–108, 152

Panel studies, 256. *See also* Surveys
Paper and pencil tests. *See* Direct response measures; Rating scales; Standardized tests
Paradigm, 34, 37, 48
Parent-Teacher Association, 192–193
Parsimony, 44, 46, 169, 282
Participants, 162. *See also* Ethics; Group discussion, recruiting; Sample; Sampling
  attrition, 115–116, 118, 260, 266
  selection, 2, 53, 115–116, 118
Phallic stage, 45
Pilot work, 53
Placebo, 119
Play therapy, 213
Political science. *See* Science, social
Poverty, 49–59, 170, 185, 198
  and crime, 54
  and families, 55, 59
  and mental illness, 52
  and migration, 52
  and rat brains, 52
  and years of education, 52, 59
Practice effects, 138–150, 156, 162. *See also* Variables, time-related
Prediction, 34–36, 39–40, 48–49
Pretest 133–134, 136
Problem solving, 12–14, 69, 225, 253
Projective tests. *See* Standardized tests
Pseudoscience, 4

Psychodrama, 286. *See also* Simulation, type B
Psychological Abstracts, 107, 192
Psychological pricing, 228, 233
Psychology. *See* Science, social

Quasi-experiments, 121, 170–172, 178
Questionnaires, 133, 176–177, 183, 207, 226, 238, 255, 261–263, 267–268, 270. *See also* Surveys

Random assignment, 58, 105, 118, 120–124, 129–131, 133–136, 143–144, 155–156, 158, 163
Random error. *See* Chance fluctuations
Random numbers, 121–124, 144, 265
Random selection. *See* Group discussion, recruiting; Participants, selection; Sample; Sampling
Rating scales, 11, 71, 73–76, 96, 181, 263, 268
  Guttman, 75
  Likert, 74
  semantic differential, 75–76
  Thurstone, 75
Rationalism, 3, 15, 33–34, 36, 44, 92, 180, 188, 206, 227
Records. *See* Archives
Reductionism, 37–39
Regression, 114, 117–118, 140, 147, 170
Reliability, 11–12, 24–26, 32–34, 49, 58, 63, 71, 87, 90–92, 94–96, 98, 107–108, 114, 125, 130, 169, 172, 176, 178, 182, 192, 218–219, 222, 224–226, 250, 259, 281, 284
  alternate form, 26
  observor, 26, 87, 93
  split-half, 26, 32
  test-retest, 25–26, 284
REM sleep, 40–41
Repeated measures design. *See* Experimental design, within-subject
Replication, 34, 91, 120, 128, 150, 152, 164, 202, 209, 256, 265
Research objectives, 50–51, 95, 108, 160, 186, 263
Role playing, 286–289. *See also* Simulation, type B
Rorschach ink blot test, 73, 176

Sample, 54, 224, 255, 264–266. *See also* Sampling

affordable, 56
cluster, 54, 265–266
of convenience, 55, 70, 266
probability, 265
quota, 266
random, 265. *See also* Participants, selection
representative, 54, 56, 221, 256, 260, 264, 271–273
size, 54, 238, 259, 264
stability, 54, 56
standardized, 256
stratified, 265
systematic, 265
of volunteers, 55–56, 266
Sampling, 51, 54–56, 152, 173–175, 192. *See also* Sample
  a population, 54, 166–167
  random, 54–56, 177, 221
  representative, 256
  stratified, 56
Schizophrenia, 209–210
Scholastic Aptitude Test (SAT), 73
Science, 4–6. *See also* Goals of science
  and misrepresentation 5–9
  methods of 2. *See also* Data, methods of collection
  physical, 2
  social, 2, 10, 13, 21, 24–25, 31, 41, 56, 58, 61, 77, 81, 84, 90, 168, 180, 186, 201–202, 205, 207, 256–259, 286, 288
Scientific understanding, 36, 48
Sentence processing, 42–43
Sentry Insurance study, 268, 270–281
Sequence effects, 125
Simulation, 1, 12, 49, 51, 60–61, 79, 214, 282–289
  blends, 283, 288
  type A, 283–285
  type B, 283, 285–289
60 Minutes, 7
Sobell study, 6–9, 291, 297
Social work. *See* Science, social
Sociology. *See* Science, social
Split-plot design. *See* Experimental design, mixed
Standardized tests, 71–73, 76. *See also* the names of specific tests
  achievement, 73

Standardized tests (*Continued*)
   aptitude, 71–73
   interest, 73
   personality, 73
   projective, 176–177
Stanford-Binet IQ Test, 72
Statistics, 21, 258. *See also* Correlation
   and analysis, 124
   analysis of variance, 23
   factor analysis, 31
   mean, 21–23, 79, 150, 159–160
   standard deviation 21, 79. *See also*
     Error, variance
Stroz Interest Blank, 73
Subjects. *See* Participants
Surveys, 12, 49–50, 56, 60–61, 85, 102,
   172, 183, 192, 201–202, 227, 237,
   255–281. *See also* Interviews;
   Questionnaires
   by mail 267
Synesthesia, 217

Tachistoscope, 68
Tape recording, 233–234, 253
Testing, 114, 117–118, 140
Test performance
   and anxiety, 110–111
   and expected test, 105–106
Tests, 11, 183, 263. *See also* Standardized
   tests
Theory, 5, 34–48, 106, 167, 257–258. *See*
   also Models
   and bridge principles, 40–41, 46
   and clarity/precision, 46
   deductive, 40–42
   and deductive capacity, 46
   and empirical support, 45–46
   and falsifiability, 44–45
   functional, 40, 42–43
   and generality, 46–47
   and individual differences, 47
   inductive, 40–42
   and internal principles, 40
   and logical consistency, 46
   mathematical, 46
   and parsimony, 46
   and predictive capacity, 46
Theory of reasoned action, 260–261,
   263
Time series design, 170–172

Transfer, 139–140, 147, 284–285, 287.
   See also Differential transfer
Trend studies, 256

Unobtrusive observation. *See*
   Observation, unobtrusive

Validity, 11–12, 24, 27–34, 49, 58, 63, 71, 79,
   87, 90–92, 94, 96, 98, 107–108, 131, 162–
   163, 169, 172, 176, 178, 182, 192, 203,
   224–226, 229, 250, 259, 281, 284, 287
   concurrent, 29–30, 284
   construct, 31–32
   content, 28
   convergent, 31–32
   criterion-related, 29–31
   discriminant, 31–32
   ecological, 166–167
   external, 27, 128, 152, 163, 166–167,
     183, 218, 221. *See also* Generality
   face, 28–29
   internal, 27, 112–121, 126–128, 163, 165–
     167, 183, 218, 221, 256. *See also* Control
Variables, 13, 50, 65, 90–91, 93–95, 102,
   106, 162
   confounding, 4, 11–12, 116–117, 125–
     131, 138–139, 142–144, 147, 154, 158,
     162–165, 221. *See also* Control
   dependent, 11–12, 106, 108–110,
     113–121, 124–125, 127, 129,
     132–134, 136–139, 141, 145, 147,
     149, 154, 157–159, 163, 165,
     168–169, 181, 217–218, 226, 250
   external, 111–112, 118–121, 124, 127,
     129, 131, 136–139, 146, 150–152,
     155–157, 162–163
   independent, 11–12, 106, 109–121,
     124–134, 136–140, 142, 146–149,
     151, 154–165, 168–169, 176, 178,
     181–182, 226, 250, 281
   internal, 111–112, 118–121, 124, 127,
     129–140, 146, 150–152, 155–157,
     162–163, 171
   time-related, 137–139
Videotape, 70–71

Wechsler Intelligence Scale for Children,
   27, 73

Yerkes-Dodson law, 47